THE
SUGAR
KING OF
CALIFORNIA

The descendants of

Claus Spreckels
and
Anna Christina Mangels

Claus Spreckels
7-9-1828   12-26-1908

Anna Christina Mangels
9-4-1830   2-15-1910

John Dietrich
8-16-1853   6-17-1926
Lillie Siebein
9-8-1855   1-8-1924

Adolph Bernard
1-5-1857   6-28-1924
Alma de Bretteville
3-24-1881   8-7-1968

Claus Agustus
12-18-1858   11-11-1946
Oroville Dore
12-29-1863   8-22-1933

Emma Claudine
1-23-1870   5-2-1924
Thomas Watson
John W. Ferris
Arthur Hutton

Rudolph
1-1-1872   10-4-1958
Eleanor Jolliffe
3-21-1868   2-22-1949

Frontispiece. The descendants of Claus Spreckels and Anna Mangels. By permission of Adolph Rosekrans.

THE
SUGAR
KING OF
CALIFORNIA

THE LIFE OF
CLAUS SPRECKELS

SANDRA E. BONURA

University of Nebraska Press   Lincoln

The University of Nebraska Press is part of a land-grant institution with campuses and programs on the past, present, and future homelands of the Pawnee, Ponca, Otoe-Missouria, Omaha, Dakota, Lakota, Kaw, Cheyenne, and Arapaho Peoples, as well as those of the relocated Ho-Chunk, Sac and Fox, and Iowa Peoples.

Library of Congress Cataloging-in-Publication Data
Names: Bonura, Sandra E., author.
Title: Sugar king of California: the life of
Claus Spreckels / Sandra E. Bonura.
Description: Lincoln: University of Nebraska Press, [2024] |
Includes bibliographical references and index. | Summary:
"Sandra E. Bonura tells the overlooked, yet genuine rags-to-riches story of Claus Spreckels and his role in the developments of the sugarcane industry in the American West and across the Pacific"—Provided by publisher.
Identifiers: LCCN 2023034938
ISBN 9781496235114 (hardback)
ISBN 9781496239082 (epub)
ISBN 9781496239099 (pdf)
Subjects: LCSH: Spreckels, Claus, 1828–1908. | Sugarcane industry—California—Biography. | BISAC: BIOGRAPHY & AUTOBIOGRAPHY / Business | HISTORY / United States / State & Local / West (AK, CA, CO, HI, ID, MT, NV, UT, WY)
Classification: LCC HD9110.S57 B65 2024 |
DDC 338.1/7361092 [B]—dc23/eng/20240205
LC record available at https://lccn.loc.gov/2023034938

Designed and set in Garamond Premier Pro by L. Welch.

Writing and researching Claus Spreckels's immigrant experience triggered many childhood memories. My grandmother Ida Groh Hollinger, to whom this book is dedicated, left all that was familiar and dear in the little Saarland village of Wittersheim in 1912 to chase the American dream with my artist grandfather, Frederick "Fritz" Hollinger. She never imagined the hardships that lay ahead once she passed through Ellis Island. When Fritz suddenly died, she was left grief-stricken with a toddler to raise (my mother, Elizabeth), a stranger in a strange land. In an era when women could not own property, all that she had built with her husband was taken away and she was left penniless. Even though she, like others, was irrationally persecuted for her German heritage through two world wars, she prized Fritz's Certificate of Naturalization as if it were the Holy Grail. Today it is framed and displayed in my own home. By writing this book I now have a clearer understanding of the certificate's significance and the depth of love Nana had for both her homeland and her adopted country. She struggled to make a decent living, but she remained as proud as Claus Spreckels's father, who plowed his field in a black top hat. Nana wore a white hat and "pearls."

One man can rise above obstacles which
would entirely crush another.

—CLAUS SPRECKELS

CONTENTS

ILLUSTRATIONS

ACKNOWLEDGMENTS

There are plenty of people who helped me take this book from concept to manuscript. Out in front through the research process is Vinnie J. Dicks. His pep talks and unparalleled knowledge of Hawaiian history as it intersects with Claus Spreckels kept me motivated and, more importantly, focused. Out in front for the writing process is substantive editor Allan Edmands; I'm very grateful for his sharp mind and his nitpicking efforts that have seen me through three books. Out in front for the publication process is UNP's editor in chief, Bridgett Barry. Her respectful, friendly, and steady guidance once again has been invaluable. Her timely responses to this stressed-out author's annoying emails lightened my load.

Others, in no hierarchy of importance, did their part to bring the "sugar king" to life. Here's a proper thank-you to the various genealogical lines of Claus Spreckels's family whose collective enthusiasm was propelling. There are too many to mention, but Virginia Wilson and Adolph Rosekrans went the extra mile to share privately printed books on the family, personal documents, and treasured photographs. On the Anna Spreckels side of the family, Mark H. Reed in Aptos was a prized source of show-and-tell of how the Spreckelses and Mangelses lived in the nineteenth and twentieth centuries.

Even before I wrote a single chapter, I looked for inspiration and found it in a road trip through the beautiful coastal town of Aptos and the Pajaro Valley with scholars Kevin Newhouse and Robert Wall, who pointed out the fingerprints and footprints left behind by Claus Spreckels. James Perry opened his doors to the Monterey County Historical Society's archives at a time when open access was limited. Thank you!

Jim Riley's walking tour throughout the historical town of Spreckels included access to several homes to illustrate the differences in architectural plans. I'm much obliged to the big-hearted residents who opened their doors to a snoopy researcher. On my wall at home is an original oil painting of one of those Spreckels cottages to remind me of how special the village and the people of Spreckels are.

My research proceeded smoothly due to the help of some very capable scholars, who shared their knowledge with me. Derek R. Whaley, a significant train enthusiast, helped me understand Claus Spreckels's role in that industry, as did Chris Rockwell from the California State Railroad Museum. I respect guardians of history who love their work: John Hibble from the Aptos History Museum was an early steersman who helped me understand the Spreckels legacy in California. Here's a hug to Tim Fisher, who, while unrelated to the project in any way, generously let me roam at will throughout his Aptos mansion more than once so I could imagine Claus and his family in their element.

I apologize to all of the above and others if any errors have crept into this book, whether conceptual, factual, or just plain misstatements. This book could not have been finished without the contribution of all these people and more—archivists, editors, historians, families, librarians, publishers, and Carl, my very patient husband. "Thank you" doesn't seem enough.

INTRODUCTION

The inspiration for my books has emanated from the contents of a single tattered trunk left behind in the attic of an old house in Berkeley, California. The steamer trunk had belonged to teacher and newspaper columnist Carrie Prudence Winter Kofoid (1866–1942), who witnessed and wrote about a critical time in Hawaiian history: the overthrow of the kingdom. Her interactions with Hawai'i's last queen and the rebels who toppled the monarchy are uniquely chronicled in entertaining yet factual correspondence. In addition to her letters, the trunk contained an extraordinary collection of never-before-seen Hawaiiana—priceless artifacts, diaries, one-of-a-kind photographs, old newspapers, and much more—all detailing everyday life in nineteenth-century royal Honolulu.

Recognizing the historical significance of the trunk's contents, I plunged right in, and in 2012 Deborah Day's and my edited volume, *An American Girl in the Hawaiian Islands: Letters of Carrie Prudence Winter, 1890–1893*, was published. The next person I found in the trunk was a bold American social activist, Ida May Pope, who inspired and elevated an entire generation of Hawaiian women. She ultimately sacrificed her life for them but had been historically forgotten. My award-winning *Light in the Queen's Garden: Ida May Pope, Pioneer for Hawai'i's Daughters, 1862–1914*, detailing her life, was published in 2017.

Examining the trunk's artifacts for the first two books, I continually came across a name familiar to native San Diegans: John D. Spreckels. Winter, Pope, and Hawai'i's royal family all interacted with the Spreckels family in Honolulu, but I was curious to know exactly how my city's pioneer was connected to both the Hawaiian monarchy and the American teachers on assignment in Honolulu. That process left me incredulous that nobody had written the complete biography of this trailblazer who built a city with "sugar money." My award-winning *Empire Builder: John D. Spreckels and the Making of San Diego* was published in 2020.

I also found references in the trunk's contents to John's father: Claus Spreckels (1828–1908), the self-made "sugar king" who at one time was one of the ten richest men in America. I began to wonder during the writing of *Empire Builder* why he hadn't received the historical attention he deserves as one of the most important upbuilders of the American West.

There are only small parts of his life published, in decades-old material chiefly related to his controversial political exploits with Hawaiʻi's royalty. His railroad, beer, and sugar ventures are covered sporadically in various publications. In a detailed search of ancient, archived newspapers, I was startled by an open firehose of attention-grabbing articles related to Spreckels's adventures across the globe. Ever curious, I expanded my research to Hawaiʻi and Germany and found, depending on the depiction, Claus Spreckels has been cast as either a villain or a hero, with *no* balanced view to be found. I reconnected with some of his descendants and found a treasure trove in several home archives that offered a more balanced view until I at last reached an understanding of the man and the arc of his life. But it was only after going up and down California's Coast Ranges, spending time in the Pajaro and Salinas Valleys, with specific stops in Aptos, Monterey, Salinas, Spreckels, and Watsonville, talking with people whose towns and lineage owed their prosperity to Claus, that I was inspired to write his first-ever comprehensive biography. I soon found what other researchers may have discovered: distilling such an extensive life into a complete picture of this complex and colorful character was challenging to say the least.

The Sugar King of California is our quintessential rags-to-riches tale. Who doesn't love the story of someone facing impossible odds rising from grinding poverty to enormous wealth? America's mythos is based on the belief that anyone, regardless of circumstance, can get rich if they have enough gumption, grit, or ruthlessness. While there are a variety of published stories about the triumphs of immigrants, which seem to suggest that *anyone* can do great things with hard work, talent, and a little luck, I was surprised that these stories are actually rare. If America is a land of equal opportunity and upward mobility for all, why are there only a few people like him? Most underestimate how hard it is to be great at something, and then top themselves to achieve more. It was only with fierce determination and ruthless consistency that Claus Spreckels could dive into his passions and beat all his rivals on a global scale.

But there's always a cost for single-minded determination, so even though it intersects with the Horatio Alger rags-to-riches legend, this is not just a story of a poor immigrant boy who chased the American dream as far as he could take; it's a tragic portrait of a wealthy family torn apart by money, jealousy, and ego.

Meet Claus Spreckels! His story begins like many immigration stories, in a contested country pressing unwilling men into service. At the restless age of seventeen, he escaped from the family farm and the draft in the German kingdom of Hanover with only seventy-five cents in his pocket to go from absolute obscurity to dizzying heights of fame, fortune, and celebrity—all without a formal education.

Spreckels was a formidable visionary, and his industrial and agricultural enterprises ultimately transformed California industry and labor. Challenging convention with a hands-on approach, he sought industrial answers to the problems of everyday life. He operated through practical but imaginative thinking with ingenious solutions. He anticipated change—even expected change—and this was characterized in every venture.

Hawai'i was a sovereign nation under the reign of King David Kalākaua when, in 1876, Spreckels arrived from California to seize the opportunity for his San Francisco sugar refinery that was afforded by the Reciprocity Treaty between the kingdom of Hawai'i and the United States. But once he set foot in the tropical paradise, he was inspired to establish the largest and most modern sugar plantation in the world. The white businessmen who dominated Hawai'i's economy through their own sugar ventures and government positions treated the crusty Claus Spreckels with contempt. They ironically assumed an air of entitlement not warranted by what they had inherited from their humble American missionary ancestors, and their egos were boosted by their wealth and Ivy League degrees. They attempted to block his plans. But he found friends in other high places. He wasn't bragging when he said he could "rise above obstacles which would entirely crush another."[1] After occupying a position of unrivaled power and political influence in the kingdom that still has historians scratching their heads in wonder at how he did it, Spreckels wielded a clenched fist over Hawai'i's economy for nearly two decades. Cabinets were overthrown, laws were passed, grants of royal land and water rights were given. He made major technological advances throughout the Hawaiian Islands, the likes of which have never been seen before or since. He brought electricity to Hawaiʻi, irrigation to arid plains, and modernization to the sugar and transport industries. He was the king-pin in the development of the Hawaiʻi-California sugarcane industry. He opened a highway to sugar's profitable exploitation that benefited both sides of the Pacific. The reign of his friend King Kalākaua, who knighted him in appreciation for advancing and uplifting the economy, was the golden years of Hawaiian progress and prosperity, though in the end, the monarch paid for them at a very high price.

Spreckels was harshly criticized for what others perceived to be his ruthless business tactics and monopolies, yet he broke up monopolies himself to the benefit of his fellow citizens and persevered in the face of challenges and setbacks, which helped him triumph in an environment rife with cronyism and corruption. In his time he was portrayed as a ruthless predator, only concerned with the enlargement of his own fortune. He was matter-of-fact about his wealth: "Spreckels success is California's success."[2] He explained, "I'm motivated by very different rewards than other millionaires. . . . It is not money that is an object to me, but I want the people of California to be able to show that Claus Spreckels has done something for this state when his bones are at rest."[3] Spreckels created a new and profitable industry with the lowly sugar beet so that California could compete in America and, in turn, so that America could compete with Europe; in fact, a commercially viable sugar beet was his ultimate gift to his adopted country. He supplied the beet seeds for disadvantaged farmers in California's Salinas and Pajaro Valleys, personally trained them in the methods of beet cultivation and harvest, irrigated the dry valleys, and assured the farmers payment for their efforts. He built the largest beet sugar refinery in the world in the Salinas Valley, providing much needed employment for thousands in a new concept, the "factory in the fields." A self-taught agronomist, Spreckels changed the focus of a wide swath of California's agriculture from dry to irrigated crops, resulting in the vast, modern agricultural-industrial economy in today's "Salad Bowl of the World," where his white gold from sugar beets would eventually become green gold: lettuce, along with some of the best produce in the world.

John Steinbeck's imagination was captured in his seasonal work for the Spreckels sugar refinery, and immigrants later found their travails and struggles famously chronicled in his fiction. The tiny town of Spreckels, which achieved a historical designation from the Monterey County Board of Supervisors in 1991, was the location for the 1955 film *East of Eden*, based on Steinbeck's book. Claus Spreckels built this namesake industrial town in the Salinas Valley for his workers and their families to embody *his* ideas of beauty, cleanliness, efficiency—and Americanism.

At the same time Spreckels was uplifting California's vital economic and cultural development through sugar, both cane and beet, he was improving the utility, construction, and irrigation industries. He also helped resolve the state's critical transportation problems by building railroads, and his funding was essential in connecting America's shores for the first time to the Hawaiian Islands, New Zealand, and Australia with a modern steamship company flying the Spreckels flag.

Still, his accomplishments incurred a heavy personal toll. His dogged determination, so effective in business, caused prolonged periods of personal pain and contention. His dominating personality was not infinitely adaptive, and it frustrated his four sons, who were each trying to make his own mark in life. Due to their father's philosophy, "I never yet have gone into anything unless I could have it all my own way,"[4] each son—and his daughter as well—rebelled at one time or another as they grew into adulthood, and the Spreckels family kept the courts of law busy ironing out their differences at the intrigue of the public. Never was the country more stunned (and amused) as when Spreckels's son Adolph, purportedly defending his father's honor, attempted to shoot and kill the editor of the *Chronicle* but missed and was acquitted due to a "neuralgic headache."[5] The legendary Spreckels family quarrels were even discussed on the floor of the United States House of Representatives. Claus Spreckels hated losing anything but was pragmatic when he lost a lawsuit to one son, stating, "I was never beaten but once in my life, and it was by my own boy."[6]

Spreckels, rarely seen without a cigar and a smile, interacted easily with presidents, politicians, monarchs—the rich and famous—yet he remained as common, unpretentious, and comfortable as an old shoe. And whenever given the chance, he remained humble, always thankful to America for the opportunities he had been given as a poor immigrant. To that end his philanthropy was widespread with such words as "loving California as I do and being grateful for the many benefits that have accrued to me."[7] Physically ailing and suffering deep losses after the disastrous 1906 San Francisco earthquake, he was asked whether he'd return to spend his last days in his beloved mother country. He quickly retorted that while he could return to Germany and "live as liberally as the Emperor William," instead he would devote his fortune and what was left of his energy to the upbuilding of San Francisco, where his fortunes were made. He concluded, "There is no other place for me than California."[8]

I enjoy reading both the published and the unpublished histories of the founding of my Golden State, but I have not found a single pioneer who loved this state more than Claus Spreckels, who near the end of his life said, "I have never wished for any other home nor longed for anything on earth that California could not give."[9]

Claus Spreckels didn't see himself as a part of history, because he was too busy *making* history, but he did hope for someone like me to come along someday and write his biography, saying, "My life has been full of incident and would fill a book which, if not interesting, would be comprehensive."[10]

He was wrong when he said his life wasn't interesting, because it was not only interesting but downright captivating! I've struggled mightily to give you as much of the man as I could squeeze into a reasonably sized book. I've respected his legacy without, dare I say, sugarcoating it. Claus Spreckels is complex, a genius, and at times offensive, but I hope you'll come to appreciate the man as I eventually did.

THE
SUGAR
KING OF
CALIFORNIA

1   *Chasing the American Dream*

As they eagerly awaited the birth of their first child, Johann Diederich and Gesche Baak Spreckels were content with their lot in life, even though they were struggling to make ends meet as young tenant farmers. They lived in the tiny village of Lamstedt—then in the German kingdom of Hanover—on a small family homestead that had been handed down through the generations. Their thatched-roof cottage on Große Straße 25 was right below the Lutheran village church, St. Bartholomäus, which was where Claus Johann Spreckels, born on July 9, 1828, was ceremoniously baptized in the days following his birth. The church, both in good times and bad, would always play an important role for the family with such milestones as baptisms, weddings, and funerals held in the Lutheran tradition.

Even though they were mere renters of their land, Johann and Gesche were fiercely attached to it and the concomitant lifestyle. Though Johann was poor in formal education and assets, he was rich in pride, believing he was above the drudgery of his everyday life, as evidenced by his habit of trudging behind the plow while wearing an elegant and distinctive "tall, black plug [stovepipe] hat," affording "quiet amusement for his neighbors."[1] But as a high-spirited adolescent, Claus didn't find plodding behind a plow in Lamstedt as appealing as his father did.

As the family expanded to seven children, six boys and one girl, Claus, as the eldest, was required to exhibit a deep level of duty and dependability for both his parents and his siblings.[2] The entire family worked hard, from sunup to sundown, subsisting from one harvest to the next, and like other tenant farmers, they found themselves in constant debt. With nine people to be fed and clothed, Claus led by example and hired himself out to neighbors for part of the day to supplement the family's income. Even so, there was contentment within the walls of their home and pleasures to be found around the village—or in Claus's case, in the neighboring village of Mittelstenahe, where Claus fell in love with Anna Christina Mangels (1830–1910), who didn't mind being led by his overbearing personality.

But just as Claus was entering into adulthood, any semblance of contentment slowly turned to apprehension. All around him, and all across Germany, everyday life was rapidly changing in worrisome ways. The 1840s, soon to be known in northern Europe as "the Hungry Forties," ushered in a period of economic deprivation, social unrest, and political revolution of historic proportions. The immediate cause of the European famine of that decade was the massive failure of potato crops due to a blight. It was a disaster waiting to happen for Ireland because they had built a one-crop economy, based on the potato. As the blight spread across Europe, not only potatoes but grain crops failed, including the Spreckels family crops. The combined loss of two basic staple foods—potatoes and bread grains—led to historic food shortages and famine-related crime.[3] To prevent theft, military troops were regularly used to keep order among the starving population, who were finding ingenious but illegal ways to obtain and hoard food.

With the threat of eviction if his family were unable to pay their rent, Claus began searching for solutions, but he had little time to deliberate; in the middle of the deadly famine, rumors of war began circulating throughout his small village. Because Claus was approaching his eighteenth birthday, this particular rumor had to be taken seriously. Hanover had a law stipulating that at eighteen a man would be drafted into the army for two years, with "the freedom to emigrate only limited by military obligations."[4]

Claus began searching for options to relocate, even temporarily, to avoid the coming political unrest and the inevitable repression that would follow. In the beginning his parents saw the wisdom in helping Claus escape both the draft and the famine. They believed that wherever Claus ended up, he would succeed for the benefit of the family—including paving the way, if need be, for his brothers to follow in his path to safety. Putting their hope in Claus to help them out of their horrible predicament, they scraped together what little money they could part with and placed their lives in the hands of their eldest son.

Claus was likely keeping up with what printer and emigration agent Günther Fröbel was publishing. Fröbel noticed the demand among young men desperate to escape the military draft, and his popular newspaper, the *Allgemeine Auswanderungs-Zeitung (AAZ)*, provided practical advice, lists of available ships, information on what to expect at different destinations, and reports on the cities around the world in which Germans were settling.[5] As the trend in emigration continued, the newspaper covered all aspects of the immigrant experience, which would have been very helpful for Claus's brothers and friends, who would follow him to America in the coming years.

At the same time the *AAZ* came out, Claus and other young men were fed dreams of prosperity in the form of pamphlets that appeared throughout Hanover promoting emigration to the American South, specifically to Charleston, South Carolina. Claus was determined to pursue this promise of opportunity, likely factoring in that this destination was cheaper than going beyond the East Coast. Additionally, he'd have less competition, as the number of Germans then migrating to Southern states was insignificant; because the Midwest offered cheap farmland and the northeastern states were highly industrialized, of the 1.3 million who emigrated from Germany, only 5.5 percent settled in the South.[6]

When it was time for Claus to implement the heart-wrenching decision to leave his ancestral homeland for the United States, his parents had a change of heart. Even with their son's assurances that his departure was necessary to avoid possible death in military combat, even with the rationale that his leaving would result in one mouth less to feed—and most importantly, even though it was imperative and essential that he, as the eldest, make and send money home as fast as possible—Johann and Gesche couldn't bear to see Claus go and pleaded with him to stay. Their protests were seconded by their Lutheran minister and family friends, but Claus couldn't be dissuaded. Perhaps it was already evident that arguing with Claus was pointless once his mind was made up.

With his meager provisions packed and some borrowed money from an unnamed friend who had faith he'd be repaid, Claus went to Mittelstenahe and said a soulful goodbye to his Anna. It was clear to both families these two were destined for each other. Anna's younger brother Claus Mangels promised his sister's sweetheart they would both follow him to America in time. With those assurances, Claus Spreckels began the long journey to his new life.

Grocer-in-Training: Charleston

Claus sailed for the United States from Bremerhaven, the bustling port for the city of Bremen, but the name of the vessel on which he crossed the Atlantic has been lost. Passengers with the means to do so booked cabins above the ship's deck, but the only ticket Claus could afford was in steerage, the "between decks," the lightless cave sandwiched between the ship's deck and its hold.[7] For an adult traveling in steerage on a sailing ship in 1846, the average fare was 33 to 35 thalers, about $23 at the time (approximately $770 in today's money). Considering that a common farm laborer like Claus from a small village made on average 24 thalers a year, it's significant that he was able scrape the funds together at all.[8] Claus had to pay more than a year's wages to travel in the cramped, dirty confines of steerage, enduring weeks trapped in "a rolling, tumbling, dark, watery, waste-filled hell."[9]

In 1846 such a sea journey was grueling, and few amenities were provided to steerage passengers. Claus would have had to stow his meager belongings in a single regulation-size box. He was also required to bring his own food for the entire voyage. In a sailing ship, crossing the Atlantic was a slow and dangerous experience. The ship was at the mercy of both the ocean and the weather, utterly dependent upon wind for propulsion. On a calm sea with little wind, the sails would hang inoperable, and the voyage could take on average anywhere from one to three months.[10] One contemporary wrote, "Sightings of whales and icebergs alleviated some of the tedium, but when there was no wind, . . . the boredom is hardly to be tolerated."[11] Besides the boredom, it's likely that Claus suffered deep hunger, rationing his provisions very carefully, not knowing how long his journey would be.

When the ship finally anchored in New York harbor, six miles south of the dock, anxiety set in on every deck, regardless of a passenger's status. Before a single person could disembark among the general population, a doctor would board, looking for the telltale symptoms of smallpox, yellow fever, typhus, cholera, or other infections obtained on the voyage that would require the passenger to be whisked off in a small boat for quarantining. Once the ship was allowed to dock, nerves were again frayed when a second clearance by a medical doctor was required.

Cleared from the medical checkups, a disheveled Claus finally put his feet on solid ground and was thrown into a mass of weary immigrants, all trying to figure out their next moves. As Claus made his way through the waterfront, he brushed past a diversity of people that he would never have encountered in the narrow cultural borders of Lamstedt. One diary entry of the era voiced what many must have felt after leaving the ship: "I felt somewhat uncomfortable. The frantic hurry of the people, the hundreds of cabs, wagons, and carts—the noise is indescribable. Even one who has seen Germany's largest cities can hardly believe his eyes and ears."[12]

Claus, a lad who had never ventured far from his home village, then had to figure out how to get from New York to South Carolina. Though his method of transportation to the South is unknown, it likely reflected the limited funds he had left. After he exchanged his money—a single German thaler amounting to a pitiful seventy-five cents ($27 in today's money)—at the port of New York to pay for his fare, he knew he'd have to employ the "Spreckels formula" of "work, work, work!"[13]

Though South Carolina's rural agricultural Lowcountry region would have been a logical choice for a young farmer such as himself, Claus chose instead to settle in the city of Charleston, a vibrant seaport central to the important cotton and rice trades. It was also a city that prided itself on its sophisticated Southern culture and was well known for its lavish lifestyles, horse racing, and diverse architecture. The emerging metropolitan city was a far cry from the simple farm life in Lamstedt, and this was exactly what Claus wanted. With his whole life ahead of him, it must have been frightening yet exciting for him to ponder his future in a strange country.

In America Hanoverians referred to themselves as German, even though Germany wouldn't exist as a political entity until 1871; they related to their cultural identity rather than their birthplace.[14] At the time, German immigrants filled an important gap in Charleston's economy "as grocers, bakers, dry goods merchants, commission brokers, tailors, and shoemakers."[15] Claus learned that working in a grocery store rather than on a farm was the most common apprenticeship, and being centrally located as opposed to isolated on a distant farm would provide more opportunities for inculcation into the American way of life. In 1851 there were 125 applicants for American citizenship from the kingdom of Hanover, and more than 40 percent listed their profession as grocer.[16]

Charleston had an active German Friendly Society, which offered practical assistance to newly arrived immigrants by helping them secure positions in German-owned businesses as well as providing social occasions to aid in the transition from European to American culture. Germans, more than most, maintained strong cultural ties to their homeland and protected one another in practical ways. In South Carolina this community was vital because white Southerners had begun to exclude them over the issue of slave ownership, a practice deplored by most Germans.[17]

Through the society, Claus found his first job as a clerk in a German-owned grocery store. The pay was low—a paltry one dollar a week—but it included room and board, so he was only too happy to accept the position. It's likely the storeowners were also from Hanover because Charlestonian German grocers, themselves former farmers, would often hire untrained men from their home country over experienced grocers from another country.[18]

As a grocer in training, Claus demonstrated the same determination and reliability that had made him a popular hired farmhand in Lamstedt: "My labor was in demand, and I got better wages than the other boys."[19] Claus stated that he had "kept an eye" on how his boss ran the grocery business, all the time considering ways it could be improved, "so that he, the dollar-a-week clerk, would know how to run his own business better, when he had one to run,"[20] a strategy he would employ many times over the next decade. After he passed the one-month probationary period, it seems the owner didn't want to lose his industrious young grocer, because Claus proudly recalled: "I then got $4 a month and was raised $2 a month progressively until I was receiving $16."[21] His parents were delighted when Claus, true to his word, included money with his letter announcing his progress.

Claus quickly recognized that his future options would be limited unless he learned English, so he began to acquire the language by diligently inter-acting with as many sympathetic Americans as he could. He attributed this same attention to the minute details of every task—deploring any mistakes, even minor ones, applied to learning both the grocery business and the English language—as the most important factor in his success. Despite his thick German accent, his language skills were impressive and, coupled with his strong work ethic, soon led to his promotion to manager.

A year and a half after Claus's arrival in Charleston, the store owners announced their retirement, and Claus bravely asked to buy the store with a meager down payment and the rest on credit. Without hesitation they agreed to his terms and recommended Claus to their vendors, who also extended him credit, which greatly assisted his prospects for success. Their faith was not misplaced. Claus lived frugally and repaid the entire amount, about $1,200, within the year. Indebtedness apparently didn't appeal to him, as he would later repeatedly announce, "I make a strict rule of cash purchasing."[22]

Claus sent many letters home to his sweetheart in Hanover. At his urging, in 1849, when she was nineteen, Anna immigrated to New York with her younger brother, seventeen-year-old Claus Mangels, who himself faced a military draft. Anna was the eldest of seven children and knew how to run a household and take care of younger children. She easily found domestic work—providentially in the home of a wealthy sugar refiner—and waited for her beau. Once Claus had established himself in a newly built, three-story, red brick dwelling at 60 Anson Street in the heart of Charleston (still standing today),[23] he traveled to New York and married twenty-two-year-old Anna Christina Mangels on August 11, 1852. It was becoming clear to those left behind in Lamstedt that the couple might never return.

Life was promising for the newlyweds when they returned to Charleston and began married life as shopkeepers in the neighborhood now called Ansonborough.[24] As with many of their shopkeeping neighbors, the ground floor of their home was used for their business, and the top stories were their living space. With their both working and residing on the same street, the lines between business and social activities were often blurred, and Claus and Anna found themselves deeply immersed with people of every background. Down the street from the boldly named "Spreckels Store" was a cigar shop, run by the Cuban immigrant Rafael Morallo Morillo. Perhaps this is where Claus developed his lifelong habit of smoking the best Cuban cigars money could buy. The bustling street was scented with rich cigar smoke mingling with the delicious yeasty aromas from Edward Stehle's popular bakery. Other neighbors included a bottler, a bootmaker, a drayman, a barber, a watchmaker, a midwife, a tailor, and other grocers from every part of Europe.[25]

To increase revenue and compete with other grocers, Claus applied to the city of Charleston to sell alcohol. His liquor license was approved on October 2, 1852. The signatures of those who vouched for him on the license were mainly of German origin, revealing that he had established a strong ethnic network in Charleston. Claus began to sell alcohol—or, as the license stated, "retail spirituous liquors"—in the Spreckels Store, and indeed his income increased.[26]

Anna, like her husband, detested idleness, and soon put her baking talents to use in the shop. Claus partitioned off a small area of the store for her, but he soon needed to expand the space when Anna's delectable German baked goods far outsold the other food products.[27] When it comes to breads and sweet pastries, especially delicate strudels, Germany has more variety than any other country in the world, and the Spreckels Store became stiff competition for the popular bakery run by its neighbor Edward Stehle.

A year after their wedding, Anna might have sought the assistance of Mrs. Albright, the local midwife. On August 16, 1853, she gave birth to their first child. Since the father of each parent was named Johann (John), no favoritism was shown in naming him John Diedrich Spreckels.[28]

Although the Spreckelses' home was free of strife in those early days, the same couldn't be said of the world outside their door. The issue of slavery had begun to divide the nation in the 1830s, and South Carolina was a stronghold of proslavery sentiments. By midcentury tensions with Northern states were high and soon to become worse. German immigrants in the slaveholding states had earned a reputation for tolerance and liberalism regarding race, which put them at odds with the established white communities.[29] And vice versa. For example, when Texas publisher Ferdinand Lindheimer ran an editorial in his German-language *Die Neu-Braunfelser Zeitung* (now the *New Braunfels [TX] Herald-Zeitung*) suggesting that fellow Germans go along with the Confederacy and their right to own slaves, German transplants became so incensed they broke into Lindheimer's newspaper office that very night and threw his printing press into the Comal River.[30]

Claus's opinions about individual liberty simply didn't allow him to accept the popular racial ideologies of the proslavery majority around him. In Charleston this attitude drew sharp criticism from his non-German neighbors, many of whom resented Germans who did business with Blacks. Historians now suggest that in Charleston, "German grocers undermined the slave system to a significant degree" by acting as "bold breakers of the law" against selling liquor to the Blacks, a practice that had been illegal in South Carolina since 1831. By flouting this law, Claus and other immigrants were challenging the established institution of racial division.[31] In the 1850s conflicts between native-born white Southerners and immigrant German grocers were at an all-time high over the sale of liquor to this population. The police force, mainly Irishmen who made up the largest group of immi-

8 Chasing the American Dream

grants in Charleston, continually harassed German grocers by arresting and fining them.[32]

Soon it was South Carolina, rather than Hanover, imposing personal restrictions and sanctions on Claus, which he found unbearable. According to Spreckels family lore, when Claus was found to have blatantly broken the law by selling alcohol to Blacks, slave and free, and Charlestonian authorities were poised to come down hard, they sold their prospering grocery store and fled town.[33] And they did so quickly to avoid severe penalties: stiff fines and perhaps imprisonment. Luckily, they had somewhere to go: Anna's brother was living in New York, himself working in a grocery store.

New York Misery

In 1854 the Spreckels family arrived in New York, trepidatious about starting all over. Earlier Anna's brother Claus Mangels had unsuccessfully tried to entice his brother-in-law into a grocery store partnership in New York.[34] But the disturbing events in South Carolina now changed everything, and the two Clauses went into business together, presumably sharing living quarters.

Remembering how the liquor license had significantly increased his grocery revenue, Claus totally devoted the new store to selling "liquors." *Trow's New York City Directory (1855–1856)* identifies its location at the corner of West Broadway and Worth Street.[35] Claus and Anna arrived at a time when city officials were trying to reduce crime in lower Manhattan. Officials encouraged new merchants, likely at a reduced rent, to help transform the neighborhood into the city's new dry goods district.[36] German businesses were thriving in New York City, not only in the heavily German neighborhoods but all over the vast city. Claus applied the business experience he had gained in Charleston, and the store prospered beyond expectations.

Nevertheless, neither he nor Anna acclimated to the congestion, crime, rampant disease, or climate. In fact, Claus made it well known they were both miserable in New York. Homesick and pregnant, Anna survived the sweltering summer months of 1854 only because Claus promised her they would return home for a visit if they saved enough money. Their second son, Henry, was born in November. Because Claus was an astute businessman and lived frugally, they were able to take six months off in 1855 to introduce toddler John and baby Henry to their grandparents, who were surely overjoyed by their children's achievements in America. The severe agricultural crisis that had gripped Lamstedt, indeed all of Europe, had diminished, which meant the urgency for Claus to provide for his parents had also eased. Hope was in the air.[37]

Claus's younger brother Bernhard had immigrated to San Francisco in 1849 and owned a small dry goods grocery store there.[38] On his own way home to Lamstedt in 1855, he stopped in New York to visit with Claus and Anna, who had returned from their own visit to Lamstedt.[39] He told of numerous lucrative opportunities in a city still feverish from the Gold Rush. Claus, miserable, restless, and bored in New York, was intrigued by his brother's stories and decided to make California his permanent home, sight unseen. He was oblivious to newspaper stories of sickly and disillusioned adventurers who had returned home after failing to strike it rich in the West. Any misgivings that Anna, now pregnant with their third child, Adolph, might have had didn't stop Claus. For $8,000 (about $270,000 in today's money), he sold his shares of the New York store to his brother-in-law Claus (who would later follow them) and then packed up his family once again. In June of 1856 they began the long and grueling trek to California.[40]

The pursuit of Claus's dream to go west required fortitude. The family journeyed two thousand miles by ship down the East Coast and then across the Caribbean Sea. Rather than following the route most travelers undertook, a thirteen-thousand-mile voyage around Cape Horn at the tip of South America, they took advantage of a grueling "short cut." Using an array of transportation methods, they crossed forty-seven miles of malaria-laden wetlands in Panama. Although arduous and full of peril, shaving off eight thousand miles was worth the hardship for the ever-efficient Claus, who was grateful that his family had avoided the dreaded tropical fever that cost so many their lives. They also escaped being mugged or murdered by robbers who waited in the dense jungle for travelers carrying valuables to and from California.

At the other side of the isthmus, the fatigued Spreckels family was more than ready to catch sight of the Bahía de Panamá (Panama Bay), where they boarded a wooden-hulled side-wheeler steamer, the *John L. Stephens*, driven by a massive single-cylinder steam engine equipped with a thirty-foot paddle wheel providing power to assist the sails. On this final stretch of the journey to San Francisco, the family endured another unpredictable and dangerous ocean voyage.

San Francisco After the Gold Rush

On July 1, 1856, eight days before Claus turned twenty-eight years old, the *John L. Stephens* steamed through the Golden Gate into San Francisco Bay and landed on Central Wharf.[41] Claus and Anna, holding their two small children tightly, made their way down the pier. They saw a city that had transformed itself in just ten years from a sleepy hamlet of around two hundred to a thriving town of nearly fifty thousand.[42] The increase in population was due to the thousands of men who had rushed to California's Sacramento Valley in 1849 to pan gold-bearing streams or to dig gold nuggets out of the Sierra Nevada earth. When the easy-to-find gold was gone by 1855, disappointed 49ers returned to the coast and settled in San Francisco.

San Francisco was not unique among cities in having a seedy side, but there was a sense among those who spent time indulging in "sins" that they could enjoy themselves more openly in this far western city than they could in their places of origin. A large portion of the population was young, single men who were bold, speculative, and enterprising, seeking money any way they could get it. Gambling was a principal industry, and murders, robberies, and public hangings were alarmingly prevalent. It was truly the wild, wild West following the Gold Rush era. Recorded reminisces from German newcomers, used to law and order, indicate they were overwhelmed by the tumultuous, sinful, unsettled, and chaotic culture.[43]

In the months preceding Claus's arrival, seven thousand armed citizens, intolerant with the apathy shown to criminal behavior, had formed a Committee of Vigilance to put an end to the disorder.[44] Luckily for the Spreckels family, after the mob violence of the vigilantes, citizens had approved the Consolidation Act in April 1856, merging San Francisco's city and county into a single body. This act promised to curb the politicians' extravagant expenditures and institute political reform to curb criminal behavior.[45]

Many young, disillusioned former miners, out of money, stayed in California to provide goods and services to the miners. In 1852 Domingo Ghirardelli opened a chocolate factory and the Studebakers built carriages for gold miners. Other entrepreneurs established Folgers Coffee and Schilling Spices to meet the needs of San Franciscans at the end of the Gold Rush.[46]

When Panama steamers started dumping shiploads of passengers into San Francisco, more wharves were constructed to accommodate them, providing the richest source of income for the city. Many land-grabbing schemes were publicized about wily men anxious to lay claim to lots on the waterfront. Shops, eateries, and offices clustered together on the creaking wharves for the convenience of those in shipping-related trades. All along the waterfront, clever opportunists turned abandoned vessels left behind from the Gold Rush pioneers into warehouses and lodgings.[47]

Claus joined the fray of those who went into business to supply goods to the former 49ers. Unlike others who were forced to become laborers, however, he had the advantage of being flush, still having much of the money from selling his shares in the New York store to Anna's brother.[48] With those proceeds, he purchased the grocery store of his lovesick brother Bernhard, who was moving back to Lamstedt to marry Juliane Hink. The family grocery store was situated on the northwest corner of Powell and Filbert, fronting Washington Square in today's North Beach district.[49] Claus soon found that location too isolated to grow, so he relocated Spreckels & Co. to Pine Street near today's Chinatown.[50]

In San Francisco Claus found a city where he could put down roots for his growing family. Unlike New York, the city was small enough to easily navigate, and the temperate climate was agreeable. Anna and Claus seemed content in these early days and began to raise their family and save a little money for a house. John found those childhood days on Pine Street sentimentally "unobtrusive" and quiet. Both of his parents emulated a "no nonsense" attitude, combined with Anna's "old-fashioned principles—obedience, thrift, thoroughness, simplicity and, above all, honor and truth." There was no "mollycoddling," and young John didn't dare disobey his father; hence, his only remembered childhood punishment was for his "incurable propensity" for "strumming the piano" instead of doing tasks.[51]

A grocery venture was a logical investment for Claus, but in just a few months he knew he had made a mistake. All around him the city was vibrating with an entrepreneurial spirit, yet he was twenty-eight and bored with stocking and selling groceries. Motivated by all he saw and felt around him, Claus wanted to take risks, to be one of the entrepreneurs who seized the opportunities in the aftermath of the Gold Rush. His "restless energy and ambition" was nothing short of palpable, and he began to seek new opportunities.[52]

1. The face of stubborn determination. Claus Spreckels (1828–1908). Courtesy of Terrence and Virginia Wilson private collection.

Hoping with Hops

After a decade working as a grocer, Claus's entrepreneurial drive couldn't be contained, and he was ready to step away from the safety of his grocery business and risk his earnings to become a professional beer brewer. Many of Claus's countrymen who had arrived in America alongside him joined the growing beer industry in such German-heavy cities as St. Louis, Chicago, Milwaukee, and Philadelphia. As the number of breweries and bars increased, the religious-based temperance movement, along with other social reformers and politicians, began to blame German immigrants and their breweries for the nation's growing problems surrounding alcohol.[53] But those claims never stopped the Germans or their breweries from expanding.

A beer lover himself, Claus thought most West Coast beer tasted horrible, because it was shipped from the East Coast and spoiled in transit. As a result, a handful of local home brewers had begun specializing in "quick-brewed beer," but because it was brewed in only three days, it was "tasteless."[54] Claus recognized a gap in the San Francisco market that he intended to fill. A persuasive entrepreneur, in 1857 he convinced his brother-in-law Claus Mangels (now in San Francisco) and his brother Peter Spreckels to pool their money and enter the brewery business.

For Claus, bringing family into the business was not only traditional but also practical: working with people he cared about would be both professionally and personally rewarding. It was well known that he had a hard time trusting many people outside his tight-knit German family when it came to money. In years to come, he wouldn't have to look too far from his nuclear family for business partners, though. By the time the family's Albany Brewery debuted in the spring of 1857, Anna had given him three sons: John was three, Henry was two, and Adolph only two months old. They moved to reside above the brewery, which enabled Claus to ensure that his high standards were always kept. While the smell of fermenting beer likely permeated every nook and cranny of their home, life looked bright.

Their extended family grew as well. When twins Agnes and Anna Grosse arrived on the San Francisco scene from Westphalen, Germany, Claus's and Anna's bachelor brothers coordinated their proposals: twenty-two-year-old Peter Spreckels married seventeen-year-old Anna on January 5, 1862, and twenty-nine-year-old Claus Mangels married Agnes later that same year.[55]

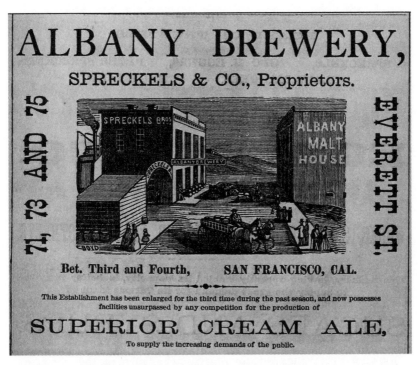

ALBANY BREWERY,

SPRECKELS & CO., Proprietors.

71, 73 AND 75

EVERETT ST,

Bet. Third and Fourth,   SAN FRANCISCO, CAL.

This Establishment has been enlarged for the third time during the past season, and now possesses facilities unsurpassed by any competition for the production of

SUPERIOR CREAM ALE,

To supply the increasing demands of the public.

2. Brewing steam ale gave the Spreckelses credibility in their German American community and provided the manufacturing experience necessary to succeed in sugar. *San Francisco Directory*, 1874.

The twin sisters were only too happy to give up the life of "sandwich girls" to join in the brewery business. Claus's brother Diederich, eight years younger, had also found his way to San Francisco and joined the growing family brewing business.[56]

It was easy for Claus to persuade the family to enter this business by showing them how the opportunity was lucrative due to a lack of serious competition. But rivalry showed up around the same time their Albany Brewery opened. German immigrant John Wieland, a gold miner turned baker turned brewer, bought San Francisco's Philadelphia Brewery in 1856 and elevated its status, much to the chagrin of Claus.

The Albany Brewery, downtown on Everett Street (now Natoma Street), advertised "superior cream ale to supply the increasing demands of the public."[57] The brewery prospered beyond expectations and soon expanded across the road to include a saloon, which Claus named the Albany Malt House. At the time, "Albany cream ale," brewed from pale hops in Albany, New York, was famous for its smoothness and high alcohol content. Claus was producing and publicizing this American popular type of beer, rather than the familiar German lagers, to win over the West Coast the same way that easterners had been won over. While Wieland concentrated on traditional Bavarian lagers, Claus strategically went in another direction with cream ales before brewing lagers himself. Then he went in still another direction with his invention of "steam beer," a workingman's beer—sturdy, carbonated, and cheap.[58] After boiling, the beer was cooled outside in the open evening air. When the heat from the boil swirled up and mixed with the chilly fog, it was a memorable and steamy sight.

With employees under him for the first time, he quickly learned the difficult lesson that an errant employee could easily harm his business. Managing people who were not invested in the profits of the company cost him much needed sleep. Claus recounted a time when he was forced to micromanage the brewery or risk spoiled product:

> You know in brewing great attention has to be paid to the thermometer. If the mercury goes too high the beer will turn sour and spoil. The men would all knock off at a certain hour and think no more of business, but I have frequently gone into the brewery after all hands have left and found the thermometer making unpleasant records, and I have slipped on my overalls and worked all night by myself. Why at one time I only took four hours sleep in the twenty-four for months.[59]

Over the next few years Claus continued to build his brewery business, but frustratingly, he was always second tier to John Wieland in brewing prominence.[60] Nonetheless, Claus fell into a comfortable routine, both at home and at the brewery, experimenting with beers, especially German lager, which became so popular that it won a top award at a district fair.[61] He also came up with clever ideas to market his beer, such as taking five-gallon kegs to the newspaper offices with the "polite request" to evaluate its qualities. Then newspapers, such as the *San Joaquin Republican*, reported that it "was superior in its line" and they could "conscientiously recommend it to the public."[62] Working at the Albany Brewery, with the fine, rich perfume of malt, hops, and yeast, pleased Claus, but the money was not what he imagined it would be. While the brewery provided a good income, it was not enough to elevate the family's living conditions, considering all the ways he had to split the earnings among others. While he gave Wieland a run for his money, Claus realized the brewery business would never be a money maker, and it wasn't a profession that needed elevating. He was out to make his own mark of significance and realized that it wouldn't be in beer. In time, Claus and John Wieland became the best of friends, and Claus would act as a pallbearer for Wieland's premature funeral in 1885, when he died along with his daughter Bertha in a kerosene explosion in the basement of his house.

Claus was going through the motions as brewery owner when providence struck. The Albany Brewery and Malt House were located near the city's sole sugar manufacturer, the San Francisco and Pacific Sugar Refinery. Its massive brick building, five stories high, had been established in 1857 by the flamboyant, rich Englishman George Gordon, regarded as the life of every party, on the northwest corner of Harrison and Price. Gordon's refining techniques were anything but advanced, and while the refinery was lucrative, it seemed more like one of his numerous hobbies than a career.[63] Claus listened to the complaints of Gordon's refinery workers as they nursed their beers after work and learned that in the process of refining, a significant quantity of the sugar liquor overflowed and went to waste. In one of the refining process steps, washed sugar crystals are dissolved in water to yield a syrup referred to as melt liquor. Wasted product along the way would negatively impact the gross yield, a thought that horrified frugal Claus, who said, "If men can run liquor into the sewers day after day and night after night, and the firm can still make a good profit, those profits must be enormous!"[64] At that time Claus had no idea just how enormous those profits would be.

White Gold

Back in Germany the Spreckels family stirred sugar into their morning coffee—sugar made from beets rather than cane. Claus was surprised to discover that America's sugar came strictly from cane. Although the two sugars are virtually indistinguishable from each other in both taste and appearance, the process of cultivation is completely different.

In America the refining process involved mechanically crushing the sugarcane to extract the sweet juice, which was then heated to reduce its water content. The resulting thick and sticky syrup was poured into a variety of shaped molds to dry. Manufacturers sent their sweet product to grocers across the country in solid form that depended on the preferred shape of the large mold—often in tall cones, large blocks, or loaves. Once sold, the grocer or distributor portioned off the customer's desired amount using "sugar nippers," a specially designed tool that resembled pliers. The chunk of hard sugar was then pounded, ground, or grated, depending on the recipe. A savvy grocer with a portable mill to grind hard lumps of sugar into fine granules could easily become popular with a customer. These processes begged to be advanced. Claus, never one to embrace a nostalgic vision of the good old days, likely looked restlessly ahead to see how America's refinement of sugar could be improved.

Sugar was not always available to common people. In colonial times it had been a luxury item—expensive and scarce. In the days of George Washington, when dentistry was virtually nonexistent, a person's smile could reflect one's socioeconomic status.[1] The affluent Washington himself, who had a great affinity for sugar, had only a single natural tooth left by the time he was inaugurated as president in 1789. That year the first U.S. Congress, installed under the newly adopted Constitution, provided a "sweet deal" for American cane growers by imposing tariffs on imported raw sugar as a means of insulating them from overseas competition.[2] After President Thomas Jefferson, a lifelong farmer who prioritized agriculture in his administration, carried out the Louisiana Purchase in 1803, the sugar plantations in Louisiana would come under the control of those American growers.[3]

Laboring in the cane fields or sugar mills was one of the most dangerous agricultural and industrial tasks to be found. Backbreaking work on the sugar plantations meant that enslaved people had short life expectancies, many dropping dead after working only seven years. Enslaved children toiled alongside the adults under the constant threat of boiling kettles, open furnaces, and grinding rollers—as well the master's whip.[4] This "white gold," as it came to be called, was an important fuel for the slave trade when Claus arrived in America.

Refining the cane, however, was not Louisiana's job. The raw sugar was shipped to the East Coast, packed in large wooden barrels called hogsheads that were marked with the name of the originating plantation.[5] By 1860 the sugar-refining business had exploded and had become central to New York City commerce and industry. There were more than twenty-six different refineries that could pick up those hogsheads, turning New York into the sugar capital of the world.[6]

After the Mason jar was invented in 1858, fruit canning—which required sugar—expanded across the country, particularly in California, a state on its way to becoming a principal producer of grapes, citrus, apples, peaches, and other delicious fruit. But that all changed when the American Civil War began in 1861. To block the transport of both merchandise and recruits, railway stations became the targets of attack, and the trains themselves became targets for destruction by the forces of both the North and the South. When the South shrank its transport of raw Louisiana sugar to the North, the West suffered. Small grocers in San Francisco could no longer afford the staggering price of sugar, and sugar once again became a household luxury.

Sleuthing by Moonlight in New York

The inspiration to change the direction of his life came to Claus in the winter of 1863, when he realized this was the time to get in the game of sugar refining due to the supply demand.[7] Claus informed Anna that he was going to New York, the epicenter of sugar refining, to learn the trade *on the job*. He reasoned the only way he could launch his own business was to roll up his sleeves and learn the techniques firsthand, even if that meant living across the continent and enduring hard work and low wages for an extended period. Family and friends thought this decision was foolhardy and strongly advised Claus to forgo this new undertaking. Their chief argument was the "heavy outlay of capital" to build a refinery when there was already one big enough to meet the city's needs.[8] But Claus wouldn't be deterred. He recognized that brewing was giving him no challenge, no sense of satisfaction, and little return for his investment. More importantly, he was facing midlife and desired purposeful work, where he could make his mark.

Furthermore, Claus told a stunned Anna that he'd be taking their son John, not yet ten years old, along with him on this expedition. There would be no arguing with Claus. He had worked alongside his own father as a child and knew the satisfaction of reaping what he sowed. John, his eldest, would follow suit, even if it meant moving close to the site of the ongoing Civil War. This war was the first conflict for which Americans could absorb battle news even before the dead were buried. Horrific eyewitness accounts were relayed via telegraph to the country's newspapers, printed almost immediately, and then read voraciously by a nation desperate for all war news. Even so, Claus wouldn't be dissuaded from going to the East.

And it was getting worse: President Lincoln's later famous line "If slavery is not wrong, nothing is wrong" was made manifest on January 1, 1863, when his Emancipation Proclamation went into effect, ostensibly freeing all slaves in the rebellious Confederate states. The chaos that followed the president's decree illustrated the bitter divide among Americans over the issue of slavery. Despite the highly publicized news about the pandemonium occurring specifically in New York, Claus and John packed their bags and set out via the Isthmus of Panama. The nearly two-month perilous journey was all too familiar. Staying behind were Claus's five youngest children—eight-year-old Henry, six-year-old Adolph Bernard, five-year-old Claus Augustus "Gus," two-year-old Anna Gesina, and infant Louis Peter. The Albany Brewery was left in the hands of Claus's capable partners.

As intended, Claus was hired as a laborer at the sugar refinery owned by Charles Wright Durant.[9] Claus worked the moonlight shift—twelve hours a day, six days a week. Toiling under gaslights was dangerous, as sugar is highly combustible when it's finely divided and dispersed as a dust cloud in the air. Newspaper articles were replete with horrific stories of explosions that occurred at sugar refineries. In poorly lit conditions, this would render Claus's shift particularly hazardous. But working through the night enabled him to keep an eye on young John during the daylight hours. Claus said that his focus was singular: "I waded right in. I went to learn the trade and I learned it."[10] John, for his part, was bored in the boarding house. He was also deeply homesick and recalled that this "lonesome" time in New York cemented his love for California.[11]

During the day, John's sugar training took place when they traversed New York's cobblestone roads by horsecar and visited other refineries to compare the best practices of refining methods. At every refinery, Claus was notably observant of every detail and doggedly asked questions until he got the right answer.[12] Although John disliked the entire experience, he learned the valuable lessons of hard work, including persistence and being methodical, and saw by his father's example that there's no shame in starting from the bottom.[13]

Claus believed he had seen the last of wartime drafts when he fled Hanover—where conscription was certain—because America had never drafted men for war. But the Civil War changed everything. When the National Conscription Act was enacted in March 1863, it touched off the worst rioting in New York that Americans had ever seen. Claus and John, in the very heart of the city, were nearby the violent rampaging of those opposed to the draft. The police force had been reduced because men were away at war, leaving the city painfully vulnerable. Over four terrifying days rioters set buildings on fire, cut telegraph lines, and ripped up railroad tracks. Hundreds upon hundreds of people were wounded or killed.[14] Despite the chaos in the city, however, Claus kept a singular focus on sugar.

By the end of that sweltering summer, Claus believed that he had assimilated the technical methods of refining and made plans to return home to California. As luck would have it, an opportunity arose to buy the necessary equipment to open his own sugar refinery in San Francisco. After some persuasive bargaining, he purchased machinery at a rock-bottom price from New York's newly bankrupt United States Refinery. Claus, trusting no one, supervised the packing of the refinery machinery to ensure it would arrive intact on its lengthy journey around Cape Horn to San Francisco.

The Bay Sugar Refinery

When Claus and John arrived home in the fall of 1863, they were met by Anna who was overjoyed with emotion when her firstborn walked in the door "alive and well."[15] It was a wonderful reunion, but Claus was distracted with all he had to do to get his new sugar venture organized in time for the machinery in transit to San Francisco. Even so, the separation must have been hard on both him and Anna, because his future practice was to take the entire family with him on business trips.

Claus was confident he could make the process more economical than the refineries he'd seen in New York, and knew without a doubt that George Gordon's San Francisco and Pacific Sugar Refinery was way behind technologically and would be easy to beat. He wanted out of the brewing business completely, but he realized he needed the Albany Brewery and Malt House income until he could get the refinery up and running. He recalled that he was stretched thin: "I kept the brewery going all the time" until I could get the refinery "in a working condition."[16]

Meanwhile, he managed to persuade his twenty-four-year-old brother Peter and his thirty-two-year-old brother-in-law Claus Mangels to join him in his new venture. Although they believed in Claus, they didn't want to abandon the Albany Brewery, which by this time had become a large-scale producer of beer in San Francisco. As additional relatives immigrated to San Francisco from Lamstedt, it became even more important to keep the Albany Brewery in the family.

Claus's youngest brother, Hinrich "Henry" Spreckels, arrived in San Francisco in 1864 at the age of twenty-two. Fourteen years older, Claus may have felt more fatherly than brotherly. Young and muscular, Henry was installed at the brewery to handle the heavy wooden kegs full of beer; he would then make deliveries by horse-drawn wagons throughout the dusty roads of the city. Before long, Anna's sister Sophia and her husband, Claus Brommer, arrived from Hanover and joined in the prosperity of the brewery.[17] The brewery provided a vital means of employment for the new arrivals and kept the expanding family unit together.

Claus Spreckels immersed himself in planning for the Bay Sugar Refinery Company. In the best of times, he was described as outgoing and jovial; during this time, however, he was characterized as driven, ruthless, and impatient. Both at home and at work, he was accustomed to getting what

3. Claus sits proudly. He passed his pride to his two eldest boys, Adolph Bernard (*left*) and John Diedrich. Courtesy of Terrence and Virginia Wilson private collection.

he wanted, and he had little patience for business partners, family or otherwise, who were foolhardy enough to question his decisions or priorities. In addition to his partners Peter Spreckels and Claus Mangels,[18] Claus enlisted two Hanoverian transplants, Hermann Meese and Louis Meyer, as investors. Even though each of the five men had equal shares, Claus proclaimed that he alone would guide the company as president.[19]

Schooling the Boys

Claus hadn't gotten the opportunity for much schooling as a child, but he didn't want to deny his boys that opportunity. Throughout his single-digit years, John's formal education had been inconsistent, but with Claus busy getting the refinery up and running, it was time to remedy that. Somehow, Claus came to believe in the structure of early boarding school training, with the added benefit that it would relieve worn-out Anna of the increasing responsibilities of their growing family.[20]

At eleven, John was sent across San Francisco Bay to the newly created College of California, a boy's academy in Oakland designed to prepare secondary students for higher education.[21] Though nonsectarian in its mission statement, the boarding school was run by ultraconservative ministers of the Congregationalist and Presbyterian faiths, unlike the more liberal Lutherans, who would have been the Spreckels family's preference.[22] Worldly and focused, John had no outward troubles, unlike his brother Adolph.

Adolph argued against leaving home for the first time, but Claus believed the school would provide him the much-needed structure he appeared to lack.[23] Accompanied only by his mother on the big day, Adolph hated the boarding school the moment he saw it and clung to her arm as they inspected the "bare, dingy room" he'd share with several boys. Adolph was "doggedly silent," and thoughts of "incipient rebellion" began even as his mother "kissed him good-bye" and "expressed her maternal confidence that he would be a good boy." Catching sight of his mother crying into her handkerchief as her carriage rounded the corner caused him to fall to the ground, as "pent-up feelings freed themselves in a sob." Within minutes, the school bully called out, "Crybaby!" A fight ensued, which Adolph continued the next day. Adolph didn't yield well to authority, and his punishment was "doubled" due to his "spirited argument" with the principal. The conflicts continued throughout his time at Oakland College and gave him a lifelong determination to "beat any bully to the punch."[24] This attitude would prove deadly as he grew.

If You're Not First, You're Last

The Bay Sugar Refinery Company was established in a large two-story brick building on the waterfront at Union and Battery Streets, at the foot of Telegraph Hill near Law's Wharf. By all accounts, the fledgling operation was a financial success from its formal incorporation in January 1864; it was capitalized at $250,000 in one thousand shares of $250 each.[25] Due to his sleuthing among the New York refineries, Claus knew just what type of people to hire. Where he got an accomplished workforce, skilled foremen, and technicians is anybody's guess, but the Bay Sugar Refinery began operation in record time due to his expert selections, and he was finally able to sell his shares in the Albany Brewery.[26] From this point forward, nothing would steer his attention from building a sugar industry.

Claus made all the necessary purchases of the coarse brown raw sugar to be shipped to his refinery. When it arrived, all hands were on deck to attend to the principal task of removing the brownish color and foreign "impurities" (minute insects) by implementing the technical procedures he had mastered in New York. When sugar is first crystallized, it's brown, but to please the eyes of consumers and tickle the palate, it's transformed into a sparkling white.[27]

The preference of white over brown sugar traces its roots back to brothers William and Frederick D. Havemeyer, who had learned all aspects of sugar refining in London and brought them to New York in 1807. Their refinery, later the Domino Sugar Company, led the efforts to gain control of America's sweet taste buds. The Havemeyers convinced the public that brown sugar was of inferior quality due to impurities to restrict price competition with the established brown sugar industry. They effectively launched a nasty smear campaign, supplying false information to the public with warnings of eating the "dangerous" brown sugar.[28]

Employing racist tactics, books of the day went so far as to equate the luxury of white sugar with whiteness by including images of dark-skinned people gnawing on sticks of sweet sugarcane in faraway lands. These pictures were intended to promote the supposed purity of white granulated sugar to a refined civilization who had better table manners than did "savages."[29]

Recalling an incident in the late 1860s, Black politician John P. Green said that an employer had denied him the privilege of sweetening his cup of coffee with white granulated sugar, instead "restricting [him] to some very dark-brown sugar," illustrating that sugar was a contested marker of the color line, enacted every day at the sugar bowl.[30] With the shift in public perception, refiners needed to master the techniques to obtain the high-quality, sparkling white granulated sugar, the product most preferred by the those who oversaw the sugar bowl in the homes.[31]

When the Bay Sugar Refinery's sparkling white product entered the market at lower prices, due to Claus's cost-cutting innovations, George Gordon's established San Francisco and Pacific Sugar Refinery was forced to drop prices or lose customers.[32] Gordon felt blindsighted by Claus Spreckels, who seemingly out of nowhere began to corner the market. Local capitalists quickly grasped there was money to be had in sugar. But whenever rumors began circulating that there would be yet another rival refinery in the city, Claus's instant reaction was to expand and enlarge operations before any rival could catch up.

Claus's two nonfamily business partners, Meese and Meyer, categorically rebuffed his expansion plans to "double" the size of the refinery.[33] They were living comfortable lives in San Francisco and didn't see the need to risk their refinery's dominant position in the market; they told Claus that his plans were too grandiose so soon after the founding of their successful refinery. Despite his passionate entreaties, his partners stood firm for their comfortable dividends over risk. Claus was incensed.

Opportunity and Heartbreak

Claus startled the business community when he declared in 1865 that he would sell out and start "afresh rather than being hampered by the conservatism of frightened little men."[34] He publicly vowed to never again give up control in business with anyone who dared to hold him back. He sold his shares in a huff and received a substantial payout. Hermann Meese became president and Louis Meyer secretary of "his" Bay Sugar Refinery. This was a bitter pill for Claus to swallow, but he'd get his revenge because he was anything but finished with sugar refining. He had found his passion.

Claus should have been joyful at fulfilling his dream of starting his own sugar refinery, but his experience was otherwise. In December 1863, a month before the opening of Bay Sugar Refinery, Claus and Anna experienced a parent's most feared tragedy—the first of seven in a short time span—with the death of nine-year-old Henry. The official reason for his death is unknown, but it could have come from one of the myriad nineteenth-century causes: accidents, tuberculosis, dysentery, typhoid and scarlet fever, diphtheria, smallpox, measles, influenza, whooping cough; the list is long, and children especially were susceptible to such perils.

More than likely, Henry died of cholera, the "epidemic disease of the nineteenth century, as plague had been of the fourteenth."[35] Many victims of cholera, both dead and alive, disembarked regularly on the wharves of San Francisco from the infested, overly crowded Panama steamers. After two decades of numerous cholera outbreaks and epidemics, the U.S. surgeon general's office in 1875 would bemoan the fact there was an attitude toward sanitation in San Francisco that could most kindly be described as laissez-faire.[36] Raw sewage commonly tainted the water supplies, which caused acute diarrhea. Thousands of lives could have been saved if the situation had been treated seriously.

Cholera was a quick killer and yet another indication the Spreckels children might have succumbed to the pestilence. Henry's dreadful death was followed in rapid succession when two other Spreckels children also lost their lives to conditions or incidents lost to history: Louis Peter, sixteen months old, on January 22, 1864, and the family's first girl, Anna Gesina, age three, on February 19, 1864. One wonders if the emotional blow of tragedies in rapid succession factored in Claus's abrupt and emotional departure from the Bay Sugar Refinery.

Going Undercover

As Claus was debating his next moves, the *San Jose Mercury* noted that nobody in the country was considering the sugar beet as a replacement for sugarcane. They reported new and exciting data on beet cultivation and expressed surprise that an entrepreneur hadn't taken advantage of the opportunity, because "there's money in it!"[37] The data came from several scientific experiments conducted in the summer of 1861 with San Jose farmers who were asked to grow beets to determine their success in California's soil.[38] Unlike the case with other vegetable plants, the unusually shaped sugar beet seed made the tasks of germination and establishment much more difficult than with the typical round or oblong shape. But the results were nonetheless impressive: the necessary quantities of alkali were found in the soil, enabling the sugar content of the beet to exceed that in Europe's beet by 15 percent or more.[39] These results illustrated that growing beets in California for the manufacturing of sugar was both practicable and *profitable*. It was time for the state to step up and make its mark.

After reading the results Claus became intrigued, especially after discovering that he would save a considerable amount on the machinery used to manufacture beet sugar. Not only was the machinery tax-exempt by Congress, but by an enactment of the California legislature, producers would be paid a "premium of $500 for the first 100 bags of beet sugar, each containing one hundred pounds; adding another $150 for the same produced the next year, and $100 for the same produced the third year."[40]

As Claus, a farmer who had grown up in the center of beet production, knew full well, growing beets was not a throw-and-grow operation. They required a methodically hand-prepared seed bed. Each beet seed is actually a tiny pod containing five or six separate beet plants, so each plant has to be thinned after planting, with the farmer on hands and knees gingerly pulling out all but one tiny seedling. Harvesting proved no easier; it required a sinister-looking sugar beet knife that could easily cut off a finger.[41] The process was so laborious that farmers were relieved when their harvest finally went off to one of several beet sugar refineries in and around Hanover.

Since the entire population of Germany consumed sugar derived from the roots of beets, Claus knew the answers to the economical solutions were back home. After all, it had been a German chemist in the middle of the eighteenth century, Andreas Marggraf, who first discovered that beets contained high amounts of sugar. Some five decades later, his student Franz Achard expanded on this research and devised a scientific process to make beet sugar virtually indistinguishable from cane sugar.[42]

Claus was preoccupied with travel plans when the long-awaited news came that the Confederacy surrendered on April 9, 1865, ending the uncertainty and hardship that those four long, bloody years of the Civil War had brought to America. But the country's collective sigh of relief soon turned to mourning with the horrible news of President Lincoln's assassination on April 14. The Spreckels family left a grieving nation for Germany in the spring of 1865, harboring new ambitions while flags were still being lowered across the country. Due to the relatively new technology of the telegraph, the news of Lincoln's murder reverberated around the world and met them at every stop on their way home to Hanover.

After Anna and the children were settled in Lamstedt, Claus went undercover as a factory worker once again, this time in refinery owned by the family of Jacob Hennige, one of the founding fathers of the German Association of the Sugar Industry. Hennige's successful beet sugar refinery in Magdeburg, not too far from Lamstedt, was a good place to learn the craft of refining beets for sugar.

Historic events intervened, however, and once more affected Claus's trajectory. On October 6, 1866, ostentatious military ceremonies following a bloody war completed the Prussian annexation of the kingdom of Hanover.[43] It was clearly time to leave, which Claus did, confident that he had learned the complex combination of agricultural science, farming, labor costs, refining, waste utilization, transport, wholesale trading, and export as it related to making sugar from cost-effective beets.[44]

The Spreckelses sailed from Bremen on the SS *America* and arrived at the cold New York Harbor in December 1866 with hope in their arms, a baby boy, Louis (who held the same name of the last son they'd lost in January 1864, in the German tradition of reusing the name when a child died young).[45] Before the arrival of the transcontinental railroad (in another two and a half years), another hard journey by sea was required by Anna and Claus, who had a growing brood to manage: thirteen-year-old John, ten-year-old Adolph, nine-year-old Gus, two-year-old Edward, and baby Louis. It's unknown if they took the six-week sea voyage around Cape Horn or sailed to Central America and crossed the Isthmus of Panama by rail. Whichever way was taken, they again risked exposure to any number of deadly diseases in the crossing. It was during that sad December that baby Louis, no more than half a year old, the hope in their arms when they'd arrived in New York, died.

California Sugar Refinery

Claus arrived home to San Francisco at the beginning of 1867 bone weary but fired up with beet seeds in his pockets, ready to meet California's ever-increasing demand for sugar, but with beets. His first move was to recruit farmers willing to plant beets he promised to buy and refine. He advertised in *The Farmer*, claiming that a "man can make five thousand pounds of sugar from a single acre" and they should consider the "big profit" to be made. And it was a sure thing he told them, because even if the crop didn't sell for sugar, it would always sell for animal feed, a well-established practice in Europe. He reported that California was well suited for growing beets due to the "dry atmosphere and warm sun," which was "peculiarly favorable to the retaining of the saccharine matters of the roots." Not being completely honest, he told prospective farmers not to worry: "It is but very little work to raise an acre of beets . . . and the manufacturing is also easy and cheap."[46]

But California farmers scoffed at the prices required to grow beets. Their wheat fields could be tended by a single man, but beets required a cost-prohibitive number of forty men.[47] No amount of persuasion by Claus would work, and he soon had to concede that production costs in California would outweigh profits. Therefore, those beet seeds became souvenirs, and he pivoted back to what he knew: manufacturing sugar from cane. For the time being, he'd postpone his ambition and resume refining sugarcane on a grand scale. His goal was to go big on his second sugar venture to show his competitors, especially Meese and Meyer, that he was a force to be reckoned with.[48]

Claus moved at breakneck speed to file the incorporation papers for the California Sugar Refinery on April 3, 1867, capitalized at $300,000, with the stated purpose of "buying, importing, refining, selling, and importing sugar."[49] His associates were brother Peter Spreckels, brother-in-law Claus Mangels, and two outsiders, Frederick Hagemann and Henry Horstman. This time around, Claus Spreckels was the major stockholder and president, and because he alone held the controlling interest in the company, his fate would no longer be in anyone else's hands. He had learned his lesson.

While the buildings for the new refinery were being constructed at Eighth and Brannan Streets, Claus took off for New York to personally supervise the manufacturing of machinery based on a technique he had developed to reduce the amount of time needed to ready sugar for market. This was the era that saw the invention of the safety pin, the elevator, the typewriter, and dynamite, and now Claus's own contraption would join the list of technical innovations.[50] On March 17, 1868, his family was proud when he received his first patent for the "Manufacture of Crushed Sugar."[51] Before the year was over—there was another tragic death of yet one more infant son, unnamed. Grieving Claus began working harder on Brannan Street, welcoming teams of dray horses heavy-laden with raw sugar from the dock to his platform.

4. The impressive California Sugar Refinery. Claus pushed his sons to take on incredible responsibility at young ages, which prepared them to lead companies in their twenties and allowed for the vertical integration of the Spreckels empire. Courtesy of Terrence and Virginia Wilson private collection.

Inside, boilers were belching steam, and sugar was drying in loaf pans in the long ovens. He began refining twenty-five thousand to thirty thousand pounds of sugar *per day* instead of the typical three weeks to get that much sugar ready for market.[52]

Slowly but surely, consumers switched to the California Sugar Refinery for the ease of getting either crushed or cube sugar at a cheaper price than the other two refineries in town. Claus's local competitors, Meese and Meyer's Bay Sugar Refinery and Gordon's San Francisco and Pacific Sugar Refinery, didn't have the sophisticated machinery or access to his patent, nor did they have any idea how to make sugar by harnessing centrifugal force, thereby saving weeks of processing. Claus then invented a process for making cube sugar direct from the centrifugals.[53] The two other refineries combined couldn't compete with this amount of output, and the *San Francisco Merchant* opined that Claus had both "bled his opponents" and "slain the giants" and that was perhaps time for all other refiners to retire.[54] Soon employees from the other two refineries were pleading for employment in Claus's refinery. Not only were the salary and benefits better, but because Claus had actually lived the hardworking life of a refiner, he offered a safer and healthier atmosphere. Additionally, in German tradition, a pint of beer served at noon was an added incentive.

Customers were delighted at the novelty of using a small sugar cube, never seen before, for their cup of coffee. Grocers could now purchase granulated sugar when they wanted, instead of storing large and sticky loaves; they could easily scoop out the sweet product without the former messy hassle. Claus's invention enabled him to systematically lower prices with the goal of squeezing his competitors' profits and forcing them out of business, which is exactly what happened.

George Gordon, who fought to maintain the city's first sugar refinery, was abroad at the same time and for the same reason that Claus had been: "trying (unsuccessfully) to obtain secretive information on European methods of [beet] sugar refining," but he fell very ill and had to return home in 1868.[55] Sadly, Gordon died in the spring of 1869 at the age of fifty—some say, of a broken heart when his beloved only daughter, Nellie, eloped with a man he despised. Others said he died of a broken spirit after realizing that Claus had gained the monopoly of the sugar market and there was no way to beat or even catch up to him. The *San Francisco Merchant* was thrilled that Claus had beefed up San Francisco's economy by using local construction companies to build his refinery and employing hundreds of men at higher wages than Gordon had ever offered. The newspaper harshly opined: "We have no regret for the defeated San Francisco and Pacific Refinery and let no reader have any; it was wasteful and improvident ... a selfish monopoly—a terror rather than a friend to the merchants and no tears, that it 'fell in battle.'"[56]

Educating the Sugar Prince

A visionary, Claus was intent on creating not only a thriving company but also a family legacy. He worried the Spreckels sugar operation's modernization would be outpaced by competitors if he didn't provide a rigorous scientific education for his eldest son, John. At fourteen, it was decided that he should continue his education at the Polytechnic Institute in Hanover. Claus believed that German science was more infallible than anything available in America and wanted his son to gain the technological know-how that, in his mind, only Hanover could offer.

John arrived at the Polytechnic Institute in 1867, the same year the family returned from their father's internship at the Magdeburg factory. (Clearly, John was bouncing back and forth between San Francisco and Germany.) The school had been founded three and a half decades earlier to deal with the need for technical expertise generated by the nineteenth-century Industrial Revolution. In fact, many of the early graduates from Europe's polytechnic schools were renowned for having designed and built America's early highways, bridges, canals, and railroads. So, Claus enrolled John in mechanical engineering, an emerging field due to discoveries in physics. In Germany mechanical engineering advanced as a separate field within engineering, providing manufacturing machines and the engines to power them. The field further divided into three areas of discipline: marine, locomotive, and mill, the latter of which was all-important to sugar refining.

Whether or not John wanted to attend the Polytechnic Institute didn't matter. He was being groomed to be his father's successor, and Claus's wishes were always commands. On the voyage John, despondent at being uprooted from the familiarity of home, spent hours exploring the vessel and watching the sea. He recollected later that this long and lonely voyage to Europe was the true beginning of his "magical allurement" for the sea.[57] John's lifelong passion for engines on and off the water was ignited at the Polytechnic Institute—no doubt from the school's discipline of mechanical engineering—and would inform his future career choices, choices that would later take him far away from his father. But until then, his future was set (in fact, a year earlier, at the age of thirteen, John was already listed on company letterhead as vice president of the brand-new California Sugar Refinery).

While his young vice president was getting a technical education, the new president had become very popular in the business community. At forty, Claus sported a full, neatly trimmed beard and was the pleasant picture of a tall, well-fed, well-dressed, and prosperous businessman who always had a ready Cuban cigar. On the streets he was known as jovial—greeting friends, neighbors, and workers with a big smile, hearty handshake, and pat on the back. Inside the factory, though, he was all business, working alongside his men, dressed in overalls, his serious steel-blue eyes looking for any sign of sloppiness, laziness, or mismanagement.

At every public opportunity he thanked America for providing the liberty and economic opportunities he had been denied in Hanover. Heritage, however, was very important to Claus, and he maintained close ties with his homeland. He sent money back regularly to his family, bought his sister Anna a house, and even bought a new organ for St. Bartholomäus in the village of Lamstedt. From the windows of his childhood home, Claus's additional contribution of a church bell could easily be seen, a reminder to his parents that their great sacrifice had led to his unimaginable success. In San Francisco Claus and Anna transmitted their homeland's values and worldviews to their children around the dinner table, and they hired only Germans as household helpers to reinforce their parenting and primary language. Claus, like many other Germans, placed a high value on independence and responsibility and wanted his sons to be self-reliant from an early age, never mollycoddled by anyone.

Expanding the Business

During and after the Civil War there was a phenomenal expansion of industry, both agriculturally and industrially. In many lines of enterprise, people moved to dominate their field, including Claus. By 1869 he undertook the first of four expansions of the California Sugar Refinery on Brennan Street, which included the enlargement of both machinery and facility, due to the growing demand of sugar. In the span of only two years, he was refining an astonishing 125,000 pounds of sugar every ten hours.[58] Claus soon saw more opportunities on the horizon when the nation's first coast-to-coast railroad was completed, enabling him to ship carloads of sugar off to other states and territories.

During this time one factory in the East was turning out a million pounds a day of glucose to keep up with the demand for the adulteration of honey by sugar refiners to stretch the product and save money. As an up-and-coming sugar manufacturer, Claus was now being asked his thoughts about this common practice. His gruff response left no doubt he was appalled by both the question and the practice: "It is extensively practiced in the East—about one-fifth of the brown sugar sold is glucose. We do not adulterate here—not a pound of anything but pure sugar and syrup leaves our refinery! We have a guarantee that our product is free from all chemicals or other adulterations."[59]

All work and no play, the entire family labored from sunup to sundown to support the production of so many pounds of sugar every ten hours. With the press reporting on the never-ending expansions of the Spreckels family's sugar business, many outsiders wondered and marveled at Claus's vigor and fortitude. Mississippi's popular *Weekly Commercial Herald*, which highlighted interesting people from selected cities, ran a full-length feature story on Claus. He was compared to the likes of Josiah Wedgwood, England's celebrated pottery manufacturer; Samuel Morse and his development of the electric telegraph; Cyrus Field, who conceived the idea of the telegraph cable; Charles Goodyear, inventor of the vulcanized rubber tire; and others.[60] The *Herald* also told readers that Mr. Spreckels was "that most dangerous character"—a man with preeminently one idea: making improvements in a singular method, by fixating on the problem "night and day, sleeping and waking." This obsession, however, began to cause deep worries among the Spreckelses' inner circle. Claus's quest to build his "white gold" empire might have been too much too fast because he was showing worrisome and dangerous signs of a mental breakdown.

3

Too Much Too Fast

Even in an era when hard work and long hours were taken for granted, Claus was known as the hardest-working man under the sun. Time and again, Claus identified areas of opportunity, endured hardship to learn the necessary skills to realize his vision, and remained undeterred by failure. These strategies culminated in unprecedented success at a scale before unseen in the sugar industry. But the bright sunny days turned to a dull gray in the spring of 1869, when he experienced what's known today as a nervous breakdown.

Claus sought medical attention only after he began to display "very danger-ous" physical and mental symptoms, including loss of memory. Although no documents are available to provide further detail, his condition was report-edly grave.[1] At the time, doctors didn't have as great an understanding of mental health; however, "nervous maladies" had begun to gain attention after the Civil War, when soldiers returned home traumatized by their experience and identified symptoms such as depression, insomnia, anxiety, outbursts, and migraines.[2] Claus was ultimately diagnosed as having a "serious mental disorder of the brain."[3] Three decades later, "nervous breakdown" became the colloquial catchall for describing a period when a person's normal func-tioning becomes disrupted by extreme stress.[4]

Claus held himself to high standards and prided himself on his ability to persevere. In a cavalier statement about his own personal mental endurance, he once remarked, "One man can rise above obstacles which would entirely crush another."[5] But his nervous breakdown showed that he was as vulnerable as anyone else. What's surprising is how long it took for it to strike given the way he had been operating. He always moved with a crushing sense of urgency to accomplish his goals and desires. He rarely delegated, and even when he did, he was known to micromanage. Claus was not boasting but simply stating a fact when he recounted, "I only took four hours sleep in the twenty-four for months."[6] Claus felt the weight of his commitments and expectations, and nothing less than perfect was acceptable, but his high-pressure lifestyle was not sustainable.

Taking the "Cure" in Germany

In May 1869 the doctor's urgent prescription was for Claus to "withdraw from all mercantile matters" immediately.[7] He was told that complete rest and a change of pace were essential for recuperation. The advantages of ocean travel as a means of repose and restoration to those suffering nervous conditions were clearly illustrated in the columns of medical journals throughout the world: "The quiet routine, the absence of daily responsibilities, . . . the salt air, the constantly renewed draughts of oxygen, . . . and the irresistible charms of contact with the most sublime aspects of Nature are all influences which act as a mental and bodily tonic" for whatever might be ailing a person.[8] With uncharacteristic meekness, Claus complied.

In Claus's mind, the destination was easy. People afflicted with everything from gout to nervous disorders went to "take the waters" at spas across Europe, where withdrawing from a fast-paced life was seen as vital to both body and soul, and there was no better place to recuperate than in Germany, due to its multitude of spa towns and mineral baths as well as to its spa culture defined by its geographical isolation and dreamy romantic ambiance. In contrast, America's clinical sanatoriums functioned more like hospitals than lifestyle colonies; in the United States, Claus might have entered an established six-week "rest-cure," a popular regimented treatment for nervous illness in the nineteenth century that included "rest, a fattening diet, massage, and electricity."[9] Electricity was used to stimulate muscles, since rest cures promoted complete bed rest, a prescription Claus would never have endured. But for the Spreckels family, there was no place like the familiarity of home, and home was Hanover—now a Prussian province for the past three years.

It's easy to imagine that Anna may have been close behind Claus on the verge of her own mental breakdown. She undoubtedly suffered crushing maternal stress from the heartbreak of the clustered loss of her children— five had died within the space of just over five years. It's also quite plausible she had intense feelings of guilt and failure. Throughout it all, however, she had to uplift her grieving husband while supporting his expanding ventures, which required her full attention. She also had the responsibility for her remaining children, who certainly had deep emotions, as they were made all too aware of their own mortality with every loss of a sibling.

At the time of Claus's nervous breakdown, newspapers reported that he had San Francisco's biggest income. Even though it came at a cost to his health, he didn't want to lose that footing to any rival while he was abroad.[10] The entire extended family of employees assured him the California Sugar Refinery was in good hands and helped get him off.

Claus and Anna, along with twelve-year-old Adolph, eleven-year-old Gus, and four-year-old Edward Henry, boarded the Pacific Mail's ss *Colorado* on June 18, 1869, bound for Panama and New York.[11] The monthly departures of these three-hundred-foot-plus side-paddle steamships were red-letter days in the city of San Francisco. On "steamer day," hundreds of people flocked to the docks, waving handkerchiefs and joyfully shouting their goodbyes as the ship backed out of the wharf and headed out to sea. It's doubtful Claus hung over the ship railing jubilantly waving goodbye to anyone. The only bright spot in leaving his business as it was in the middle of expansion was that he would visit John at the Polytechnic Institute in Hanover.

Upon arrival in Germany, Anna and the children went to the familiarity of her childhood home while Claus "took the cure" in Karlsbad, Germany. Bathing in or drinking Karlsbad's mineral waters was thought to heal a wide variety of ailments, and Claus joined other patients who were put on a strict regimen that included drinking regularly from the springs. One patient graphically portrayed the grueling road back to health: "In Carlsbad [*sic*] you drink often and drink deep. Drinking is your main occupation. Your drinking glass is strapped over your shoulders as you wander, sipping from spring to spring. Your misery begins at 6 o'clock [in the morning]. If you had not been a miserable sinner, you would not be here, but you have done those things you ought not to have done, and your penalty is Carlsbad [*sic*]."[12]

Patients were expected to abide by the rules and strictly follow the rigors of the cure as dictated by the spa. The rules posted on the wall of one European sanatorium of the time indicate that when the patient entered the world of the hydropathic institution, "he forgoes the right to make his own decisions and instead is forced to submit to the regime laid out for him in the hope of improving his health and vigour."[13] This was undoubtedly a turning of the tables for Claus, who was used to living his life on his own terms. There's no doubt, however, that this time away was effective, because Claus would again return to the spa when life became too much to handle.

Old Habits Die Hard

With an unprecedented amount of time for contemplation and reflection, Claus once again reverted to thoughts of extracting sugar from beetroots. To Claus, this was an opportune time to further research sugar beet cultivation and refining while he was in Germany. Any objections by Anna to forgo expansion for the time being would have been dismissed by Claus because his "will was the law of the Spreckels household—never to be repealed nor altered."[14] It appeared the high-strung and impulsive Claus had found the perfect wife in Anna, who was calm and steadfast, the anchor at home, at sea, and abroad.

Claus couldn't wait to inform John of his renewed plans, so he traveled at some unspecified time to the Polytechnic Institute in Hanover. For the first time in his life, John was enjoying the stimulation of school and the freedom from immediate paternal oversight. Though the curriculum was demanding, he also studied music, and his happiest moments were those he could spare for his "beloved piano."[15]

But if John thought he could now make his own decisions because he wasn't living under his father's roof, he was mistaken. Claus's unexpected visit was a stark reminder that his own aspirations came after his father's.[16] John was boarding with a family who lived near the campus, but Claus soon discovered the landlady's pretty and well-endowed daughter—an actress, no less—had been routinely visiting his son's room with refreshments. Fearing that John might be more occupied with extracurricular matters, Claus moved him that very evening to another boarding house without saying a single word to him about it first. John realized there was no point in arguing with his inflexible father and grudgingly complied.[17]

John's enthusiasm for music and lack of passion for the family's sugar business were distressing to Claus. Hoping to ignite a change in his son's frame of mind, he arranged an appointment at a German sugar refinery for John to demonstrate his patented process of quick-drying sugar.[18] Unlike the more sociable Claus, John was introverted, more like his mother, and this couldn't have been easy for him to do. A short time after Claus left Hanover,

John, perhaps in anger over his father's domineering actions, started two fistfights with other students.[19]

In 1870 the village of Lamstedt was readying itself for Prussia's imminent war against France, so Claus packed up his family to head south to the picturesque countries of Switzerland, Austria, and Italy. But this was no pleasure trip. Claus bypassed the historical museums, the magnificent cathedrals, and the magical castles and visited the beet farms and sugar factories instead. He carefully noted the science and technology used, especially in places with climates similar to his locale in California. Then the Spreckels family made ready to return to San Francisco, with profound hope that the kingdom of Prussia would soundly defeat France, which it did within a six-month war that ultimately led to the creation of a unified Germany.

Home to Howard Street

When the family returned home in February 1871, the rest of their extended family and their friends were amazed at the sight of Claus "with all the vigor of youth renewed!"[20] By this time, Claus was a well-known businessman, not only in San Francisco but also across the country. His moves were followed in the press, and his recuperation and restoration were made public even outside of San Francisco.

Home was in a "roomy house" at 2027 Howard Street (present-day South Van Ness Avenue) in San Francisco's "South of Market" neighborhood, which was interchangeably referred to as the nearby Mission District.[21] After Claus and Anna moved to the area sometime in 1865, the rest of their families bought or built homes, some very ornate, up and down and adjacent to busy Howard Street. With family and employees close by, Claus and Anna's homecoming was a well-attended affair.

However, the Spreckels family that arrived back on Howard Street was not the same one that had left. Although young Gus returned with Claus and Anna, John and Adolph remained in Germany. And their relatives were apprised of their latest sorrow—Edward Henry, only five years old, had died abroad on November 23, 1869, from diphtheria. But the family held hope for the newest addition to their family, little Emma Claudine, born in Germany on January 23, 1870. This time a German nurse was in tow to ensure their only daughter, unlike her six late siblings, would live into adulthood. From the moment of Emma's birth, Claus doted on his only daughter and became fiercely overprotective of her.

Thriving South of Market

Claus was relieved to find that in his absence the California Sugar Refinery not only thrived but had a stranglehold on the local sugar market.[22] And Claus was not the only manufacturer thriving in the postwar era; these were years of general prosperity for San Franciscans (but the Panic of 1873 was just around the corner).[23] The continuing silver boom and returns of investments in the newly completed transcontinental railroad powered economic and job growth across industries in San Francisco's expansive city limits.

The area north of Market Street, on the waterfront, was characterized by a central cluster of consumer-goods manufacturers, including food merchants and processors, such as Ghirardelli's, National Flour Mills, and Schilling Spices, and clothing manufacturer Levi Strauss.[24] However, the bulk of industry headed to the South of Market area, which stretched the city southward for several miles. Immigrants-turned-industry-workers flocked to the area, far from the ocean and closer to the bay, preferring it's lower levels of fog. Thus South of Market became the city's first working-class neighborhood. While there were simple rooming houses and a fair number of small hotels to serve the transient population of single men, the streets were also lined with attractive and affordable single-family homes, both large and small. The neighborhood was vividly described by Kate Douglas Wiggin, author of the classic novel *Rebecca of Sunnybrook Farm* (1903) who was a resident at the time:

Innumerable small shops lined it from north to south; horsecars, always crowded with passengers, hurried to and fro; narrow streets intersected the broader one, these built up with small dwellings, most of them rather neglected by their owners. In the middle distance were other narrow streets and alleys where taller houses stood, and the windows, fire-escapes, and balconies of these added great variety to the landscape, as the families housed there kept most of their effects on the outside during the long dry season. Still farther away were the roofs, chimneys and smokestacks of mammoth buildings—railway sheds, freight depots, power-houses, and the like—with finally a glimpse of the docks and wharves and shipping.[25]

Claus understood that San Francisco would continue to dominate the West Coast as its commercial hub, and his prosperity gave him the confidence to begin investing heavily in South of Market property. He built a whole block of stores "to meet the growing demand" of the neighborhood.[26] South of Market was flatter than other areas of San Francisco, so the city's famously steep streets were much less an obstacle, and there was also an efficient line close to both Howard Street and Claus's sugar factory on Brannan Street. With his hires, he transformed the entire neighborhood into a vibrant one of skilled laborers whom he mostly recruited from northern Germany.[27] The streets were soon lined with German grocery stores, a thriving Lutheran church, and German restaurants, where the German language and culture created a home away from home for himself. Adolph remembered these days as some of the best of his young life, playing with the neighborhood boys, from all walks of life, in the streets and vacant lots of the community.[28] The Spreckels children now had grandparents nearby after Anna's parents, Johann "John" and Maria Mangels, along with several of Anna's siblings found their way to America.[29] Claus's roots were deepening.

A Legacy Realized

Claus put a great deal of thought and effort into creating a thriving family business because he believed in his family's loyalty and dedication. From the beginning his plan was for his sons to join him in his business ventures and to create a legacy. After he had lost so many children, it became all the more important to him that his sons enter the sugar business in different capacities.

John and Adolph didn't return to San Francisco until October 1871. Though no details remain of the circumstances, Adolph joined John at the Polytechnic Institute for a time to study mechanical engineering. This extended trip together and their first shared experiences apart from their father would solidify the brothers' relationship forever.

On their arrival home it was clear to all that, at eighteen, John had become a man. His bright blue eyes sparkled with determination, and there was an air of confidence—some would say overconfidence—that only his type of life's experience, forced independence and heavy expectations, could give. Claus eagerly welcomed John at the refinery and was happy to have him right by his side. His eldest son was proving valuable to the family business, and Claus was very proud of him. Like many first-generation offspring, John quietly helped Claus when he struggled with certain English words in his thick German accent or with their meanings. Many who did business with them remarked that Claus's eldest was a chip off the old Teutonic block. Though both men were determined and stubborn, their styles were completely different; whereas Claus boisterously demanded attention from anyone within earshot, John spoke in an even tone and never sought an audience for his ideas and opinions.

Claus was now confident that his sugar business would continue to profit and that his legacy would be secure if he carefully trained John in every aspect of the operation. John was given a salary, impressive for the time, of fifty dollars a month to work from the ground floor up and make his way through every department until he "mastered the minutest details of each and every stage in the process of refining sugar." Claus knew his money had been well spent on his son's education at the Polytechnic Institute when John detected "wasteful faults either in methods or apparatus" and provided fresh solutions. Despite this, John was not given any preferential treatment and was treated as an "ordinary workman" by his "no nonsense" father. In fact, if he ever showed the slightest disposition to forget the fact that Claus was not his father at work but his employer, Claus would promptly and effectively remind him with his "peculiar brand of gentle reminders." Outside the workplace Claus taught John the secret to success in three never forgotten lessons: "knowing how," "knowing when," and most important, "knowing *what* you're after—and then going after it in spite of hell."[30]

Adolph, at fifteen, and Gus, at thirteen, were sent to San Francisco's South Cosmopolitan Grammar School. Gus thrived but Adolph did not. Because he never expressed the slightest interest in any school subject, when the third term was about to begin, Claus asked him whether he wanted to "continue with school or go to work."[31] Adolph chose work. When it was clear he needed more training, Adolph was sent, at seventeen, to the pricey Heald's Business College for a short stint to prepare him for the back-office work of the Spreckels sugar business.

After nine months at Heald's, Adolph began work as an "office boy" at menial pay. He was resentful, stating, "[My] salary was too small to keep my end up among the young fellows whose fathers the old man [Claus] could have bought out twice over." He comforted himself by thinking about his elder brother John, who was "confined in some dirty factory in overalls boiling cane into sugar." Adolph recognized, "I was in the office selling it [sugar] in my best clothes, and it wasn't long before I concluded that I had the best job of the two." With a self-described "breezy" personality, Adolph recalled that his father didn't trust him at first. He felt Claus kept an overly watchful eye on him in the "counting room." Adolph never remembered receiving a pat on the back or any type of compliment for a task well done. Instead, his father's "unvoiced approval" came in the form of promotions, first to assistant bookkeeper, then bookkeeper, and finally secretary of the company.[32] Gus's work ethic mimicked that of nose-to-the-grindstone John and didn't need much oversight.

On January 1, 1872, Anna gave birth to another son, Rudolph. Unfortunately, he was a sickly child who suffered greatly from asthma, and his wheezing and difficulty breathing were a constant concern, particularly to Anna, who kept him close by her side.

Seeing Opportunity Everywhere

Despite the production boom following the Civil War, an industrial slowdown began, leading to the Panic of 1873. Germany decided to move to a gold standard rather than back its currency by both silver and gold, a move that forced the U.S. to follow its lead. Congress almost immediately passed the 1873 Coinage Act to gradually retire silver currency and to bolster the relative value of the U.S. dollar. Excessive speculation in railroads and real estate, currency inflation, high protective tariffs, sizable immigration, and stimulus given to industries supporting the war effort together devasted stocks, banks, and railroads, putting the monetary affairs of America into a deep crisis. The New York Stock Exchange completely shut down for ten days, and President Grant was at his wit's end to calm a nation over the cries "to hang the thieves and robbers in Wall and Broad Street."[33]

Without debt and seemingly unaffected by the financial depression, Claus began investing, taking advantage of falling prices everywhere. As a result his wealth began to increase exponentially. In October 1874 newspapers across the country reprinted an article titled "The Millionaires of San Francisco" from the *San Francisco Bulletin*, which included a "carefully-prepared list of persons whose reported wealth exceeds one million dollars."[34] Among the formidable collection of more than fifty powerful men was Claus Spreckels. The men in this list had interests representing nearly every enterprise that had shaped San Francisco and, to a great extent, the American West; most of them, if not all, interreacted with Claus in some way. The city's millionaires were larger-than-life figures who lived flamboyant lifestyles in "palaces." For example, William Ralston, head of the Bank of California, built a one-hundred-room mansion modeled after the Palace of Versailles. Leland Stanford, Mark Hopkins, Charles Crocker, and John Flood lived in magnificent mansions atop the weather-beaten hill eventually dubbed "Nob Hill."[35] These wealthy men chose this hill to escape the rowdiness of the city. Claus, though on the same list as these men, chose to live in the workingman's neighborhood instead of an expensive lifestyle above the fray. When panic struck the stock market in 1873, railroad construction halted nationwide as credit dried up, and the rich men atop Nob Hill whose wealth was tied to their railroad investments would suffer financially for another ten years. On the other hand, Claus, who practiced frugality at home and work, paid in cash, and never relied on credit to build his growing sugar empire, did just fine with some belt tightening.

Needing Breathing Space

The railroad had changed life in America forever by cutting travel to the West from months to days. San Francisco, once considered desolate and forbidding, was finally accessible to people looking for a fresh start in life. For many San Francisco residents, however, the hordes of newcomers represented an unwelcome intrusion as the unprepared city became congested. The rapid growth in population left little time to turn scrub brush into green spaces and parks. During the early days some referred to San Francisco as "Sand Francisco" due to the treeless landscape of windswept, rolling dunes. When Frederick Law Olmsted, who had created Central Park in New York, was asked by the city to design a major park, he declined, believing that no trees "which would delight the eye" would grow in San Francisco.[36] Since most newcomers became industrial workers, they headed to Claus's neighborhood. Soon that neighborhood became inundated. It would've been hard for Claus to find any separation between work and home when he strolled from the refinery to his front door, passing the homes of his many employees.

In 1876 Claus and Anna endured the seventh and last heartbreaking death of yet one more child, Edward, almost two years old. The loss of all those children with many back-to-back pregnancies took a toll on Anna's physical and emotional health. In her midforties there were numerous references to her poor health and extreme weight gain. She undoubtedly suffered some sort of maternal depletion but was also diagnosed with myocarditis, an inflammation of the heart muscle.[37] While the three older boys worked long days beside their father, Anna began to fret that Claus would have another nervous breakdown, and Claus was undoubtedly worried about Anna's own health. And both were concerned about their youngest child, Rudolph, due to his frequent and alarming asthma attacks.[38]

While convalescing in Europe, Claus had been beaten to the punch by wealthy New Englander Ebenezer Herrick Dyer. In the fall of 1870 Dyer had inaugurated the nation's first commercial beet sugar factory across the bay from San Francisco in the town of Alvarado (now part of Union City). The early financial success of Dyer's California Beet Sugar Company was due to his hiring Chinese workers for low wages. And his product was well regarded because it was filtered by bone charcoal, traditionally used by Claus and other refiners in the processing of sugarcane. This process created a brilliant-white product that couldn't be differentiated from cane sugar.[39]

Dyer's success stimulated Claus's thoughts night and day. If Dyer could do it, so could he. Until that dream could be realized, he, and Ebenezer Dyer, would learn that what goes up too fast will also come down fast!

4   *Between Heaven and Hell in Aptos*

With a new rival close by, Claus felt the familiar competitive impulse and sprang into action to achieve equal footing with beet sugar entrepreneur Ebenezer Dyer. Claus began to look outside the city for the perfect area to experiment with growing his own beet crop. While he was at it, he'd also build a second home, far away from the stress and congestion of the city. As he was pondering locations, he heard about Aptos, a lovely remote village eighty miles south of San Francisco and ten miles east of the up-and-coming town of Santa Cruz.

Aptos in the Awaswas language of the Indigenous people who first lived in the area loosely translates as "the people who live at the meeting of two streams."[1] When Mexico won its independence from Spain in 1821, the Aptos area became part of Mexico, and the government rewarded citizens with land grants, often for military service and sometimes as an inducement to settle in what was considered an undesirable outpost. Aptos—nestled between mountains and ocean in the middle of a coastal wilderness with majestic redwoods and prolific wildlife—was a somewhat neglected relic of one of those Mexican land grants, having been presented in 1833 to ranchero Don José Rafael de Jesús Castro by José Figueroa, the governor of Alta California ("upper California" [contrasted with Baja California], which included modern California, Nevada, most of Arizona, Utah, and parts of Wyoming, Colorado, and New Mexico). After California became part of the United States as a result of the Mexican War, Castro and other native Californians (Californios) were considered second-class citizens in comparison to the conquering English-speaking immigrants, but by 1858, Castro was able to legally confirm his land holdings.[2] The aging ranchero had been a shrewd businessman, and his 6,686 acres included many industries: a lumber mill, gristmill, sawmill, and wharf, a crucial piece of infrastructure for the isolated town.[3]

The area was certainly off the beaten path (one of Claus's requirements), but the trek from San Francisco would be difficult. Most passengers bound for Santa Cruz complained about the ordeals of stagecoach travel: two days from San Francisco at an average of five miles per hour in clouds of choking dust. It was also well known that on uphill grades—to make them easier on the horses—female passengers were expected to get out and walk, while the men pushed the coaches.[4]

But once he had toured the area, Claus was determined to own a huge piece of this picturesque land. When he approached the cash-strapped Castro in 1872, the timing was right, and the ranchero agreed to sell some 2,600 acres in what he called "Rancho Aptos" (today's Rio del Mar) for about $81,000. Castro was delighted when he learned that it was Claus's practice to pay in cash.[5] As for Castro, he made a tidy profit, and he and Claus became unlikely friends.

Claus now felt ready to put into practice what he had learned in Europe. He'd prove that he could successfully cultivate the beet into sugar, and he'd do it fast, with the goal of surpassing Dyer's efforts. The 1872 yield from his first small beet crop on the palisades was exactly as he'd envisioned, in terms of quantity if not quality. Claus boasted about his success to local farmers, hoping that they would feel confident enough to grow beets themselves. Growing sugar beets was a new and potentially risky practice, and there weren't many farmers willing to invest their time, effort, and money in this unknown crop, but in 1873 Claus assured a handful of locals that he'd sign contracts to buy every single beet they grew, successfully alleviating their trepidation. And if all else failed, he told them, they could use the beets as fine pig fodder, exactly what he intended to do with this experimental crop.

Moving into Frederick Hihn's Territory

It's unknown how the powerful capitalist Frederick Augustus Hihn felt when he heard that a fellow countryman, Claus Spreckels, with his pockets full of cash, had purchased large acreage in what Hihn probably regarded as *his* territory. Hihn was Santa Cruz's shrewdest businessman and foremost real estate developer.[6] As such, he was respected and hated in equal measure by the residents of the area. Only time would tell if he and Claus would become friends or enemies. They had much in common: They were the same age; both were proud Germans, having immigrated within three years of each other; both were politically conservative; both had established themselves in California as small grocers; and, most importantly, both were self-made millionaires who were unapologetic in their quest to increase their wealth. They both ascribed to the convenient philosophy that whatever benefited their bank accounts would also benefit the community.

Hihn's vast property acquisitions extended to the undeveloped coastal land east of Santa Cruz, comprising present-day Capitola and the vast timber resources in the Valencia Creek watershed, and strategic parcels of land in and near Aptos Village, adjacent to Claus's newly purchased land. One had to be careful when constructing anything near a boundary shared with Hihn's property, as members of Santa Cruz's Advent Christian Church would discover: when church workers were nearing completion of a "cement walk" in front of their church on Elm Street, Hihn ordered it ripped up, because a "narrow strip" crossed his property boundary.[7]

Hihn's main challenge in developing the area was bringing people and goods there. When his Santa Cruz stagecoach company began providing daily service in 1858 between Santa Cruz and San Jose, his property values increased significantly.[8] For twenty years stagecoach driver Charley Parkhurst garnered widespread admiration for his skillful maneuvering on the rugged mountain route. Even though he was small, he proved himself tough as nails.[9] He chewed and spit tobacco, gambled, drank, and stunned others went he went up against Hihn.

In 1864 Hihn attempted to develop land that was part of Parkhurst's farm. Parkhurst chased the mogul away and then pressed a lawsuit against Hihn for claim jumping, which was tried successfully in court on December 17, 1869. Many hated to see the way Hihn was grabbing land and foreclosing properties in the name of "development," so Charley became a local hero. In 1870 Parkhurst bought one of the properties Hihn had foreclosed on and returned it to the widow who had been forced out of her home, giving Hihn more bad publicity.[10] Charley Parkhurst's final revenge came after his death in 1879, when it was discovered by those preparing the body for burial that "he" was a "she," shocking even her closest friends but probably none more than the macho Frederick Hihn, who would realize that he had been bested by a woman.

Train Talk

During the summer of 1872, while Claus was engrossed with growing beets and wondering where to build his summer home, Hihn was scheming to bring a desperately needed railroad connection to Santa Cruz County. How to get a train to town had been a topic of conversation on every street corner and over every neighbor's fence for years in Santa Cruz. However, plan after disappointing plan to get the train had failed. In the late 1860s and early 1870s, Hihn served as county supervisor and member of the California State Assembly; in his campaign for the latter position, he had run almost exclusively on a railroad platform.[11] He hoped to position himself well with representatives of the Southern Pacific Railroad so that Santa Cruz County would reap the rewards of the railroad's inevitable expansion. Unluckily, in 1870 Governor Henry H. Haight, against all special subsidies, vetoed Hihn's railroad bill, which would have allowed for a county subsidy to help finance construction with a route up the Pajaro Valley to Santa Cruz.[12]

The defeat of the railroad bill shut down all negotiations with Southern Pacific. But suddenly, the railroad announced plans in June 1871 to extend a branch line to Salinas, with Watsonville an important stop along the way. The final alignment of the route, which opened on November 26, didn't quite meet expectations because rather than building a stop in downtown Watsonville, Southern Pacific built its line inconveniently across the Pajaro River.[13] The residents of Watsonville knew the move across the river was done out of spite because their leaders refused to subsidize SP with free land or money. The people of Santa Cruz were appalled by the actions of the railroad, but Hihn immediately set to work to ensure that all citizens in Santa Cruz County would benefit from this new railroad route.

In mid-December 1871 Hihn forced through a countywide vote for a subsidy to build a railroad between Pajaro and Santa Cruz. To nobody's surprise, the citizens of Watsonville balked at subsidizing a railroad that wouldn't directly benefit them. Its residents voted overwhelmingly against the tax, with the editor of their local paper making their point and skewering Hihn's reputation: "If a railroad is all that is required to make Santa Cruz prosperous, we earnestly hope that they may get it. But we do object to speculators bolstering up chimerical schemes for their own benefit."[14] Despite these objections, the bonds were approved, but only because Santa Cruz voters simply outvoted Watsonville voters.

The subsidy granted $100,000 toward the construction of a twenty-mile-long railroad between Pajaro and Santa Cruz, with the conditions that construction had to begin within six months and be completed within two years, and the first installment wouldn't be awarded until the first five miles were built. Subscribers were gathered, and everything was set for construction to begin, but then two different outside companies expressed their own interest in building the line. All of the stockholders pulled out, and the Santa Cruz & Watsonville Railroad collapsed. When it became clear by April 1873 that neither party would build the line and outside support was not coming, Hihn resolutely decided that it was up to him to see the railroad constructed, but he needed a rich and formidable partner.[15]

The Santa Cruz Railroad Company

It must have seemed like perfect timing to Hihn when Claus Spreckels began investing in Aptos. Hihn desperately needed an outside partner, one not biased against him as a result of past business transactions, one who could grasp how each of their investments would increase tenfold if there were a railroad to connect the area to the goods, services, and people that could make it a commercial success. For his part, Claus desperately wanted easier public access to his planned beachfront resort that he was contemplating as well as his sugar beet operation. Thus, Hihn approached Claus with a proposition. He assured Claus they would be equal partners, in control of determining the route and all the station stops. Hihn wanted a stop at the prime oceanfront acreage he had acquired earlier, at what was then called Soquel Landing. It was Hihn's goal to develop a destination spot there for nature lovers. He had laid out the plans for Camp Capitola in 1869, imagining it as the first seaside campground on the West Coast.[16] Hihn hoped that, once there, tourists, enchanted with the beauty, might be converted to future homeowners. But without a railroad, his dreams would never be realized.

From Claus's perspective, building a railroad could only benefit his new investment. These two domineering and well-known German millionaires convinced a large consortium of local investors to buy into their plan to build a narrow-gauge railroad from Santa Cruz to Pajaro and Watsonville.[17] The Santa Cruz Railroad Company was incorporated on June 18, 1873. The articles of incorporation, which committed the sum of one million dollars to the project, named seven directors, with Claus Spreckels at the top of the list, followed by Hihn and five others. The company sold stock to select community members, with Claus and Hihn acting as majority stockholders; Hihn held two hundred shares and Claus one hundred shares.[18] Claus must have been persuaded to increase his stock, because stockholders' documents from 1875 reveal that he had increased his shares to two hundred to be on equal footing with Hihn—or so Claus was led to believe at the time (Hihn eventually owned 46 percent of the stock and Claus owned only 36 percent). The remainder of the stock was sold to ninety-six landowners and businessmen in the county who held one share each.[19] Only after a number of obstacles were confronted and overcome, however, would the Santa Cruz Railroad Company achieve its objective: a finished railroad.

Experimenting with Beets

While Claus's experimental beets were still in the ground at Aptos, his beet sugar rival, the no-nonsense Ebenezer Dyer, was having "numerous difficulties" with his new partners, Augustus Bonesteel, Andreas Otto, and Ewald Klineau. So terrible were the clashes over money and operations that Dyer kicked them off his land in Alvarado and liquidated the California Beet Sugar Company in 1873.[20] Dyer alone then founded the successful Standard Sugar Refining Company, until he was forced into bankruptcy.[21]

Dyer's former partners were determined to set off on their own. Leaving Bonesteel behind due to his being hospitalized with some serious illness, Otto and Klineau left with the company's machinery and doggedly hauled it down to Soquel, near Aptos, to start afresh on land partially owned by Frederick Hihn. On October 12, 1874, the Soquel Beet Root Sugar Company, interchangeably and confusingly still referred to as the California Beet Sugar Company, was erected.[22]

Despite their machinery upgrades and the planting of high-grade beet seeds imported from Germany, it became clear to Otto and Klineau that their high expectations would never be met by the new location. They had misjudged the quality of the soil in Soquel; due to its lack of proper nutrients, it didn't produce a high-grade beet. "The soil, though good for wheat, had not, however, that under-surface moisture required for beets, and so the experiment was not as successful as desired."[23] Also, their crops barely yielded four tons of beets per acre, whereas in Alvarado, twenty tons per acre had been considered a humble yield.[24] The only solution to their predicament would be to grow the beets elsewhere and transport them to their refinery in Soquel. For this, they needed outside capital. In August 1876 they successfully recruited a few investors (unknown if Claus bought stocks) to put a total of $150,000 into their business.[25] One stockholder was Frederick Hihn, who, in addition to capital, supplied the wood to fuel the mill. But the most important investor was the wealthy John Thomas Porter, Santa Cruz County sheriff turned bank president, who offered four hundred acres of his land in the Pajaro Valley to plant beets.[26] The fertile valleys of California's Central Coast region, framed by mountain ranges to the east and west, were blessed with rich soil and benign climates. Otto and Klineau soon learned what Claus had discovered when his own experimental beet crop had failed to produce a high-grade beet in 1874: the prime alluvial soil of the nearby undeveloped Pajaro Valley was perfectly suited for growing beets.

Despite Otto and Klineau's best efforts, the reorganized California Beet Sugar Company went bankrupt for many reasons, including, first and foremost, transportation costs as well as drought conditions and insect infestations.[27] While Claus was knee-deep in expanding a new sugarcane enterprise elsewhere, Otto and Klineau's refinery was foreclosed upon. Robert Orton, in one of his last public acts as Santa Cruz County sheriff, auctioned it off on October 4, 1879, "to the highest and best bidder."[28] When the gavel came down, few were surprised that it was Hihn who bought the entire inventory for a paltry one hundred dollars.[29] This made Claus only more determined to succeed where they had failed. As for Otto and Klineau, they were fellow countrymen, and Claus would later offer them a chance of a lifetime to live and work in paradise.

The Aptos Ranch

Even though the soil was disappointing for farming beets, Aptos was idyllic for a family haven. Every Spreckels family member loved leaving the noise and congestion of the city for the tall redwoods and sandy seaside beaches. Since his parents had passed away, Claus decided that Aptos, not Germany, would now be his retreat from the storms of life.

In 1873 Claus commissioned the noted German architect Heinrich "Henry" Geilfuss to build him an enormous two-story ranch home in the architectural style known as carpenter Gothic.[30] Geilfuss was the key architect behind the quintessential San Francisco Victorian style; his houses were

5. The Aptos Ranch house, and the 2,390 acres it sat on, initially became a sanctuary for the entire Spreckels family. It was then a resort, a world-renowned horse ranch, and a gateway to the fertile fields of central California. By permission of John Hibble, Aptos History Museum.

built during the Gothic revival period and were marked by his whimsical use of Gothic detail. Claus and Anna's wood-framed ranch house featured the same ornate touches of Gothic style—board-and-batten siding, decorative bargeboards, pointed-arch windows, and a steeply pitched roof. The house sat on 2,390 acres and had fourteen-foot ceilings on the main floor; three thousand square feet of living space on each of its two floors; fifteen rooms, including ten bedrooms, a kitchen and butler's pantry, two parlors, a dining room, a card room; a full basement; and a full attic topped by a widow's walk.[31] In addition, because of Anna's weight gain, which had resulted from her "unrestrained diet," accessing the second level was a challenge for her, so Claus commissioned an elevator—the first one south of San Francisco—to be installed in the house.[32] He also built a reservoir containing millions of gallons of the purest water, piped in big six-inch mains to all parts of the property.

6. Claus and Anna Spreckels avoided society, preferring the company of their entwined extended family. Pictured are Anna's brother Claus Mangels and his first wife, Agnes Grosse, whose twin sister, Anna Grosse, married Claus Spreckels's brother Peter. In 1875 Agnes died of tuberculosis at the age of thirty-one, leaving her husband to raise four children. Courtesy of Tillmann Family Archives, privately held by Mark H. Reed.

Anna, unlike other wealthy women of the day, was never a socialite, but found her enjoyment in domesticity, surrounded by her extended family. And wherever Claus and Anna went, the circle of family followed. In 1875 sorrow struck Anna's side of the family when her sister-in-law Agnes Mangels died of tuberculosis at thirty-one. Left behind were Anna's brother Claus, now in charge of the Albany Brewery, and his four remaining children with Agnes: thirteen-year-old Anna Lisette, twelve-year-old Emma Marie, ten-year-old John Henry, and eight-year-old Agnes.[33] In 1876 Claus Mangels remarried, to Emma Zweig. The Mangelses also built a lovely mansion (still standing today), repurposing Geilfuss's architectural plan for Claus and Anna but with a reverse floorplan on a 550-acre plot of land a half mile up from Aptos Creek. Playing in the surf, running under a canopy of towering redwoods, and dining on the porch, the Spreckels and Mangels children made deep and lasting memories.

Adolph's Passion

Horses were the most-used engines in and around Aptos—both for riding and hauling people and goods in wagons and stagecoaches. Claus owned French draft horses, Percherons, which are similar to Clydesdales. These big, beautiful horses made quite an impression pulling the stately black stagecoaches in which Claus and his family traveled.

Claus loved his working Percherons, but horse racing became his new-found hobby in Aptos, and he built a racetrack for the harness racing of his trotters. In these races, the driver rode behind the horse in a sulky, a lightweight, two-wheeled, single-seat cart. One of Claus's legendary horses, Speculation, was purchased for the princely sum of $8,500.[34] Given Claus's competitive nature, it's no wonder he loved the idea of breeding and raising champions under the Spreckels name. His accomplishments in this arena were seen in the popular *Breeder and Sportsman*.

In fast horses, Claus and Adolph found common ground. Adolph's lifelong fascination with horses began in Aptos. Horse racing became his heartbeat; his intimates became the horse trainers. The Aptos Stock Farm was Adolph's baby. He had a small house built, soon called the "bachelor's cottage," that overlooked the training stalls. He adorned the walls of the cottage with pictures of his favorite horses. Watching horses out at pasture was entertainment enough for him, and he was often found seated in the stand of the training track during the morning course, holding a watch and timing the "young colts and fillies" when they were "given a full mile at speed."[35]

Rudolph also fell in love with horses at Aptos, finding them therapeutic. He remembered being a lonely, asthmatic child who didn't fit in with his boisterous brothers. He'd often ride off by himself on his pony, seeking solace and relief on the miles of bridle paths built by his father through the redwood forest. Rudolph would always go his own way in life, even if it took him far away from his family.[36]

The Newport of the Pacific

Because he loved the seaside so much, Claus expected others would too. The tourism potential of the area, particularly the estuary where Aptos Creek emptied into Monterey Bay, would be enormous now that he was helping to solve the transportation problem with the coming Santa Cruz Railroad. So, rather than retreating to the wide porch of his ranch house with a cigar and the daily newspaper, Claus began planning what the *Santa Cruz Sentinel* would soon dub the "Newport of the Pacific."[37]

Despite the uproar from competing landowners, Hihn and Claus, in charge of the train's route, strategically placed a depot closer to their bayfront properties than to Soquel, which would've been the logical choice because it had more development. Claus ensured the tracks were laid in such a way that the train would stop right in front of his newly planned Aptos Hotel.

When finished in the spring of 1875, the hotel was an imposing two-story structure with fifty rooms featuring views of the bay, the redwood forest, and the creek. The furniture was elegantly carved black walnut, always the family's choice for their furnishings. The resort had all the latest technology, including indoor plumbing and gaslights in the guest rooms and throughout the public areas. Claus enclosed a large area surrounding the hotel with a twelve-foot-high fence and stocked it with close to a hundred wild deer and elk for guests to hunt. Following paths thickly lined with redwoods down to the sandy beach, a guest could go fishing or boating from the widened wharf, originally built by Castro.

There were several separate cabins billed as "honeymoon cottages." Claus didn't stop there; gas lampposts were placed all around the grounds for the novelty of evening illumination. Via a bridge over a "moat," newlyweds were encouraged to stroll after nightfall to an island in Aptos Creek dubbed "Lover's Retreat."[38]

Claus felt enormous pressure gearing up to the formal grand opening of the Aptos Hotel. He expected dignitaries from up and down the state and wanted the event to be perfect. The hotel was a beehive of activity, and Claus had no tolerance for slacking or disrespect from his workers. On the day before the grand opening, one of the employees was caught sneaking into a servant girl's room. Claus immediately fired the twenty-one-year-old man but found him still hanging around the hotel on opening day. He was stunned. "I thought you were going away," he's reported to have told the young man, who retorted, "I will go away when I get ready and not before!" Claus, without hesitation, took him by the collar and dragged him to the door. The young man responded by pulling out a knife, but Claus, still strong

7. The Newport of the Pacific, featuring views of both the sparkling bay and the lush redwood forest, opened to great fanfare in the spring of 1875. Note the "honeymoon cottages" on top. Newlyweds were encouraged to stroll under gas lamps after nightfall via a bridge to an island in Aptos Creek dubbed "Lover's Retreat." By permission of John Hibble, Aptos History Museum.

as a bull at forty-six, wrestled him to the ground. Afterward, the story was played out, much to Claus's satisfaction, in the local papers, and his prowess garnered him respect and free publicity for his hotel.[39]

The grand opening reception on May 22, 1875, exceeded everyone's expectations. The guests included some of the most prominent people in the state, such as Governor Romualdo Pacheco. A splendid supper was served at midnight, followed by dancing until four thirty in the morning. The *Sentinel* carried the details of the event, and it was clear that Frederick Hihn, while in attendance, was neither toasted nor mentioned in any way by Claus, as would've been proper, perhaps indicating that trouble was brewing between the business partners behind the scenes.[40]

All Aboard!

Meanwhile, the Santa Cruz Railroad Company had been working to complete the railroad connecting the Pajaro Valley with Santa Cruz. With an

THESE CELEBRATED WATERING PLACES ARE REACHED BY THE
SANTA CRUZ RAILROAD, CONNECTING WITH THE
SOUTHERN PACIFIC AND CENTRAL PACIFIC RAILROADS.

8. Success! Santa Cruz finally had a rail connection to the outside world, and as a bonus both Hihn's and Spreckels's resorts became accessible to tourists. UC Santa Cruz University Library Digital Collections, Santa Cruz County Historic Photograph Collection, MS 427, box 110, folder 2.

eye toward saving money, the company's two major investors, Hihn and Spreckels, had decided to finance a narrow-gauge track, which required less dirt excavation and less material for bridges, locomotives, and cars than a standard track.

In October 1874 the first locomotive, the petite five-ton *Betsy Jane*, arrived in Santa Cruz from San Francisco. By December of that year, the first segment of the track was completed, and little Betsy Jane pulled her cars five miles from Santa Cruz to Soquel, to the satisfaction of the Santa Cruz Railroad stockholders. With the first section of tracks completed, the county was now permitted to issue bonds to continue funding the project. However, the Watsonville interests, who believed the railroad wouldn't benefit them, sued for an injunction to stop the issuance of the bonds. Hihn and Claus were furious over this action, the first of many legal actions designed to disrupt the railroad's progress. And disrupt it did. When Hihn asked Santa Cruz County for payment, officials informed him the money wouldn't be released until the city of Watsonville's legal objections could be resolved.[41]

On top of the legal issues, delay after delay occurred with supplies. Iron was shipped via the harrowing route around Cape Horn. One of the ships carrying iron rails shipwrecked, and the replacement ship caught on fire, which necessitated a layover of four months in Brazil.[42] Claus and Hihn had been assured the final rails would be in place no later than November 1875. But in December 1875 the court ruled against them in one of the lawsuits regarding the county bond issue.

One disappointment followed another until March 1876, when more of the lawsuits were decided, and the county issued $114,000 of the $240,000 that had been authorized for railroad construction. The Santa Cruz Railroad Company could now afford to complete the route. Both literally and figuratively, after a series of twists and turns, the long-awaited day came on May 7, 1876. For the first time in the history of Santa Cruz County, a passenger train would run "twenty-one miles from Pajaro Station via Watsonville, Aptos, and Camp Capitola to Santa Cruz."[43]

The company could now buy a second engine. A week later a new twenty-two-ton, "handsomely finished," and brightly painted locomotive named *Jupiter* arrived with its bells ringing and whistle blowing steam, to the delight of the crowd that had gathered in Santa Cruz to inspect their new train. Santa Cruzans marveled at the "magnificently furnished" passenger coaches with their bright red upholstery. With this powerful "iron horse" joining the stable with little *Betsy Jane*, the one daily trip between Santa Cruz and Pajaro increased to two daily trips, and as the *Santa Cruz Sentinel* gleefully noted, the "'sleepy stagecoach' era ha[d] ended!"[44] Santa Cruz finally had a rail connection to the outside world. That meant that both Hihn's and Claus's resorts were now accessible to tourists, and the coastal industries, such as timber, leather, agriculture, and lime, were more profitable, since getting their goods to market cost significantly less.

On the day the railroad opened for business, trains crowded with well-wishers left the station amid wild emotions. Along the new route, people shouted their greetings to the passengers straining to be heard over the ear-shattering sounds of bells and steam whistles of the long-awaited train. Claus was content with this outcome, as he could now bring not only tourists to his hotel and ranch but family, friends, and business colleagues. Likewise, Hihn had successfully connected his lumber lands to the Southern Pacific main line. The popularity of Claus's hotel during that first season required that it be expanded for the following 1876 season. Claus responded to this demand with a three-story addition, making the building twice as large.[45]

While John was doing his father's bidding elsewhere, it seems as if his brother Adolph enjoyed a freer range. The ledger from the Aptos Hotel for 1876 recorded both the guests' incidental charges and those of the Spreckels boys. Corks popped and French champagne flowed when Adolph was on the property. And not just any champagne: Roederer, the highest-grade champagne in the world, also the most expensive champagne the hotel offered.[46] While the ledgers show that Gus was also indulging himself, the recorded charges for sending telegrams and express freight indicate that he was at least working. The boys burned through expensive cigars as well. Gus recounted a time when Claus "took him to task" for smoking too many cigars in the earshot of his eighty-six-year-old *opa* (grandfather) Mangels. Claus himself was rarely seen without a cigar, and the reprimand seemed hypocritical to Gus. Opa was a heavy smoker as well, and he chastised Claus: "Leave the boy alone, Claus! Smoked beef lasts the longest and when you're as old as I am, it will be time to speak with authority upon smoking."[47] It seems as if the boys had an ally in their maternal grandfather, who was often with them in Aptos. There's no recording of Claus examining the hotel ledgers, but the expenses incurred reveal that his sons were indulging themselves like princes. It's probable that if Claus had known, these antics would've increased his anxieties and that he'd have curtailed the boys' spending.

Now the railroad was bringing throngs of visitors to the Aptos Hotel and to Hihn's Camp Capitola, crowds naturally drawn by the beauty of the beaches and the surrounding forests. But Claus's nature didn't allow for much rest and relaxation. While in Aptos, he worked and loved every minute of it. Claus was not the typical Nob Hill millionaire. Rather, he was proud to be a working man. Claus relayed a reporter a story of a time in Aptos when he was loading goods onto a train car in his old coveralls and slouched hat when a doctor from St. Louis, who was traveling through California for health reasons, stepped onto the platform. The doctor had an informal interest in the sugar industry and approached Claus to ask him about the famous sugar king, Claus Spreckels, rumored to live in Aptos.

"What sort of a man is he?"

"Now, you look at me, examine me well. He's a man about my size and weight and looks exactly like me; in fact you would not know us apart."

"What! You do not mean to tell me that you are Mr. Spreckels, do you?"

"I do so."

"Then, I must say, although I do not wish to be offensive, that I do not believe it."

So I said: "You would perhaps know me if you were to see me in San Francisco, but anyway there will be a handsome carriage and pair here directly. Now, if you see me get into that carriage in my dirty old clothes and order the coachman where to drive to, will you be convinced?"

This was agreed and presently the carriage arrived. I stepped in, seated myself, and it drove off. I looked around at my late companion, who immediately took off his hat and waved it around in the air.[48]

The Doomed Santa Cruz

While the Santa Cruz Railroad initially carried a significant amount of freight and passengers, financially it was never a success. The company lost money for four straight years. The annual loss might have been overcome as traffic increased along the line if other factors hadn't tipped the scales toward more financial problems. First, in January 1878 a major winter storm tore up the track along the beach. Second, in May 1880 the narrow-gauge South Pacific Coast Railroad completed its route through the Santa Cruz Mountains, providing a quicker, more direct route from downtown Santa Cruz to San Francisco markets. Third, in December 1880 the California Supreme Court ruled the county bonds had been issued illegally because the railroad never made it to Punta Año Nuevo, as specified in the articles of incorporation.[49]

Finally, it was the beginning of the end for the little railroad when, in February 1881, another significant storm tore through the area and brought down the trestle over the San Lorenzo River. Most of the stockholders of the Santa Cruz Railroad Company, including Claus, were no longer willing to repair the trestle or continue to subsidize operations in the face of competition with the South Pacific Coast Railroad. Claus may have wanted to cut his losses, but Hihn wanted to keep pouring money into the company. Against Hihn's wishes, the Santa Cruz Railroad, without funds, ceased to operate.[50]

Tensions were understandably high between former allies Claus and Hihn in March 1881, when the company declared bankruptcy. The failure of the company caused a split in their partnership. After the bankruptcy proceedings, the assets of the company went up for auction in May. They were purchased by the Pacific Improvement Company, one of the Southern Pacific Railroad's property investment firms. The SP then rebuilt the San Lorenzo River Bridge and reopened the railroad for service in June 1881. The Southern Pacific was now in direct competition with the South Pacific Coast Railroad for the San Francisco–to–Santa Cruz traffic.

By October 1881 the little Santa Cruz Railroad was no more after only five years. Hihn came out on top as the sole stockholder for the railroad company. He had accomplished this goal deliberately and stealthily right from the beginning; manuscript documents he had kept reveal that he had become the sole stockholder without Claus's knowledge. When Hihn had bought 1,000 shares of stock, Claus had bought 1,605 shares, feeling confident that he'd retain some control over the company's assets. But Hihn's meticulous records and notes reveal that he had secretly bought an additional 1,522 shares in his sister Emma's name, with the following handwritten annotation: "purchased to prevent S. [Spreckels] obtaining control."[51]

At some point during their working relationship, Claus had granted Hihn a license to use a logistically important road that crossed over Claus's property. After the partnership ended, Claus retaliated and legally revoked that license in 1881 and then closed the road permanently. Hihn, furious, sued Claus for access, lost, appealed, and lost again.[52]

The directors of the Southern Pacific Railroad knew they would benefit from Santa Cruz's tourism, and in November 1883, the Santa Cruz Railroad was converted to standard gauge and absorbed into the Southern Pacific.[53] The two years of railroad upgrading construction, from 1881 to 1883, severely affected access to Claus's Aptos Hotel. The public, however, had a new option in the area. They could easily access the brand-new Hotel Del Monte in Monterey, built and owned by Southern Pacific, which conveniently provided excursion trains nearly to the hotel's doorstep at its opening in 1880.[54]

Sadly, the beautiful Aptos Hotel sat empty for so long that it became obsolete. Many believed this was Southern Pacific's strategic plan all along to knock out Claus's hotel as competition for their resort. When the Aptos Hotel closed, everything was left where it stood—the furniture, bedding, chairs, and dishes. The neighbors in the area helped themselves. With the abandonment of the hotel, there was little else for Claus to do but move on. He had lost a lot of money building the hotel, but he was nothing if not thrifty, and he'd recoup some of those losses by tearing it down a little bit at a time to reuse the lumber and the cottages for future projects.[55]

Perhaps the bitterest pill for Claus among the cascading events that led to the distressing failure of his hotel was the irony that his own investment in the Santa Cruz Railroad brought down his Newport of the Pacific by attracting competing investment from others, especially the Southern Pacific. More troubling, he had been bested by Hihn. Despite the Aptos Hotel's short-lived success, however, Aptos would remain Claus's favorite place to "rusticate." He was so invested in the community that he deeded land and built buildings for two public schools.[56] Though never one to stay still for long, Claus uncharacteristically took some time to assess his position. He was not used to being bested. The one thing he knew without a doubt was that in Aptos he had found his personal paradise, and he'd need a refuge because his mind was about to spin off in a thousand different directions.

5   *Threats, Opportunities, and the Reciprocity Treaty*

As Claus was investing millions of dollars in and around Aptos, a rumor began circulating among American sugar refiners that made his blood run cold. The U.S. Congress was considering a reciprocity treaty with the island kingdom of Hawai'i to end the mutual tariffs that prevented the two nations from importing each other's goods. Such a treaty, in Claus's mind, threatened all that he had built to date. Cane sugar was Hawai'i's main export to the U.S., and a cheap supply of this milled superior product that could bypass his refinery would cause nothing but trouble for him. Such an arrangement would compromise his profitable business. "I fought it," he said, "as I saw it would ruin the refining business."[1]

Claus was hardly alone in opposing the treaty. Even though the merchants of San Francisco favored the treaty, because the city was the gateway to the U.S. for Hawaiian goods, sugar refiners in San Francisco and New York and sugarcane planters in the South vehemently opposed the treaty because they feared the competition of foreign, duty-free sugar. Additionally, Claus and other U.S. refiners mass-produced fine white sugar, and their refining methods also created a surplus of light-yellow "coffee sugar." The low-grade sweetener appealed to a secondary market.[2] The refiners were afraid that Hawaiian sugar would drive them out of business because the "higher-grade Hawaiian-milled sugars, known as grocery grades, went to market without further refining."[3] By cutting out the middleman and dispensing with tariffs, Hawai'i's grocery-grade sugar, known to be superior in both taste and color to coffee sugar, would end up in stores at a competitive price point. Of course, customers would switch to the more affordable option.

Had Claus still been a San Francisco grocery store owner, he would've profited from this arrangement. But being a sugar refiner put him in an altogether different position. He began to mentally calculate what his loss would be when Hawaiian sugar went directly from the dock to the stores. He couldn't let that happen—at least not without a fight.

The treaty under congressional consideration was a free-trade agreement, and in time it would be identified as the Reciprocity Treaty of 1875. Tariffs or taxes levied on imported goods were the federal government's dominant source of revenue. So, it was a big deal for the U.S. to negotiate this type of treaty.

Thomas Jefferson had initiated the first protective tariff focused on foreign sugar, in favor of insulating Southern sugarcane planters from overseas competition. But the Civil War had changed everything. With a Union embargo on Confederate sugar, planters in Hawai'i eagerly stepped in to take Louisiana's place as the source for raw cane sugar. This expanded market brought an astonishing economic boom for island planters. In 1860, on the eve of the war, Hawai'i exported 7,659 tons of sugar to the U.S., and by 1865 the amount had increased tenfold to 76,590 tons.[4] No wonder Mark Twain, on a newspaper assignment in Hawai'i, proclaimed that Hawai'i was "the king of the sugar world."[5]

Following the Civil War, however, Hawai'i's sugar boom abruptly ended. A broad panic in the American stock market subsequent to the war plunged the kingdom's sugar planters into a general depression.[6] The remedy, in the eyes of the planters and the Hawaiian government, would only be found in a reciprocity treaty that would place their sugar and other products on the duty-free list. In exchange, American merchants would enjoy a market for their wares in the islands. The treaty would convert Hawai'i into a virtual one-crop economy in which sugar was king.[7]

Hawai'i's king David Kalākaua, who had taken the throne in 1874, saw the potential benefits of the treaty for his national economy. But gaining the support of his own legislature, comprising both Hawaiians and non-Hawaiians, would prove to be tricky. Some Native Hawaiians, the Indigenous population, tended to distrust him, because when the last of the kings of the Kamehameha dynasty died, Kalākaua had been elected and hadn't earned the throne by blood. Despite the king's efforts to reintroduce traditional culture and customs that had been banned by the missionaries, distrust remained among his own people. On the other hand, his election campaign slogan of "Hawai'i for Hawaiians" didn't endear him to the *haoles* (whites) in the Hawaiian legislature. In his advocation for the treaty, King Kalākaua was forced to walk a tightrope between the two groups. The only practical solution was to promote prosperity for the islands as a whole in the hope that it would benefit the entire public—leaving, of course, an ample portion for the king's expenses.

Kalākaua didn't just have to convince his own government; he also had to garner the support of the United States government. His goal was to gain enough public support to sway the U.S. Senate to draft a reciprocity treaty that would do away with the 30-percent sugar tariff.[8] Kalākaua left Honolulu at the end of 1874 with Henry Alpheus Peirce Carter, who was the U.S. minister to Hawai'i and the partial owner of a sugar plantation, to embark on a goodwill tour of the United States that conveniently coincided with the negotiation of the Reciprocity Treaty in Washington DC.

The king was interviewed across the country by curious press whose racial biases at times were clear. *Harper's Weekly* was amazed at how the king, "only two or three generations removed from barbarism," could speak several languages besides Hawaiian—"English, French, German, and Portuguese!" Kalākaua's knowledge of American politics and history astonished dignitaries, who had no idea that the king's academic curriculum had been American. The king received honors at all his stops. As the first reigning monarch ever to visit Washington DC, he was royally entertained for two weeks and spent considerable time with President Ulysses Grant, who apparently got along splendidly with the king.[9]

Fighting the Treaty

On March 18, 1875, the Senate finally approved the treaty. In addition to allowing tax-free trade for many products between Hawai'i and the U.S., Kalākaua ceded to the U.S. certain rights to Pearl Harbor, rights that would later expand.[10] But even though Kalākaua signed the treaty on April 18 and President Grant added his signature on May 31, it still took a year for Congress to pass the necessary legislation to fully implement it because of the bitter opposition from California's sugar planters.

Claus led that fight. In hope of preventing ratification of the treaty, he successfully recruited the support of San Francisco's rival refinery owners—

including his former partners Hermann Meese and Louis Meyer. Once adversaries, they now came together to oppose the proposed treaty and sent an urgent protest to the California delegation in the United States Congress to stop it. Claus spent $2,800 ($71,550 in today's dollars) out of his own pocket to send the petition, but it's not clear what those funds were used for.[11] Claus's main arguments against the treaty were that it would cause damage to home industry and consumers, violate the favored-nation clause, and create a monopoly. Most notable was his reasoning that the beneficiaries of the treaty would be the planters in Hawai'i, predominantly Americans, who Claus claimed were "self-expatriated" citizens. Why, argued Claus, would the U.S. government "kill the fatted calf" for disloyal Americans who, for all intents and purposes, relinquished their citizenship by living in a foreign land? [12]

The "expatriated citizens" Claus referred to were the descendants of American missionaries (mostly Congregationalist) who had sailed to the kingdom of Hawai'i in twelve separate companies, the first one in 1820 and the last in 1848.[13] The companies included well-accepted ordained ministers, physicians, teachers, farmers, and printers. Once satisfied that the Native Hawaiians were successfully educated and, more importantly, evangelized, the sponsoring organization, the American Board of Commissioners for Foreign Missions, withdrew its financial support. Some missionaries went home to New England, but some stayed. Many of their children, the self-proclaimed "missionary sons," were now the prosperous sugar plantation owners. Born in Hawai'i, these second- and third-generation missionary sons were bilingual and bicultural, and they were the principal industrial leaders of the islands. Many of them had gone to the United States for their education and returned as doctors, lawyers, and merchants. They partnered with the Hawaiian government and monarchy when it was to their financial advantage, but their intent, as history illustrates, was clearly to have the upper hand in ruling.[14]

Washington politicians were not amused by Claus's bold and nervy request for an exemption. In March 1875 a politician retorted in the *Pacific Commercial Advertiser*: "This is an age of cheeky documents, but about the most cheeky document of which we have heard for some time is the protest of the San Francisco sugar refiners against the Reciprocity Treaty."[15] The politicians were outraged that Claus and the other refinery owners opposed the treaty out of greed and at the expense of Pacific Coast consumers.

The United States clearly saw the advantage of a closer relationship with the strategic Central Pacific nation, as steamships were shrinking the distance between continents. Behind closed doors, the U.S. favored the treaty on political rather than commercial grounds. Years later the Senate Committee on Foreign Relations revealingly reported the treaty "was negotiated for the purpose of securing political control of those islands, making them industrially and commercially a part of the United States, and preventing any other great power from acquiring a foothold there."[16]

Looking Out for Number One

Those delegates in Washington needn't have troubled themselves further over the "cheeky" refiner, because Claus made a complete reversal on his stance in regard to the treaty after a visit by Carl Pflüger in the fall of 1875. Pflüger was managing H. Hackfeld & Company, a prospering sugar agency, for his brother-in-law, German entrepreneur Heinrich "Henry" Hackfeld. He was also acting as the representative for the other sugar agencies across the Hawaiian Islands who were desperate to get the treaty in place.[17]

H. Hackfeld & Company had one singular focus: to manage, finance, and control Hawaiʻi's sugar industry and all associated businesses. Sugar agents made large commissions from the oft-struggling sugar planters who considered these middlemen a necessary evil. Planters turned to agents such as H. Hackfeld & Company for financing, warehousing, marketing, and selling their crops, and ordering supplies and equipment. It was common practice for the sugar agency to advance money to the planters until their crops could be harvested and sold. Considering it took two years to grow sugarcane, agents were vital. While helpful, the arrangement often resulted in a debtor-against-creditor resentment.[18] Plantation managers had their hands full "fighting drought, pests, labor shortages, and a hundred and one other hazards" that beset life on a sugar plantation and needed these agencies to survive.[19]

Pflüger boldly encouraged Claus to reverse his well-known stand against reciprocity or at least remain neutral. Otherwise, he threatened, island sugar planters would withhold the next year's crop from his and other smaller San Francisco refiners, all of whom relied upon Hawaiʻi's raw sugarcane for their refineries. The full details are unknown, but Claus's views were promptly changed, and he wired the California delegation in Washington that the

California refiners had removed their opposition to the treaty. This led some congressmen to loudly and publicly conclude that this hasty reversal was a collusion between California refiners and Hawaiian planters to defraud the government.[20] With no time to investigate, the treaty went through by special protocol on September 9, 1876.

Pflüger might have been patting himself on the back, but it didn't take long for Claus to identify his opportunity in this defeat. An idea began to ruminate: If he could bypass the agents in Honolulu and contract directly with planters in Hawai'i for their entire production of sugar for the following year, he'd ensure that his California Sugar Refinery had a surplus at a significantly reduced cost. Then he wouldn't need to continue buying raw sugar and paying commissions to agencies in Hawai'i, the Philippines, China, and Java. He deduced that with the reduced duty on Hawaiian sugar, the islands were now the *only* place he would need to go for his refinery's sugar. It's easy to imagine his exuberant anticipation at the prospect of a two-cent-per-pound discount on a product that sold for eight cents.[21]

John, Sleuthing in Paradise

There's little doubt that, as part of his concession to Pflüger to stand down, Claus negotiated a job for his son. As vice president of the California Sugar Refinery, John, at twenty-three, was managing men twice his age and had become his father's right-hand man in all financial matters. The son of a prominent sugar refiner would be of great help to Pflüger—or so he was likely told. The highly successful H. Hackfeld & Company would be a perfect place for John to learn the ins and outs of the Hawaiian sugar industry from the agent's perspective. John, a stickler for details like his father, would be a great asset for Hackfeld, but his covert role was to establish positive relationships with Hawai'i's planters. It was Claus's goal to convince them to bypass their sugar agencies and to sign contracts directly with his California refinery.

John left the foggy San Francisco Harbor for the 2,500-nautical-mile voyage on the Pacific Mail Steamship Company's ss *Granada* on Sunday morning, January 9, 1876. When he arrived in Honolulu eight days later, the dock was much improved from when Hackfeld had arrived twenty-six years earlier. The odorous "slaughterhouse and meat market that projected over the water" had been replaced with a proper wharf,[22] now a crowded hub for commerce, and thousands upon thousands of baskets of raw sugar from the other islands of the Hawaiian archipelago were continuously loaded onto sailing vessels or unloaded from them.

John disembarked into the waterfront mayhem on a Monday, the start of a workweek. Honolulu itself was no longer an "overgrown village" but had become a thriving business community with a population of fifteen thousand, a good fifth of whom were foreigners from all over the globe. By then, the city had several well-defined streets dotted with wooden houses that were slowly replacing the "little grass shacks" later made famous in song, along with a post office, a hospital, a jail, lodges, and a forty-two-room hotel.[23] The hodgepodge of buildings reflected the mix of extreme wealth and extreme poverty that defined Honolulu. Interspersed in the neighborhoods were churches of varying denominations surrounded by beautiful foliage; but a trek beyond one of those fragrant church arbors could easily lead to dismal lanes of squalor.

John realized that he was a long way from home when he saw women with long, swirling skirts riding astride horses. Back home, such a sight would've caused a scandal, but Honolulu was well filled with lady equestrians riding as only the men would have done in San Francisco. In addition to horseback riders, the busy and dusty streets were crowded with every manner of commercial vehicle—water wagons, trams pulled by mules, bicycles, and horse-and-buggy combinations of many varieties had found their way to Honolulu.

Fort and King Streets constituted the main business thoroughfares of Honolulu, and H. Hackfeld & Company was centrally located, occupying a "solid block on fort street."[24] The business section was characterized by a canopy of shade trees that lined the dirt road, frequently dotted with rain-filled potholes, hitching posts, and the clapboard structures that typified a small western town. Captivated by the tropical paradise, John fell in love with Hawai'i. His words tumbled onto paper as he sought to aptly describe the "abundant vegetation, bright flowers" among "the beautiful scenery of cliff and vale and waterfall, of coral reef and breaking sea and quiet lagoon."[25]

Walking a Cultural Tightrope

As Hawai'i's new ruler, Kalākaua fought for the Reciprocity Treaty, but others in the royal family were dismayed and denounced the treaty as a dangerous step toward annexation.[26] Emma Kalanikaumaka'amano Rooke, queen consort of King Kamehameha IV, was much beloved among Hawaiians.

After her husband's death in 1863, she ran for the title and office of queen of Hawai'i against the charismatic David Kalākaua who aspired to be the king. Her defeat in the hotly contested election created mutual animosity between them. Peter Young Ka'eo, a Hawaiian high chief and politician exiled on Moloka'i because he had leprosy, wrote many letters to his cousin Queen Dowager Emma about the kingdom's business. In a letter dated March 14, 1876, it's easy to see the Reciprocity Treaty was unwelcomed among important members of the Hawaiian royalty. Young Ka'eo reproved Kalākaua's role in the treaty. In his opinion, the United States' sole intention was "to win us." He further warned, "They will have the Center of the Pacific Ocean. Kamehameha V was not a man to be trifled with, and the Yanks knew it, but this one [Kalākaua]—'Humph.'"[27]

Like his two predecessors, Kalākaua believed that Hawaiians were better off under the guidance of a ruler of absolute power. The king understood, however, that Hawai'i also had to modernize and adjust commercially and industrially to a rapidly changing world. But this was not easy because the king had to please both Native Hawaiians and especially the wealthy haole ruling class (the missionary sons).

After the benevolent works the first generation of apolitical missionaries had accomplished in the first part of the nineteenth century, the schism between their descendants and Kalākaua grew progressively wider and increasingly contentious, and with good reason. Along with other heirs to the Hawaiian throne, he had been raised, educated, and Christianized by American Congregationalist missionaries in a strict, austere boarding school, the Chief's Children's School. In an unparalleled partnership between the monarchy and these missionaries, sixteen royal children, including David Kalākaua and his sister Lydia Lili'uokalani, had been sequestered in a heart-rending manner. Isolated from their families and culture, the children had been immersed in learning the English language and groomed for future leadership using an advanced American curriculum taught by two New Englanders from Connecticut, Amos Starr Cooke and his wife, Juliette.

Cooke left behind twelve leatherbound volumes of private diaries full of intense self-admonition, frustration, and confessions that spanned his decade raising the kingdom's royal children. The diaries chronicle numerous occurrences of withholding food, locking the little children up in the dark outhouses, and lashing with a leather whip for minor offenses. David

Kalākaua entered the boarding school at only three years of age. Cooke's diary reveals the young David had been punished severely several times, had incurred persistent illnesses, and had suffered serious accidents involving horses until his twelfth birthday, when the school was dismantled. In the summer of 1849, at around thirteen years of age, David went home, somewhat a foreigner in his own land. Amos Cooke documented his own internal struggle in such a way that it's not surprising to learn that he died in 1871 at an "insane asylum," a strong indication that his treatments with the small royals were precursors to an undiagnosed mental disorder, known today as Huntington's disease.[28]

Given his negative experience at the boarding school, David Kalākaua had reason to distrust the missionary community when he became king. But he had to tread softly because not only were the missionary sons running the economy through their sugar enterprises but, as Hawaiian-born subjects, at least fifteen of them also held political appointments.[29]

Like others who were deprived in childhood, Kalākaua became prone as an adult to excessive and indulgent habits, such as smoking, gambling, and drinking. From the point of view of the missionary descendants, the Christianized king had begun to revert to spiritual darkness. The men who'd attended church with the king throughout their boyhoods were alarmed when he resurrected the hula dance, whose gestures the early missionaries found lewd and immoral. They were also shocked when the king reincorporated *kahunas* into his royal rituals. (In ancient Hawaiian healing traditions, the *kahunas* were the medical doctors who communicated with the spirit world, and the missionaries had denounced them as pagan practitioners long before.) To the missionary sons, Kalākaua's actions indicated the kingdom was moving backward, not forward.[30]

The First Sugar Plantation

Once on the job at H. Hackfeld & Company, John Spreckels found that not all the white businessmen running sugar plantations in Hawai'i were descendants of the missionaries. The first to domesticate sugarcane had, in fact, been three aspiring, young, secular venturers from Massachusetts. In the summer of 1835 William Ladd, Peter Brinsmade, and William Hooper formed a plantation enterprise called Ladd & Company. After seeing the tall, wild sugarcane rippling in the trade winds all over Kauai, they had known the land was right. They began the first commercial sugar-growing enterprise on what would become the Kōloa Plantation.

Courtesy of King Kamehameha III, who clearly saw a financial profit for his kingdom, Ladd & Company received a fifty-year lease on close to a thousand acres at $300 a year—the first major land lease in Hawaiian history.[31] They also received permission to hire twenty-five Hawaiians to work the land. They agreed to pay a tax to the government for each man employed and "satisfactory wages" to the workers. In return, the king and governor of Kauai would exempt the workers themselves from paying taxes.[32]

Much has been written about the heavy taxation and cruelty inflicted on commoners if they were lax in performing labor for their chief. Native Hawaiian historian David Malo reported that commoners often lived in a state of "great dread," fearing the death penalty or expulsion from the land.[33] On September 12, 1836, William Hooper wrote down his thoughts on the matter:

> Just one year to day since I commenced work on this plantation, during which I have had more annoyances from the chiefs and difficulty with the natives . . . than I ever tho't possible for one white man to bear, nevertheless I have succeeded in bringing about a place, which if followed up by other foreign residents, will eventually emancipate the natives from the miserable system of "chief labour" which ever has existed at these Islands, and which if not broken up, will be an effectual prevent[a] tive to the progress of civilization, industry and national prosperity.[34]

Within a year Hooper, in charge of the plantation at Kōloa at only twenty-six years old, had transformed both the land and the labor structure there. Ladd & Company gave the local workers free housing but didn't pay them cash. Instead, they issued scrip, tokens that could be exchanged for goods only on the plantation. Thus, Hooper created both a wage-earning labor force and a consumer class dependent on his store.[35]

Seeing the profits Ladd & Company were making, missionary families— including the Alexanders, Baldwins, Castles, Cookes, Rices, and Wilcoxes— began to found their own sugar plantations and acquire leases on royal lands from the Hawaiian government. But the new plantation owners soon found it took a lot of manpower (and it was indeed only men who were employed) to grow and harvest sugarcane over the two-year period of a crop, and manpower was in short supply. The declining population of Native Hawaiians, who historically worked for their chiefs only on a temporary basis as a kind of labor tax, didn't enjoy working year-round for foreigners. Nor did they adjust well to the backbreaking work of clearing land, digging irrigation ditches, planting, fertilizing, weeding, and harvesting cane in daily ten-to-twelve-hour shifts.[36] Plantation owners became frustrated with the job performance of the Hawaiians, who, they felt, lacked a capitalist work ethic and required constant surveillance.[37] The question was how to keep up with the demand for labor. The only answer: import it.

China was the first to answer the call, and soon Chinese migrants represented close to 5 percent of Hawai'i's population, almost as large a group as the whites.[38] This new workforce toiled long hours for little money. They were supervised by *lunas*, the bosses, who were mostly Native Hawaiians in the beginning days. The friction between the groups was constant. Feeling lonely and living in strange new circumstances, many workers turned to smoking opium and became horribly addicted.

Steaming into Hawai'i with the Treaty

The Hawaiian people had no idea how significantly life as they knew it was about to change. On Thursday, August 24, 1876, at 2:00 p.m., the ss *City of San Francisco*'s steam whistle was first heard and then spotted outside the Honolulu harbor. The ship was festively adorned with colorful bunting over the tops of the masts from bow to stern. Soon, word spread like wildfire. The decorations certainly meant that good news was on the way! Even before the first tender left the steamer, crowds assembled on the dock to hear it, and there was "electricity" in the air.[39]

When the first U.S. dignitary stepped off a small boat, the hushed multitude waited in expectation. A paper was unfolded and read: "The treaty bill passed the Senate on the 14th of August by a vote of 29 to 12, was signed by the President on the 15th, and at once became law."[40] This was met with silence. The transoceanic telegraph cable hadn't yet reached Hawai'i, so the stakeholders in the sugar industries were not present. The American representative was probably stunned—surely, he had expected at least one cheer. Sugar may have been a dominant fact of economic life across the Hawaiian

Islands, but few at the dock would've been sugar planters who understood the significance of the announcement and whose wealth would now grow with access under the free trade agreement to U.S. markets.

Right behind the U.S. politician, a portly gentleman with a precisely trimmed salt-and-pepper beard quickly disembarked and sidestepped around the commotion. Claus Spreckels had managed to get passage on the very ship that carried the news to Hawai'i that Congress approved the appropriations necessary to put the treaty into effect.[41] Claus rarely traveled without his family, so it's no surprise that his wife and younger children Emma and Rudolph followed after him. Adolph, nineteen, and Gus, eighteen, had been left in San Francisco to watch over the refinery. The whole family was pleased to be reunited with John, but the dockside reunion was short lived. Anna and the children had to be set up in the Hawaiian Hotel so Claus and John could take off for the other islands. They had plenty of work to do in a short amount of time. The treaty would come into effect in a month's time, and they had to act before the market could adjust to the new economics.

Over the course of three weeks, with John by his side providing introductions where necessary, Claus visited the biggest sugar plantations throughout the islands and offered to buy their future crops in cash. The price agreed upon for the entire future crop was equal to that of an equivalent quantity of Manila "extra superior" sugar in San Francisco, including duty, which Claus believed was an overpayment that would generate goodwill. The planters were admittedly overcome by his "sharp-elbowed ways" but were pleased, at that time, to sign contracts ensuring them a better price than they had ever received to date.[42] Thus, the planters reaped the benefit of their lost duty, and Claus secured his dominance of the market.

Inspiration in Maui

The most providential visit Claus made was to Maui, the second-largest island of the Hawaiian group, to inspect the flourishing sugarcane culture in the center of the island. Central Maui, frequently called the isthmus, is a narrow bridge of land between the two volcanos that formed the island. Once covered by water, the isthmus was created by lava flows from Mount Haleakalā and then strengthened by surface soils that washed down from the West Maui Mountains. Here in the hot, dry, windswept climate is where the sugarcane thrived—when rain could be had.

John arranged a visit with the prominent missionary son Samuel Thomas Alexander. Six years prior, Alexander had teamed with his childhood friend, another missionary son, Henry Perrine Baldwin, to start a sugar business. Together they purchased land in central Maui and planted their first crop to mark the start to what would become Alexander & Baldwin Inc. Since "two thousand pounds of water are needed to produce one pound of sugar" their sugar business—which included the Haiku Plantation and Mill—was marginal.[43] At the time, they were trying to solve the water problem by capturing the rainfall that fell regularly in the mountains. They had just obtained a well-publicized government lease authorizing them to build a seventeen-foot trench for water, soon to be called the Hāmākua Ditch. The term *ditch* is both humble and misleading. Humble because these water development systems were often intricate and quite large. Misleading because they were not merely trenches dug in the earth but were composed of flumes, siphons, and tunnels.[44] Claus was more than anxious to see the engineering work in progress. He knew the Reciprocity Treaty was predicated on full government support of sugar planters transporting water out of the watershed, because otherwise, investors, like himself, wouldn't be attracted to Hawaiʻi, and the only way to get the water to the dry plains of Maui was to build ditches.[45]

Having grown up in Hawaiʻi—or "tropical New England," as many had described the missionary community—the conservative, proper, forty-year-old Samuel Alexander had an easygoing temperament. He was likely overwhelmed by Claus, who by then was described as having an "emphatic but by no means unpleasant manner of speaking" with a "military bearing, and of a somewhat gunpowderly temperament."[46] Alexander consented to be his guide, and off they went to tour Hawaiʻi's first major irrigation project.

Claus promptly evaluated and grasped the importance of the ditch he saw under construction. During the trek, Alexander also shared with him the urgency to complete it due to a strict deadline. Their lease stated that if the Hāmākua Ditch was not completed by September 30, 1878, all rights would revert to the government.[47]

Claus and John were patting themselves on their backs after securing signed contracts for more than half of Hawaiʻi's sugar crops by circumventing the established sugar agents.[48] Claus's quick action gave him virtual control of the Hawaiian sugar crop. But he understood that he might not always be able to retain this dominant position and owning half of a small plantation and securing contracts with planters wouldn't be enough. The time crunch Alexander and Baldwin were under to complete the ditch might have stimulated Claus's calculations in a thousand different ways, because that very same day, with the unsuspecting Alexander as his guide, Claus began to consider the possibility of establishing his own sugarcane plantation. Perhaps, if they failed to meet the deadline, he could convince the Hawaiian government to allow him to finish it and use it for his own envisioned crops.

Imagination Running Wild

On September 11, 1876, Claus and his family set off for home. Claus's visit to Hawaiʻi was short but fruitful—he made every moment count and his refinery was assured product at a remarkably low price. John remained behind to complete paperwork for the co-purchase of a small Maui sugar plantation, the Waihee, with pioneer sugar planter Captain James Makee.

On the voyage home, Claus calculated over and over the risks and rewards of establishing and running a sugar plantation so far away. The rewards won out. If he could streamline his operations by taking direct ownership of sugar crops rather than relying on external contractors, planters, or suppliers in the form of sugar agencies, he couldn't lose. But during the week's crossing of the Pacific Ocean, he began to formulate a much bigger plan—he would become the largest producer of sugarcane in the kingdom by modernizing the process, and he knew just where to do it.

According to Hawaiian legend, the volcano Haleakalā—which is frequently referred to as the "House of the Sun"—is the spot where the "trickster" demigod Māui ensnared the sun, freeing it only after it promised to linger longer in the sky. Haleakalā was designated "the sublimest spectacle" Mark Twain had ever seen—and a place of "incomparable grandeur" by Jack London.[49] Claus decided he'd build his own sugar operation in the shadow of this picturesque monument despite an existing rival company. Face to the wind, Claus must have realized he was one of the very few Americans, if not the *only* American, to take advantage of the Reciprocity Treaty of 1875. But he couldn't have known that his strategic timing would make him the world's undisputed "sugar king."

6   *Storming into Hawai'i*

While Claus was upgrading equipment in the California Sugar Refinery in anticipation of a great haul of Hawaiian sugarcane, harsh judgments were being made. His success was denounced by jealous competitors on the East Coast once they realized that they had been bested, learning the majority of duty-free sugar crops were going to Claus's refinery on the West Coast. Claus, who embraced the motto "If you're not first, you're last," unapologetically defended his strategy and actions by claiming, "I went to the islands for self-protection."[1]

Meanwhile, John was given a new assignment. This one would whisk him temporarily far away from his Hawaiian paradise where he had agreed to run his father's operations to the congested city of New York, which he loathed. As his father's proxy in Hawai'i, John would have to learn the proper grading of raw versus refined sugar to avoid the tariff as dictated by the Reciprocity Treaty. He would also need to learn about acquiring high-yielding varieties of sugarcane that would resist tropical diseases. The examination of sugarcane juice is a vital process of sugarcane agriculture. John needed to learn up-to-date laboratory analysis of sugar: all the steps for determining the right purity, the right levels of sucrose content, and more. Not reading about it, doing it. On the job, the Spreckels way.

John left for the East Coast at the beginning of 1877 to work in a "sugar laboratory," studying advancements in all aspects of sugar analysis. In the aftermath of the Civil War, sugar refining was New York City's most profitable industry. John went to work at a refinery in the neighborhood of Lower Wall Street, in the heart of the raucous district where the coffee and sugar trade thrived together. Businessmen in tall silk hats greeted one another with their canes raised high as they elbowed through the throngs going to work. Horses pulled coaches in a variety of sizes in an ever-so-slow transit. In the stores that sold sugar, the lumpy lower grades were manually ground and repacked in barrels. One elderly man, a former errand boy on Wall Street, remembered how the schoolboys would gather around the back of stores, fascinated at "the negroes" laboring away, grinding the lumps into granulated gold using sugar mills.[2] Wall Street auctioneers stood on barrels of sugar, selling off both sugar and coffee in a rowdy atmosphere that was a sharp and unwelcome contrast to easygoing Hawai'i, a place John now loved and wanted to return to.

The New Mrs. Spreckels

John had purposely chosen lodgings far from the fray in Hoboken, New Jersey. With its waterfront location opposite New York, Hoboken had established itself as a water transportation center and a major port for transatlantic shipping lines. It also had ferries, which left packed with commuters for Lower Manhattan throughout the day. He recalled that the "morning and evening whiffs from the sea were a tonic" from the stress of working in the congestion of New York.[3] During one of these wistful daily commutes across the Hudson River, he met and fell in love with a beautiful young woman from Hoboken.

Lillian Caroline Siebein was a spunky twenty-three-year-old with blue eyes and a petite figure, standing at five feet two. From the beginning, the pair had much in common. Like John, she was the offspring of parents from Hanover, she spoke German, she had lost siblings, and she was musically proficient. Lillian's father (also named John) was a ship chandler. John and Caroline Siebein gave their daughter permission to marry this handsome, bright entrepreneur, but John Spreckels didn't ask his parents' permission: "I didn't ask anyone when I picked out a girl I liked and that was all there was to it."[4] After a whirlwind courtship, Lillian agreed to go west with him, and they quietly married in New Jersey on October 29, 1877, with none of his family in attendance, a fact that demonstrated John's first step of independence.

John and Lillian boarded their first-class passenger car for the three-thousand-mile, ten-day train trip in November. Theirs was a comparatively comfortable experience, with roomy seats that converted to sleeping berths and with porters attending to their personal needs. In contrast, those who were unwilling or unable to pay the premium fare had to sit in noisy cars

9. Lillian Caroline Siebein Spreckels (1855–1924). The talented singer charmed young John during a stint in New York, and he surprised his family with his spunky bride. Courtesy of Terrence and Virginia Wilson private collection.

fitted with rows of wooden benches and would've had to fight for floor space when they rolled out their bedrolls at night. Regardless of status, everyone endured stifling conditions as they traveled though some western states and territories. According to one first-class traveler, "Sand got into everything. I know I ate my 'peck of dirt' as windows and ventilators were closed and soon it became stuffy."[5] Even under these difficult conditions, though, few complained, considering the six months or longer (eight to twenty miles per day, depending upon weather) it formerly took to cross the county in a covered wagon (which necessitated many miles by foot) or to sail the Cape Horn route, which covered eighteen thousand nautical miles. After Lillian was introduced to the large Spreckels and Mangels families in San Francisco, the newlyweds left for a short honeymoon at the family ranch in Aptos.

Newlyweds in Paradise

Claus still needed John to continue solidifying the Spreckels sugar interests in Hawai'i. Six weeks after the wedding, the newlyweds arrived in Honolulu on Thursday, December 13, 1877. Downtown Honolulu was the business, social, and cultural center of Oʻahu. Its rich theatrical history had begun with the opening of the Thespian in 1847, which included a royal box for King Kamehameha III.[6] The growing population of American merchants and their families were hungry for familial cultural entertainment, such as concerts, plays, musicals, and operas—and, apparently, that included John and Lillian, who shared a passion for music.

Lillian knew she was a long way from Hoboken when she performed two vocal solos at a benefit in the Honolulu Music Hall under the watchful eyes of King Kalākaua and Queen Kapiʻolani.[7] John knew these carefree days with his bride in the "moonlit Hawaiian evenings of dance and song and fun" in "fairyland" would always be considered as the best days of his life.[8] The Music Hall, complete with a royal box for King Kalākaua and Queen Kapiʻolani, would become the center of John and Lillian's social life in Honolulu. The brick building, which seated eight hundred, was built by wealthy Englishman William G. Irwin, a close friend of King Kalākaua who had been in Honolulu since he was a child.[9] So close was the friendship, in fact, that the king gifted Irwin the entire island of Lānaʻi. Perhaps it was at the Music Hall that John made the most important connection to help the Spreckels sugar business move forward and thrive: he went to work for Irwin's company, W. G. Irwin & Company, a direct competitor to H. Hackfeld & Company in financing, warehousing, marketing, and otherwise managing Hawaiian sugar enterprises.

John in Charge

John and Lillian traveled on the *Likelike*, a small interisland steamship named for another of Kalākaua's sisters, Princess Miriam Likelike, to Maui, where John would oversee the Spreckels sugar operations. The wooden passenger-freight steamer left Honolulu twice a week at 4:00 p.m., when the winds were somewhat lessened. Nonetheless, the miserable travel conditions included strong headwinds, and the rolling of the sea between the islands was legendary. The bright and beautiful leis that were around the necks of the passengers were forgotten the minute the ship left the narrow coral reef harbor. A soil engineer from San Francisco, on a typical interisland trip, hadn't been sufficiently warned: "In an hour after we leave Honolulu, the deck is practically cleared of passengers except those who are heaving over the rails. The sounds of wailing and groaning are heard all through the vessel from the lower cabins. Ventilation is generally poor and what with the smell from sugar, bananas, mangoes, and other fruits, even hardy sailors have been known to 'bite the dust' crossing those channels."[10]

The captains encouraged those who felt ill to leave their cabins to vomit over the rail, but many couldn't even stand up to do so. Very few repeated the experience a second time if they could avoid it. John and Lillian were relieved as Claus had been to disembark the next morning at 9:00. Claus, in particular, succumbed to the severe sea sickness on the passage to Maui and viewed the trip as a necessary evil—but with a vow to build a better vessel for interisland trips.

John, the newlywed, was content to spend his time in paradise overseeing the construction efforts of Spreckelsville. Because there was no access to telegraph cable in Hawai'i, father and son instead communicated by letter. This slow pace of communication enabled John to be free of Claus's direct supervision as he managed the family's business interests. John was paid a salary of $250 a month (about $7,300 in today's money), an amount he considered skimpy compared with the magnitude of his administrative duties and the great wealth of his father. That said, not only was John in complete charge of the family's businesses, but he also began to make some of his own ventures, which would pay him "handsomely."[11] The planters in Hawai'i regarded John as a force to be reckoned with. He negotiated sugar crops at a low fixed price and convinced them they would certainly benefit if prices later plummeted.

The Princeville Plantation Company on the island of Kauai, under the ownership of William Allen, traditionally held back part of its sugar crop for the local retail market, so locals could avoid paying a premium. Allen was struggling to make the plantation viable financially and had seen his fair share of problems. Unlike Maui, Kauai, known as the "garden island," received ample rainfall—so ample that in some years, the rain washed the cane completely away, whereas in other years, the cane rotted in fields of sitting water. Because of these problems, Allen was in deep debt to his Honolulu agent, Brewer & Company.[12] John offered Allen the same "Spreckels deal" that he had been presenting to other plantation owners: he'd buy the entire sugar crop, and nothing less, at a fixed price. (The "nothing less" of this deal would, of course, deprive the local area residents of their favored price.)

The obvious advantage for Allen to John's proposal was that he'd know how much money he'd make as soon as the crop was shipped to San Francisco. And by selling directly to the California Sugar Refinery, he'd cut out the sugar broker agency and save that percentage. Recognizing both the advantages and drawbacks of the Spreckels deal and their monopoly in the sugar industry, William Allen wrote to his father at the end of September 1879:

> John Spreckels . . . bought all the crop. . . . We were completely in his hands. He would have all or none, and as Spreckels controlled all the refineries, we could not send our sugar to an open market with but one purchaser and that him, so we have sold. Everything looks favorable for a large crop next year, say 40,000 tons, so you see Spreckels' purchase was no small one, at least $4,000,000.[13]

Soon, the Princeville Plantation Company declared its first dividend, and William Allen was delighted.[14] Their previous broker agency, Brewer & Company, however, was anything but jubilant. Since the Spreckels family bought the entire crop, there was no need for the agency to do any of the marketing, sales, or transportation.

Solidifying Control of Maui's Sugar

When other plantation owners signed contracts with Claus (or with John), the sugar factories and agents were essentially cut out of the process. For everyone except the Spreckels family, these became "poor years for the sugar industry" in Honolulu.[15] Peter Cushman Jones, who was associated with Brewer & Company, recalled that once the Reciprocity Treaty of 1875 brought Claus to Hawai'i, those were "the hardest and saddest years in all [his] business experience."[16] Jones despised King Kalākaua, calling his rule a "demoralizing sham," but he came to hate the interloping Spreckels men even more.[17] The Hawaiian sugar industry's hatred of Claus was just beginning, and they would soon reorganize into one big association in their fight for survival.[18]

Even in the midst of expanding the refinery, Claus had devoted much of 1877 to researching sugarcane cultivation and the weather in his chosen location. The key obstacle to his success as a planter was obtaining water, as demonstrated by Alexander & Baldwin's water engineering efforts. Before investing a fortune into building a ditch of his own in Maui, he calculated the island's rainfall for an entire year to see whether it would receive enough rain if diverted. He explained his strategy to the German newspaper *California Demokrat*:

> Careful observation for the past year has shown that the clouds passing over the mountains, with the dew, gave an annual amount of moisture equivalent to a rain-fall of 100 inches. This moisture created many small streams, whose waters were wasted by running into the sea, and the point to be gained was to prevent this waste by diverting the water from its natural channels and conveying it to the lowlands by ditches or canals and using it for irrigating purposes.[19]

Assured with the results of his research, he found the solution to accessing the rainfall in the German immigrant Hermann Schüssler, the chief civil engineer of San Francisco's Spring Valley Water Company. Schüssler, a thirty-five-year-old rising star and Switzerland-trained civil engineer, was already exerting a profound influence on the development of San Francisco's water supply, so his price was certainly high when he agreed to build a ditch in Maui. Although Claus as yet owned neither land nor water rights in Maui, he was confident he'd get both. He had plenty of money and was confident the kingdom would grant him the same water rights that Alexander & Baldwin had.

Anxious to get things started in Maui, Claus and Anna, along with eight-year-old Emma and six-year-old Rudolph, boarded the ss *City of Sydney* on May 13, 1878. Left behind were Adolph, who was content to stay and manage the books and, more importantly, his social life out from under his father's prying eyes, and steadfast Gus, who oversaw the factory operations. Gus, now nineteen, had entered the refinery business at age fifteen, and it was clear to all that he had "sugar in his blood," so Claus felt confident leaving him in charge.

Claus's family checked into Honolulu's elegant Hawaiian Hotel, which had been sponsored and financed by the coffers of the Hawaiian kingdom in 1871 under King Kamehameha V. Like other guests, Claus and Anna were impressed at the opulence of the three-story-high hotel, crowned with an observatory cupola from which to view the sparkling ocean. The interior featured glittering crystal, polished rare woods, overstuffed silk couches, and fine artwork.[20] Claus left Anna and the children behind to enjoy the billiard room, shaded courtyards, cool piazzas, and expansive lawns bordered by colorful and fragrant shrubs and trees, while he went off to Maui on May 28, 1878, with Schüssler—Claus to acquire land and Schüssler to survey the slopes of Haleakalā. The *Pacific Commercial Advertiser* expressed hope the "millionaire sugar king" would find "sufficient inducement to warrant the investment of some of his capital in the Islands."[21] He did.

On June 20 Claus purchased an undivided half interest in sixteen thousand acres in Maui's Waikapu Commons from American businessman William "Henry" Cornwell for $20,000.[22] He then secured a thirty-year lease on twenty-four thousand acres of crown lands in the Wailuku plains of central Maui. These investments received favorable press, and the editor of the *Hawaiian Gazette* expressed wonder there were not more entrepreneurs like Mr. Spreckels who were full of "courage and pluck."[23]

For his part, Schüssler assembled a surveying party that consisted of eight Native Hawaiians familiar with the wild landscape, an accomplished Japanese cook, and a mule driver. Their headquarters was romantically described in the press as a pitched tent in the native forest adjacent to a "little brook that flowed through beautiful tropical vegetation."[24] In reality the ground consisted of dangerously loose lava rock, and the iron-rich dirt and mire stained everybody and everything the color of blood. In addition, everyone had to be on high alert because "every mile or so, the forest floor [dropped] off into a savagely steep ravine," where plenty of mules slipped down the mountainside.[25]

The locals laughed at the survey party because even if the Spreckels operation was somehow successful in corralling water, the land itself was at the foot of Haleakalā, and the soil, covered in volcanic dust, was considered poor. It was specifically stated the land "looked about as valuable for agricultural purposes as a flagstone walk."[26] However, Claus, the farmer's son, had already discovered he could remedy the situation by breaking up the crust that had formed over the soil and mixing it with a "small quantity of vegetable mold."[27]

While some of the locals laughed, others watched and worried—especially, the taro farmers. For thousands of years they had diverted streams into taro patches and corralled fish into ponds. But their efforts to redirect water for nourishment paled in comparison to the radical manipulation of the ecosystem soon to take place under their noses. The Hawaiian word for water is *wai*, and the word for wealth is *waiwai*, *wai* doubled, demonstrating the immense value of fresh water to Hawaiians.[28]

It took the energetic Schüssler less than two weeks to provide an exact survey of the entire ditch.[29] His written plan was ambitious and costly. It involved carrying water thirty miles from the top of the mountain, almost twice as far as Alexander & Baldwin's Hāmākua Ditch. Schüssler's extensive irrigation system consisted of "building 45 miles of canal, about 20 tunnels, and crossing 31 large ravines (some of them 2,000 feet wide and 400 feet deep) with iron pipe."[30]

The Midnight Deal

The pressure was now on for Claus to get the official water rights. On June 24, 1878, Claus formally petitioned King Kalākaua and his cabinet ministers to lease a seventeen-mile irrigation system for $500 a year that would originate on the northeast slopes of Haleakalā.[31] With Schüssler's detailed plans attached to his request, Claus expected a rubber stamp. Kalākaua's cabinet was composed of Dr. John Mott-Smith, a dentist, as minister of the interior; Henry A. Peirce Carter, a sugar agent, as minister of foreign affairs; John M. Kapena, former governor of Maui, as minister of finance; and Alfred S. Hartwell as attorney general.[32]

But things didn't go the way Claus imagined. In a cabinet meeting on July 1, Hartwell and Mott-Smith convinced the other members to unilaterally reject Claus's request because of what they called a "perpetual monopoly" by an outsider.[33] Claus was outraged. The king and cabinet members knew the Reciprocity Treaty had been predicated on the Hawaiian government's allowing American investors to transport water out of the watershed if needed, and the only way to get the water to the dry plains of Maui was to build ditches.[34] The cabinet members also knew it would take a vast investment to tap the copious groundwater of the island mountains to create a dependable irrigation system, an investment that only someone like Claus, with the resources of his profitable California Sugar Refinery behind him, could make. But they were willing to turn him away, even though it meant losing a big influx of money and jobs for their economy, because they despised him. As educated men, Mott-Smith and Hartwell looked down on the unschooled Claus. And Peirce Carter, a full partner of Brewer & Company, was bitter about having been cut out as the sugar agent for the Princeville Plantation.

Without those rights Claus had no water, and without irrigation his land was useless for growing sugarcane. He had to act fast to get the decision reversed. King Kalākaua enjoyed parties, fine cigars, fine champagne, and rich food, which earned him the dubious title of the "Merrie Monarch." The very day he was denied the water rights, Claus sent an urgent invitation to Kalākaua to meet him that evening at the Hawaiian Hotel for an extravagant get-together in a private dining room. With Claus was British businessman, courtier, and politician George Walter Macfarlane, whom Claus had met through the island's sugar commerce. Macfarlane, a good friend of the king, knew the right tone to take on the subject of water privilege. Also present for the party was Sam Parker, major landowner on the Big Island (the island of Hawai'i); William H. Dimond, one of the most prominent businessmen in Hawai'i; and Hermann Schüssler, Claus's civil engineer.[35] To Claus's great relief, Kalākaua accepted his invitation. In fact, the king might just have strolled down the koa wood staircase, since he had permanent quarters in the hotel, Suite 17, for his well-known adulterous encounters.[36]

Claus was sparing no expense in his effort to persuade (in fact, to empower) the king to reverse the decision of his cabinet. He made sure the king was served the Hawaiian Hotel's finest food and French champagne.[37] As Claus and Kalākaua both enjoyed decadent pleasures, the two men bonded well. Claus, neither Hawaiian nor associated with the Congregationalist Church, was a breath of fresh air for a king who constantly had to straddle the diplomatic line between Native Hawaiian traditionalists, who scorned the king's weak connection to the Kamehameha dynasty, and the ultra-conservative haoles in the government. The convivial Claus, possessing an apparent unfathomable wealth, shared his Cuban cigars with the fun-loving but perennially cash-strapped king and toasted the kingdom's advancements that (he assured Kalākaua) only the king could bring about.

What passed between Claus and Kalākaua that night has long been the subject of rumor. Allegedly, Claus offered the king a personal gift of $10,000 and a loan of $40,000 at 7-percent interest, which would settle his existing notes, which required 12-percent interest.[38] But what is known is that around midnight, after an evening of too much drink and merriment, the group left the Hawaiian Hotel and headed for the nearby palace. With Claus and Macfarlane looking over the king's shoulder, letters were drawn up and signed with the king's seal, which informed the four cabinet members that, effective immediately, they were fired with no reason given. To add to this insult, the letters were delivered to each cabinet member's home by a royal messenger at around 1:30 a.m. that morning.[39]

The next day the king appointed a new cabinet, consisting of Samuel Gardner Wilder, Honolulu's British attorney, replacing Mott-Smith as minister of the interior; John M. Kapena, formerly the minister of finance, replacing Peirce Carter as the new minister of foreign affairs; Simon Kaloa Ka'ai, replacing Kapena as minister of finance; and Edward Preston, replacing Hartwell as attorney general.[40] Kalākaua knew the cabinet under Wilder would advance his reputation for enterprise. When the new cabinet met on July 8, they granted Claus the desired water privileges for thirty years at $500 per annum, exactly what he had asked for. The terms of an 1865 statute rendered the crown lands inalienable, and thirty years was the maximum permissible length for a lease of the lands. Claus, further exploiting his influence over Kalākaua, was also promised the rights to Alexander & Baldwin's Hāmākua Ditch if they failed to meet their government-imposed deadline of September 30, 1878. (Later, with John on the scene to witness it, Claus disappointedly heard the news they had completed the ditch on time. Samuel Alexander and Harry Baldwin were proving to be worthy competitors.)

Although Claus had successfully persuaded Kalākaua to dismiss all his cabinet ministers and appoint new ones who would see eye to eye with him on his need for water rights, the king acted in his own interest, wielding his constitutional rights to shed the restrictions placed on him. Defending his agreement with Claus, he asserted the Hawaiian government was "not now ready or willing to undertake such works and incur such expenses."[41] In other words, the Hawaiian kingdom, ever in debt, would be unable to develop or control water projects that should have been government-funded; Claus, in the king's eyes, was a savior.

The outrage from the missionary-descended haoles in the cabinet and their families in charge of the business community was substantial. Indeed, they looked upon Claus—who had no connection to either the Congregationalist Church or the Indigenous Hawaiians—as an intruder and treated him with undisguised hostility. They described Claus rather unkindly as "short, squat, and pudgy," with a penchant for "crusty, arrogant and demanding" behavior. They abhorred his lack of social graces and his "boorishness," and vowed to refuse him entry into their social circles.[42] They stepped up to denounce

Kalākaua's gambling, dancing, drinking, and "panky"—vices they said led to Claus's immoral influence on the kingdom.[43]

The Hawaiian Commercial & Sugar Company

Claus's mind was spinning in a hundred different directions when he left Hawai'i on July 9, 1878. He had legalities to untangle. Hawaiian laws barred foreigners from running corporations. Therefore, to establish a controlling company for his Hawaiian ventures, Claus filed for incorporation in San Francisco and founded the Hawaiian Commercial & Sugar Company on September 30, 1878. "The authorized capital stock was $10,000,000, represented by 1,000 shares having a par value of $10,000 each."[44] The directors under Claus were Frederick Low, ex-governor of California and a prominent Republican; William Babcock, former president of the Spring Valley Water Company; Hermann Schüssler; and Herman Bendel, a prominent San Francisco businessman.[45] Of course, Claus was the majority stockholder with holdings that amounted to $5,200,000. The ambitious purposes of the Hawaiian Commercial & Sugar Company set forth in the charter were to build and maintain ditches for irrigation of lands in the Hawaiian kingdom; cultivate, mill, and sell sugar; build mills, railroads, wharves, and other necessary structures; acquire lands, leases, and water rights; and build or buy ships to ply between the Hawaiian Islands and other ports.[46]

While Schüssler went on to Pittsburgh to procure the materials and equipment needed for the construction of the ditch, Claus assembled a workforce. For months he advertised daily in Honolulu's *Pacific Commercial Advertiser* for "Ditch Builders" to construct the largest irrigation ditch that had ever been undertaken in the islands. Excitement abounded among the unemployed, especially when the *Advertiser* reported a rumor that Claus would employ "natives" to work as common laborers and pay between fifty cents and one dollar per diem. The editor noted the wages were unreasonably high and speculated they would demoralize the labor market and cause "serious injury to the native Hawaiians."[47]

However, with Indigenous Native Hawaiians tragically declining as a race, Claus needed to find enough field laborers to work on the ditch and then later transition them to building the mills and readying the fields. Although Chinese laborers were working around the islands on plantations, the sentiment against them was becoming quite negative. So, Claus sent recruiters to

Portugal and to the Cape Verde Islands, a Portuguese possession off the coast of Africa. Claus believed workers from these regions were already acclimated to the tropics and familiar with sugarcane agriculture.[48] On September 30 the first shipload of Portuguese contract workers arrived in Honolulu to implement Claus's dreams.

Moving Heaven and Earth for Water

In the fall of 1878 Schüssler, by then fully invested as a major stockholder, returned to Hawai'i to begin building the ditch from isolated Hana to central Maui. To undertake this monumental endeavor, the Hawaiian Commercial & Sugar Company employed four hundred men and put one hundred head of oxen and sixty mules to work carrying lumber and dynamite. San Francisco's Risdon Iron Works supplied the pipes that would cross the ravines, pipes that measured an astonishing twenty-one thousand feet.[49] The Spreckels Ditch, once completed, was thirty miles long with a capacity of sixty million gallons of water per day.[50] Nobody in Hawai'i had ever seen the likes of it! (Some of the Spreckels Ditch can still be seen today along the road to Hana.)

Singlehandedly overseeing all of the construction and laborers was John, who some believed to be a carbon copy of his father. Those who knew him intimately, however, were aware that even though father and son shared the same work ethic, John was painfully shy in large gatherings and disliked being thrust into the spotlight, which seemed to follow his father everywhere. It's unclear when he earned it, but his most prized possession was a shipmaster certificate that authorized him to oversee all aspects of any large ship's operation, at sea or in port. Fiercely proud of what it had taken to achieve this, he stated more than once, "I know what manual labor means. I have earned a Pilots and a Masters license at sea."[51] Art, music, and the sea, rather than sugar refining, fed John's soul. He was also focused on supporting his own growing family, as Lillian gave birth to their first child, Grace Alexandria, on September 16, 1878. Life looked bright and promising for John, but he had a vision for his future, and it didn't include working on a sugar plantation, or in a refinery. In his words, he had plodded along doing his father's will but "kept his eyes wide open" and finally saw the opportunity he had been waiting for.[52] However, he needed to bide his time and consider when, how, and where to tell his imposing father about those plans.

7   *Branching Out*

Claus's dream from the moment John had been born was for him to follow in his footsteps. To that end, John, without question, was the favored son, and Claus invested heart and soul into teaching him all he knew so that one day he would have a successor for his sugar empire. But John was born with the same entrepreneurial impulses as his father and was itching to branch out and make his own mark—away from sugar. He needed a clever solution to get out from the career path his father had chosen for him and into his own passion: the sea.

John's solution for self-employment while getting his father to financially invest in his scheme was to start a small shipping business to convey freight between San Francisco and Hawai'i, giving the family control over the transport of their raw sugar. Of course, he'd tell his father, although he'd be earning freight income from other businesses, the most important cargo carried would be the sugarcane prioritized for their San Francisco refinery. And the ship that would ply the sugar over the Pacific Ocean would cunningly be named the ss *Claus Spreckels*.

John conferred with Adolph and together they cooked up the plan to help them individuate from their father. Adolph was the most frustrated son of Claus; because of his father's "tireless energy and constant effort without rest or diversion," he never seemed to understand Adolph's need for fun. In addition, Adolph was tired of being a "controlled employee under salary" for their father. While John was adventuring out and about, Adolph was kept busy as secretary of the company, managing the financial books of ever-increasing assets with no appreciable salary advance. In his words, his salary was "entirely out of proportion" with his personal and social needs. At this point, he was twenty-one, a "world-loving youth" who didn't have "the slightest desire to anchor his nose in mires of ledgers, bills of lading, freight transportation, factory wages and the calculation of profits" for such little money.[1] Adolph had an image to uphold: he had an active social life in San Francisco as the life of every party, always picking up the check and always with an eye out for a pretty girl. His father deplored his womanizing, overspending, and indolent ways.

Brothers United: The Pitch

This long-planned proposal for independence, as remembered by Adolph, sprouted from John's "inventive mind" and went from "slumbering" to "well-grounded." Claus's dictum when being asked to join any outside venture was, "Give me some business reason. The sentimental ones don't interest me."[2] Adolph crunched the numbers, and John looked into rational options. It didn't take long for the sons of Claus Spreckels to provide the facts that not only could they compete with the existing freight companies, but they would efficiently beat them at their cost, with an improved method, Spreckels style.

In an era before shipping containers revolutionized the business, loading and off-loading of cargo was expensive and time consuming. Shipping merchants set their own freight rates, and abusive practices often entangled them with companies where they were hurt financially by exorbitant rates and inconsistent schedules.[3] In Honolulu John had seen the frustration first-hand among plantation agents who contracted for transport of sugarcane. He had learned a lot working at H. Hackfeld & Company, which acted as the brokerage agent for transporting sugar across the seas.

John and Adolph told their father, who valued efficiency above all else, that they shouldn't rely on the current freight companies with their unpredictable schedules.[4] With Spreckels efficiency, they told Claus, all that would be fixed when they built the ss *Claus Spreckels*.[5] Why should Claus pay an outside, undependable shipping company to deliver the cane when John could do it better, faster, and cheaper while ensuring the proper storage of the cane? John explained all this and more to persuade Claus to finance his venture with $2 million in capital.

Claus agreed that if his family shipped the Hawaiian sugarcane to their California refinery, they would have a monopoly on all aspects of the sugar production. But he challenged John to formally enter a proper competitive

10. John Diedrich Spreckels (1853–1926), dubbed the "Sugar Prince" from a young age. Courtesy of the Society of the California Pioneers, C018220.

11. Adolph Bernard Spreckels (1857–1924), a notorious ladies' man. By permission of Adolph Rosekrans.

bid to transport his sugarcane.[6] John recalled that he got the job only because he quoted a bid with "lower freight rates" than what "the old established shipping firms" were charging his "old man."[7] Of course, John's bid was accepted, but this ordeal was meant to be educational.

J. D. Spreckels and Brothers

The firm J. D. Spreckels and Brothers opened an office on California Street in downtown San Francisco, and the shingle read, "General shipping, commission, importing, and exporting."[8] The brothers' company name followed an American tradition: "J. D. Spreckels and Brothers" meant the firm was headed by an older brother, with two or more younger brothers serving under him. As John was the eldest brother and the founder of the company, only his name would be spelled out. John was president, and Adolph was vice president. Claus insisted that he himself along with Gus, while only advisors, be equal financial partners. The fact that Gus, less than two years younger than Adolph, wasn't given any official title other than "advisor" hinted to the fact he and John didn't see eye to eye. But everyone knew, due to John's well-known lack of tact, the shipping operation was John's and that his father and brothers were to remain in the background.

To ensure quality with a known entity, J. D. Spreckels and Brothers commissioned Matthew Turner, a prolific builder of commercial sailing ships, to build an impressive 247-ton, two-masted schooner, 132 feet long with a 32-foot beam, for their fledgling company.[9] The *Claus Spreckels* was built in an astonishing seventy days.[10] On her maiden launch on June 4, 1879, Turner himself took the helm. While testing maneuvers in San Francisco Bay, he inadvertently cut through a regatta and struck a yacht, carrying away its mainsail. This mishap was hotly contested by dozens of San Franciscan yachtsmen, who shared their disgust in the local press at being "run over" by the massive *Claus Spreckels*.[11] The irony was certainly not lost on those who went up against Claus in business matters.

When the *Claus Spreckels* took off for Kahului, Maui, several days later, it made big news—the Spreckels brothers completed the trip in a record nine and a half days.[12] Adolph found it "surprising" how quick the money was coming in as they transported "steel rails, pig iron, coal, pressed brick and machinery for other companies."[13] With money pouring in, the second ship, the Turner-built brigantine *John D. Spreckels*, went into service in 1880. At 300 tons, it was bigger than the *Claus Spreckels*. When the two ships left on the same day in February 1880 for Hawai'i, the first bound for Honolulu and the second for Hilo, there was much interest in which vessel would win. The *Hawaiian Gazette* projected a win by *Claus*, who would never "permit himself to be beaten by juniors of the family."[14] Both ships arrived in ten and a half days, calling the race even—but those in shipping quietly knew which ship was the real victor, because the distance to Honolulu was a bit longer. New ships, one after another, were added until the company had nine "good ships, of varying rig and tonnage."[15] To honor their mother, John and Adolph named a very special ship *Anna*.

The lifelong business partnership of John as president and Adolph as vice president was just getting started. Even though they had branched off, however, they were still expected to manage some aspects of their father's sugar business interests. Adolph apparently didn't mind sitting at a desk, managing their joint partnership and operating in his brother's shadow, while John, out in front, began investing deeply and widely, an activity that would soon worry Claus. Whether or not Adolph had full confidence in his brother or was just apathetic is unknown, but there's no record of any tension or of Adolph questioning or challenging any of John's business decisions. When a close friend of the brothers was asked to comment on their different approaches to business, the answer was, "That's easy . . . J.D. did the hunting, and A.B., the retrieving; J.D. paved the road, and A.B. found the loaded specie wagon to drive over it."[16] John recounted that financial discussions between the two of them approximated to the following: "Oh, by the way, A.B. I'm thinking of putting a few millions into so and so." The response was always, "Sure! Go ahead, J.D., fifty-fifty, of course."[17]

Grooming Gus: Inspecting the Ditch

With his two eldest sons branching off, it was time to groom twenty-year-old Gus. (The third son, Claus Augustus, always went by "Gus" to distinguish him from his father.) Gus had a marked resemblance to his father; though he stood slightly above Claus at five feet ten and a half inches, he did have the same bright, steel-blue eyes.[18] Moreover, his interests in the sugar business, his personality, and his mannerisms had become more like his father with the passing years.

Claus and Gus arrived in Hawai'i on April 22, 1879, anxious to see how construction on the thirty-mile Spreckels Ditch, interchangeably dubbed the Haiku Ditch, was progressing in Maui. First, they inspected their rival's Hāmākua Ditch, completed the year before. Alexander and Baldwin's joint effort had been harrowing and required great speed on their part, since they understood that if they hadn't been able to complete it by the deadline imposed by the government lease, their ditch, and the flowing water within it, would have transferred to Claus. Henry Baldwin, with nerves of steel, had been the hero of the project. Despite the fact that he was handicapped by the loss of an arm in a previous sugar mill accident, he swung perilously on a rope over the treacherous 450-foot Māliko Gulch, using his legs and his left arm—thereby proving to reluctant laborers that if he could do it with one arm, they could easily do it with two.[19] Alexander and Baldwin finished the ditch a few days before their deadline—much to the satisfaction of their missionary-descended "cousins" in Honolulu who were eager to put their new rival in his place.

Upon inspection, it was clear that Schüssler, working systematically and rapidly, was near to deliver exactly what he'd promised Claus: millions of gallons of water.[20] When the Spreckels Ditch was completed in September, the success of this irrigation project was publicized far and wide. It surpassed the size of any ditch that had been constructed in the American West: thirty miles long and delivering about fifty million gallons of water daily (compared with Alexander & Baldwin's seventeen-mile Hāmākua Ditch, delivering some forty million gallons). The Spreckels Ditch cost $500,000 (compared with the $80,000 price tag of the Hāmākua Ditch).

Claus and Gus also inspected the progress of the experimental planting of thirty acres of sugarcane on the formerly dust-dry leased land.[21] The hired agriculturalist, a soil chemist, was pleased to show Claus that his faith in the soil remediation, by using fertilizers, was not misplaced, because the small crop was thriving. Claus looked over his large acreage and clearly saw into the future, when the wide, grassy leaves of thousands of fourteen-foot-tall sugarcanes would be wafting in the warm trade winds of Maui.

With a projected yield of three thousand tons of sugarcane in 1880, Claus had but a short time to direct the building of a mill to process that crop and get back to San Francisco to further expand operations.[22] Once home, he sent engineer Joseph Moore and his machinist son Andrew recruited from

Risdon Iron Works. Their monumental task was to design the mill to be able to process twenty tons of sugar in a ten-hour day.[23] Accompanying Claus was Charles Watson, the engineer and plant manager from the California Sugar Refinery, who would remain behind to ensure that everything was completed the Spreckels way. With Claus breathing down their necks, "Mill Number 1," as it came to be called, would be completed in time.

Buying Crown Lands

With millions being poured into the kingdom of Hawai'i, Claus was beginning to worry how he could safeguard his vast financial investments. He reasoned that before he began to pour even more money into developing additional mills and equipment, he somehow needed to acquire ownership of the royal land he was leasing. Even though he had a thirty-year lease, he feared that at any time, a government authority, on a whim, would demand more money or the land back, as he knew had been done time and again in the kingdom of Hanover.

Leasing crown lands was an important source of income for the Hawaiian government. But purchasing acreage owned by the monarchy was another matter. On January 23, 1865, the Hawaiian Supreme Court had upheld the Act to Relieve the Royal Domain from Encumbrances, and to Render the Same Inalienable, which stated, "Crown lands shall [remain] inalienable and shall descend to the heirs and successors of the Hawaiian Crown forever."[24] This obstacle may have seemed insurmountable to other investors, but Claus was not deterred.

He found a backdoor to gaining land by getting the Hawaiian legislature to deed him "24,000 acres of the Wailuku Ahupua'a on Maui from the Crown Land inventory."[25] He put himself in this position through a deal with Princess Ruth Keʻelikōlani, supposed heir to the vast Kamehameha estate, which encompassed 9 percent of the private land in the kingdom.[26] The princess, who stood six feet tall and weighed more than four hundred pounds, intimidated Hawaiians and non-Hawaiians alike with her rigid stance and formidable appearance. Claus, however, was not daunted, and in a controversial transaction in 1880, he gave her $10,000 in exchange for "any rights in the Crown Lands to which she was entitled" as a royal successor.[27] This illicit real estate deal occurred after Claus lent the princess $60,000 at 6-percent interest so she could pay off burdensome loans she was carrying at 12 percent.[28]

The transaction caused a huge uproar with cries of "land grabber." In 1880 the going rate for land in Maui was about $1.50 an acre, making the crown lands worth around $1.5 million. Princess Ruth's claim to a half interest in the lands would then be estimated, not at the paltry $10,000 Claus paid but at $750,000.[29] The sale was hotly contested and legally questioned throughout the Hawaiian kingdom. First and foremost, members of the ruling monarchy believed that Princess Ruth's legal claim to the crown lands was debatable because she "had no estate, right, title or interest of any description in the crown lands."[30] Lili'uokalani was angry: "Mr. Spreckels paid the Princess Ruth $10,000 to release her claim to a small tract of these lands, although she had never ascended the throne."[31] It was true the princess herself never took the throne, and some royals, behind her back, questioned her self-claimed close genealogical relationship with the Kamehamehas.[32]

Claus sought legal advice in both San Francisco and Hawai'i to ensure he had a plausible claim to the land, and came away with conflicting opinions, but most concluded that his position was "legally weak." Nevertheless, some haoles in the Hawaiian legislature were more than happy to assert that he had good title to those crown lands: his real estate deal would set a precedent for the sale of prime crown lands, and if he could own some of the best agricultural lands in the kingdom, perhaps they could too! However, those legislators who claimed that Claus had a weak legal case "feared the power of his money to hire the best legal talent and, one way or another, get title to half the crown lands."[33] Realizing they couldn't finance a long and drawn-out lawsuit by Claus, the Hawaiian legislature, out of sheer frustration, was persuaded to quiet any subsequent claims of his by passing the contentious Act to Authorize the Commissioners of Crown Lands to Convey Certain Portions of Such Lands to Claus Spreckels in Satisfaction of All Claims He May Have on Such Lands. Since Claus had previously been leasing the land under a thirty-year contract for $1,000 per annum, he settled the case for $30,000 in "lost lease money and the future value of less than .05% of the Crown Lands."[34] Once this compromise was signed on August 11, 1882, the kingdom finally conveyed the 24,000 agricultural acres to Claus.[35]

Princess Ruth had been suffering from heart disease for some time and likely paid little attention to all the legal commotion surrounding the act.[36] She died at fifty-seven, just nine months later. In her will she left everything, including 353,000 acres of Kamehameha lands, to her cousin Princess Bernice

Pauahi Pākī Bishop, thereby making her the richest woman in the kingdom.[37] Bernice had married Charles Reed Bishop, an American with no missionary affiliation, who thus became the kingdom's richest man. And he had already begun to vocalize his strong distaste for Claus.

The legal issues surrounding Princess Ruth's 1880 conveyance of her interest in the crown lands continued to be debated all the way into the late twentieth century, when the Hawai'i Supreme Court, in 1987, decided "she had no legal right" to give Claus a deed for those royal acres.[38] Nevertheless, Princess Ruth had been shrewd because she knew her claims to the lands were worthless: previous court cases had already decided that crown lands belonged only to the ruling monarch. She was land rich but cash poor at the time she met Claus. She pocketed $10,000 from the deal and reduced the interest on her loan payments, and Claus got the land, thereby protecting his investments. In the end, it seems they both got what they wanted.

Relocating the California Sugar Refinery

With the assurance of a steady stream of raw sugar from his Hawaiian plantation, and America finally entering into another period of prosperity, Claus believed it was time to relocate and upgrade refinery operations. The 1880 announcement of the expansion caught the attention of agricultural reporters who thus sought after Claus, now uniquely both planter and refiner. In one such interview, he astonished a reporter when he boldly reported that "eighty million pounds" of his Hawaiian sugar would be arriving by 1881 and that Hawai'i, not Louisiana, would be America's new sugar source.[39] This was big news!

Claus purchased just a little over six blocks on the bay shore of Potrero Point, adjacent to the Southern Pacific Railroad tracks. This industrial district, two miles south of the city, was a perfect choice for a massive refinery. He was joining a cluster of other heavy industries that were shaping not only the city but the American West; locomotives, cable car equipment, the legendary battleship *Oregon*, as well as iron and steel for many of San Francisco's buildings came from Potrero Point. Many of these trades also needed the natural deep-water access for ships.

Claus hired the eminent German engineer Teile Henry Müller to design the new refinery. Müller had been educated at John and Adolph's alma mater, the Polytechnic Institute in Hanover.[40] He assured Claus that no other refinery in the country would have more modernization and innovation than his and that he alone would have a "vacuum pan the largest in the world—seventeen feet in diameter!"[41]

The local press reported that Claus contracted with local suppliers for all materials, with the stated purpose of boosting the economy. Furthermore, effective immediately, the public was told, he'd be hiring "an average force of two hundred men" to construct the buildings, small houses for married men, and hotels for the other employees of the refinery.[42] On a bright day in May 1881, four hundred people, including family, reporters, and distinguished San Franciscans, boarded tugboats for the cornerstone ceremony at Potrero Point, to watch Claus, full of smiles, pick up a ceremonial silver trowel and symbolically spread the first mortar to place the solid granite cornerstone of the outer wall to commemorate the dedication. One side read "California Sugar Refinery, 1881" and the other side "Claus Spreckels."[43]

Ex-governor Frederick Low said the refinery would "employ some hundreds of men directly and other hundreds indirectly" and that it would "contribute largely to industries of San Francisco." Then he turned to the man-of-the-hour and repeated Claus's well-known mantra, "Spreckels success is California's success." At the conclusion of an overly long speech, a catered lunch was offered to all. One reporter noted that "as the champagne was more plentiful than sugar, tongues were loosed, and cheerful speeches made."[44] It was one of the happiest days in Claus's life. Anna and all their children stood by, full of pride and emotion for how far they had come as a family.

When the twelve-story facility was finished, it presented "the appearance of an enormous fortress to those approaching San Francisco from across the bay."[45] Hundreds of newly hired men received salaries ranging from fifty-five to sixty-five dollars per month, which Claus reported were "much higher than [those] paid in the East." He sweetened the handsome salary with "a weekly allowance of five pounds of sugar and one gallon of syrup to each married man, while beer furnished the hands twice a day."[46]

With his first refinery on Brannan Street, Claus had been forced to use seven "four-horse trucks" in rotation to transport sugar to and from the refinery.[47] To streamline operations in Potrero Point, Claus had a four-hundred-foot-long wharf built, so that ships heavy-laden with raw Hawaiian sugarcane could easily slide up alongside the refinery for loading and unloading. He went further with new technology: a tunnel was constructed under the bay

THE NEW CALIFORNIA SUGAR REFINERY, SAN FRANCISCO.

12. The new refinery at Potrero Point. Completed in 1881, the twelve-story facility presented itself as an enormous fortress to those approaching San Francisco from across the bay. Courtesy of Terrence and Virginia Wilson private collection.

whereby eight thousand gallons of water per minute could be raised for the purposes of cooling and condensation.[48] Potrero became a flurry of activity, with workers moving between the "main refinery, charcoal house, warehouse and melting room, boiler room, engine room, machine shop, cooper's shop and coal sheds."[49]

For an area geographically cut off from the heart of San Francisco, Claus had a reservoir built, capable of holding seven million gallons of fresh water furnished by large artesian wells. On the flat land surrounding the waterfront, economical housing for both single and married men was built. Once stores and restaurants were added, the Potrero Point neighborhood developed as an informal company town for the hundreds of Spreckels employees. On Sundays, Hobbs Wharf was busy with hundreds of bamboo fishing poles rising in the air with silvery smelt for the evening meal.[50]

By the sheer number of references in the newspaper regarding the construction of the new refinery, it was clear that San Francisco was watching

13. The Sugar Mansion in the Makiki neighborhood of Honolulu was for many years the finest private residence in the city, being second only to the ʻIolani Palace. Courtesy of Terrence and Virginia Wilson private collection.

everything Claus was doing. With the optimistic belief the refinery and the Maui plantation would coexist and operate as an integral part of his sugar empire for the rest of his life, Claus sought out every innovation to ensure that his new enterprise would continue to thrive.

The Sugar Mansion

With his Hawaiian-Californian relations securely tied together, it was time for Claus to branch out and build a home in Hawaiʻi. Anna and the children more often than not accompanied him on every business trip, and the family found the tropical warmth and humidity of Hawaiʻi a welcome climate for body and soul. Their new home would be on the island of Oʻahu. Claus bought the lot for $5,000 at auction in 1880 in the Makiki neighborhood, on a plot of land fronting Punahou Street.

Henry Geilfuss's architectural plans, for the third time, were thriftily repurposed. Inside his new tropical mansion, the same floorplan as he had in Aptos would generate a feeling of warm familiarity. But Geilfuss designed an elaborate ornamental tower for this mansion, giving it the appearance of an ornate wedding cake. After the house was painted white, it became known colloquially as the "Sugar Mansion."[51] Claus always gave Anna free rein with decorating their homes. Her artistic tastes were wide-ranging. She brought in furnishings, paintings, and statuary from around the world, including luxuries never before seen in the islands. When the mansion was completed, the press called it the "grandest habitation barring those of royalty."[52]

Henry Berger, leader of the Royal Hawaiian Band and King Kalākaua's personal bandmaster, was frequently found at lavish dinner parties in the Spreckelses' ornate ballroom, conducting his cotillion string orchestra under soft candlelight. It was beginning to look to others as if the king had a social rival. The power of Claus's celebrity in Honolulu is plain, and—just as was the case in San Francisco—Hawaiian newspapers were watching his every move.

But Claus was never comfortable in such an ornate atmosphere; he was his happiest working around the expansive tropical garden, where he was seen wearing a black silk skullcap and smoking a cigar. When in Hawai'i, which was not as often as he had imagined when he built the house, he would "stir things up, and make new plans." The *Gazette* described a beehive of activity: "He usually makes things hum wherever he goes."[53] Once you were invited to his home, you never forgot the generosity of Mr. and Mrs. Spreckels, but if any person were ever to stand in Claus's way even once, there would never be another chance to visit the home, for while Claus was a generous friend, he was an unrelenting enemy.[54]

Oceanic Steamship Company: A Dream Realized

Having two massive projects going on simultaneously required intensive oversight by Claus, and because an ocean separated these endeavors, a long voyage was needed each way. John and Adolph, sensing the time was right, pitched their proposal for expansion. Not only would their diversification into a luxury passenger line make their father's travel more comfortable, but the timing was perfect in many ways.

Mail delivery in the islands was accomplished by the slow and unpredictable Pacific Mail Steamship Company, which had a lucrative contract from the U.S. government to carry mail across the Pacific. This meant that news, whether of national importance or the deeply personal, could take months to an entire year to reach its recipient. Because of this alone, many American expats living in the Hawaiian Islands described a deep sense of isolation that often led to dark depression. Pacific Mail had earned a bad reputation for a number of reasons, including the fact that it was the prime carrier of Chinese immigrant labor for the sugar plantations during the era of anti-Chinese sentiment. But the primary complaint was its irregular mail service due to mechanical challenges. The dissatisfaction was well documented by those living and doing business in Hawai'i. Their "ships came and went as they pleased," and their "flying visits were not long enough for passengers to spend money sight-seeing, or for businessmen to arrange freight."[55]

By 1880 it was clear to anyone in the shipping industry that sails were giving way to steam. John and Adolph easily saw a huge commercial opportunity to branch out from carrying freight to carrying passengers *and* freight. Passenger steamship services were becoming an increasingly popular means of transport and the brothers had to move quick to avoid potential competition in the Pacific.[56]

Claus, well impressed with the financial returns of J. D. Spreckels and Brothers, agreed to invest in his boys, knowing they could elevate the steamship industry and pleased they were manifesting the philosophy *If you're not first, you're last.*[57] To the amazement of all on the sidelines, the brothers incorporated the Oceanic Steamship Company in San Francisco in December 1881, with twenty-eight-year-old John as president. "Capital stock was 25,000 shares of par $100.00," with Claus and his sons holding 14,500 shares.[58] The company's articles of incorporation ambitiously stated the brothers' extensive purpose:

> To carry on and conduct a general freight and passenger business by sea, and to that end to build, buy, own, charter, hire and sell steamships and other steam and sailing craft, and operate the same between San Francisco and the Hawaiian Islands, and from and to other ports and harbors on the Pacific Ocean and elsewhere, and to purchase, sell, own and operate coal mines, tenders, warehouses, and all other property necessary, proper, convenient and auxiliary to or for said business; and to invest its funds and earnings in the stock of other corporations.[59]

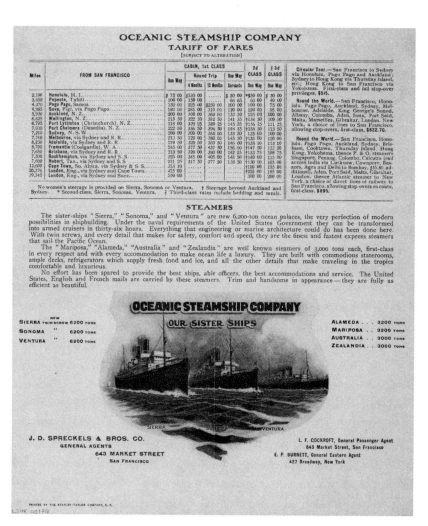

14. The Oceanic Steamship Company set a new standard for luxury sea travel. UC San Diego Library.

Sailing ships were still useful in part because they were cheaper to build and run and didn't require deep harbors. To that end, the J. D. Spreckels and Brothers' ships were "turned over" to the Oceanic Steamship line for continued service. The new firm began with a chartered steamer, the *Suez*, to operate until the firm's own ships could be built. In 1882 Oceanic commissioned two elegant steamers from William Cramp & Sons Shipbuilding Company, the *Alameda* and the *Mariposa*, to be built in Philadelphia. Leaving nothing to chance, as he learned from his father, John went to Philadelphia himself to supervise the details.

On the bright morning of Tuesday, July 31, 1883, Claus, Anna, thirteen-year-old Emma, and eleven-year-old Rudolph ran from their staterooms to get the first look at Honolulu from the rails of the *Mariposa*. On this, her maiden voyage from San Francisco, the entire family jubilantly realized they had broken all previous records, with the time of five days and twenty-one hours.[60]

When the *Mariposa* rounded Koko Crater at 10 a.m., the lookout on Diamond Head ran down the mountain to telephone the palace with the news that Hawai'i's first steamer had arrived. The government went into action. The Royal Hawaiian Band was rousted from their homes and put aboard a tugboat to musically guide in the *Mariposa*. The soft air was then loudly pierced by a twelve-gun salute from the shore battery. The Spreckels ship hadn't been expected this early, but a distinguished reception committee, including Governor Dominis, Princess Lili'uokalani's husband, was quickly organized. When Captain Horace Howard slid the *Mariposa* into dock, rope ladders were dropped so that members of the hastily put together welcoming delegation could clamber up the sides of the ship to get the first look. When the proud Spreckels family descended the gangplank, they were pleasantly surprised that King Kalākaua had sent his private carriage to transport them to their Punahou home. It was noted that a band of schoolchildren played "Hail to the Chief" when Claus entered the royal carriage.[61] It's unlikely the Hawaiian children knew that this was the official arrival anthem for the president of the United States, but it's curious as to who would've ordered this particular piece to be played. After royal celebrations for an entire week, thousands of people, including the king and his sister Princess Likelike lined the shore to bid aloha to the family whose steamships would advance the kingdom in a thousand different ways but none more importantly than bringing timely communication from the outside world.

Not many Americans had ever visited the tiny kingdom of Hawai'i, and John saw the value of tourism as a separate venture rather than something ancillary to the trade and cargo operation. The Oceanic Steamship Company challenged the widespread belief that ocean travel was boring and uncomfortable. In the era before the iconic hula girl, Hawai'i's romance was symbolized by an alluring, scantily dressed female situated against a backdrop of coconut palms, mountainous islands, or sandy beaches on Oceanic brochures. Part of the line's success was linked to its first-ever all-inclusive package deals to the islands, which included hotel, sightseeing, and even volcano excursions, all of which immediately stimulated the local economy. John wrote one of the earliest published tourist articles encouraging Americans to board his ships and discover "La Dolce Far Niente," or the sweetness of doing nothing (something he nor his father could personally actualize). He said, "There is but one Pacific Ocean, but one Hawaiian group, [and] to sail for a week over the clear and calm waters of the one and to luxuriate in the tropical beauty of the other are pleasures not to be duplicated the world over."[62]

Not all who heeded the call were born sailors like John. For some, it was difficult in the extreme to appreciate a transoceanic voyage. Carrie Winter was one passenger who found the journey less appealing after suffering debilitating seasickness. On her voyage to Hawai'i aboard one of the Spreckels ships, she wrote a vivid description of her experience. It's clear the romance of the handkerchief-waving departure at the wharf disappeared along with the coastline as the steamer departed San Francisco's harbor.

SS. ZEALANDIA, AUGUST 27, 1890

When we reached the ocean, the ship began to rock and roll. Oh the misery of what followed. I did not leave my state-room till Monday morning. Saturday night was the worst though. We were on the storm side and every crack was stuffed tight. Not a bit of fresh air till Monday. The waves pounded, way above us on the hurricane deck, the boat rocked so that I had to hold on all the time to keep in my berth the awful sounds, and smells!!! The sickness was bad enough but then there was that indescribable feeling of being poised in the midst of the air and sky and water and swaying there with nothing to grasp.[63]

Her narrative changed soon enough, however, during the latter part of the seven-day cruise. Once she discovered the romance of moonlit nights on deck, she could feel what had constantly lured John Spreckels to the sea: "For us every day dawned clear and beautiful and every evening saw the sun sink into the ocean in a blaze of glory, leaving its glow in the sky long afterwards, while every night the stars and moon seemed brighter."[64]

Voyaging on big steamships was a relatively new mark of high status, and the Oceanic line was among the first to provide an extravagance on par with fine hotels and restaurants. The luxuries of the Spreckels ships became newsworthy, with travel journals across the country lauding the ships: "To say that this fine fleet is furnished with all the modern improvements does not fully convey the extreme comfort, which is enjoyed in the voyage. The state rooms are furnished with . . . electric lights, the table is up to the standard of the best first-class hotels ashore, and good order and cleanliness everywhere prevail."[65]

One thing John shared with his father was his dislike of mingling with the high-society crowd where pomp and circumstance were required. Finally, far away from the sugarcane fields and the hot boilers of the refinery, John was happily on board his ships, not to lounge on the deck or entertain guests as a rich shipping magnate but to assist in all aspects of navigation. He was often seen smoking a cigar and swapping yarns of navigational challenges with the captain or with some rough-and-ready shipmates in the pilothouse.[66]

When an opportunity to deliver the mail arose in 1885, the Spreckels reputation to meet deadlines became vitally important. The Pacific Mail Steamship Company had withdrawn from its monthly sailings between San Francisco, New Zealand, and Australia. John wasted no time in pursuing and winning the contract, adding "an additional $150,000 a year to the Oceanic Steamship's coffers."[67]

When John added the *Zealandia* and *Australia* to his line in 1886, the Hawaiian flag flew from the masts because, as John explained, the ships had been built in England, and this fact "forbade the use of the stars and stripes."[68] One year later he strategically hired American shipbuilders to heavily alter the *Australia*. He then petitioned Congress to acknowledge his newly modified American ship, and by a special act of Congress, the *Australia* was granted her American registry. The British ship now flew Old Glory from her mast, and the Spreckels ships were the only ones flying the American flag in the South Pacific.[69]

John had first journeyed aboard a Pacific Mail ship from Panama to California, tightly holding his father's hand at the age of three; now, as president of this major shipping company, he had taken over the Pacific Mail's routes. He was doing more than transporting cargo, passengers, and mail to and from the Southern Hemisphere; he was finally making his own mark and living his own dream, not his father's.

8 *Vilified for His Overnight Monopoly*

When Claus first began to achieve success in the sugar industry, the press extolled him as an immigrant who achieved the American dream through hard work and sheer ingenuity. He was often celebrated for employing hundreds of men in a downturned economy and providing reasonable hours, safe working conditions, and high wages. Andrew Carnegie, on the other hand, had appalling working conditions in the steel mills. When he began to give his profits away philanthropically rather than raising his impoverished workers' pay, labor leaders and clergymen condemned him. Carnegie argued that by keeping his profits high, he could serve society with such charitable acts as funding libraries across the nation. But during the infamous Homestead Steel Strike, nearly four thousand workers snarled at that logic, asking, "What good is a book to a man who works 12 hours a day, six days a week?"[1] Carnegie is on record for replying, "If I had raised your wages, you would have spent that money by buying a better cut of meat or more drink for your dinner. But what you needed, though you didn't know it, was my libraries and concert halls. And that's what I'm giving to you."[2]

Claus's views were well represented by John when he was asked what he thought about Carnegie: "I do not believe in indiscriminate charity. We have too much of it, and it tends to pauperize men and make drones out of them. I believe the best charity you can give a man is work, and [to] pay him so well that he is satisfied. I believe that the man who works is entitled to be comfortable, and I try to make everybody who works for me feel so."[3]

Even though there were no specific federal or state statutes prohibiting monopolies, there was a growing general sentiment resisting monopolists. The term *robber baron* was being attached to such tycoons as Carnegie, Vanderbilt, and Rockefeller, who were building massive empires at the expense of poorly paid factory workers. But as his wealth increased, some in the press began to apply the label to Claus.

Claus's increasing fortune generated an amazing amount of envy from other capitalists, but the label of robber baron couldn't stick. His loyal workers were powerful evidence that he was not an exploiter of labor. And because he didn't monopolize the sugar industry through the formation of a trust by corruption and the exploitation of workers like other sugar refiners had, it was a conundrum to easily define him. Also, nothing he did was illegal—there were no laws preventing him from gaining unfair advantages over competitors. Claus simply found weaknesses and exploited holes in the capitalist system for his personal gain, and he consoled himself as he amassed a fortune that Americans were also benefitting mightily with a cheaper, high-quality product due to his efficiencies.

Closing a Loop with William Irwin

With the establishment of the Oceanic Steamship Company, Claus's monopolistic control of the Hawaiian sugar industry was almost complete. All that remained was for him to become his own sugar agent: setting the price of sugar and initiating (and signing) his own contracts. He had to enter into a business partnership with an established sugar factor who would act as a front and would ensure that his holdings were well represented. Such a partnership would help tighten the link in his chain of control. He looked for an influential man who understood all aspects of the Hawaiian sugar culture, one who could diplomatically straddle the line between the missionary descendants and the monarchy. He found these qualities in the wealthy, British-born sugar agent William G. Irwin, who ran a leading sugar factoring business in Honolulu and whom John had already worked with. Claus and Irwin incorporated a formidable partnership in 1881, doing business as "Sugar Factors and Commission Agents" under the name W. G. Irwin & Company.[4] Claus was the "Company" and a 50-percent partner. Now he was his own agent for his Spreckelsville plantation on Maui and his other smaller investment plantations across the islands. Irwin and Claus were balanced opposites. Irwin's good looks, trim physique, easy manner, crisp British accent, and courteous demeanor would help iron out the wrinkles Claus typically created during his business dealings. When William Irwin's island colleagues had asked him why he'd partner with a monopolist, he replied that it was simply a matter of "business, of pure, competitive dealing," and besides, Claus was "one of the smartest businessmen in America."[5]

With his new partnership with Irwin, Claus had closed the final loop. He now controlled every stage of the production and distribution of his product—through land leases that became titles, water rights that resulted in sugarcane production, a sugar agency to control multiple plantations and transactions, and a steamship line that monopolized transpacific sugar transport to his personal sugar refinery. Claus had created an unassailable monopoly, through bare-knuckled, unapologetic competition.

The Public Reaction

His monopolistic control of the Hawaiian sugar industry propelled him into the international spotlight. Claus had power over his family and over the people he employed, but the press was beyond his sway. And with this unplanned celebrity, he gave up a significant part of his private life. Every link he had forged in the chain to his monopoly was dissected and disseminated, framed and reframed by the press in constantly changing viewpoints. He could hardly keep up.

Portland's *Oregonian* published "That Fraudulent Treaty," in which Claus was harshly singled out as the treaty's sole beneficiary with the stunning accusation that he had actually costed the government: "The treaty of reciprocity with the Hawaiian Islands is therefore merely a treaty for the benefit of Mr. Claus Spreckles [*sic*], and it costs the government more than two million dollars a year and the consumers of the Pacific coast an equal annual sum."[6]

To help repair Claus's reputation, Scotsman John Walker, minister of finance for the kingdom, wrote a response in the *Advertiser* (withholding the fact that he was a new business partner with W. G. Irwin & Company): "As to the unfair advantage our free sugar gives to the one man, we know nothing about; we simply know that Mr. Claus Spreckles [*sic*] came here and offered to purchase our sugars, and we did just what the people of any other country should or would have done—sold them at the best price we could get."[7]

Henry Alvin Brown, former special agent for the U.S. Treasury Department, also singled Claus out and told Congress in no uncertain terms the American people were losing money on the treaty. He called on Congress to "abrogate this unjust treaty and put a stop to the ever-increasing subsidy now annually drawn from the people of this country to support Hawaii and enrich a few monopolists, under the guise of a 'commercial treaty' or 'foreign policy.'"[8]

The Vilifying of Sir Claus

Never imagining the fallout that would occur, King Kalākaua sent a delegation to San Francisco to confer upon Claus the degree of "Knight Commander" in a public ceremonial knighting on March 29, 1879. The Royal Order of Kalākaua was awarded in four grades for exceptional service to the kingdom. (Not being a head of state, Claus ranked third from the top.) The insignia of the Commander Cross, an ornate gold Maltese cross surmounted by the Hawaiian crown, was ceremonially presented in a solemn ceremony to a beaming Claus with the following words: "I am commissioned by His Majesty Kalākaua, King of Hawaii, the honor of conferring upon you, in his name, the decoration of the Commander's grade of the Order of Kalākaua assuring you, sir, that His Majesty fully appreciates the energy and industry manifested by you to advance and develop the productive interest of Hawaii, which you have inaugurated, and which must conduce to the growth and prosperity of the Hawaiian Kingdom."[9]

Claus's being knighted by a small Pacific island nation was laughable to Michael de Young, the editor of the *Chronicle*. De Young colorfully entertained San Franciscans with his tabloid-style journalism and found ample fodder in the honorary knighthood to get even with "*Sir* Claus," who'd publicly called him a "disgrace to journalism." In a variety of articles covering the sugar industry, de Young used every opportunity available to ridicule Claus as "Lord Sugar Barrel," "Kanaka Knight," "Commercial Monarch," and more.[10]

According to Article I, Section 9 of the U.S. Constitution, "No Title of Nobility shall be granted by the United States." In fact, the federal government's personnel are prohibited from receiving any office, title, or emolument from foreign states without the consent of Congress. The clause does not prevent a U.S. citizen who was not employed by the federal government—a citizen such as Claus Spreckels—from accepting titles of nobility from royalty, although a proposed amendment to the Constitution, approved by supermajorities in Congress in 1810 but never ratified by three-fourths of the states, would've revoked the citizenship from such a recipient.[11] When, for example, it was learned that sometime after 1874, two U.S. naval officers who'd assisted with restoring civil order after a riot in Honolulu had been knighted as Claus had been, the medals were hastily confiscated by the State Department. Behind closed doors in the House of Representatives but on public record, New York representative William E. Robinson snickered at the absurdity of the knighting by a king whose name you couldn't even pronounce and wondered why naval officers would even want them.[12] He asked, "Are not these men contented with the honors which America gives them?" In the same session, King Kalākaua was ridiculed as the "Dark Prince and Prince of Darkness" now "owned" by another king: Claus Spreckels. When Robinson stumbled on pronouncing the king's name, he stated: "Kalakaua, or kill-cow, or however you may pronounce it. We will call it 'cow' because you are making a bull of conferring such an order." The record shows that laughter erupted throughout the House.[13]

Cussed in the Street

In this depression-ridden era, many viewed the influx of cheap Chinese laborers as unwelcome competition for a scarcity of jobs. Socialists, thousands of them, regularly voiced their anti-Chinese sentiments on the infamous "sandlots" in front of City Hall. They were led by the fiery Irish seaman Denis Kearney, prominent in the Workingmen's Party of California. It seemed that nobody could stop him as he delivered inflammatory speeches inciting San Franciscans to grab their muskets and stop the Chinese men as they disembarked from ships.

In one of his well-attended sandlot tirades, Kearney singled out "Claus Spreckels, the biggest damned thief whoever went unhung." He cursed, "God Damn him, I am man enough to tell him so to this face."[14] This after he'd told the crowd that Claus ignored the unemployed locals to favor cheaper laborers from China. Kearney shouted to the rowdy mob that the men Claus hired to work for him were "crawling, creeping, festering, stinking, maggot-producing insects that go to make up the lying, thieving, stealing, nasty, murdering, treacherous, lousy, God-forsaken, hell-bound classes who seek to crush out the respectable and honest portion of the people," by which he meant white, unemployed, local men.[15]

Kearney continually cited his First Amendment rights to freedom of speech, but the public defamation of a leading citizen was viewed as crossing a legal line. This was just the excuse the police were looking for to arrest Kearney on the charge of using "incendiary language." The headline read, "Dennis Kearney Jailed for Cussing Claus Spreckels Name in Public."[16] Out on bail, Kearney returned to the sandlot and told the press, "If I were to call the Emperor of Russia the worst name in the dictionary, it would be fine, but you must not say a word against Claus Spreckels. Why? Because he was knighted by King Kalākaua of the Sandwich Islands."[17]

Ona Miliona

Claus was not the kind of man to thoughtfully consider the anticipated press coverage on his actions. When any steamer arrived in Honolulu with suspicions of smallpox, cholera, measles, or any other contagious disease on board, the ship was abruptly rerouted to "Quarantine Island" (today's Sand Island) near the harbor entrance. Due to thousands of immigrants being transported in to work on sugar plantations, the Board of Health had their hands full dealing with irate ship captains losing both money and time. There were even irate passengers who refused to quarantine—passengers such as Claus Spreckels. The Board of Health was serious in its effort to mitigate the racial extinction of the Indigenous Native Hawaiians, who were declining at an alarming rate from a variety of diseases, so quarantining was strictly enforced.

Claus and Anna arrived in Honolulu at 3:00 a.m. on the first Sunday of June 1881 on the *City of Sydney* and somehow knew they were at risk and began packing. Passengers were told to stay on board, but Claus and Anna, fearing a forced quarantine, hurried down the gangplank. Meeting the steamer at this ungodly hour was the president of the Board of Health, who objected to Mr. and Mrs. Spreckels's departure from the ship and insisted they go directly into quarantine for six days.[18] Claus, likely overly cranky from a lack of sleep, forcefully declined, and he and Anna, demonstrating a complete lack of respect and regard to the order, somehow ended up in Maui via the *Likelike* despite the quarantine laws.

Word spread fast throughout the Hawaiian community that if you were Claus Spreckels, you were not obligated to follow the same laws ascribed to ordinary Hawaiians. In the Hawaiian language Claus was referred to as "Ona Miliona"; whether the moniker was derogatory or just a neutral recognition of

15. Claus Spreckels at fifty-one. There were many references to his eyes: "They are clear blue, and are at once shrewd and searching, but they are so quick in movement that they give the observer a distinct impression of his secretiveness and even of cunning" ("Claus Spreckels," *Harper's Weekly*). Courtesy of Terrence and Virginia Wilson private collection.

his wealth is unclear, but having more than a million dollars was almost inconceivable at the time. The Hawaiian newspaper *Ko Hawai'i Pae 'Aina* ran the headline "Rich Are Treated Differently." In the article the editor demanded an explanation from the government for this unequal treatment and requested the same independence from the laws as that granted to Ona Miliona.[19]

16. Anna Spreckels at forty-eight, the perfect partner for Claus. Courtesy of Terrence and Virginia Wilson private collection.

Even though Claus had begun to be vilified in some press stories for his "overnight" monopoly, he defiantly justified his having seized opportunities, averring the reason his competitors couldn't survive against his lower prices was because he was offering a better product. Consumers purchasing from the California Sugar Refinery didn't pay unjustifiably high prices for inferior-quality sugar. He had efficiently improved his sugar product at every stage of production while lowering the costs for consumers. Why should there be any complaints?

Like Rockefeller with his monopoly on oil, Carnegie with steel, and Vanderbilt with steamships, Claus dominated the sugar sector, crushed small competitors, and consolidated his power. At every opportunity he said he was making the sugar industry more efficient and safer for workers and was doing his best to grow the industrial strength of California, the state he was becoming more loyal to with every passing year.

The *San Francisco Merchant*, a commerce magazine that measured the pulse of the growing city, opined:

> Would that kind Providence send California more "monopolists" like Mr. Claus Spreckels, who would save the poor from extortion, furnish employment to the industrious, and trade to the enterprising merchant, and give wealth to the country and all who are bound up in interest in it, even while making from themselves and their families colossal fortunes. And would that all millionaires would wear their honors so lightly among their fellow men as Claus Spreckels and Sons.[20]

9   *Raising Cane in Spreckelsville*

With outright ownership of the land in Maui secured, it was full speed ahead for Claus to develop the Spreckelsville Plantation. He was an expert on converting raw cane sugar into food-grade white sugar, but now he'd have to grow his own supply—and that meant he simultaneously would need to be a sugar planter, miller, and refiner. His goal was to implement technological and accounting sophistication not seen or heard of on any other plantation in the islands. Those who knew Claus knew that Spreckelsville would be more than just a resource outpost for his California refinery; his operations there would be a labor of love and a chance to stretch his mind and learn.

Securing Laborers

With five hundred acres of sugarcane planted by the end of 1879 and the now-operational ditch system providing the irrigation needed, Claus had the daunting task of securing labor for Maui on a scale sufficient to implement the technological expertise that would turn his crop production into a massive enterprise. Labor notices offering higher wages in Hawai'i caught the attention of suffering workers internationally, who imagined better opportunities on the islands.[1] Thus, Claus began earnestly recruiting from all over the world, with the largest numbers coming from China, Portugal, Japan, and the Philippines. By the time the first crop was ready in 1881, Claus had 1,150 laborers: "800 field hands of all nationalities, and 350 white men."[2] Because of his fast recruitment, his yield amounted to an impressive three thousand tons of sugarcane.[3]

Claus employed two distinct types of plantation laborers—independent and contract—with wages dependent on the skill level of the job. The larger group was the independent laborers, who were engaged at twenty-two dollars per month, from which they paid the plantation for food and housing on the property. Laborers under a three-year contract, on the other hand, received ten dollars per month, with board and lodging provided by the plantation. Claus preferred independent workers because he found them cheaper in the long run. In his view, laborers on "long contracts" often shirked their work and seemed sick more often than independent workers, and yet they still had to be fed, housed, and paid.[4] The salaries were generous at a time when typical wages were eight dollars plus food or eleven dollars without, and laborers could eat well on three dollars per month. The *Pacific Commercial Advertiser*, under Claus's influence, noted that his laborers were "purportedly paid well and fed well."[5] The fact remained, however, that after finding and training the labor, keeping them was just as challenging. One plantation manager explained, "If I were to wrong or abuse one of my men, he would persuade a dozen or twenty others not to re-enlist when their terms are out."[6]

Claus later found himself in trouble when he employed labor agents to secure 2,500 workers from Puerto Rico. The greedy agents, working on commission, turned out to be inhumane. Once on the U.S. mainland, the agents tightly packed the recruited laborers into sleeping cars and guarded them closely as they traveled by train from New Orleans to San Francisco. In one instance, a group of 194 Puerto Ricans reached California three days before the steamer to Maui was scheduled to leave. The agents consequently forced the migrants to camp out in the desert three hundred miles east of El Paso to prevent them from escaping into San Francisco's general population. To Claus's chagrin, a *New York Times* journalist reported on this horrific situation with his sensationally titled article, "Men Say They Were Kidnapped for the Spreckels Sugar Plantation—Closely Guarded on Train." The labor agents had enticed the men ("decoyed" them, according to the article) to board a ship, "ostensibly to land on the other side of their island"—that is, still in Puerto Rico. Imagine their surprise when a short cruise turned into a journey to a foreign land. Waylaid for three days in the desert, these workers shouted their situation to anyone willing to listen. Unfortunately, the outcome of this situation and Claus's response are unknown. Journalists had frequently noted, "Mr. Spreckles [*sic*] is an easy man to get access to, but it is another matter entirely to draw any information out of him."[7]

Managing the Laborers

By 1882 Claus had the largest sugar plantation in the world. Because he couldn't be in Hawai'i more than once or twice a year, Claus relied on John and insisted that his managers maintain copious records on all features of production. He required daily reports on every employee, the number of hours worked, and systematic cost records so that he, in San Francisco, could figure the cost of all crops at any stage on a field-specific basis.[8] No one before had utilized this disciplined, clock-ordered management on any plantation, and his rival planters realized how far behind they were in every way.

A loud plantation whistle measured each workday at Spreckelsville— starting at 6:00 a.m. and ending at 4:30 p.m. Any complaint about the starting hour would've likely been countered with the statement that workers on neighboring plantations started their workday at 5:00 a.m. Lunas would rout late workers out of bed and unceremoniously march them to the fields.

Immigrants worked side by side on a wide range of rotating tasks. With no common language, they gradually developed a plantation pidgin that was an amalgam of English, Hawaiian, Chinese, Portuguese, Japanese, Tagalog, and so on. Field hands learned different skills because it takes almost two years for a sugarcane crop to mature and they rotated with the seasons. While one crop was being planted, another was growing, and still another was being harvested.[9]

One of the most tedious and backbreaking tasks was hoeing weeds. In heavy clothing covering their faces and hands to protect themselves from yellow jackets and spiny needles, workers had to "hoe hoe hoe for four hours in a straight line and no talking."[10] But harvesting was the most laborious task: "Mature Hawaiian cane, about fifteen to twenty feet tall, with a tough stalk and narrow, serrated-edge leaves that can grow to between five and six feet long projecting from the cane, must be cut close to the ground, where the sugar content is highest. The sucrose in cane degrades soon after cutting and so must be milled within twenty-four hours of harvesting."[11] With this short time window, lunas could be overly harsh to rush the workers.

The mill was a "machine in a garden" that rushed through thousands upon thousands of sugarcane stalks, squeezing out the juice and then crystallizing it into raw sugar.[12] Once the cane was pressed, sugar boilers heated the extracted juice in a series of cauldrons in which water was evaporated and impurities removed. A sugar master closely watched the boiling liquid until sucrose crystals began to form. Mill hands then moved this muddy-looking substance to large cases, where it cooled and formed crystalline sugar and molasses. Once the mixture was cool, workers transferred it to vessels that drained the molasses from the sugar, a process that took weeks. After draining, the sugar was ready to be packaged for storage, shipment, and sale.[13]

Innovations

Seeking to reduce the manual labor associated with planting, Claus implemented new technology. He contracted with Charles Carson Coleman to use his patented cane planting machine, which did the work of "ten men." The machine was mounted on wheels and drawn by two or four animals. It "opened the furrow, dropped the cane seed piece, and buried it, all in one pass."[14]

Bringing in Hawai'i's first steam plow created more than a little excitement not only for the field hands relieved from backbreaking hoeing but for curious onlookers throughout the kingdom. Claus provided a demonstration for King Kalākaua of his "huge puffing monsters" easily turning over and loosening the top layer of soil, removing crop residue and weeds and thereby making it easier for the cane to take root.[15] His "monsters" paid for themselves after plowing fifteen acres per day, reducing the cost of manual labor and the need for draft animals. A pair of steam engines, one placed on either side of the field, were used for plowing. Each engine would turn a large-diameter winding drum. A long wire rope was wound onto the drum and used to pull the plow or cultivator back and forth across the field.[16]

Mill Number 1 was successfully processing twenty tons of sugar daily, but it was not enough. Construction of three more mills got underway in 1881, with major improvements based on trial and error with Mill Number 1.[17] The four mills were housed in one complex (northeast of today's Kahului Airport, near the juncture of Stable Road and Hana Highway). The crop for 1882 was estimated at twelve thousand tons, four times greater than Claus's first sugarcane crop in 1880 (planted in 1879), and this yield was equal to the entire output of Hawai'i before the Reciprocity Treaty of 1875.[18] Claus not only wanted higher yields but, more importantly, an enhanced sugar quality, which necessitated that he micromanage the experimentation of different varieties of cane until he was satisfied. He enthusiastically pioneered the use of

17. The Spreckelsville sugar-refining operation. While other plantations used mules, oxen, and the poor backs of men, Spreckelsville applied railroad technology to get cane from field to mill to ship, requiring minimal hand labor. Claus was also the first onshore user of electric lighting in all of Hawai'i. Library of Congress Prints and Photographs Division, HABS HI, 5-SPRK, 1–2.

advanced milling and harvesting techniques. Thanks to the ingenuity of the Risdon Iron Works' engineers, Spreckelsville introduced five-roller grinding, replacing the customary three-roller system for extracting juice from the cane, to reduce sugar loss and add a 10-percent yield.[19] The hydraulic attachment assured the same pressure was exerted by the rollers regardless of the amount of cane passing through them. The resulting bagasse (the fibrous matter by-product) had only 38-percent moisture and could be burned immediately without further drying.[20] These assembly-line procedures effectively reduced manpower and increased quality. How would the other planters ever be able to catch up?

Transporting milled sugar from Maui to San Francisco initially involved incurring the time and expense of first transshipping it from Kahului's tiny boat harbor near Spreckelsville to Honolulu. Claus had that boat harbor dredged and transformed into a bustling port for oceangoing steamships, such as those in the Spreckels Oceanic line. It was now Maui's only deepwa-ter port. Three miles east of Wailuku, situated on Kahului Bay, the harbor became not only the hub of sugar production but an urban center for the islanders. The term *kahului* translates as "winning" in Hawaiian, and this was most appropriate: Claus had helped Maui become the second most prosperous port of entry for the islands. Wailuku now surpassed the former capital and seaport of Lahaina as Maui's major town. Kahului Bay became a lively destination spot after Claus created a wharf; large warehouses to store such things as gunpowder, oil, flour, animal feed, lime, cement, and salt; and an impressive general store (with a small branch for the workers in Spreckelsville itself), which carried everything from "two penny nails to a silk dress," brought in from ships around the world. Such delicacies as truf-fles and such extravagances as silver tea sets made the store the largest and best-appointed in the islands, bringing in about $50,000 a month—thereby putting money back into Claus's pockets while he managed the Spreckelsville payroll going as high as $39,000 per month—and simultaneously elevating services for the community.[21]

While other plantations were still using mules, oxen, and the poor backs of men (bags easily weighed 125 pounds!),[22] Claus contracted with clever entrepreneur Thomas Hobron to construct a narrow-gauge railroad. Spre-ckelsville discarded the customary oxcarts and now benefited from twenty miles of movable iron track threading throughout the plantation, requiring minimal hand labor. The short track could serve all the cane fields between the port of Kahului and central Maui. But, whereas other planters hauled their product by oxcarts to a designated loading area, Claus had an imagi-native industrial spur, a secondary track, constructed that would enable the Kahului Railroad to stop directly at Spreckelsville for the loading of cane. Then, at the port of Kahului, the product was efficiently transferred directly onto a Spreckels ship.[23]

The most sweeping and complex technological change in American man-ufacturing was the electrification of factories. Claus became the first onshore user of electric lighting in all of Hawai'i. To see history in the making, hun-dreds of people traveled from every island to witness the marvel of electricity on the evening of September 22, 1881. With the flip of a switch by John, the darkened mill became infused with, as the press described, "concentrated daylight."[24] Because the mills were an unbearable sauna during daylight hours, workers were thrilled to have the option to work a night shift during the grinding season.

With neighbors watching the development in astonishment, Claus found a way to further stimulate economic development in Maui. He encouraged local farmers and small planters to cultivate their own sugar crop on portions of his land. For those without the capital, Claus lent money for this singular purpose at 7 percent a year, when the going rate was 9–12 percent a year compounded quarterly.[25]

Living in Spreckelsville

When the whistle ended the day of hard work at 4:30 p.m., hundreds upon hundreds of men trudged back to Spreckelsville, the town built around the factories and fields. Whether it was in the hot cane fields or in one of the rumbling sugar mills, the work was physically arduous, and the workers were not inclined to keep their barracks tidy after a long hard day. On other plantations in Hawai'i, workers of different nationalities were usually segregated in separate buildings, a situation the laborers themselves preferred. Segregating the workers supported the planters' strategy of "dividing and controlling their work force," not only to prevent strikes but to foster a useful competition among the nationalities—for example, in keeping their barracks clean.[26] But Spreckelsville purposefully differed with the segregation philosophy: "The result of this mixing of all races in one village has been the disappearance of racial antagonisms and jealousies and the development of mutual respect. There is a community spirit growing up among the laborers and a good deal of competition in the matter of flower gardens and tidy lawns."[27]

Spreckelsville didn't mirror the crowded barracks and unsanitary work camps of other plantations; such conditions weren't tolerated. Both Claus and John required their integrated camp to look spick-and-span at all times, and they put untold pressure on the mangers to ensure it. Many visitors were stunned that Spreckelsville was tidy, inside and out, "a picture of cleanliness and order [where] all the buildings were constantly receiving a fresh coat of paint."[28]

Claus's workforce initially consisted primarily of single men, and keeping them content with their lot could be a challenge. Before the 8:30 p.m. whistle signaled "lights out" in the barracks, workers sat around the fire and nursed their blistered hands. They might talk about the harsh treatment by the lunas or reminisce with each other about their home countries. Workers who were single, lonesome for family left behind, sought solace in drinking and gambling.[29]

Eventually, Claus preferred employing married men with families and provided not only cottages for families but also a school for children. As an employer to hundreds of men in California, he had found married men more dependable. Families were even given small plots of land to grow their own fruits and vegetables and raise small animals. Spreckelsville morphed into "a permanent village with good streets, filtered water for domestic purposes and tap or ditch water for irrigating lawns and gardens." There was a proper church, clubhouse, baseball diamond, and parks. Cottages were uniquely built with a bit of space between them: "Instead of being bang up against one another like city tenements, they are spaced not less than forty feet apart."[30]

At Pa'auhau, a plantation partially owned by Claus's on Hawai'i Island, Andreas Otto had been recruited by Claus to be the manager. Otto was exasperated when workers began brewing their own beer and getting too drunk to rise out of bed in the morning. He recorded in his diary, "They made some beer out of syrup and got drunk on it. We give them no more syrup, but they get liquor somewhere on the plantation." One Filipino worker said "everyone" knew how to make "swipe wine." "You just ferment molasses with water and yeast and in a week it's ready. And if you distilled that, you got clear liquor ten times stronger than any gin you can buy from the store."[31]

Young men needed healthy outlets to combat the structure of plantation life, and recreation was a sound defense against misconduct at Spreckelsville. Nothing was more popular at the plantation than a simple baseball game featuring the "Spreckelsville Nine." This friendly competition bonded the workers to one another in rich ways when they went out into the community on their day off.

Recruited from all over the world, workers introduced a wide variety of ethnic foods to one another, mainly after the noon lunch siren. The aluminum double-decker kau kau tin (*kau kau* means "eat" in Hawaiian) was given to each worker to carry their own lunch into the fields. The meal typically consisted of leftovers from the previous night's dinner. There was no electricity or refrigeration, so much of the fish and meat was dried or canned, and in the fields, men from different cultures sat together and shared from their kau kau tins. One recollection went like this: "We get in a group and we spread our lunch cans on the ground and eat together. We pick from this guy's lunch and that guy'll pick from my lunch and so forth." The Japanese laborers typically took "little rice balls with an *ume* [pickled red plums] inside," the Portuguese took "bread with cheese inside," and the "Filipinos spread *bagoong* [salted fish] over their rice." Koreans ate *kimchi*, made from planted vegetables and pickled red peppers.[32] Back at the camp, the workers' wives and children were also mingling and sharing their ethnic dishes with one another while their husbands were in the fields and factory (and the plate lunch was born!).

John was the one overseeing the practicalities surrounding the electrical lights that would permit the mills in Spreckelsville to operate night and day. He was by the king's side when he and his entourage personally inspected and marveled at the lit-up night.[33] And John vowed to light up the king's palace (though, it would be another five years before the 'Iolani Palace had electricity).

Queen Emma was also sent an invitation to view firsthand the "concentrated daylight." After her defeat in a hotly contested 1874 election for the Hawaiian crown against Kalākaua, the result was mutual animosity between them. So, she made sure that her visit to the mill was at a separate time from the king's and that she came with a large contingency. Three hundred employees of the Hawaiian Commercial Company made sure that she was royally entertained by the quickly formed Spreckelsville Brass Band.[34] Queen Emma described her visit on November 27, 1881:

> Last night Mr. J. D. [John] Spreckels called and invited me to go & see the electric light which they use at the mill, so this evening we started by train with a party of nearly 600 people. . . . Everything is carried on in the most extensive scale, and the newest inventions are used of machinery, etc. Mr. Spreckels showed us the electric machines where electricity is made & conducted through wires, to every part of the mill. You have seen the light no doubt, so can fancy how like unto day was the entire interior & exterior of [the] building.[35]

John and the Hawaiian Royals

After the festivities surrounding the electrical phenomenon in Spreckels-ville, Queen Emma, like Kalākaua, expressed a great interest in advancing the kingdom technologically. To that end, she once again met with John to view more inventions at the Spreckels mansion in Honolulu. John may have strategically chosen one particular day in March of 1882 to give this tour. After picking her up in an open-air carriage to ride across town, John purposely directed their route past the government building on King Street where the kingdom's sugar plantation owners and agents were having a closed session of important meetings hosted by King Kalākaua himself.

A pressing concern was the uncertain future of the 1875 Reciprocity Treaty, which was due for review in 1884. But this particular meeting—a meeting of "the Sugar Planters of this Kingdom"—had been called because "Hawai'i's system of immigrant labor contracts was under attack by sugar interests in the United States, who charged the contracts represented a species of human bondage." In response to this threat, Hawai'i's planters, mainly the tightknit group of missionary descendants, organized the Planters' Labor and Supply Company at this meeting to respond to the "malicious slanders" of their sugar industry.[36]

Upon seeing the large number of men gathered outside the building, Queen Emma quickly covered her face with a veil. John "firmly demanded" that she remove it because he wanted to make sure the meeting attendees saw his exalted company, but she flatly refused. The public viewed Emma as an enemy of the king, which is precisely why John had been so eager to be seen in her company. When the queen dowager asked John why he was not attending the very important sugar plantation meeting, he replied that he "did not want to socialize with liars or those who break their promises to friends as David Kalākaua [had done] to his father"—apparently referring to some royal edict that was not in the Spreckels family's best interest. Emma scolded him for speaking badly about his friends, whereupon John snapped they were *not* his friends.[37]

After touring the Spreckels mansion, she told a confidante that "John Sugarcane" was ostentatious and a "pretentious show-off."[38] From then on, Queen Emma maintained a strong dislike toward the young Spreckels. In her royal role, she was used to absolute submission from her subjects and was appalled at the aggressive nature of foreign businessmen like the Spreckels family.

Reorganizing the Hawaiian Commercial Company

Claus was burning through money; by the end of the first year operating the Spreckelsville plantation, he had spent a veritable fortune and thereby stimulated Hawaii's economy in many different directions, which deeply impressed the king.[39] But as Claus continued to modernize and pour more and more money into Hawai'i, those heavy investments were starting to land him in financial difficulties. He had no recourse but to reorganize the controlling company in 1882 in order to sell stock to the public. The Hawaiian Commercial & Sugar Company was thus incorporated in San Francisco to take over the assets of the three-and-a-half-year-old Hawaiian Commercial Company. The *Hawaiian Gazette* allayed any fears over the company's name change, stating that "with the aggregation of brains, business enterprise and capital," this new company would "infuse new life and health" into the kingdom of Hawai'i's sugar production.[40] Capital stock of the new company, informally referred to as the "Hawaiian Company" consisted of 100,000 shares of $100 each, with the same stated purpose as those of the previous company. Upon public issue that year, the stock sold around $60 a share. By the fall of 1884, the new company was deeply in debt, and the share price fell to 25¢. A personal loan by Claus of $1 million and authorization by the directors of a bond issue moved the price up to $8 a share in 1885.[41] This action would be a highly contested; his enemies would charge that the Spreckels interests were manipulating the stock.

Claus, through the Hawaiian Commercial & Sugar Company, was operating the largest plantation in the Hawaiian Islands. The *Gazette* certainly understood the economic significance of Spreckelsville:

> Claus Spreckels has certainly made out of what was once considered worthless land, a waving plain of cane. One must ride through these acres and acres of cane to fairly understand how great the enterprise is: one must compare the sweep of bright green crops at the base of Haleakala with the few patches upon the low lands of west Maui, to fully realize how much more has been done.... If this is gathering wealth to the owners, it is also scattering money among the Hawaiian people.[42]

It wasn't long before other planters, most of whom despised the interloper, realized they were technologically backward and needed to emulate Spreckelsville's methods—its entire production processes—if they were going to survive. The problem was, they didn't have the same capital. During these days, when it seemed that sugar would forever power Hawai'i's economy and his bank account, Claus could never imagine the Spreckelsville Plantation, the largest and most magnificent in the world, would in a relatively short time slip away from his grasp, taken over by the ones he had sired, trained, and loved.

10   *The Kingdom in Crisis*

In January of 1881 David Kalākaua became the first head of state in the world to circumnavigate the globe. He had suffered his share of difficulties during his nearly seven years on the throne and decided he'd travel to find solutions "that would protect [his] native Hawaiian people and strengthen [his] nation." He believed that gathering ideas firsthand from other nations, "Constitutional Governments," was the only answer for a stronger Hawai'i. Before he left, he went for prayer at Kawaiaha'o Church and told his people another reason for the journey was that he was ailing in heath and sorely needed the recuperation.[1] When he arrived in Sacramento in February, the *Sacramento Bee* met the king's train:

> Quite a large crowd had collected at the depot to see this genuine, living representative of modern monarchy, who proved to be rather portly and generally fine-looking man of middle age, dressed in plain citizens garb, rather dark-skinned, and sporting a pretty fair set of side-whiskers. His countenance bore a genial expression, and the impression that one could get from a brief glance at the royal gentleman would be decidedly a favorable one.[2]

Claus was conspicuously by the king's side in San Francisco for the eleven days he was royally received and entertained by dignitaries. Their close friendship was noted by those in high places, who reported the king spent two private days with Claus at his Aptos Ranch, riding throughout the coastline redwoods.[3] From his prized herd of horses, Claus selected on the spot two handsome bay horses and a thoroughbred colt as personal gifts for Kalākaua.[4] The world was on notice that Claus was more than an investor to the king of Hawai'i; the king was a close friend.

Royal Extravagances

During the nine months that David Kalākaua toured through the courts of the world, a hot rumor was generated by a *New York Times* editorial: "It is an open secret that Kalākaua, King of the Hawaiian Islands is on a voyage around the world for the purpose of selling his kingdom."[5] The editorial pointed out the extensive American interests and wondered what would happen to the islands in the hands of another country; it brazenly suggested that annexation was a viable option. Picked up by major newspapers, this story sped across the country and to Hawai'i. Outraged, Queen Emma wrote a heated letter to British commissioner James Hay Wodehouse, stating, "I consider that America is now our open enemy" and that "the Native Hawaiians are one with me in the love of our country and determined not to let Hawaii become a part of the United States of America."[6] Even after a prompt denial by the Hawaiian minister to the U.S., Elisha Allen, the rumor spread. Informed of the story, Kalākaua paid it no heed; his islands were not for sale, and with his next moves, he was going to make sure the world knew Hawai'i was an absolute monarchy.

The king arrived home on October 29, 1881, racing to reach some unspecified zenith. He began withdrawing great sums of money from the royal treasury to build himself a proper kingdom. The sugar boom, mainly due to Claus's efforts, was bringing into the kingdom heretofore-unseen revenue. Before he'd left on his tour, he had his palace, little more than a spacious bungalow, demolished and the bones of Hawai'i's former rulers relocated to an impressive new mausoleum. All this to make way for the construction of a stately palace fit for the kind of king he wanted to be seen as.

When the stately 'Iolani Palace was completed in 1882, its cost was $343,595.[7] The inside was ornately finished with rare woods. There was a regal throne room where mockers said the voyage had gone to the king's head and now he loved to "play the sovereign" according to rules like those of England's Buckingham Palace.[8] In Kalākaua's view, however, the money had been well spent because the palace verified the legitimacy of his monarchy. Royal balls at the palace, where you never knew whom you might meet, became legendary, and an engraved invitation embossed with a gold crown was highly coveted by Hawaiian society. The king extended invitations to many foreign naval officers in port, many artists, many authors, many

18. The royal House of Kalākaua. *Clockwise from top right*: Kalākaua, Liliʻuokalani, Leleiohoku II, ʻIolani Palace, Kaʻiulani, Likelike, Kapiʻolani. *Center*: Government building. UC San Diego Library.

musicians, many a poor foreign missionary teacher, and for sure, any Spreckels family member.

The most coveted invitation, after the ʻIolani Palace was complete, was "to have the honor of being present at the 'Coronation Ceremonies of Their Majesties the King and Queen' on 'Monday, February 12th, A.D. 1883' at '11 o'clock. a.m.'"[9] Captivated with the court rituals he had witnessed on his world tour, Kalākaua moved to imbue his own reign with a similar ceremonial presence. The self-coronation took place outside the palace with flashy pomp on the ninth anniversary of his election to the throne. A pretty little bandstand was built on the grounds just for the occasion. The two jeweled crowns were reputed to cost $10,000 apiece. Kalākaua crowned his own head and then Queen Kapiʻolani's. The whole affair cost $30,000 (about $903,000 in today's money), and the crowd of eight thousand subjects gathered for the magnificent pageantry no doubt concluded their kingdom was prospering.[10] But, behind the scenes, there was nothing but frustration and disgust by those in the government who paid the bills. Claus, who had been vocal in his opposition to the great outlay of money for the theatrics, was nowhere to be seen.[11]

No other non-Hawaiian name evoked more respect in the community than that of Charles Bishop. As the husband of the beautiful great-granddaughter of King Kamehameha I, the founder and first ruler of the kingdom of Hawaiʻi, Bishop garnered admiration. His wife, Bernice, had inherited staggering amounts of royal wealth while her prosperous husband earned his own fortune in ventures from banking to agriculture. When the Bishops boycotted the event over the expenditure, their absence spoke louder than words.

Meanwhile, outside the palace and behind guarded doors, the king entertained his cronies at his other "palace," the infamous Royal Boat House at the foot of Richards Street. Welcomed along with Claus into the inner sanctum were the likes of Robert Louis Stevenson, who noted the king could hold his liquor "like a mountain with a sparrow on its shoulders."[12] Gossip insinuated that "buff bare" hula girls entertained the men and high-stakes poker games stretched into the morning hours. Here "deals were made, and trades consummated."[13]

Ousting Moreno

Most if not all of those "boat house deals" were denounced by the white fundamentalists in the kingdom's government. Attempting to circumvent the naysayers, Kalākaua began entertaining ambitious types, along with Claus Spreckels—people with big ideas, people like Celso Cesare Moreno and Walter Murray Gibson. Being with restless people inclined to take risks motivated the king; they were the opposite of the conservative sons of missionaries who surrounded him in the government.

First Moreno, an Italian with a checkered past, was appointed by the king in 1880 to be the new minister of foreign affairs within nine months of his arrival. Under Moreno's influence, a series of extravagant bills appeared in the legislature calling for enormous subsidies to provide innovations like a transpacific cable. When long-distance communication was being sent by signals over telegraph cables seemingly to everywhere *but* Hawai'i, the king understood this project was realistic to help Hawai'i keep up with the rest of the world. But the conservatives found it outlandish and too expensive to consider. The Hawaiian-language newspaper *Ko Hawai'i Pae 'Aina* began denouncing the agitation against progress and the blatant disrespect of their sovereign ruler.[14]

However, in a move that would compound his growing troubles, the king, under Moreno's sway, granted a license for the sale of opium to a Chinese company for a $70,000 bribe.[15] The prohibition of this highly addictive drug in the kingdom had deprived the king of substantial revenue from licensing fees and customs duties, and Moreno saw the license as a way to help the famished budget of the king. When news of this transaction trickled out, apoplectic shock waves spread throughout every sector of the community, even in the king's own family. Outraged over this and other acts, the legislature banded together, defeated most of Moreno's bills, then demanded that he be terminated. Moreno had only been in the government two weeks and the king refused, wanting to give him more time. Their next bold step was to recruit Claus, their heretofore adversary, to help them rid the kingdom of the spendthrift. Claus never hesitated to spend millions on improvement and development in the kingdom, hoping to gain in the end, but he had little sympathy for some of the other extravagances Moreno was pushing for, especially a steamship line that would compete with his. Claus was the king's primary creditor, and hoping to be paid back someday, he successfully convinced Kalākaua to terminate Moreno.[16] After Moreno's termination, a new cabinet composed of Missionary Party affiliates took over the legislature, suddenly depriving the missionary sons of any grounds to complain.[17]

Walter Murray Gibson Recruits Claus

After the ouster of Moreno, the legislature had another problem to deal with when the world adventurer and charismatic Walter Murray Gibson was then appointed minister of foreign affairs. After having been stripped of his Mormon affiliations by Brigham Young over corrupt land ventures on the island of Lāna'i, Gibson became a newspaperman using the slogan "A Friend and Champion of the Hawaiian People." He was enormously popular with Native Hawaiians after encouraging the lifting of the missionaries' ban on the hula and with his stance on elevating healthcare for the dying populace. He was easily elected in 1879 to the Hawaiian legislature. In 1880 he bought the *Pacific Commercial Advertiser* for $15,000 with money loaned by the government but supplied by Claus (who used advertising and editorial space to his advantage), with the stipulation the loan would be repaid by doing government printing. Banding together, the white businessmen promptly removed all of their own advertising from the *Advertiser*, hoping in vain it would shut down.[18]

Claus Makes a Mint

On his world tour, Kalākaua was convinced Hawai'i needed its own coinage to truly be a sovereign nation. The king, encouraged by Gibson, believed that establishing new coinage, distinctly Hawaiian, would "add to the prestige of the kingdom" and stimulate national pride if nothing else because this issue was becoming a matter of paramount importance to the king. The Indigenous Hawaiian population was sinking into a deep apathy because of the gradual decline in its numbers and the domination by foreigners in their government, factors that were spelling the end of the old Hawaiian culture.[19]

Out of the jumble of foreign currency brought to Hawai'i, American coins were the standard of exchange, a fact that reflected the high degree of integration of Hawai'i's economy with that of the United States.[20] The only place to exchange currency was at the one and only bank in Hawai'i: Bishop & Company. Gibson found the bank reticent to fund the king's improvement projects, such as roads, bridges, wharves, and schools. But this might have been because the king was known for frequently transferring legislative appropriation from one project to another on a personal whim, which resulted in neglected public projects.[21]

In 1882 Gibson saw a "fascinating opportunity" to get the king his own coinage. He'd combine the authority given to the kingdom by the 1880 Coinage Act with the powers awarded by the new National Loan Act of 1882. This statute authorized the government to borrow up to $2 million to cover the budget deficit at an interest rate not to exceed a modest 6 percent.[22]

Gibson believed the right combination of actions, coupled with "flattering the king and profits for Spreckels[,] could be joined to provide the solution."[23] Gibson, with no accessible funds, asked Claus if he'd be interested in ushering in a bit of competition by creating a rival bank by using his money to buy "new money" for the kingdom. New money would be the only way to break up Charles Bishop's banking monopoly, and Gibson went to work to untangle the many complexities imposed by Hawai'i's law.[24] Claus agreed to the transaction, which would in effect be a loan by him to the Hawaiian government. In September 1882 he entered into a formal agreement for coining a sum of gold or silver not to exceed $150,000. He would spend $850,000 ($25.6 million in today's money) to buy the silver and have it minted into a million dollars' worth of coins. First, Gibson needed to pass a law to make this happen, but since he was the chairman of the Finance Committee, this was an easy sell. In Hawai'i's legislative session of 1882, he pushed through an appropriation bill calling for the minting of silver coins in San Francisco. In 1883 Claus became a temporary agent of the Hawaiian government, which empowered him to have one million dollars of silver coins minted in the United States.[25] The coins were to carry a portrait of Kalākaua on the face and the royal coat of arms on the reverse.

The first Kalākaua silver pieces, $130,000 in half dollars, arrived at Honolulu on December 16, 1883, and Gibson patted himself on the back. His king had been honored, there was new cash for the government to spend, and Claus profited nicely from his investment. There was the predicted uproar throughout the business community on a variety of monetary issues. William Castle, Sanford Dole, and William Smith investigated the coinage arrangement and sued to halt it from being carried out. They laid out the astonishing facts: Claus had spent $850,000 to have silver minted into a million dollars' worth of coins, which gave him a profit—or seigniorage (the value that governments enjoy when the cost of minting coins is lower than their face value in exchange)—of $150,000 ($4.5 million today). The three investigators learned that the U.S. Treasury Department was also somewhat mystified by the Gibson-Spreckels arrangement; it was the department's policy to coin silver at cost for other governments, and their agent was surprised the Hawaiian government itself didn't collect the seigniorage rather than reward it to a private individual.[26]

The suit was dismissed on technicalities, but the court determined that it was illegal to exchange gold bonds for silver coins because gold was legal tender and the coins were not. That is, the bond couldn't legally be placed except for par value in gold coin of the United States. The court issued an injunction to that effect to the minister of finance on December 14, two days before the first shipment arrived. To solve the impasse, Claus set up a bank that could distribute the coins through cashing checks and through other normal banking transactions. Unfortunately, the Claus Spreckels & Company Bank had barely opened when it was shut down because it was found "to be out of step with Hawaiian banking laws."[27]

During the following year, however, those laws were conveniently changed to allow the new Spreckels bank to be established on April 28, 1885, on Fort Street. Claus was now competing with Bishop & Company, which had been the kingdom's lone banking firm for almost thirty years. The competition of the two banks was welcomed by just about every sector in the community, even by those who legally tried to stop him. Having competition in the banking services for the first time was good for the economic life of the public, as Bishop's bank was forced to compete with the Spreckels bank to offer better rates and services.[28]

By that time, the million dollars in coin had been delivered to Honolulu, and the legislature was obliged to pass a bill declaring the coins legal tender. Claus then used $500,000 in coin to buy Hawaiian bonds of that amount. He put the other half million into circulation through his bank with William Irwin and advanced $130,000 to the Hawaiian government as a special loan. Now the government owed him, in bonds and notes, a total of $630,000 ($19.7 million in today's money). Claus's neat profit in the coinage transaction brought harsh criticism from Peirce Carter, the Hawaiian minister to Washington, who sneered that "probably the next move will be to declare photographs of Mr. Spreckles [sic] legal tender for any amount."[29]

The Tide Turns against Claus

Furious that Claus Spreckels had to lend their government money and then made a $150,000 profit on the coinage transaction, the kingdom's sugar industry increased their complaints to the legislature about government extravagance and about how they, along with other men of means, were being taxed to death. They didn't object to spending for immigration of field hands, for harbor and road development, or, up to a point, for education or public health. But they bitterly resented having their tax dollars wasted on fripperies at the 'Iolani Palace, which resulted in a sorely depleted till.[30] Their colleagues in the legislature felt the same way. In their views, the world tour, the erection of a palace, the raising of the statue of Kamehameha I, uniforms for the Royal Hawaiian Band and the Royal Guard, the minting of the Kalākaua coins, and the elaborate jeweled crowns and coronation in 1883 were all theatrical effects arranged by Gibson to elevate Kalākaua and to prepare him for an imaginary dominion. They were determined to put close restraints on Kalākaua's extravagances. The opposition was led by Sanford Dole, then serving his second term in the legislature, and the newly elected Lorrin Thurston. They were both lawyers from missionary families, and their antagonism ran deep and bitter to the ministry of Walter Gibson, who encouraged the overspendings. With the extreme amount of wealth that Claus was amassing through the sugar industry, he was now being accused of financing the king's expensive habits and of using those loans to control the king and his cabinet.

11   *Adolph Shoots to Kill*

It was 5:00 p.m. on November 19, 1884, and the fog, like clockwork, was beginning to blanket San Francisco. Michael de Young was heading back into his office at the *San Francisco Chronicle*, which he owned, when he heard his name. He turned around to see Adolph Spreckels—who had followed him into the building. Adolph was aiming a pistol at the publisher. He fired it. A bullet struck de Young's left shoulder, and as he stumbled, Adolph fired two more shots. One hit his left arm, and the other missed its target, stopped by children's books that de Young was carrying to bring home to his son.

Hearing the gunfire, George Emerson, a *Chronicle* employee, grabbed a revolver from a desk drawer and ran into his boss's office. Quickly assessing the situation, he fired. The bullet struck Adolph's left arm. Adolph looked down at his wound, thereby enabling another newspaper staffer, G. Chesley, the chance he needed to wrestle away Adolph's pistol. In the end, it took three men to overpower Adolph, a brawny twenty-seven-year-old.

Adolph was taken to jail, then rushed to the hospital. Emerson's bullet had gone through Adolph's left arm, below the shoulder. While being stitched up, Adolph, it was reported, "chatted pleasantly" with hospital workers. After the procedure, he "donned his coat and smoked" while Claus and brother John posted the $5,000 bail. Adolph was back at Howard Street just after 7:00 p.m., surrounded by a "host of friends." Charged with "assault to murder," Adolph chose not to make a public statement. Nor did any member of his family. He stayed behind closed doors, ensconced in the family mansion with "special policemen" prohibiting access to all but relatives and legal counsel.[1] Meanwhile, de Young's injuries, while not dangerous, required hospitalization to remove the bullets from his arm and shoulder.

"'Mike de Young Shot! Attempt at Murder by a Man Who Didn't Like Criticism." So read the *New York Times* headline about the story that was reported across the nation. "A man who didn't like criticism" was putting it mildly. Adolph's armed attack on de Young was the tipping point in a long and bitter conflict between the Spreckelses and de Young. At its heart was a series of anticorruption articles in the *Chronicle* that went after Claus Spreckels, now known as San Francisco's "toughest citizen." Among the article's many inflammatory accusations were that Spreckels's Hawaiian Company was defrauding stockholders, that the plantations were little more than slave camps, and that Claus acted as a pimp for King Kalākaua, providing women for the king in exchange for plantation acreage.[2]

Incensed, Claus retaliated with personal attacks against de Young in various local weeklies, including the *Pacific Commercial Advertiser*. He also threatened to sue the *Chronicle* for libel in the amount of $100,000, calling the paper a "disgrace to journalism."[3] It's unknown why the threat never resulted in legal action, although it might have been due to another of Claus's concerns: he was heavily in debt.

Claus always moved fast, and Hawaiian Commercial & Sugar Company quickly grew indebted after a series of expansions. In 1882 stock valued at $60 a share on the San Francisco market plummeted to a mere 25¢ in the autumn of 1884. Claus desperately worked to maneuver the stock price upward. The first adjustment was to give the company a $1 million personal loan that he had borrowed. An authorization of a bond issue by the directors was an important decision. These measures, in addition to the forecast of a good sugar crop in 1885, helped boost the price to $8 a share.

Just as Claus's finances were improving, however, the *Chronicle* published a scathing editorial. It informed the public that his company was swindling shareholders by manipulating stocks with his own money to increase the value of its shares. This piece hit the streets strategically just days before a major stockholders' meeting on November 17, 1884. "It is doubtful whether the Commercial ever made any money at all," the *Chronicle* wrote, adding that Claus had to borrow the money to pay dividends and keep up the company's successful image. The *Chronicle* then went so far as to say that Claus could be "indicted and convicted."[4] That editorial went one step too far for Adolph, a hotheaded but softhearted young man under his swagger, who, though he seemed an unlikely assassin, decided to seek his revenge.

The Wild West's Newspaper Wars

The Spreckelses were, in fact, not the first to have a violent encounter with the *Chronicle*'s brass. Slander, libel, distortion, defamation, scandal, and corruption were commonplace in the tumultuous early days of San Francisco's newspapers—and so was fierce rivalry for circulation and advertising. Many of the early newspapers following the Gold Rush era were founded with a shoot-to-kill attitude. The *Chronicle* was one such free-for-all newspaper that reflected the rowdy nature of San Francisco in the mid-nineteenth century. The founders were the feisty de Young brothers, the sons of Jewish immigrants, who had come to San Francisco during the Civil War. Losing their father on the westward journey from St. Louis forced them at such a young age to be overly industrious to help their newly widowed mother. Michael and his brothers, Gustavus and Charles, were fortunate to earn a meager salary as typesetters for a small Jewish publication, the *Weekly Gleaner*.[5] Their newspaper careers began as enterprising teenagers when they borrowed a twenty-dollar gold piece from a sympathetic landlord to bankroll the printing of a publication designed to look like a playbill. Their *Daily Dramatic Chronicle* touted itself as an important record of local affairs, but it was little more than a gossip sheet that soon annoyed the city's elite, who valued their privacy.

Because of their bold, scandalous reporting, prominent San Franciscans never considered the de Young brothers as anything more than amateur journalists. But that would change in little time. Three months after their paper's debut, President Abraham Lincoln was assassinated, and this shocking event was the catalyst that altered the public's perception. The president's death, on April 15, 1865, at 4:22 a.m. Pacific time, gave the de Young brothers the scoop of the century. The tragedy occurred too late for the city's established morning newspapers, such as the *Alta California* and the *Examiner*, but the de Young brothers' paper had no deadline and wasted no time putting out an extra edition. The day's *Dramatic Chronicle* was snatched up in record numbers by frantic San Franciscans eager to read about the death of the president. This timely reporting suddenly legitimized the de Youngs' position as competitive journalists. Taking advantage of the change in public opinion, the brothers moved quickly to morph the *Dramatic Chronicle* into a more substantial newspaper. After a few twists and turns, their new *Daily Morning Chronicle* hit the streets on September 1, 1868.[6]

Bold and brash, with no father to guide them, Charles, twenty-two, and Michael, just nineteen, began to publish personal insults about powerful men and their families in an attempt to influence the political debate, because, as Michael once testified in court, the *Chronicle*'s "columns were always for sale."[7] The brothers weren't above taking a payoff to squelch any story, because with this business model, they would need money to fend off libel suits.[8] At its founding, the *Chronicle* was incorporated in Nevada, a shrewd decision that made it difficult for Californians to file such suits.[9] One county commissioner, upset with the *Chronicle*'s campaign in 1871 against a favored municipal judge's reelection, went so far as to severely pistol-whip Michael, to cheers across the city.[10] The de Youngs' style of reporting emphasized sensationalism over facts, and the *Chronicle* soon became the most-read paper in San Francisco, to the amazement of its rivals. However, the newspaper's success would set in motion a chain of events that would lead to murder and attempted murder, in which Adolph Spreckels would have blood on his hands.

The Murder of Editor Charles de Young

Scandal and mayhem followed in the de Young brothers' wake. Their reputation was rooted in their high-profile rivalry with Isaac Smith Kalloch, who didn't care to settle his differences with the de Youngs in court. Kalloch was a Baptist minister running to become San Francisco's mayor. He was solidly supported by the Workingmen's Party. Charles de Young, who was backing another candidate, became relentless in his efforts to destroy the minister's status amid his rising popularity with the working class. Charles launched a barrage of anti-Kalloch propaganda and went lower by digging up a two-decades-old story of an unfounded adultery charge from Kalloch's days in Boston. Kalloch then responded in kind from his pulpit, denouncing the "bawdy house breeding" of the de Young boys and implying that Mrs. de Young had run a bordello back in St. Louis.[11] This accusation against his mother was enough for Charles to ambush Kalloch on the streets of San Francisco and shoot him. Incredibly, Kalloch survived the two bullet wounds, one only two inches from his heart.

San Franciscans showed their sympathy for the minister: he was elected in a landslide and became the eighteenth mayor of San Francisco in 1879. Pending the trial and free on bail, Charles de Young spitefully persisted in his mission to destroy Kalloch's mayoral career. The continued insults ultimately became too much for Isaac "Milton" Kalloch, his thirty-year-old son, who stormed into the *Chronicle*'s newsroom on April 23, 1880, and fatally shot Charles.[12] Attorney Henry E. Highton was retained to defend Milton Kalloch. The plea was justified self-defense after Highton found an observer, John Clementspaw, who inexplicably was willing to perjure himself (he was already serving time in San Quentin for perjury), testifying that he was walking by and saw Charles fire the first shot. When the jury foreman declared young Milton not guilty, Highton was so astonished at his contrived victory that "he swallowed his tobacco cud."[13]

Adolph's Trial

Michael, now going by the tonier "M. H. de Young," took over the *Chronicle* after his brother's assassination without changing the way the paper did business, and it was only a matter of time before history repeated itself. Maligning a Baptist minister was one kind of provocation, but taking on the mighty Claus Spreckels was another thing entirely.[14] Claus spared no expense in Adolph's defense. He assembled a team of attorneys headed by the cunning Hall McAllister, well known in national legal circles as a force to be reckoned with. McAllister was from Georgia and projected himself as a cultured Southern gentleman. A "tall, well-built, large-framed man of fine appearance," he commanded a courtroom like his father and grandfather before him.[15] He knew the law so well that "he could cite cases by the hour from memory, giving the number and page of the report in which they were found and the points discussed."[16]

The second in command of the legal team was chosen shrewdly. British-born Henry Highton—the same lawyer who had defended Milton Kalloch in *his* shooting of a de Young—was a stern-looking, highly religious man who had "no patience with infidelity, or atheism."[17] In legal circles, Highton was known for relentlessly standing over a jury box, inundating members with long and drawn-out speeches in an effort to "cover up a crime beneath an avalanche of words . . . adjective upon adjective, substantive upon substantive, verb upon verb, particle upon particle."[18] But the real reason Claus wanted him to defend Adolph was because Highton had become famous for securing the astonishing verdict of "justifiable homicide" in Kalloch's murder of Michael de Young's brother Charles. If he had done it once, perhaps the Spreckels family could get lucky with another such verdict.

By April 1885 the Spreckels legal team, including attorneys Ralph Harrison and Dr. Edward Taylor, decided on a plea of "emotional insanity, provocation, and self-defense."[19] McAllister explained the defense of "emotional insanity" was due to "the repeated publications in the *Chronicle* accusing the defendant's father of 'fraud and dishonesty,' which profoundly 'affected his mind.'" Adolph's fragile mind, claimed the attorney, was due to a previous accident. Therefore, the shooting was committed "while under the influence of a morbid and uncontrollable impulse," which was actually "a condition of mental disease" and an established term defined by law writers as "impulsive insanity."[20] (Behind the scenes, McAllister was painfully familiar with mental illness, which had brought on his father's early death. And, unbeknownst to most, McAllister himself was in the early stages of "softening of the brain," and would be dead within only three years of the trial.)[21]

The prosecution team of Alexander Campbell and Reuben Hedley Lloyd loudly and strongly condemned Adolph's plea as ridiculous, asserting that "criminal acts imply a co-existence of intent and act, and that no persons can have the intent who are idiots, lunatics or persons affected by insanity."[22] This point was well taken, given Adolph's casual behavior after the crime in the presence of police officers. Regardless, with fingers crossed, the defense stood by its argument of emotional insanity due to provocation, on the one hand, and self-defense, on the other hand.[23]

Attempted Murder—or Self-Defense?

Adolph's trial attracted extensive, emotionally charged coverage across the country.[24] The public's insatiable desire to glean information about the case is reflected in the sheer number of reports with sensational headlines. Newspapers were quick to direct readers to the vigilante tactics and the Wild West atmosphere of San Francisco journalism. Numerous stories characterized the assassination attempt as "cowardly" and "brutal." Closer to home, however, many privately and publicly implied that Adolph had rendered what amounted to a public service—since de Young was so hated.

The stakes were high for father and son. To help repair any loss to the family's reputation, Claus paid $25,000 ($780,000 in today's money) to publish an overly long speech in defense of Adolph. The justification of the shooting, though, was mostly overshadowed by the defense of his business practices in Hawai'i. To spread the word, he acquired space as supplements in nine leading newspapers and magazines.[25] These mass-produced sections totaled an astonishing thirty-two columns, over four full pages.[26] Claus simplified the event for the reader, explaining that Adolph had entered the *Chronicle* office with "proper indignation" and with the sole purpose of convincing de Young to "put an end to the attacks which were embittering the lives of his family and of himself." His defense was that when de Young put his hand in his pocket, Adolph naturally assumed de Young was pulling out a pistol, so he fired away. When all the "clerks and employees" went to the aid of their boss, "there was nothing left" for poor Adolph to do, if he desired to live, "other than to advance as rapidly as he could and paralyze the obvious intention of Mike de Young [and] to shoot him."[27]

Jumping the Gun

Adolph's high-profile trial began on May 25, 1885, in an overly packed courtroom in San Francisco's Superior Court, presided over by the steadfast judge Dennis J. Toohy. Claus and sons John and Gus were front and center, where they would remain throughout the trial in full solidarity with Adolph. Fifteen-year-old Emma and thirteen-year-old Rudolph stayed home with their anxious mother, awaiting updates.

From the outset of the trial, the collective energy from the defense team was palpable in the courtroom. A parade of witnesses, mainly employees of the Spreckels companies, testified to Adolph's kind and peaceful nature. The prosecution brought forth its own parade of witnesses—mainly *Chronicle* employees—who vouched for de Young's own nice character. The defense strategy was painfully clear to the nation's reporters from early on in the proceedings. Many newspapers reported the Spreckels legal team would stall, muddle the facts, and overload the case with extraneous details in an effort to bore the onlookers, wear down the prosecution, and confuse the jury.

To set the "insanity" stage, Dr. R. H. Plummer, the Spreckels family physician, testified that Adolph had a "nervous and excitable" temperament, "one in which impulse predominates over reasoning power." The doctor gave a lengthy account of when Adolph had been thrown from a buggy five years prior, in 1880, and had "sustained a concussion of the brain." During his ten-day convalescence, he "suffered acutely and was repeatedly out of his mind." This event, and the medical procedures that followed, the doctor told the court, caused "lingering severe headaches" that made Adolph "excitable and nervous" and surely played a role in the unfortunate shooting.[28] Claus took the stand to corroborate the doctor's testimony and solemnly add that his son was "suicidal after the buggy incident."[29]

With the insanity stage set, Adolph, well-coached by his lawyers, stepped into the witness box. He calmly told the court that he merely wanted to talk with the editor and was forced to protect himself after de Young "thrust his right hand into his right hip pocket" when he saw Adolph. He had no choice but to "jump the gun," he told the courtroom.[30]

In the six long weeks that followed, the defense team continued to take the court far away from the crime of attempted homicide. McAllister, with his commanding voice, tired both jury and spectators when he recited the entire history of the jury system since Tacitus through the Saxons and the Normans up to the present. He recited poems and quoted William Shakespeare, Daniel Webster, William Gladstone, and the Bible. Despite strong objections by the prosecutors, an entire day was devoted to the history, geography, ethnology, and economics of the Hawaiian Islands.[31]

The defense called a stream of witnesses to debunk the *Chronicle*'s charges regarding Claus's business practices. The prosecution continually objected, reminding the judge that they were present not to try the case of de Young against Claus Spreckels but the case of the people against Adolph Spreckels, a man charged with attempted murder.[32] The judge overruled the objections because the defense established their right to prove that the *Chronicle*'s lies about Claus led to Adolph's temporary insanity.

One comment—from Claus—prompted an outburst of laughter in the courtroom. His statement on the witness stand gave onlookers a peek behind the curtain of his power in Hawai'i. He testified that he had long ago turned the deeds of his sugar plantation holdings over to the Hawaiian Commercial & Sugar Company. When he was asked by the prosecuting attorney if being a foreigner made that act necessary, he replied that by law, foreign companies "could not hold real estate." But then he reported with a smirk that a new law had recently changed this. Laughter erupted around the courtroom when he added, "I had the law passed myself."[33]

An Emotional Appeal

After six weeks of testimony, the defense finally rested its case on June 30, 1885. The prosecution and defense attorneys took completely dissimilar approaches in their closing arguments. Approaching the jury, the defense adopted a friendly and conversational manner. The attorney delivered the facts of the case with a voice that expressed sympathy and outrage over the course of events that had led a devoted son to protect his beloved father against repeated lies that threatened their collective well-being. Then, making the most of hyperbole, he delivered an eloquent outpouring of emotion for both father and son:

> Can you not, gentlemen, appreciate his feelings when, day after day and year after year, these slanders and calumnies were published in this paper against his father. . . . Here is his father, the author of his being; the man in whose breast he nestled as a child; the man around whose neck he has wound his tiny arms; the man whose knee he has climbed as a boy, to be fondled and caressed; the man who has provided for him in childhood and boyhood; who has nursed him in youth; who has furnished him means for all the wild enjoyment of youth; the man who has guarded, protected and instructed him, taught him his duties to others, his duties to himself, given him a place in the business world; fixed on him a name and a position; given him all that he has and all that he is. That . . . he has seen that father growing gray in his labors and efforts, not so much for his own personal prosperity as for the future prosperity of his children. And, gentlemen, cannot you understand, can you not appreciate what his feelings must have been in his weakened and enfeebled mental condition when, day after day and week after week and year after year, slanderous and calumnious lies of all kinds . . . ?[34]

The defense's oratory was likened to a dramatic performance that appealed to the sympathy, prejudice, and emotions of the jurors, with such comments as, "I ask you if you [were the father, would you] not be proud of such a son?"[35]

Prosecutor Alexander Campbell delivered a lively closing argument. He pointed out that his opponent was trying to embellish and exaggerate the facts because the real facts of the crime were too damaging. His voice laced with sarcasm, he told the jury that Adolph Spreckels was a spoiled rich kid who was lucky that de Young didn't die: "[Adolph] receives yachts and fast horses and all the luxuries which a wealthy young man of the period must delight in, you are then told that—and I again use the language of counsel—after this beautiful picture has been drawn you are asked *not* to convict. If there was anything in that transaction for him to rejoice over, it was that his son escaped the guilt of actual murder." Campbell made a point of reminding the jury that the unheard-of double defense of insanity and self-defense was a travesty upon the court and a fraud upon the law.[36]

> It is evident from the very nature and character of these two defenses, so utterly inconsistent, where one, if it is true, shows that the other is false. If this man was insane, if he did not know that what he was doing was wrong, he did not act in self-defense. . . . If he did act in self-defense, why this parade of insanity? As a defendant he is insane, and as a witness he is perfectly sane.[37]

The law, Campbell proclaimed, holds every man equal, and if the jury allowed the Spreckels family to be their own judge and jury, they should consider what message they would be sending to the community:

> Suppose that he had been libeled for three or four years, as the gentlemen say, in the *Chronicle* columns, what then? Would that justify Adolph Spreckels in going down to the *Chronicle* office and shooting Mr. de Young? . . . Do you not see at once that absolute anarchy would be introduced into the community; that every man would become his own judge, his own jury and his own executioner; that for every slight or fancied insult the trigger of the pistol would be invoked as the remedy? How long would there be order, or decorum, or decency, or anything but a state of absolute chaos in the community if such things were permitted to exist.[38]

The prosecutor reviewed the hard facts of the crime, which he followed by translating legal concepts into easily understood words. He compared those words to everyday events in life, rhetorically asking the jury to consider the kind of society they wished to have for their children. It was a strong closing argument, and it must have made the Spreckels family worry mightily.

The Shocking Verdict and Aftermath

The verdict arrived, at last, on July 1, 1885. It came in fast—some say too fast. It seemed as if after six long weeks of service, the worn-out members of the jury needed only a few hours to deliberate, reaching a unanimous verdict right after a hearty lunch. They returned to the courtroom at 5:15 p.m., when it was reported that "a death[-]like silence ensued in the brief second that elapsed between the Judge's question to the jury and the foreman's reply that a verdict had been arrived at." Claus had left earlier and hadn't returned in time to sit behind his son in his darkest hour. Adolph, it was noted, "chewed a toothpick and pulled on his mustache," while John's lips visibly trembled.[39]

Then came the stunning announcement: "We find the defendant, Adolph Spreckels, not guilty!" Family, friends, and employees "rushed frantically" to the defendant's table. In disbelief, reporters took in the howling and stamping of feet "unparalleled in any judicial records." "Chairs were overturned or thrown into the air as the easiest method of removing them; hats touched the ceiling and startled the sleepy spiders, who were unprepared for so sudden an invasion of their judicial quarters; the hands, arms and legs of John and Adolph were eagerly seized. Had they possessed a hundred or centipedes more of these appendages there would not have been arms and legs enough for everybody to seize upon."[40]

Judge Toohy's bellowing of "Order! Order!" was drowned out by "Three Cheers for the judge, jury, and Adolph." The vindicated Adolph was then "hoisted on high by the throngs and carried out into the corridors, down the stairs, and into the streets." When Adolph spotted his father returning, he broke into a run. One reporter described it as an "emotional sight to behold with tears streaming down both their faces."[41]

The verdict of not guilty was condemned in papers from coast to coast. The acquittal was a genuine astonishment to the outside journalists who had covered it. The *New York Times* pointedly noted that "money can do anything in this city" (San Francisco).[42] Many wondered that if the trial had been conducted outside of the *Chronicle*'s reach, the outcome might have been different. In San Francisco, of course, many speculated the poor reputation of the *Chronicle* helped the defense, with de Young perhaps getting what he deserved; in fact, it was generally agreed that de Young's murder would've been a community service.

12   *Beets Now or Never*

News coverage of Adolph's trial revealed the extent of Claus's control over the Hawaiian government to the mass public. People on the streets of Hawai'i learned for the first time that Mr. Spreckels was not only the kingdom's major taxpayer but Hawai'i's chief creditor and holder of $1.3 million in unpaid government bonds.[1] In the days following the trial, Charles Reed Bishop, fed up with all the unfavorable news, began to criticize Claus: "It is strange that the King does not see that he and his family are being made tools of by Claus Spreckels."[2] Heretofore, the sugar planters in the legislature had been afraid of the wrath of Claus, but now empowered by the powerful Charles Bishop's public stance as well as the negative editorials over the Spreckels shooting, they began an uncompromising and ruthless attack.

Who's the King?

Lorrin Thurston in his *Daily Bulletin* reported that while Spreckels was a benefit to the economic growth of the islands, his excessive influence in the kingdom's affairs was now a threat to the nation and he must go. With the disclosure of the kingdom's debt, including specific references to Kalākaua's personal extravagances and the massive debt incurred by loans to both kingdom and king from Claus Spreckels, the fury began. To further infuriate the Native Hawaiians, Thurston boldly referred to Claus as "King Claus" and "His Majesty, King Spreckels," initiating others to do the same.

Soon, Princess Lili'uokalani began wondering aloud just who was actually the king of Hawai'i, her brother or Claus Spreckels. Kalākaua became weary of the implications that he was under the control of the sugar king and came to realize that his once strong alliance with Claus, which spanned over two decades, had to end. The only way out, he calculated, was by relieving himself of all debt so he could distance himself once and for all.

Gibson's solution for the king to get out from under the debt was through a substantial loan. Because this would add even more to the government's debts, Dole and Thurston, the legislators constantly in opposition to the king, profoundly objected. Surprising them, Claus backed up their objections. His protest, however, was personal: more loans could threaten the stability of the sugar market in which he was heavily invested. Claus told Kalākaua that he'd rather "see him going barefoot, as an independent King, than to see him rolling in luxury for a few years and then to find his kingdom slipping from under his feet."[3] With the urge toward financial prudence, Claus then railed at Gibson for suggesting a massive loan, who then complained to his diary: "He is as ruthless as he is shrewd . . . an irascible old millionaire who addresses one in a most insulting manner."[4]

Claus's Reign Ends

To Claus's dismay, Hawai'i's legislature reluctantly introduced the Loan Act, which authorized the additional debt. Claus realized his influence had waned when, on September 1, 1886, Kalākaua secured a loan from London financiers to help pay off the kingdom's debts.[5] To protect his interests, Claus brought a proposed amendment to the act, demanding that he "be given priority in any payment of interest or principal."[6] As the debate over this amendment proceeded, Claus, watching from the gallery, broke protocol to shout directives in a "raised voice." If his finances were not given priority, he told the king, he'd "demand immediate payment on his loans and would never make another penny available!"[7]

He correctly surmised the vote on his amendment would test the strength of his control in Hawai'i. It was voted down, 23 to 14. Henry A. Peirce Carter, the Hawaiian representative, wrote on October 22, 1886, that Mr. Spreckels "made his dictations as to the terms to be accepted by this country so offensive that the king and his ministers and the assembly deemed it essential to their best interests of the country to break off all relationships with him."[8] With Claus's hasty departure in 1886, the time was now ripe for the kingdom's fundamentalists and its allies to act.[9]

Kalākaua's Reign Ends

In January 1887 Dole and Thurston recruited like-minded men into a secret organization to determine how to handle Kalākaua and the current cabinet headed by Gibson. The so-called Hawaiian League, composed mostly of those who operated lucrative sugar plantations, began their moves to strip the king of his authority. At 2:00 p.m. on June 30, 1887, nearly four hundred members held a mass meeting. Their major concerns were Kalākaua's mismanagement of funds and his acceptance of a bribe of $71,000 in exchange for his bringing back the licensed monopoly to sell opium. The meeting resulted in a list of demands and a new constitution, drafted by Thurston, they would force the king to sign. Their timing was strategic: the king's wife, Kapiʻolani, and his sister Liliʻuokalani were far away attending Queen Victoria's Golden Jubilee in England, and Claus was now out of the picture.

On July 6 Thurston led a group of men who handed Kalākaua a pen and told him to sign the new constitution. After hours of argument, protest, and inquiry, the king found himself in a futile position. Faced with a purported threat to his life and weighing the improbability of successfully refusing, Kalākaua sullenly affixed his signature to the document. He then had to accept that Gibson and his cabinet had to go, replaced by Lorrin Thurston who became minister of the interior.

When the sun set that evening over the shores of Hawaiʻi, the king's signature ushered in a new era. The document became known as the Bayonet Constitution because it was signed under the threat of assassination. This constitution eliminated every vestige of the king's monarchical powers and placed all executive power in the hands of the new four-member cabinet. Thurston later entertained a crowd with a story of what Kalākaua's surrender reminded him of: "I remember reading somewhere of a man who was going to shoot a coon, and the coon said: 'Don't shoot; I'll come down.' The King is the coon and this meeting is the gun."[10]

Claus's reaction to the Bayonet Constitution was one of grief for his old friend who had helped him become sugar king, but in the immediate days, he was callous in his assessment of the king for news-starved journalists in San Francisco:

The King for a long time has been led by gin-drinking adventurers. Men with nothing to lose and everything to gain by leading His Majesty into escapades and upon a course of wildest dissipation. He is easily approached when sought at the drinking or gaming table . . . [he] cannot be reached by calm reason but can be ruled by the gin bottle; that is his divinity, and whoever worships at the shrine of Baccus will find an open-armed welcome from him.[11]

David Kalākaua, once so strong and cheerful, became silent and withdrawn. He believed he had disappointed his family, his kingdom, and himself. All the drama soon exasperated his health conditions. It had been known that he had been suffering from heart, kidney, and liver problems. To make matters worse, his beloved younger sister, Princess Miriam Likelike, only thirty-six and the mother of eleven-year-old Princess Victoria Ka'iulani, died following a miscarriage on February 2, 1887. "Sadness seemed to be in the very air. The sky was dull and overcast; scarcely a breath of wind was stirring, and but a few faint rays of sunlight penetrated the prevailing gloom"—so reported the *Advertiser* in the days following her death.[12] Although the people didn't yet realize it, the reign of Kalākaua would be considered the golden years of Hawaiian progress and prosperity, which in the end had been paid for at a very high price.

Building a Farm Industry with Beets

The idea to revisit his dreams of refining beets was just the distraction and intellectual challenge Claus needed after the turbulence in Hawai'i. It had been twenty-two years since he worked as a common laborer in Germany to learn the processes of making sugar from beets, but in the end, his timing had been off. The motivations now were the same as then, however: to build a farm industry in California to replace the need for importing sugar once and for all for the United States. California's first beet sugar manufacturer, Ebenezer Dyer, had been making a go of it again with his Standard Sugar Refining Company, until two of his boilers blew up in 1886 and put him out of business. Claus didn't know if he would resurface or not.[13]

Every instinct Claus had told him in 1887 that was now or never due to several factors. Hawai'i's planters, resentful of his domination over the affairs of their kingdom, would never renew their three-year contract with him (due to expire in 1890); as a result, a new source of raw sugar would have to be found. With the expected end of reciprocity, beets were a way to get ahead.

They would ensure that he had material (new word) to refine for sugar. He was also in a struggle for survival with a powerful sugar trust newly formed in New York. He either had to strengthen his position on the West Coast or leave the refining business altogether.

This was the time to build a beet industry and turn California into an economic powerhouse. It wasn't more money he needed; in fact, he said, "I'm motivated by very different rewards than other millionaires."[14] He regarded himself a state nationalist rather than an agriculturalist; that is, he claimed his motivation for beet farming was for California's prosperity.

Rejuvenation and Rediscovery

Claus was at an age to think about retirement—indeed, he was well past it for a man of his generation—but he had no intention to retire to his porch in Aptos. Inching toward the age of sixty, Claus was still the proverbial picture of health. His piercing blue eyes, wide smile, firm handshake, and the ever-present cigar in hand fooled most observers, but Anna knew the stress and strain of building his sugar empire on both sides of the Pacific had taken its toll. She worried about his diabetes and high blood pressure and his chronic cigar smoking. More than his health issues, he had other weaknesses to deal with: namely, his tendency for intense outbursts of anger.

Seeing familiar symptoms, Anna began to worry that Claus was headed into another nervous breakdown as she watched him grapple night and day with the complexities of initiating a beet sugar industry. At her urging, he saw his doctor who "warned him that he was headed for an early grave."[15] As before, the prescription was to check into a European health sanitarium in order to calm frayed nerves and lose weight.[16] As he had the first time around, following the spa treatment, he'd use the opportunity to roam around Europe with the ever-faithful Anna by his side to study the latest technology of beet manufacturing from seed to sugar that had occurred since his previous visit twenty-two years earlier. He needed to become extremely well versed in the science of beet farming because he alone would have to teach California farmers.

John Gets a Bug

While Claus was rejuvenating in Europe, his eldest was on an expedition of his own. John had grown up with little playtime under Claus and was now making up for it with his sailing hobby. In July of 1887 he was at the end of a race from San Francisco and stopped at San Diego Bay to restock the *Lurline*, named after Gus's daughter.[17] After dropping anchor and going into town, John was introduced to the town's leaders who made him aware of a looming threat to San Diego's development. The Santa Fe Railroad, indispensable for growth, was on the verge of abandoning the city due to the lack of a local coal supply. They "begged" the "Sugar Prince" to invest in their city by building a wharf and coal bunker.[18] No begging was needed for a Spreckels, who knew a solid opportunity for investment when he saw one. Already, the J. D. Spreckels and Brothers company had been transporting building materials and merchandise to various ports around the Pacific, making the brothers a fortune. John quickly foresaw the immense returns on an outlay of $90,000. He predicted that he could easily step in to become the largest supplier of coal, oil, cement, wood, fertilizers, and more for the struggling town of San Diego, desperate to grow.[19] He instructed the town's leaders to tell their railroad contacts he'd advance them all the coal they needed on credit if they would agree to keep the line running until the Spreckels's wharf and coal bunker was finished.[20]

Before John left, he toured Coronado Island with a visionary entrepreneur named Elisha Spurr Babcock Jr. who was in the process of elevating Southern California's boom to his financial advantage. Even though neither he nor any of his investment partners had any hotel experience, they intended to develop a superlative master-planned community anchored by a resplendent hotel, with a sweeping fairytale silhouette and a whimsy of red turrets and towers, which would be called the Hotel del Coronado.[21] This was the fantastic dream—still under construction then but displayed in the blueprints of the celebrated architect brothers James and Watson Reid—that inspired John's imagination during the summer of 1887. Recalling this inspiration, John exclaimed, "The San Diego bug got me!"[22] And in due time, this "bug" would take him far away from his father, Claus.

Results of Claus's Study

Claus and Anna took months visiting factories and fields in Germany, Austria, and France, absorbing facts and figures all along the way. The success of a beet farmer is measured by two basic figures: "the number of tons to the acre and the average percentage of each beet that is sugar."[23] For the eighteenth-century German pioneer chemist Andreas Marggraf, a 6-percent yield was considered good. Since then, the beet had been selectively developed and extraction techniques improved. Claus heard boasts from farmers who were yielding as much as thirty tons to the acre, with beets that contained 15-percent sugar. He learned that from a refiner's standpoint, beets of 12-percent sugar were considered good and 14-percent was a profitable average, so the boasting farmers were right to be proud. Since beets were sold to the refinery by the ton, the more tons per acre, the more money that could be made. Fifteen tons to the acre was regarded as an excellent yield.[24] Claus vowed to himself to match and even beat this number in California.

Claus favored automation, with up-to-date plans and equipment. He was buoyed by all he had learned and felt confident enough in his knowledge to go to a well-known manufacturer of machines for beet sugar factories in Grevenbroich and order a complete outfit capable of refining 350 tons of beets per day.[25] Even with the site for a factory unconfirmed at this point, it seemed a good idea to him to get the equipment ordered, especially since it would enter the United States duty free. He also purchased 30 tons of the best beet seed he could get his hands on to be delivered to San Francisco by the end of December 1887.[26] Since beets are planted in spring and harvested late in the fall, appropriate fields had to be identified quickly. Claus was anxious to get home and put his plans into action.

On September 17, on their way home with a layover in London, Claus was interviewed by a reporter. The incorporation of a beet sugar company when no other existed in America was radical and warranted the attention of the press. The article put Europe's sugar manufactures on notice they would soon have stiff competition because Mr. Spreckels, "the Sugar King," intended to make "California the greatest sugar producer of the world," using beets.[27] He explained that sugar refined from beets and cane were chemically identical, but "the sugar that is made from the beet is more powerful, it possesses a greater sweeting faculty than that which is made from the sugar cane."[28]

On October 7 Charles Reed Bishop, worried about that declaration, called Claus a "big bragger" but predicted the sugarcane culture in Hawai'i could be "ruined" if he were to succeed: "Mr. Spreckels expects to make himself the most popular man in the U.S., if not in the whole world[,] by introducing beet culture for sugar making in all parts where vegetables grow well and will be 'Sugar King' not only of the Pacific Coast of the whole Republic."[29] Back home and acting quickly, Claus founded the Western Beet Sugar Company, with a fully subscribed capital stock of $500,000. It was incorporated on October 17, 1887, with the following directors: San Francisco mayor Edward Pond, James Burgess Stetson, Leon Sloss, M. P. Jones, John Koster, and Meyer Ehrman—all under President Spreckels, who owned 85 percent of the stock.

Watsonville

More than a decade had passed since the Pajaro Valley's alluvial soil was proven to be well suited for planting beets. Claus now set his sights on the fertile valley, which was covered in a deep layer of rich soil deposited by millennia of periodic flooding of the Pajaro River.[30] Otto and Klineau had failed primarily because of the high transportation costs to get the harvest to their Soquel factory for refining. Claus knew that he'd have to build a "factory in the fields" to avoid the same failed outcome.

Based on the successful beet-growing regions he had seen in Europe, Claus knew the temperate region of the Central Coast, cooled by fog and ocean breezes during the summer and without winter frost, would be ideal. Watsonville was the only town in the valley drained by the Pajaro River, which ran a sixty-mile course from the Coast Ranges to Monterey Bay. Nearly a hundred miles south of San Francisco and, more importantly, not too far from his Aptos Ranch, Watsonville is where he wanted to build his beet refinery.[31]

The beginnings of the coastal agricultural town of Watsonville are mired in legal battles and local legend. Judge John Howard Watson was prominent in laying out the town of Watsonville in 1852 on one square mile near the banks of the Pajaro River. Watson obtained a portion of the Bolsa del Pajaro land grant in south Santa Cruz County for $4,000 from Sebastian Rodriguez, a Mexican land grant recipient. Watson, a notorious ladies' man, had a hot temper and "a reputation for smutty language." He was said to be "a little devious in his business dealings."[32] Because of this, the legality of Watson's possession of land was questionable. Even though he never stayed around, the ranching town curiously became his namesake.[33]

This was the Wild West in many ways, as reported by a correspondent of the *Santa Cruz Sentinel* who had the misfortune of spending the night in the "quiet village" of Watsonville on October 25, 1856. He was startled awake at about 6:00 on a Sunday morning to the sounds of fifteen to twenty gunshots in the streets below him. After the reporter "hastened to the scene of action," he learned the unrest was over stolen horses from the Pajaro Valley that had been taken by Mexicans "armed to the teeth." The reporter recorded that a small group of these Mexicans were attacked as they rode through town by a group of "Americans" who "sallied forth from their place of rendezvous with guns and revolvers, some with one in each hand, and demanded the parties to stop." It's unclear why the firing began, but each side would accuse the other of firing first, with the reporter concluding that "God Almighty and the recording angel only knows." After a wild pursuit throughout the hills, one wounded Mexican gave himself up. Back in Watsonville, he was tied to the town's flagpole ("Liberty pole")—to the shock of the reporter, who looked up and sadly wondered if the "stars and stripes" would catch a breeze and unfold to highlight "the unpatriotic and unchristian act below." Later, without judge or jury, the prisoner was led "down to the river and across to the nearest tree," where he was lynched. The reporter was so horrified that he used an alias to write his account. It's unlikely that he ever went back to Watsonville.[34]

Pajaro Valley was called "Spud Valley" in early days because of the over-abundance of potato farms, an overproduction that ultimately plunged farmers into deep debt. By the late 1860s most of the potatoes and cattle ranching had been replaced by the growing of grains, and nearly two thousand people, mainly farmers, called Watsonville home.[35] In 1868 a city government was organized; elections were held, and tiny Watsonville, surrounded by farms and fields, became an incorporated municipality. The town comprised a barber shop, a lively saloon, a livery stable, a general store, and a community hall grandly known as the Opera House—all lining a small commercial district along Pajaro Street (now Main Street).[36]

No other industry had more influence, good and bad, on the development of California than did the railroads. Towns were created or destroyed, whole ways of life improved or oppressed by the political decision of where to route a train. This is no less true of Watsonville than it is for many other small towns throughout the country.

On July 17, 1871, the Southern Pacific began constructing a forty-five-mile branch line toward Watsonville and Salinas.[37] Nearby towns were stunned when the SP diverted the course from coming through Watsonville proper because city leaders failed to offer the railroad executives enough incentives and subsidies. Francis Wyckoff, member of the Board of Aldermen for the city of Watsonville, explained that he was the reason: "The railroad surveying parties and engineers came down the coast to lay out the railroad. 'If you want this railroad to go through your town, you'll have to give us a little cumshaw, a little money.' . . . [I] told these engineering and survey boys to go to hell. So, they said, 'All right, we'll put your goddamn town out of business.'"[38]

So, out of spite, the railroad rerouted the line two miles away across the river and called the station "Pajaro." Wycliff said, "After the train came in, the local residents had to cross a bridge over the river. Of course, you couldn't get across that bridge and get over to Pajaro to catch the train unless you took a hack [a six-seater wagon pulled by two horses]."[39] As a clever solution, citizens began to develop an industrial area between Watsonville and the Pajaro Station, and the inconvenience seemed less annoying.

When the Southern Pacific roared into the Pajaro Station on November 26, 1871, life forever changed for the community; their role as a commercial center for Pajaro Valley was solidified despite S P's efforts. After Watsonville transitioned itself from a gritty farm town to become the center of agricultural business for all the surrounding smaller communities, more people came to live and work there. "Dry goods stores flourished and related services such as barbers, coopers, cobblers and blacksmiths set up shop on and around Main Street."[40]

Inspiring the Farmers

Claus's success as a beet refiner would be wholly reliant on successful cultivation, subsidized by willing farmers with their own land and equipment. The feisty Pajaro Valley farmers would have to be convinced. To get the ball rolling, he invited two of Watsonville's most prominent citizens to his home in Aptos to discuss business: Judge William Gaffey and William Radcliff, a banker and the editor of Watsonville's *Pajaronian*. As a good poker player, Claus knew he'd have to keep his cards close to his chest; with a straight face, he stated that he'd be building a beet refinery "somewhere" in California.[41] Even though towns up and down the state expressed their great interest in the enterprise, there was only *one place* he wanted his refinery to be: Watsonville. Naming several towns that had already begun courting him, he let it be known that Watsonville could rise to the top of the list *if* his requirements were met.

The first requirement to make the enterprise worth his while was to contract with enough farmers in the Pajaro Valley to grow at least two thousand tons of beets yearly.[42] For the plan to work, Watsonville's city leaders (and then Claus) would have to convince the farmers to embrace a whole new concept of farming, one that was disconnected from their current practices; that is, they would need to grow produce for a factory to refine rather than for the kitchen table. Also, because of the labor-intensive methods required to cultivate beets, a higher standard of skill and attention would be required.

Farmers would also have to increase their hiring of seasonal laborers. For every man they might have hired to work in wheat fields, forty-one men were needed in the cultivation, harvesting, and processing of sugar beets.[43] On the large farms and ranches, migrant workers had always arrived at the moment of high demand in agriculture—the planting and the harvesting. The transient worker's life was not an easy one under any circumstances. They had reason to complain about the physically hard work, and like any outdoor worker, they sweated in the summer and froze in the winter. One such laborer, circa 1880, succinctly summarized some of the problems: "Oh, we were always scratching. We ate burned beef. We drank filthy water. Our bunkhouses were crowded. Sometimes we lived with the chickens and the cows. We were always dirty. We never had any money. We stank to hell." With no union tradition in the fields to guide them, farm laborers tended instead to vote with their feet. Workers simply left employers when the pay was too low, food or living quarters intolerable, or dangers too great to bear.[44]

Cultivating beets would be a hard sell, but Radcliff and Gaffey were stimulated after the meeting in Aptos with Claus. They were convinced the new Western Beet Sugar Company could put Watsonville on the map as an agricultural force. Because they understood how Claus's capital investment could transform their region and community, they vowed to do their best to convince farmers and find appropriate land for the refinery.

Their first attempt to motivate farmers was with a full front-page interview with Claus on October 20, 1887, in the *Pajaronian*. The article was long and drawn-out, written in a question-and-answer format. In it, Claus described the precise steps of beet sugar production, from seed to cultivation, the relationship between farmer and factory, the refining process, and the mutual financial benefit for all "partners." The Pajaro Valley farmers from "foothills to flatland" were told they were about to receive the opportunity of a lifetime, because through them, America was about to enter in a new era! An open invitation to attend a get-together, conducted by Mr. Spreckels himself, on

November 5 at the Opera House in Watsonville was strongly encouraged if farmers wanted to increase their standard of living. The *Pajaronian* told the valley farmers the grain they were growing would never pay as much as a beet crop would and that "every friend of progress should attend [the meeting]."[45]

The *Pajaronian*'s published appeal to their valley's famers was picked up in other newspapers. As Claus predicted, it opened a floodgate of interest. News that the newly formed Western Beet Sugar Company's offer to build a refinery, contingent upon agreements from local farmers to grow the beets, spread like wildfire around the state. The *Sacramento Daily Record-Union* reported that in just over two weeks, Claus had been "promised" an "enthusiastic reception" with more than "twenty invitations . . . from the Boards of Trade of Chico, Sacramento and Los Angeles, and other organizations in Stockton, Fresno, Redding, Napa, Santa Rosa, Martinez and other places."[46] Their eager appeals for Claus to visit their town came with offers of free land for the purposes of the refinery.[47]

On the appointed Saturday (November 5, 1887) at 2:00 p.m., the town's meeting hall, the Opera House, was packed from wall to wall with farmers, making this the largest business gathering ever held in Watsonville.[48] Seven different metropolitan newspapers had traveled to the town, lending an air of importance to those who gathered to hear Claus's proposal. On the stage were three of Watsonville's most prominent pioneers: William Augustus Sanborn, Albert North Judd, and Charles Ford. Right on time, as usual, Claus and Gus walked through the door. The farmers were anxious to get their first look at the famous sugar king, reported as being of medium height, compactly built, and neatly dressed. They saw what was described:

> He has the face of a typical German, with the high cheek-bones, fair skin and blue eyes of the Fatherland. His eye is as clear as that of a young man, and his skin though browned by exposure, is also clean and healthy. His round head is covered with a thick growth of hair, rapidly changing from gray to white. This is the only indication of his years. He has the alert look and movement of a man of thirty, and in his steel-blue eyes is a look which goes far to reveal his character.[49]

Charles Ford had been in Watsonville since the days when it consisted of "two wooden buildings and a large tent."[50] As the president of the bank and Watsonville's wealthiest citizen, Ford acted as master of ceremonies.

He introduced Claus as "a typical Californian." After Claus began talking "farmer to farmer," his listeners were surprised by his heavy German accent. It was noted they listened with "strained attention" until they got used to his speech's cadence.[51]

Claus told them that he had been born into a farming family, that he had lived their lives, that he understood the hardships. He knew that every farmer in the room existed on the margins of profitability. After recounting his recent European findings on "the sugar beet and sugar making industry," he told them in no uncertain terms that he was "convinced beyond all doubt" that "California could raise sugar beets profitably and the Pajaro Valley was the place to do it."[52] He outlined the economics of beet culture and crop rotation methods. There wasn't a question he couldn't answer as it related to farming. Claus realized that he needed to provide incentives to convince farmers to grow sugar beets when almost every other crop was easier and cheaper to grow. He told the farmers that he'd provide the German seed pods. Thus, farmers were guaranteed a risk-free investment, at least as far as the seeds were concerned, and Claus was guaranteed a steady supply of raw material that would meet his quality standards. He told them he'd pay for a refinery if they would agree to "cultivate a certain number of acres of beets each year, according to German methods—which was crop rotation, and fertilization. . . . If the first factory is not enough—I will build another or if is not large enough—I will make it larger, but this I will guarantee—a profitable sugar industry for California is under my supervision."[53]

Claus then described the "German factory system," where the refinery was "owned by the farmers themselves." He said if the local farmers chose to go on this cooperative method, "he would contribute $100,000 toward their $300,000 investment" ($3.1 million and $9.4 million, respectively, in today's money). To assure them of success, he'd guarantee management of their farmer-owned refinery. Or, if this idea was not appealing, he said, the Western Beet Sugar Company would both "build and operate the plant," but it would need donated land.[54] (This second way is how he went; the first option was not appealing to the farmers.) Claus's speech was widely applauded, but only a few farmers signed a commitment before leaving the meeting. These were not the type of people to hastily make decisions, and before they placed their signatures on any document, they needed the privilege of weighing the matter at home, at the saloon, or in the streets.[55]

After Claus and Gus left the meeting, a committee was appointed to select a suitable site for the refinery, one that was at least twenty-five acres and near transportation. The site they found was on the edge of town, on Walker Street, alongside the train tracks. The very next day, Ford and some others formally called upon Claus, offering this site for his inspection. But because of the lack of commitments at the Opera House meeting, Claus "cagily played for time" and said he might be back in three weeks to investigate the site.[56] After a nail-biting three weeks of waiting, Watsonvillers were relieved when Claus finally inspected the site on November 26, 1887. Claus liked what he saw.

On December 1, 1887, Claus, inundated with offers of free land up and down the state, formally told the Watsonville committee that their time of indecision was up. Claus was holding out for an agreement stipulating that if the "people of the Pajaro Valley would buy the land near the depot and deed it to the Western Beet Sugar Company, beet contracts would be drawn up immediately for the farmers to sign," with a December 7, 1887, deadline.[57] As if they knew this stipulation might be coming, the committee had been circulating subscription pledges throughout the Pajaro Valley during the month of November. Claus had met his stipulations.

Watsonville Wins!

On December 14, 1887, Claus accepted the site in Watsonville at a cost to the contributing farmers of nearly $400,000 ($12.5 million in today's money). On December 15 the *Los Angeles Daily Herald* pronounced, "Watsonville Wins!"—news that disappointed rival farming communities. The report continued, "Claus Spreckels has accepted the site offered by the people of Pajaro valley for beet sugar evaporation and was in town to-day signing contracts with farmers for raising beets. He agrees to pay a minimum price of $4 per ton."[58]

At the same time Watsonvillers were leveling the land for the future beet sugar factory, Claus was testifying on March 23, 1888, in Washington DC, before the House Committee on Manufacturers. Due to public concern with the growing problem of trusts and monopolies, state and federal governments began serious attempts to regulate big businesses. The committee requiring Claus's presence was tasked to investigate the New York Sugar Trust and their impact on consumer pricing. Claus, as a West Coast competitor, was important to their investigation. The committee was concerned the Spreckels refinery in San Francisco would keep raising the price of sugar to match that of the New York Sugar Trust. If so, it would smack of collusion. Displaying offense at such a question, Claus strongly maintained his autonomy as a sugar refiner: "I came here from Germany for liberty, gentlemen, and liberty I will maintain."[59] No doubt after meeting him, it was evident to all in attendance that this man could never be under anyone's thumb.

Recognizing the unique opportunity, he redirected the conversation to lobby for domestically grown beets: "We can make our own sugar in America, and it is about time we do!" Adding, "This country has made discoveries in beet culture and machinery, which would make domestic sugar production a success." He boasted of his invention that would produce "90 per cent of pure sugar from beet juice" and proposed that if other states replicate his methods, "the United States could supply the world with sugar if the industry was developed."[60] His optimism, combined with his affable and dynamic personality, generated a positive response among the House members, and after the assembly, he was introduced to President Grover Cleveland.[61]

Meeting the president was an honor, but he was anxious to get home to find out if the thirty tons of beet seeds had been distributed in Watsonville. He was elated to learn that on March 25, 1888, more than 175 farmers, in their horse-pulled wagons, waited in line at the refinery's under-construction Walker Street location to get their seeds.[62] With the assurance of beets in the ground, Claus's anticipation was intense as he got ready for his second cornerstone-laying ceremony of a new factory.

Weary, if not downright exhausted from the arduous cross-country travel, Claus, accompanied by Anna, Rudolph, and Emma, arrived at Watsonville's depot on the morning of Saturday, April 28, 1888, for the celebration. As they stepped down onto the platform, they were not prepared for the mass delegation, all dressed in their Sunday best, awaiting them. When the Watsonville Band started playing rousing tunes to welcome the family, Anna, known to be shy, likely blushed and moved behind her husband. The mayor of San Francisco, local dignitaries, and people from many counties north and south escorted the Spreckels family in a parade all the way to the three-story Mansion House Hotel, in the heart of town. Since 1871 it was the valley's most elegant hotel, boasting that former president Ulysses Grant had even spent the night there. At the hotel, the family was treated to a lavish reception followed by another parade to the Walker Street site where firecrackers were shot in the air to signify their arrival.

Speeches were made, hands were shaken, prayers were given, and songs were sung, before Claus, in a time-honored tradition, stepped up to the hollowed-out space left empty in the construction of the corner of the building. After he guided the granite block in place, "a delegation of young Watsonville ladies showered bouquets upon Mr. Spreckels until he was completely covered from sight." According to the *Pajaronian*, "No corner stone was put in place in California, accompanied by such a public demonstration." Looking sheepishly in the middle of the festivities, "Mr. Spreckels probably for the first time in his life felt like retiring under the fence." When he was asked to say a few words, he couldn't say much except that the "warmth of the public" before him made this "one of the happiest days" of his life.[63]

A Finished Factory: Beets on Board

With the completion of the factory, hundreds of acres of beets were being harvested. Three hundred seasonal workers all worked together at the factory during the season or "campaign." There was a "between-season" crew of one hundred year-round factory employees living in the area or commuting from Salinas, four miles away. A steady stream of small-time farmers began to make their way to Watsonville, hoping to get contracts for planting beets in their fields.

The refinery had a capacity of 350 tons of beets per day, which would convert to 40 tons of sugar. Soon, the refinery had to be enlarged to a capacity of 1,200 tons. Unfortunately, the refinery was handicapped by the freight rates and time schedule of the Southern Pacific, which hindered the timely transport of the beets by farmers up and down the valley, sometimes for "weeks at a time," causing a degradation of the sucrose content.[64] To remedy this situation, Claus got to work and built a narrow-gauge steel railroad to travel twenty-five miles with side tracks; he named it the Pajaro Valley Railroad (PVR).

Claus cleverly built the tracks directly to the deep-water shipping point at Moss Landing, where the Pacific Coast Steamship Company went directly to San Francisco. He and others could now avoid using the Southern Pacific altogether.[65] Farmers were elated to access Claus's train to ship their other crops of grains, apples, and dairy products to San Francisco markets at significant savings. The steamship charged farmers $3.75 per freight ton to San Francisco while the SP charged $4.75 per ton.[66] Claus was delighted to break up SP's monopoly and cut into their profits.[67] Even though the line cost Claus $2 million ($63 million in today's money), it was well worth it for the goodwill it created for the citizens in and around the valley. People were astonished at his "proverbial energy" and his ingenuity and commitment to the new industry.

Claus, the Expert

Claus's success in Watsonville generated a widespread interest in beet cultivation. Inquiries reached Claus from across the country. The most important questions farming communities wanted answered related to "preparing the soil, selecting the seed, cultivation, harvesting and marketing of the crop."[68] The inquiries were so great that Claus drafted a lengthy letter to Edwin F. Smith, secretary of the California State Agricultural Society, including complete information on the cultivation of beets and outlining what was necessary in erecting a beet sugar operation. Claus had become the country's foremost expert on the subject. Meanwhile, the demand for Spreckels beet sugar soared. At its peak, Claus's Watsonville refinery was processing an average of 359 tons of beets per day, yielding 45 tons of sparkling white sugar.

The Watsonville refinery became the largest sugar factory operating in the country.[69] On May 12, 1888, an eastern newspaper noted the sugar king, even though in his seventh decade, and a "millionaire many times over," had just found his purpose in life, or in Claus's words, his "lifework."[70] Claus wanted it known that wealth wasn't the motivator: "It would kill me to fail in what I undertake to do. It is not money that is an object to me, but I want the people of California to be able to show that Claus Spreckels has done something for this state when his bones are at rest."[71]

Claus's success attracted the attention of two other wealthy sugar refiners from New York, the Oxnard brothers, former cane sugar refiners. They knew all too well that Claus knew what he was doing and quickly followed suit in California in 1890 with their own Chino Valley Beet Sugar Company (later the American Beet Sugar Company).[72] The Oxnards weren't viewed as rivals but partners in order to propel California's agricultural economy forward.

The year before starting his own beet sugar company, Henry Oxnard appeared before the U.S. House of Representatives and argued persistently for a two-cent federal bounty on domestically produced sugar. At that time, Claus and the Oxnard brothers differed in their attitudes toward proposed tariff legislation. Claus believed he could obtain more protection for his interests by discouraging the importation of foreign sugar, so he himself journeyed to Washington in February 1889 and appeared before the House Ways and Means Committee to argue against the passage of the legislation. Joseph McKenna, U.S. congressman for his district, pointedly asked Claus what effect, if any, the proposed law would have upon his interests. Claus responded that he wouldn't invest in any additional factories, which would curtail further employment. He emphatically asserted that with the right education for farmers and under the proper conditions, enough sugar could be grown in the United States to supply all its consumption needs. No outside source should be considered. The congressman wondered if it was realistic, to which Claus replied, "If you assure us [American sugar growers and refiners] that there is not to be any change in the tariff and you had one hundred Claus Spreckels, I think we could."[73]

The passage of the McKinley Tariff Act of 1890, in spite of Claus's initial objections, annulled the exclusive reciprocity between the United States and Hawai'i beginning in 1892. But it did provide a federal bounty of two cents per pound on all domestically produced sugar and allowed for the free importation of beet seed and sugar machinery. This was the first piece of national legislation aimed at supplying the United States with enough domestically grown sugar to meet consumption needs. Thus, the act had some beneficial effects upon the fledgling beet sugar industry spearheaded by Claus. During the four years the law was operative, some $6 million was invested in beet sugar factories throughout the nation, and Claus's expertise was sought time and time again. Also, the amount of beet sugar produced in the United States—and in California, in particular—doubled in each of the two successive years following the enactment of the law.[74] As the largest sugar refiner in the country, it might have been time to slow down and enjoy life a bit, but severe challenges lay ahead: Claus would be battling not only with another sugar king but with his own children.

13   *Sugar and Strife*

In the late 1880s the California Sugar Refinery had only one local competitor, the very small Bay Sugar Refinery. Claus was the top sugar refiner, as well as the leading grower and importer of Hawaiian sugar, on the Pacific Coast. Indeed, his output of sugar was more than could be consumed on that West Coast. Never afraid of competition, Claus decided to ship sugar across the country and compete with the East Coast sugar refineries, never imagining that this business decision would mark the end of the Spreckels family solidarity.

Third-generation German American entrepreneur Henry Osborne "H. O." Havemeyer was the East Coast's own millionaire "sugar king." His Sugar Trust was one of the twelve holding companies setting the Dow Jones Average. He was as aggressive and outspoken as Claus was. With more notoriety on the East Coast, Havemeyer was widely considered to be the second-most significant trust organizer after John D. Rockefeller, and the newspapers frequently villainized him as a robber baron. Havemeyer's ruthless business tactics, focused on eliminating competition, were legendary.

Upon learning the West Coast sugar king was encroaching on his territory, Havemeyer was straightforward about his monopolistic intentions; in 1887 he invited Claus to join the Sugar Trust, asserting that cooperation was far better than competition, and fully expected him to accept as had other refiners. If Havemeyer thought the two sugar kingdoms could merge, however, he was sorely mistaken. The zealously independent Claus flatly refused a partnership, despite the fact the collaboration would have augmented his wealth. He revered independence much more than he valued profit, declaring at one point, "I never yet have gone into anything unless I could have it all my own way."[1]

The Battle of the Two Sugar Kings

Outraged and incensed by the rebuff, Havemeyer decided to institute an aggressive campaign to drive Claus out of the refining business altogether. His first action was to go to San Francisco and purchase Claus's single competitor, the Bay Sugar Refinery, and rename it the American Sugar Refining Company. Havemeyer promptly slashed sugar prices to below cost. The bargain prices impelled many of Claus's customers to transfer their business to his competitor; in fact, the Hawaiian planters jumped ship for the American Sugar Refining Company as soon as their contracts allowed. They were delighted to have their sugar refined by anyone other than Claus Spreckels.

Seeing business slipping away, Claus had to plan his next steps carefully and strategically. Meanwhile, everyone walked on eggshells around Claus while he contemplated many different scenarios. Incensed, Claus declared to anyone within earshot, "This trust has trampled on my toes and I won't stand it!"[2] In early 1888 he decided the only way to get full revenge was to return the favor and build a massive refinery in Philadelphia, "enemy territory," an area under the control Havemeyer's Sugar Trust.[3]

The press went wild with his stated intentions. Before Claus left for Philadelphia, his friends, employees, and their wives gave a surprise party for him to show him their full support and wish him "success in his new enterprise."[4] After speeches, gifts, and cheers were given, Claus "completely broke down and wept like a child at the token of his affection and esteem of his 1,600 employees." It was noted that many of refinery's "rugged working men" were so moved to see "their chief in tears" that they too broke out in "audible sobs."[5]

In May 1888 Claus found a site for his operation fronting the Delaware River on Reed Street, which had access to cheap coal, an abundant water supply, and first-class transport facilities. He allocated nearly $4 million ($125 million in today's money) to construct the most modern and highly efficient refinery of the time.[6] The first of his refinery's twenty million bricks were laid that summer, and Claus couldn't begin to anticipate the agonizing hardships that lay ahead of him.

Some Payback and Its Reversal

While construction was underway on his Philadelphia refinery, Claus was about to enjoy a much-needed breathing spell back in the West. On November 5, 1888, action was brought by the district attorney in San Francisco Superior Court to terminate the franchise of Havemeyer's American Sugar Refining Company. The suit charged the new refinery was actually part of an organization violating California's new and untried antitrust laws. It was generally suspected that Claus had used his power and money behind the scenes to bring about this lawsuit, but nothing was ever proved. The court action dragged on for fourteen months, due to postponement after postponement because John Searles and Henry Havemeyer, as officers of the Sugar Trust, simply ignored all summons to testify in San Francisco. Thus, on January 7, 1890, the lower court decided the American Sugar Refining Company must close for business. Searles and Havemeyer immediately appealed the decision. Nevertheless, the no-nonsense superior judge William T. Wallace, known far and wide as a merciless dispenser of justice, ordered the refinery shut down.[7] There was nothing but rejoicing within the walls of the Spreckels refinery and home.

The immediate result of Judge Wallace's decision was a sugar famine in San Francisco. Claus's California Sugar Refinery was now the only place to buy sugar. Claus summarily pulled out his blacklist. Wholesalers who had transferred their patronage to Havemeyer, those who had publicly criticized Claus over his business activities, reporters from the *Chronicle*—there was now no sugar available to them. Not only were Claus's critics unable to buy sugar from his refinery but they also couldn't buy it secondhand from other merchants, who feared that resale to those on the blacklist would jeopardize their own future sugar supply. To the question "How is Mr. Spreckels to know if you sell sugar to any of the boycotted firms?" one merchant was quoted in the *Chronicle*:

> Oh, he's a sharper.... You observe that all my barrels have numbers on them. Those numbers tally exactly with a tabulated list of customers on file at the refinery. Then since the boycott has been instituted, each barrel bears another private mark by which it can be identified. To complete this system of surveillance, Spreckels probably hires men to spy around the various boycotted stores to see whether they have any barrels secretly purchased from accepted customers of the refinery.[8]

Claus's retaliatory measures were frustrated on June 9, 1890, when the state supreme court reversed the lower court's decision and declared that the

American Sugar Refining Company could reopen for business. Judge Wallace received a "hand slap" after being found guilty of contempt for having thrown Havemeyer's refinery into receivership while the case was under appeal.[9] By the time Havemeyer reopened for business in San Francisco, Claus's new Philadelphia business, the Spreckels Sugar Refining Company, had already been in operation for six months, with $5 million of paid-up capital stock, almost 100 percent of which Claus owned.[10] Claus hired five hundred men, and the fight for America's sugar market, no holds barred, began in earnest.

Gus and Rudolph: A Lifelong Partnership

Ceremoniously and full of fatherly pride, Claus put Gus in charge of the Philadelphia refinery. Gus and his wife, Oroville Dore, whom he had married in 1883, and their four-year-old daughter, Lurline Elizabeth, were enthusiastic at the prospect of a new adventure and the news that Gus would be receiving a hefty yearly salary of $24,000 ($750,000 in today's money).[11]

Seventeen-year-old Rudolph was the only brother with no clear direction in life. Likely owing to his childhood struggles with asthma, which kept him from straying too far from home and his mother, he was known in the family as a mama's boy. After Anna had lost so many children, she became overly cautious, keeping such a careful watch on her youngest that Rudolph missed plenty of school. When Claus unexpectedly dropped by the house one afternoon, he found his youngest lounging with a novel, with servants and his mother attending to his needs. Claus, very much displeased, looked him straight in the eye and gave him exactly one minute to choose which direction his life would take: school, a trip around the world with a tutor, or life in the family business. Without hesitation, Rudolph chose business, knowing full well his father's preference. With the choice made, Claus ordered him to pack immediately and sent him to Philadelphia so that his brother Gus could induct him into the family business.[12] Thus began a lifelong partnership between Claus's two youngest sons as they presided over the Philadelphia refinery, a decision Claus later deeply regretted.

Rivalry and Dirty Tricks

The East Coast public found the West Coast Spreckels family's competition with the Sugar Trust intriguing and entertaining. The press frequently cartooned the portly Havemeyer, in a black frock coat and silk hat, as a capitalist class enemy. To easterners, Claus was David confronting the Goliath of the Sugar Trust, and standing alone without being forced to join the trust, he was venerated as a prominent symbol for private entrepreneurship.

Faced with aggressive competition from the Spreckelses' Philadelphia refinery, the Sugar Trust was forced to lower their prices. Havemeyer's organization persisted in trying to partner with the Spreckelses, but Claus stubbornly and proudly refused; he was more inclined to bolster his public status and the success of his own Philadelphia plant, saying, "I came here to fight the trust, and I have fought it, and I intend to keep on fighting it."[13]

If the Spreckels men wanted to embrace competition, Havemeyer and the Sugar Trust were up to the task, but they would fight dirty. Gus loathed the Sugar Trust's underhanded methods, which were typical of hostile takeovers. Some of the scurrilous antics and sabotaging operations the Sugar Trust resorted to included breaking various types of expensive equipment and depositing dead rats in vats of sugar liquor. Any mention of a partnership with the trust enraged Gus, so disgusted was he by Havemeyer's unethical tactics, which kept him and his brother working overtime to monitor every plant operation vulnerable to potential sabotage.

Gus at thirty, so like his father, worked hard, determined to make the refinery a success. In the first month, the refinery turned out 200 to 700 tons a day. But, with unremitting pressure, Gus kept production on the increase, so that in one's year time, by February 1891, he was turning out 3,500 tons daily, putting the Philadelphia refinery among the top five refineries in the United States.[14]

King Kalākaua Dies

It was big news when King Kalākaua arrived in San Francisco on December 4, 1890. His arrival was greeted with great pomp and ceremony by the U.S. military, unaware the monarch had come seeking medical treatment. With Gus and Rudolph in Philadelphia, the king, back on good terms with the Spreckels family, visited with Claus, Anna, John, Adolph, and Emma all at different times and dates. John and Adolph took Kalākaua sailing aboard the *Lurline*.[15] But during all these visits, it was clear to the Spreckels family the king's health situation was dire.

San Francisco was having an exceptionally cold winter, and the Spreckels family encouraged Kalākaua to go south to and recuperate at the Hotel del Coronado, where many went specifically to improve their health. The "Del" under John's ownership had achieved a level of distinction that had eluded even the dreams of its founders. After a couple of weeks in frigid San Francisco, the ailing king was undoubtedly anxious to get there.

Kalākaua arrived in San Diego on December 28, 1890, and the *San Diego Union*, owned by John, reported that he was "one of the most enlightened and thoroughly able monarchs of modern times, a patron of art, science and literature, a friend of liberal government and a wise and sagacious ruler."[16] The king was awed by the Del calling it "the grandest hotel [he] ever saw."[17] On New Year's Eve the king was entertained lavishly in the hotel's beautiful Crown Room. But it was clear by his royal attendants that their king needed to leave. The entourage left the following day, stopping along the route for numerous public appearances despite his infirmities. On the journey north, he developed a "fever accompanied by nausea, vomiting and diarrhea" and then suffered a stroke.[18]

Once back at San Francisco's Palace Hotel, U.S. Navy medical inspector George W. Woods was urgently commissioned to assess the king's situation on January 7. Dr. Woods confirmed what those who traveled with him suspected, the king would die in a foreign land. When death was immanent, Claus's presence was requested, and he "hovered in the room" with his old friend until the bitter end.[19] At 2:35 p.m. on Tuesday, January 20, 1891, Dr. Woods wrote, "His Majesty, King Kalakaua I of the Kingdom of Hawai'i, ceased to exist," with the final diagnosis: "Bright's Disease with Uremic Blood Poisoning."[20]

The king of Hawai'i who had made Claus the king of sugar was no more. For Claus, there was nothing but sadness. His emotions were being stretched thin with the trust war, and now he had to deal with this big loss, for despite what anybody alluded to, their friendship had been genuine.

Partnering with the Enemy

New York, like California, had become trust conscious, and Havemeyer's Sugar Trust monopoly was being scrutinized in the courts. In their investigations, the New York Senate Committee on Laws decided the Sugar Trust was illegal because it was merely an unincorporated stockholding trust, engaged in the business of manufacturing and controlling markets without any corporate responsibility. Havemeyer's trust was formally dissolved, and its stock was changed to stock in the American Sugar Refining Company, a corporation.[21]

This then motivated the Sugar Trust to wave the white flag in its battle with the Spreckelses. John Searles, the secretary and treasurer of the trust and often called the "brains of the company," offered Claus, through Gus, a juicy offer: they would settle for a minority interest in the Philadelphia operation, and Claus could retain the majority ownership.[22] Outraged at the ridiculous idea of partnering with the enemy, Gus forcefully declined and then wrote to his father about the insulting offer.

The fierce price war that Claus had been waging for two long years had taken its toll on his emotional and physical health. He began to realize that crossing the country by rail, even in his luxurious private car, was getting all too much. On one of his homebound trips from Philadelphia, the *Overland Flyer* "struck a broken rail" in Nebraska, and Claus's car rolled down a twenty-foot embankment. While many passengers were "seriously hurt," Claus escaped major injuries, but he was shaken up pretty badly, both physically and emotionally.[23] He was ready to lighten his load and spend his time and energy on influencing beet cultivation throughout California. But any settlement would be on his terms.

Claus, without telling Gus, invited Searles to come west in early April 1891 for the purpose of negotiating a deal. Because Claus didn't want to be seen with the enemy after all his public denunciations, they secretly met in San Diego. In an isolated corner of the Hotel del Coronado, John Searles and Claus drew up an agreement.

To avoid falling afoul of the California antitrust laws, that day's contract was sealed between Claus, Searles (secretary-treasurer), H. O. Havemeyer (president), and Theodore Havemeyer (vice president), his father—and not the corporation. The Philadelphia refinery was sold to Havemeyer's American Sugar Refining Company for $7 million. But Claus retained majority control with 55 percent of the stock. For Havemeyer's western holdings, there was a 50-50 arrangement, and a new company, launched as the Western Sugar Refining Company, was organized and capitalized for $1 million with the stock equally divided between them.[24] Western then leased the Spreckels San Francisco refinery for $50,000 a year. The agreement between Claus and Havemeyer guaranteed that each would stay out of the other's territory permanently, but in terms of profit, Claus was the clear victor.

Even while the secret meeting was taking place, Gus was dispelling rumors to the Philadelphia press. Believing with his whole heart what he thought was true, he emphatically repeated that his father would never make a deal with the trust, the Spreckelses' Philadelphia refinery would remain independent, the rumors were false, and "there was no more reason for talking about the matter."[25] Therefore, when Gus learned about the deal made behind his back, he was apoplectic. Time after time, Gus had seen his father go into competition with an adversary, inevitably forcing that adversary to surrender. He didn't understand why his father would merge with a hostile enemy, especially considering the underhanded trickeries he and Rudolph faced on a daily basis. Gus was profoundly offended by his father's disloyalty in keeping him out of the negotiations, considering that he was the vice president and general manager of the Philadelphia operation and, most egregiously, his son.

The Family Breakup Begins

The Sugar Trust war may have ended, but it was only the beginning of a family war. Gus was so aggrieved that he decided to quit the family company and go out on his own. He informed his father that after an agreed-upon transition period, he'd be leaving to start his own refinery because he could no longer trust him. Claus was so traumatized by this news that he packed up and left for another stint in a health sanitarium in Germany to soothe his frayed nerves.

But the worst was yet to come. The originally well-timed transition period of Gus's resignation abruptly ended when Adolph, going through the financial records, supposedly found that $250,000 ($7.8 million in today's money) from the proceeds of the sale of the Philadelphia refinery had gone missing on paper. He accused Gus of stealing it. When Claus returned from Europe, he met with Gus at the Philadelphia refinery and pored over the figures. Gus reported of this meeting that as far as he could tell, his father "was satisfied with [his] account." Yet back in San Francisco, Adolph soon convinced his father of Gus's role in the missing funds, and Gus was denied access to the financial records by which he might prove his innocence. Intending to humiliate his brother, Adolph demanded an extensive written statement detailing Gus's accounting. Gus, insulted and furious, quit on the spot. When his father published statements calling him an embezzler, Gus published a letter of his own to his father.[26]

Philadelphia, November 24, 1891

Dear Father:

The other day you said that my explanation as to what became of the money paid by the Havemeyers was perfectly clear to you. This afternoon Adolph informed me that the matter was not clear to you, and that you had instructed him to investigate further into the matter. He insinuates that I have stolen the money, and says that for my own justification it was necessary to make a detailed statement. All that I can say is that every cent that has ever passed through my hands is still there. It was my earnest desire to settle everything as amicably as possible and to resign my position only after you had become familiar with many of the details of the company; but I can no longer remain in an office to be thrown in contact with him, who is evidently determined to put me under a cloud, and bent on blackening me in your eyes, in order that we might part with an unfriendly feeling. He is not satisfied with the breach he has caused in our business and family relations, but now stoops to this base and cowardly accusation. I therefore enclose herewith my resignation.

I have always worked in your interest as faithfully, honestly and conscientiously as any man could do, and no one deplores more than I do the way things have turned. In conclusion, I want to say that I part with the best of feelings toward you knowing full well that you are being wrongfully influenced against me, and that in time you will see things in a different light.

Your loving son,
Gus

John was frustrated with the family turbulence that took him away from a variety of capital improvement projects he was spearheading in San Diego, a city he was falling in love with. John had been forced to spread himself thin, reluctantly taking over the reins of all his father's businesses during the Sugar Trust war, and the press took notice: "The sugar king's colossal fortune has been amassed by his own indefatigable industry, [but] the ability of his son, John D. Spreckels, in guarding those millions, proves him a worthy second to his father."[27]

But John wasn't interested in being "a worthy second" to his father. Family members fully expected Gus to always be in that role. Gus and his father shared not only their temperaments but also their zeal for sugar cultivation and refining. With Gus now estranged, John, as the eldest son, was forced to dutifully, but resentfully, step up once again, with no end in sight. Since the family warfare seemed permanent, John and Adolph, in 1892, banded together and removed Gus from the "Brothers," buying out his interest in J. D. Spreckels and Brothers (the company organized to hold stocks and bonds and operate the assorted wholly owned interests). The brothers believed that since Gus neither contributed money nor time to the business, he should be grateful to get any profits.[28]

But the beginning of harassing their "disloyal" brother had only begun. Citing the fiscal losses as a result of the McKinley Tariff Act, Claus informed the stockholders of Hawaiian Commercial & Sugar that the company was in financial straits. Under California law, Claus was able to levy a stock assessment of five dollars a share, which he promptly did. His justification would "discharge his liability and to provide for necessary expenses." When some of the fifteen shareholders representing 10,000 shares out of a total of 100,000 refused to pay, those 97,550 shares were declared in default. The Spreckels interests immediately swooped in and bought all the outstanding stock at a bargain.[29]

John and Adolph went on record for paying their assessment on their shares, but they purposefully left Gus out, and considered his 900 shares forfeited. Through his lawyers, Gus said that he'd pay the assessment and asked for the reinstatement of his shares.[30] His older brothers, who had taken over the management of the company, refused.

The Overthrow of the Queen

While Gus contemplated his next legal steps to restore his shares in the Hawaiian company, Lili'uokalani was attempting to restore her sovereignty. When she began her reign, she was determined to negate the Bayonet Constitution her brother had been forced to sign, which authorized the sitting monarch to reign but not to rule. She firmly believed in the divine right of absolute monarchy, so she privately drafted a replacement constitution and waited for an opportunity to proclaim it publicly and thereby reclaim her sovereignty. The date she chose for the proclamation was Saturday, January

14, 1893, and when that day was over, the lives of the Hawaiian people would be changed irrevocably.

The haole elite, protecting the power they had wrested from Kalākaua six years earlier, labeled the queen's move to institute a new constitution revolutionary and three days later staged a coup. The so-called Committee of Safety, organized by the Hawaiian League, was composed of thirteen members, a cross section of Honolulu's leading white residents, led by Lorrin Thurston, who planned the overthrew of the monarchy to put a more stable government in charge until the time they could ensure that stability through annexation to the United States.

Pleading for their "safety," the Committee of Safety was able to gain the support of John L. Stevens, U.S. minister to the Hawaiian kingdom, and Captain Gilbert Wiltse of the USS *Boston*, the fully armed warship then anchored in Honolulu's harbor. The queen surrendered peacefully to avoid violence, believing wholeheartedly this wrong would be undone by the American government under anti-imperialist Grover Cleveland, who in less than two months would succeed President Benjamin Harrison (who had already sent a treaty to the Senate authorizing the annexation of Hawai'i).[31]

Lili'uokalani knew Lorrin Thurston's missionary grandparents, Asa and Lucy Goodale Thurston. They had arrived in 1820 with their hearts opened wide to serve the Hawaiian people; they built churches and schools and were among the first to painstakingly translate the Bible into the Hawaiian language. Never could Asa and Lucy have dreamt that their grandson would someday accomplish such an act to gain economic and political control over the island nation they had served so humbly.

By the end of January 1893, it was widely known there had been a coup d'état in Hawai'i by American merchants and sugar planters. As soon as ships arrived at the dock in San Francisco with this stunning and inexplicable news, headlines across the country proclaimed that Queen Lili'uokalani had been deposed. More shocking to the American correspondents was the news their own citizens were the revolutionists who had succeeded in overthrowing the government of Hawai'i.

March 29, 1893, was an important day for both annexationists and royalists. Newly inaugurated President Cleveland sent James H. Blount on a fact-finding mission to investigate the true conditions of the coup d'état and the role Americans had played in the event. American teacher Lilla

Appleton, in Honolulu, described the ostentatious patriotic efforts of the annexationists, who by an abundance of American flags, hoped to portray Honolulu as American as apple pie: never before has there been so gorgeous a display on any Fourth of July as that which greeted Commissioner Blount. Long before the steamer touched the wharf, a multitude of banners were fluttering in the breeze. On one street, a single flag (Hawaiian) was conspicuous among its foreign associates.

That spring found politics virtually at a standstill in Hawai'i, now administered by the Committee of Safety's new Provisional Government, while Commissioner Blount investigated the situation. Feeling safe during this time, Claus, Anna, and John arrived in Hawai'i on April 18, 1893, to see if they could facilitate the reestablishment of the monarchy. Claus attempted to gather support for the queen's restoration from fellow plantation owners and convince them that backing down from the coup d'état would be in their best financial interest—that if the islands were American, there would be a big labor problem for the plantations (that is, the Chinese Exclusion Act of 1882, which restricted Chinese immigration to the United States, would apply to Hawai'i, which had relied on Chinese labor for decades)—but he was rebuffed just as William Irwin had been in his own attempts.[32] In fact, he was told the Provisional Government they had installed was now appealing to Washington for Hawai'i to be fully annexed by the United States. Some planters only supported annexation for fear of financial repercussions by the Provisional Government if they didn't.

Claus Spreckels & Company Bank, located in the heart of Honolulu, had become an important institution over its eight years of operation.[33] The bank had elevated Hawai'i's status and had connected the islands with international financial markets throughout the world. Before the queen's overthrow, the Spreckels bank had been making extensive loans to those who were now members of the Provisional Government of Hawai'i. Lili'uokalani's diary entry on May 29, 1893, and more like this illustrate she believed Claus would be the means to restore her to the throne: "Claus Spreckels called at quarter to 12 noon . . . says that when he draws money from them they will fall to pieces."[34] Claus told the dethroned queen on May 29, 1893, that he'd embarrass her enemies, demand immediate and full repayment, and thereby put an end to their so-called government. To Claus's surprise and disgust, though, the usurpers somehow raised $95,000 to satisfy the loans. Members of the Spreckels family then vigorously used every method of public communication at their disposal—chiefly the *Pacific Advertiser* in Honolulu and their *San Francisco Call*—to struggle against the usurpers' Provisional Government and to support the restoration of Queen Lili'uokalani.

An Unhappy Birthday

Ever nervous of its day-to-day legitimacy, let alone its long-term prospects, the Provisional Government had to get rid of the queen's most powerful supporter, the leading royalist, Claus Spreckels. On the morning of July 9, 1893, which happened to be Claus's sixty-fifth birthday, a death threat was attached to the Spreckels mansion's gate.[35] It was a placard with an explicit threat of assassination. Above the skull and crossbones was a scrawled message in red ink to clearly stimulate blood, which read: "Gold and Silver will not stop lead!!!" Below the warning was a crude sketch of a coffin, daggers, and bullets. This was frightening enough for Claus to demand round-the-clock police protection while his family boarded up the mansion and planned their exit. Ironically, it was the chief of the police himself, Harry A. Juen, who placed the placard, a concession he agreed to after refusing to take part in dynamiting the Spreckels mansion at the suggestion of another police officer loyal to the Provisional Government.[36]

Ten days later, Claus, Anna, and Emma made their way to the harbor, still under police protection, to board the *Australia*. The *Hawaiian Star*, the voice of the annexationists, parodied the departure: "Ex-King Claus was the cynosure of all eyes. He paraded the deck absolutely embowered in leis and wreaths, his head rising amid the expanse of roses and posies like a pumpkin in a big flower patch."[37] The Royal Hawaiian Band played from the wharf, and Claus ordered champagne to be delivered to the crowd, mainly comprising those loyal to the Hawaiian monarchy who were grateful to have had the support of the Spreckels family. Behind the beaming smile of that family, though, there was nothing but heartbreak at the turn of events.

With the overthrow of the queen came disillusionment and uncertainty in the islands, and Claus wondered if he would ever return. A later attempt to restore Lili'uokalani to her throne ended horribly with the mass arrests of royalists. Claus offered a million dollars to the cause, and it had been whispered that John had looked the other way when the queen's supporters surreptitiously transported guns and ammunition on a Spreckels ship to

19. Praise in Hawai'i for Claus Spreckels for his loyal support of the monarchy and for being the greatest entrepreneur to have ever landed on Hawai'i's shores. The profusion of fragrant long leis draped over the Spreckels family conveyed a great amount of affection, admiration, and respect (ca. 1904). Courtesy of Terrence and Virginia Wilson private collection.

support the royalists in Hawai'i.[38] The Spreckels family was publicly implicated by Hawai'i's former minister of foreign affairs John Adams Cummins, who after being arrested for conspiracy, confessed that he had a letter from the queen telling his aide to go to San Francisco, where he'd be furnished funds by Rudolph Spreckels with which to purchase "248 Winchester carbines, 80 revolvers and thousands of rounds of ammunition."[39] The press implied that Rudolph should be arrested for conspiracy, but in the end, nothing happened.

Lili'uokalani was charged with treason and imprisoned in a wing on the second floor of 'Iolani Palace. The entire Spreckels family, while fractured within the fold, were united in respect for the Hawaiian monarchy and told Lili'uokalani to "fight it" to the end and assured her of their financial assistance.[40] Claus assured her that he'd help pick a loyal cabinet should she be restored.

Both sides waited expectantly until July 17, when Mr. Blount delivered his report to President Cleveland, condemning the actions of the Americans who overthrew the monarchy. Given his power to reverse any of the acts of the American military officers respecting the coup, he ordered Captain Wiltse of the USS *Boston*, "You are directed to haul down the United States' ensign from the Government building, and to embark the troops now on shore." Lilla Appleton recorded the annexationists' shock when the Hawaiian flag was rehoisted: "Everybody was surprised, native and foreigners, when a few days after [Blount's] arrival the Stars and Stripes were silently lowered from the capital building [*sic*] and the Hawaiian flag was silently raised in its place. Could Cleveland have heard the private howl which went up from many a throat."[41]

Sanford Dole, who declared himself president of the newly proclaimed republic of Hawai'i, had to respond to the demand of President Cleveland to return the government back to Queen Lili'uokalani, abolish his republic, and restore the monarchy. Dole brazenly declined to abdicate and told the president of the United States that he now had no right to interfere in Hawaiian matters.

Hawai'i's newly empowered regime was considering retaliation against Claus for "meddling with Hawaiian politics" by "confiscating his property."[42] Hearing the threats from credible sources, Claus quickly transferred his holdings for safe keeping under the names of his youngest children in July of 1893. Five thousand shares of Pa'auhau Plantation stock was put under Rudolph's name and his entire Honolulu real estate under Emma's name, a move he'd sorely regret.

Beaten by Gus

Heretofore, Rudolph had stayed out of the family disputes, even though Gus, in his belief, had been wrongly accused by Adolph of embezzling money from the company in the sale of the Philadelphia refinery. But when his father and brothers "stole" Gus's nine hundred shares in Hawaiian Commercial &

Sugar Company, this propelled him, at twenty-two, to finally choose his side in the out-of-control family war, and he stood with Gus.[43]

Many other shareholders threatened legal action after losing their stocks in Hawaiian Commercial & Sugar Company but never followed through. But a Spreckels goes after what belongs to a Spreckels, and Gus filed suit in December 1893 and asked for "transfer of these shares to his name, an injunction to avoid foreclosure by the bondholders, and punitive damages of $2,500,000."[44] He then shrewdly asked a stockholder of record, Horace M. Wooley, to join the lawsuit, claiming "stockholders were defrauded of a large sum of money."[45] Gus needed Wooley, who "by virtue of this position had the right to demand inspection of the company's books."[46] He was confident of a good outcome, knowing his father's activities for the past ten years could be viewed negatively—including, Gus alleged, keeping "$500,000 worth of sugar off the market, to make the company seem poorer than it was."[47]

The public geared up for a sensational trial, but instead, an out-of-court settlement, a "secret agreement of compromise," was reached with no details forthcoming to the public.[48] Whether or not Claus simply ran out of steam or didn't want his company's book scrutinized is unknown, but the case settled in just six weeks, and on January 6, 1894, Gus gained control of the Hawaiian Commercial & Sugar Company and the Spreckelsville Plantation. To further infuriate his father, Rudolph was named as the director.[49] Anna was inconsolable at the turn of events.

Rudolph sailed to Hawai'i for a firsthand look at the operations at the Spreckelsville Plantation and saw "neglect, mismanagement, extravagance and stealing." He quickly attributed the financial losses to the absence of John and Adolph's oversight, which had been turned over to them by their preoccupied father.[50] Rudolph and Gus believed that a bit of modernization and some belt-tightening could turn operations around because Spreckelsville was still the crown jewel amongst Hawai'i's plantations. And to their delight, a few months after beating their father out of Spreckelsville, a Democratic Congress replaced the McKinley bill with the Wilson–Gorman Tariff Act in 1894, which lowered tariff rates and instantly put fresh capital in their pockets.

Emboldened, Gus sought his revenge in another area of the family business: the Oceanic Steamship Company. Gus appeared at the annual stockholders meeting in January 1895 with some aggressive demands that were rebuffed by the company's president, his brother John. Upset by the rebuff, Gus filed a legal action three months later, a writ of mandamus, which would have enabled him to inspect the Oceanic records in a forced stockholders meeting had the judge not ruled in John's favor. John was thoroughly outraged at Gus's attempts to "vex and harass the other stockholders."[51]

Probably to protect their father's emotional state of mind, John and Adolph didn't tell Claus about Gus's provocative actions within the inner sanctums of the Oceanic Steamship Company. But a newspaper reporter inadvertently dropped the bombshell during a casual interview with Claus on the streets of San Francisco. Caught unawares, the family patriarch couldn't contain his anger toward the "family villain":

> I never whipped him in my life, but I feel like going out and cowhiding him now. This is a piece of blackmail—that is what it is. He is trying to force himself upon us in that company when he knows we do not want him there. That boy cannot bulldoze me that way. He and his younger brother are trying to beat me out of millions of dollars, but they will never do it.[52]

He then barked at the reporter: "I will show the people how those boys will die in the gutter and why they ought to."[53] This last published comment regarding his "death in the gutter" drove Gus to sue his father on April 5, 1895, for slander, claiming that his "reputation and prospects" were damaged over the false accusations of embezzlement. To make the point that it was not money he was after but an opportunity "to clear himself of the charges," he asked for only three hundred dollars.[54]

The family's dissension was blazoned through the public courts, and family members aligned themselves on opposite sides—John and Adolph sided with their father, Gus and Rudolph sided with each other, and Anna was distraught in the middle. The trials and tribulations of the wealthy Spreckels family were a veritable soap opera, and the press followed their every legal move with great fervor: "The Spreckels family is not popular. The Spreckelses fight. They fight hard. But they don't fight together. They are not a unit. The family fights inside as well as out, and not all the members speak to one another. They differ among themselves in character, tastes, methods, purposes and, apparently, morals. All they all seem to have in common is a certain aggressive independence."[55]

When Claus's deposition took place, he and John were seated across the table from Gus and Rudolph. The tense scene was vividly described in the *Chronicle* under the headline "Claus Spreckels Declined to Answer." It was noted the "uncooperative" Claus literally created a smokescreen; whether it was sabotage or nerves or both, he lit up cigar after cigar, creating billowing "clouds of smoke" throughout the courtroom while refusing to answer "hundreds of questions" from Gus's coughing attorney.[56]

As the legal probing continued, Claus watched Rudolph whisper something into the attorney's ear, which prompted him to turn and ask Claus, "[Was it] not fact [that] one day on the deck of the steamer during a voyage to Hawaii you told your son Rudolph that your goal was to 'squeeze out' your shareholders?" Stunned at his son's disloyalty, Claus's eyes "misted with tears."[57] The tears then moved to an emotional spectacle, which one observer never forgot:

> His face became livid with rage. From head to foot, he quivered. Surely that old man presented a pitiable spectacle. Finally, after a great effort, he recovered himself to struggle to his feet. Then clutching the back of his cha[i]r to steady himself he glowered at Rudolph shaking his pointed finger at him all the while like an unfortunate suffering from palsy. He tried to talk, but his emotion overpowered his efforts. His mouth opened and shut but no sound came from those bloodless, quivering lips.[58]

While the spectator waited for a "pistol shot to bring the affair to a finish," Claus found his voice: "You ingrate! You unworthy son! You are worse than an ingrate! I disown you. I don't want to have anything to do with you, you who would lie about your own father."[59] After this outburst, Claus fell back in his chair, shook violently, and then closed his eyes as if dead, prompting his attorney Samuel Morgan Shortridge to run across the street for a shot of brandy, which quickly revived Claus.

During the day's questioning, Gus's attorney was able to produce the startling evidence the "missing" $250,000 allegedly embezzled by Gus had actually been "used to pay a draft drawn by Adolph Spreckels."[60] The revelation that Adolph had not shown this report to his father and had apparently created a smokescreen of his own might have influenced the next surprising move: instead of showing up for a second hearing, Claus accepted the judgment of slander, paid Gus the $300 in damages ($10,100 in today's money), and left for a health sanitarium in Europe. He had a lot to think about on that trip, particularly about how Adolph, by accusing Gus of embezzlement, might have deflected attention from his own misappropriation of funds.

Beaten by Rudolph

After the slander lawsuit was settled, Claus, still bitter, left instructions with his attorneys to retaliate against Rudolph for his defection with the single-minded purpose of getting the Pa'auhau Plantation stocks returned. The five thousand shares of stock worth $500,000 had been yielding about $60,000 per year in income for Rudolph, and Claus felt the ingrate didn't deserve any more.[61] In 1891 California had passed the first of its laws that would give a wife some control in the disposition of a couple's community property. Prior to this, the husband was considered the legal owner of the marital property. Claus and his lawyers appealed to that statute, using his wife's legal rights as a guise. His lawyers argued the value of the stocks gifted to Rudolph must be returned because Anna hadn't consented to the action back in 1893. Everyone who knew Claus knew Anna was never consulted on anything of this nature, but they considered this was a legal wrangling that might work.

That argument failed in court, however, because the written-consent statute couldn't be applied retroactively to community property.[62] The court ruled the gift was valid and Rudolph could keep the stocks. After his loss, Claus's bitterness almost sounded like pride in a later interview: "I was only beaten once and it was by my own boy."[63] John used the *San Francisco Call* to denounce the California Supreme Court's decision with the following headline: "Wives Declared to Have No Right in Community Property."[64] The family's archenemy, the *Chronicle*, spun the story differently: "Rudolph Spreckels Defeats His Father!"[65]

Claus, brokenhearted, with no other male heirs in sight, began turning over $26 million in cash, property, and securities ($876 million in today's money) to his eldest sons. Although Claus retreated from Hawai'i in 1894, John and Adolph continued to manage plantations (Kilauea Sugar Co., Hutchinson Sugar Co., and Pa'auhau Plantation Co.) interests and the Oceanic Steamship Company through J. D. Spreckels & Brothers under the direction of William Irwin, who had proved his loyalty and friendship to the Spreckels family in a multitude of ways. With that huge gift of money, Claus, in his seventh decade of life, fully expected his eldest sons to pick up the slack in his various businesses so he could focus on his passion, developing the sugar industry for California, while he still had time.

Losing Spreckelsville

Gus and Rudolph weren't able to gloat for too long over their victory at outmaneuvering their father out of Spreckelsville, because they were soon to get payback. Prominent planters in Hawai'i knew full well the underlying worth of the plantation and were determined to bring it under their control. Missionary sons James Castle, Samuel Alexander, and Henry Baldwin worked covertly with a minority stockholder to buy stock to successfully accomplish their mission in 1898. Gus and Rudolph were summarily thrown out of the company and thus began the move by the missionary descendants, out from under the monarchy they overthrew, to control the sugar business in Hawai'i and begin their own formidable reign. Even though they had been outwitted and forced to sell, Gus and Rudolph walked away with a hefty profit of $2 million in 1898 ($68 million in today's money). And just like that, Claus's magnificent Spreckelsville Plantation slipped away from its namesake family, and Claus was further heartbroken.

It seemed the feuding would never die. Even though the press said that wealth itself was stoking the family's highly publicized feuds, those who knew the family said that pride more than money was the real motivation. Thus, the final accounting from his sugar war in Philadelphia: gained, millions of dollars; lost, two sons and, later, a daughter.

14 The Divided House of Spreckels in Pacific Heights

That "necessity is the mother of invention" was never put to better illustration than in the development of the cable car system to crisscross San Francisco's hills in the late 1870s. Cable cars enabled those with the means, such as the Spreckels family, to move up and get away from the congestion of the working-class neighborhoods. Soon, a previously inaccessible hilly area with magnificent vistas of the sparkling bay transformed into Pacific Heights. More than a third of the families listed in *Our Society Blue Book*, a compilation of California's "people of social standing" with great wealth and power, had moved up to the Heights toward the end of the nineteenth century.[1] Magnificent mansions began popping up like storybook castles on the Heights, but Claus was content to remain below on his beloved Howard Street, where he could stroll up and down the street, cigar in hand, waving to his neighbors, who were also his extended family and employees.

But with the financial success of his Western Beet Sugar Company in Watsonville, Claus, with urging by John, Adolph, and Anna, decided that it was their time to move up to the new money district alongside other millionaire merchants and manufacturers. A move up to the Heights, however, meant for Claus a move away from the familiarity of his German way of life, which he had almost single-handedly built for himself in the South of Market and Mission area. St. Markus Kirche, the largest German church in California, had been within walking distance and had been providing most of the social activity he required. A proud Lutheran, he donated a Schoenstein organ and chandelier to "St. Marks." So, with great sentiment, he decided to not completely do away with their community roots; he would move to Pacific

Heights, but he'd also keep their home on Howard Street, a decision that would soon prove to be a good one.

In 1896 Claus and Anna acquired a choice lot on Van Ness Avenue and Clay Street to build conspicuously. The avenue had been named after San Francisco's seventh mayor, James Van Ness, and was one of the widest in its day. The rows of stately eucalyptus trees on either side of the unpaved avenue completed the picture of wealth and beauty. Every house had one or two ornate iron hitching posts in front for visitors.[2]

Claus hired the Reid brothers, celebrated for their whimsical architectural design of the Hotel del Coronado. The plans dictated a three-story, head-turning mansion that when built, for a rumored $6 million ($202 million in today's money), would be one of the most expensive private California homes of its time. Its design resembled the German hunting lodges and summer residences that were in fashion during the era of Kaiser Wilhelm II. Built from brownstone mined in Connecticut, the mansion was unique and would simply be referred to as "the Brownstone."

When asked what the residence would ultimately cost, Claus shrugged his shoulders. "I told the ladies [Anna and Emma] to spend as much money as they wanted to on the shanty." For a man who loved the outdoors, one item of importance was "fresh air every ten minutes," and to that end Claus worked with the builder to arrange the house in such a way as to have proper ventilation. The second was for the house to be "thoroughly fire-proof."[3]

In their nod to their love for Hawai'i, Claus and Anna had the library walls paneled in rare Hawaiian woods.[4] Anna and Emma ("the ladies") did spend as much as their hearts desired on the new mansion: the marble in one hall alone cost over $100,000 ($3.4 million in today's money).[5] Unheard-of luxuries were found in their stone mansion, including forced-air heating and cooling and indoor plumbing for the fourteen bathrooms. One of those bathrooms, attached to Emma's suites, cost a staggering $10,000 ($340,000 in today's money), because nothing was too good for daddy's darling girl. "The faucets are all of solid gold, and so is the piping for the shower and needle stream."[6]

When completed, the mansion rivaled in its opulence those of J. P. Morgan, John D. Rockefeller, and Andrew Carnegie. In 1897 the *San Francisco Call* gushed over the magnificence of the new mansion for a public who would never see the interior:

20. Emma Claudine Spreckels (1870–1924). Nothing was too good for Emma, the apple of her father's eyes. Courtesy of Terrence and Virginia Wilson private collection.

21. The Brownstone on Van Ness. The head-turning mansion, resembling a German hunting lodge, was one of the most expensive California homes of its time. Courtesy of Terrence and Virginia Wilson private collection.

[It is] floored with mosaics, wainscoted with Algerian marble, whose decorated panels show the luxury of the art of the Renaissance; the walls covered with priceless tapestries from the looms of France, and divided by columns of polished marble; surrounded at the second floor by a balcony railed by red marble and paved with mosaic, curving on each side into projecting alcoves overlooking the floor below; the noble hall rises through two floors to the height of thirty-four feet, and is roofed with art glass through which the light streams soft and mellow as the beams of a summer moon when all the sky is cloudless.[7]

If Claus worried about feeling isolated, he needn't have been, because members of the Mangels side of the family also moved up, as did John, Lillian, and their children, Grace, Lillie, Jack, and Claus Jr.—right around the corner to an ostentatious Italian Renaissance mansion. Like Claus, John didn't believe his daughters should attend college, but he was a thoroughgoing progressive when it came to preparing his daughters to be self-reliant in the real world. John had seen how his father had doted on his sister, Emma, who had little outside interests, and wanted more for his own daughters. He purposefully gave them a broader perspective than most females of their time had. He encouraged them to do everything their brothers did, including owning and driving cars.[8]

The Heartbreaking Elopement

On one occasion, Claus sent Emma with a bevy of servants to attend to her needs on a volcano excursion. After many days on the island of Hawaiʻi with Emma, Iretta Hight, a young American teaching in Honolulu, wrote in her diary that she felt sorry for the twenty-year-old Spreckels daughter, for despite her wealth, Emma seemed to have low self-esteem: "Miss Emma impressed me as being a girl of good sense and kind heart lacking only some strong and true friend to lead her out. It sounds egotistical to say that I pitied her but such was the fact. She has so little within herself that she is wholly dependent upon others for her happiness."[9]

Without an outlet for any meaningful exercise, except for the occasional horse riding while in Aptos, and with such a rich diet, she, like her mother, had become overweight. In addition, her looks were unremarkable compared to the beautiful and stylish women that attracted all four of her wealthy brothers. She was painfully conscious of her failure to meet society's beauty standards and perhaps believed that handsome gentlemen of her own age were off limits, considering her plain appearance an obstacle. But her father didn't share her opinions. For Claus, nothing was too good for his Emma, and he reserved all his fatherly affection for her. Among the prime parcels of real estate he owned on Market Street in downtown San Francisco, he built an ornate office structure in 1895 and, to no one's surprise, named it the Emma Spreckels Building.

Claus always looked disdainfully at San Francisco's socialites who, in a display of untrammeled wealth, strolled through the city's streets with nowhere to go. They just wanted to be seen. To that end, Emma didn't participate in a pompous debutante ball when she came of age—her nonparticipation was unheard of, considering the Spreckels wealth. Around the country, however, the reformer Mary Livermore was urging parents to "train their daughters for self-support because their chances of getting a good husband were dwindling."[10] Claus was keenly aware of the changing times. The four-year Civil War had cost an estimated 620,000 men their lives, creating more "spinsters" in Emma's generation than any other in American history.[11] She didn't have to worry, however, because her wealth alone assured marriage, and with the ostentatious mansion in Pacific Heights under construction, wealthy eligible men were on notice that she had her own money.

Regardless, Emma's lack of social life was uncommon for a young lady of her standing; her life mainly consisted of mingling with the Mangels cousins. With so many marrying around her, thoughts of finding a love match was never far from her mind. But her thoughts were not of finding a Prince Charming but rather finding companionship with the right man, since she didn't need to worry about financial security. She was looking for someone who would be kind and treat her well with love and respect. And she soon found whom she was looking for, right under the nose of her oblivious father.

Christmas 1896 in the Howard Street home was difficult for everyone. It should have been a sentimental time, since they would be moving up to the Brownstone in Pacific Heights, but the holiday was overshadowed by sadness. The very mention of Gus and Rudolph or their families was forbidden at all times. But it was especially difficult for Emma, who was keeping a big secret. She was planning to elope with her father's card-playing friend after her parents left for Aptos to celebrate a quiet New Year's Eve. Her chosen groom was Thomas "Tom" Palmer Watson, a divorced man more than twice her age at fifty-five, born and raised in England. Tall and thin with salt-and-pepper hair, a receding hairline, and a long muttonchop beard, he was not especially handsome. A grain broker of some significance, Tom had been in and out of the Spreckels house to play poker. Somehow, he and Emma had developed a clandestine relationship, even under the hawk eyes of Claus.

Emma had never before done anything sufficiently imprudent to incur the wrath of her father, but on Wednesday, December 30, with no family to spy upon her, Emma dressed in a fur-collared, blue tailored suit and quickly walked down the stairs to meet her groom. After Tom put Emma's small hand satchel on the back of the carriage, they sped away toward the train station to board a car for the sixty-mile trip south to San Jose. At the Santa Clara County clerk's office, officials had lots of questions, since Tom was English and previously married. Once the questions were satisfied and a license secured, Emma and Tom walked over to Trinity Episcopal Church, where Reverend John B. Wakefield married them in the vestry, with his daughter as witness, as previously arranged by Tom. All involved vowed to keep their marriage secret until "it was a matter of public record."[12]

For three days the Watsons enjoyed each other's company at San Jose's exquisite Hotel Vendome, set on thirteen beautifully landscaped acres. With great reluctance, they returned to San Francisco because it was time to face the music: Claus and Anna were back on Howard Street. Emma checked into the handsome California Hotel and began to plan the best way to present to her father the news of her marriage. It's unclear how the news was ultimately given, but it was met with expected hostility. Through clenched teeth, Claus told Emma that not only was Tom after the Spreckels fortune but he could easily make her a widow before her own mother.

The romantic marriage of a rich girl to a comparatively poor man caused a stir of great magnitude in the San Francisco gossip circles. The press sardonically congratulated Tom on his marriage and good fortune because Emma, not quite twenty-seven years old, was worth millions and would be an heiress to even more upon the death of her father.[13] Indignant from the gold-digging insinuation, Tom arranged for his new bride to sit for an interview with the *Examiner* to give her side of the story:

Mr. Watson and I have known each other for over ten years, and we thought enough of each other to become united in marriage. . . . If we are satisfied, I cannot understand why other people should not be. It is a matter with which the public has no concern. We would have been pleased beyond measure to have been able to come back to San Francisco quietly and in a manner to ward off notoriety, but it seems we are not to enjoy that pleasure. Papa and my brothers are too sensible not to look at the situation the way I do [and] I am confident they will applaud my course.[14]

No applause from Claus would ever be forthcoming over this "love match." Not only did his "ungrateful" daughter marry without his consent, but she had also married, in his view, an "elderly fortune hunter," putting his hard-earned wealth at risk.[15]

To prove to her father that Tom had married her only for love, Emma immediately quitclaimed her expensive Honolulu real estate and an endowment worth $1.5 million ($50.5 million in today's money) that had been given to her by her once-doting father.[16] She retained, however, possession of the gorgeous Emma Spreckels Building her father built for her in downtown San Francisco. Not knowing what else to do and overcome by his feelings of betrayal and rejection, Claus vowed never to see his daughter again, and Emma made it easy by moving to Lower Kingsford, England.

Claus did what he typically did in times of grief: immerse himself in work. Anna, however, stayed behind closed doors, immobilized by the painful turn of events. One gossip columnist reported that it was "Mrs. Spreckels's habit to sit at a window hoping that her daughter would someday look in her direction."[17]

The Family Expanding

After living through the betrayal and bitterness of his sister's situation, John saw the importance of ensuring that his daughters were properly presented to society. The debutante ball of 1899, showcasing San Francisco's most elite young ladies, was an extravagant event: "The Spreckels, though exceedingly rich people, paid little attention to fashionable society before the debut of the two daughters. The transformation of young and bashful debutantes into ladies of fashion does not take long, and by the time the palatial home of the Spreckels on Pacific Avenue was completed, there were no smarter debutantes in town than Miss Grace and Miss Lillie."[18]

Society pages speculated on who might be worthy enough to enter the Spreckels family and become John Spreckels's sons-in-law. While the gossiping wags chewed on this question, however, the debutantes' college-student brother was able to keep a budding romance secret. Society was stunned when it was neither Grace nor Lillie who married first; it would be their younger brother, John Jr. "Jack," who was not quite twenty-one and the apple of his grandparents' eyes.

Claus and Anna's grandson Jack Spreckels—handsome, tall, fair-haired, blue-eyed Jack—had arrived at Stanford as a millionaire's son with a hefty allowance. *The Wasp*, a widely read satirical weekly, noted that Jack didn't have "the heavy Spreckels beauty of his sisters, but rather the delicate beauty of his mother [and] if he were a girl he would be decidedly pretty."[19] Whether he was "handsome" or "pretty," girls were quite impressed with the heir to the Spreckels fortune. But the one who captured his heart was Edith Marie Huntington, the grandniece of the wealthy and famous Collis P. Huntington, one of the "Big Four" who had invested in the Central Pacific Railroad as part of the first U.S. transcontinental line.

During his second year at Stanford, Jack announced his intent to marry eighteen-year-old Edith. When this broadcast, society pages pointed out that even though all the sons of Claus Spreckels married poor girls, his grandchildren must marry into money because of John's fear "that his children [would] be married for money"—that is, they should marry into the same social class to prevent being taken advantage of.[20] The press speculated that Edith, heir to the vast Huntington fortune, earned full approval on this fact alone. After the honeymoon, Jack and Edith also set up housekeeping in another Pacific Heights mansion built by John. One day short of nine months, Edith gave birth to Claus and Anna's first great-grandchild, Marie Spreckels.[21]

Claus and Anna's granddaughter Lillie beat her older sister, Grace, to the altar when she married the wealthy and popular Henry "Harry" Morgan Holbrook. Gossips wondered what Lillie saw in a man fourteen years older, a known hard drinker and pleasure seeker.[22] But Harry Holbrook, with his place in a wealthy and prominent family as the only son, was good enough for John, and the proposed marriage was viewed as a financial merger rather than as a love match. Their elaborate wedding, with more than four hundred

22. Jack Spreckels, Claus's first grandson, standing between his father, John, and his uncle Adolph. Note the Royal Hawaiian Band with their ukuleles in the background, shipped in for a special Christmas celebration. Courtesy of Terrence and Virginia Wilson private collection.

attendees (mainly Spreckels employees), was covered extensively in the society pages across the country. Papers snobbishly noted the presence of many "common people" at the 1905 wedding while praising the Spreckels family "for their loyalty to old friends and faithful employees." But it seemed as though all eyes were on the seventy-six-year-old Claus, after he broke down crying when Lillie, on the spur of the moment, left the aisle, ran over to her grandfather, and threw her arms around him. Nobody present would ever forget the touching scene when "the old gentleman [became] much affected by the tenderness of his grandchild."[23]

As a wedding gift, John, to keep his expanding family near him in Pacific Heights, presented them with "one of the handsomest homes on Pacific avenue."[24] Harry preferred life in society more than the home, however, and the mansion became lonely for Lillie until their one and only child, Harriet, was born six years after the wedding. By then, the drinking lifestyle had caught up with Harry, who became sick, and Lillie became his miserable caretaker until she couldn't take it anymore.

Next to the altar was Grace, John and Lillian's firstborn. More than "Daddy's little girl," she was Daddy's buddy. She enjoyed being outdoors and traveled with her father all over the world on his ships and up and down the coast in his cars. *The Wasp* went so far as to say what many were thinking: "Grace is regarded as his favorite child, and naturally anybody aspiring to win her would find the X-ray of parental scrutiny more than usually penetrating."[25]

Apparently, one man withstood John's scrutiny and approval. Alexander "Alec" Hamilton was busy running the large and prosperous Baker & Hamilton hardware store in San Francisco. Grace fell hard for Alec, but the society pages didn't gush over her choice of a man sixteen years older than her: "He is a handsome man of fine physique, though in recent years he has taken on a trifle too much flesh for perfect symmetry. Some 10 or 12 years ago he was as trim and attractive a chap as one can see anywhere."[26]

Grace, who was becoming more and more like her father and grandfather, declared that she wouldn't be "goaded" into having an extravagant wedding like her sister had had. Society papers noted her "aversion" to fussy events.[27] And if that were not enough, Grace refused all the preliminary festivities her contemporaries planned, including the requisite engagement party. The couple had a small and simple ceremony, in the white-and-gold drawing room of her parents' palatial mansion on Pacific Avenue.[28]

Rudolph's Distant Marriage

It was only by reading the *San Francisco Examiner* that Claus and Anna learned their estranged son Rudolph had married a beautiful blue-eyed, petite, but poor socialite, Eleanor "Nellie" D. Jolliffe, on August 5, 1895. Anna likely pored over every detail of the wedding in the society pages. A sketch alongside the story showed that handsome Rudolph now sported a trendy handlebar mustache. When Nellie was asked why she didn't have the large wedding that society expected her to have, she cited the recent "annoyance" of the Spreckels family litigation as a major reason.[29] The heartbreak of missing the wedding of her youngest child must have been unbearable for Anna. Representing the groom's side of the family was Gus as best man, his wife, Oroville, and their ten-year-old daughter, Lurline Elizabeth Spreckels.[30]

Just after they were married, Rudolph and Nellie moved into a Pacific Heights mansion at the northwest corner of Pacific Avenue and Gough Street, which was noted for its dazzling Italian marble. It was just two blocks down from John and Lillian, but there might as well have been hundreds of miles between them because the brothers never acknowledged each other's presence, even when they passed on the road.

The first few years of their marriage were happy and bright. Unlike her estranged in-laws, Nellie Spreckels took full advantage of the fashionable address to host luncheons, teas, and dinners for San Francisco's well-heeled set—until a tragedy curtailed her festiveness: their four-year-old son Rudolph, who had never met his paternal grandparents, died in 1891. According to *Town Talk*, "The boy's death was caused by a sad mishap. He had an ear-ache and his nurse poured what she thought was oil in the ear; but it turned out to be carbolic acid. All that could be done to relieve the little sufferer was tried, and an operation was performed, but it was of no avail."[31] Many stories throughout the years following the death of young Rudolph were along the lines of "the once beautiful Nellie Joliffe is but a shadow of her former brilliant self."[32] Even after Nellie gave birth to Howard (born 1898), Eleanor (1902), and Claudine (1906), photos of her reveal a perpetual sadness.[33]

Adolph, Out of the Fray at the Palace Hotel

With no marriage plans in sight, the freewheeling bachelor Adolph was now going by "Dolph" to the ladies and close friends, and by "A.B." to his colleagues.[34] Adolph took up his private residence in the Palace Hotel, built in 1875 at the corner of Market and New Montgomery Streets. Seven stories high, it was San Francisco's first luxury hotel and was the largest in the world, covering an entire block and able to accommodate 1,200 guests.[35] Hotel life, a common option for single men, offered a gregarious existence not possible in the home of Claus Spreckels. Surrounded by opulence, dozens of California's prominent families resided in the suites on the top floors of the Palace, including the family of Leland Stanford, ex-governor of California. The saloon of the Palace concentrated local political and business life, and all topics spoken over gin and whiskey were off the public record. The Palace had been built for a crowd, and Adolph's bachelor life was spectacularly and notoriously public. The hotel's unprecedented luxury quickly made it a popular social gathering for the rich and famous, the world's most influential individuals, many of whom recognized Adolph—not for Spreckels sugar but for horses.

The ownership of magnificent champion horses provided a step up in the social strata for Adolph, a step apart from his brother and the rest of his family. As other family members were moving up to Pacific Heights, Adolph bought a large parcel of land in Napa, a gateway to the lush agricultural valley northeast of San Francisco. With no expense spared, his five-hundred-acre Napa Stock Farm became a sportsman's paradise. John became the silent partner in the horse breeding and racing operation, leaving the development and management as a thoroughbred breeding operation to his brother, just as Adolph did for John's development of San Diego.

Adolph was more easygoing and laid back than his father and brothers, but even so, he was "inflexible as destiny" and "more than willing to settle any matter with his fists if required."[36] Once he had discovered his passion in the horse business, he demonstrated the same entrepreneurial and managerial acumen that his father and brothers were known for. Adolph earnestly produced fine racing stock and sent his horses to the country's major tracks, where they won races. Morvich, a crippled colt Adolph bred and regrettably sold, went on to become the first California-bred Kentucky Derby winner. After Adolph was recognized for his equestrian accomplishments, he was asked to serve as San Francisco park commissioner. The city leaders were happy he stayed on through three terms because he energetically helped develop Golden Gate Park into a masterpiece.

For Adolph, the swanky Poodle Dog Restaurant was his favorite retreat from high-pressured business. While the bottom floor was a respectable place for a married couple to partake in an elegant French dinner, the second floor had private dining rooms suitable for secret dinners with the opposite sex. On the third, fourth, and fifth floors were "cozy rooms for private assignations only whispered about." The Poodle Dog's elevator operator for floors three through five became rich on the tips provided "for service."[37] The operator might have been getting paid from both sides, because the *Chronicle* often made racy jokes about the Poodle Dog Restaurant and the indecencies that took place in the private rooms upstairs involving certain patrons. While Anna and Claus worried about Adolph's free-for-all bachelor lifestyle, John knew his brother's deep dark secret: he was living with an incurable sexually transmitted disease—syphilis.[38]

CLAUS SPRECKELS BUILDING

23. The Claus Spreckels Building, interchangeably known as the Call Building, was, when completed in 1897, the tallest building west of Chicago. It became the most recognizable San Francisco landmark. Courtesy of Adolph Rosecrans.

The Claus Spreckels Skyscraper

As Claus aged, he saw San Francisco grow the way he had hoped it would and began investing in real estate. John was supervising the creation of what would be a San Francisco landmark ensuring the name Spreckels would never be forgotten: a skyscraper as the new headquarters for the *San Francisco Call*. Claus had bought the *Morning Call* from the publisher of the *San Jose Mercury News,* Charles Morris Shortridge, the brother of John's best friend, who had recently purchased it when it went on the auction block in 1895. Behind the scenes, many believed that Shortridge, in a secret handshake, had bid on the paper using Spreckels money to keep the price in check. Once the purchase was complete, the paper then "sold" to the Spreckels family two years later at a reasonable price.

John officially took over the *Morning Call* in 1897 and renamed it the *San Francisco Call*. It then became known as a "feisty, in-your-face newspaper."[39] Henry James, a former columnist, described his years working under John as a "pleasing memory." He recalled the news staff became fiercely loyal to the man who paid them well and greeted everyone by name, as his father had taught him, with a "hearty handclasp."[40]

The new "Call Building," interchangeably known as the "Claus Spreckels Building" and, curiously, sometimes the "John. D. Spreckels Building," was built to house the *San Francisco Call*. The tall, 75-foot, narrow tower, topped by a baroque terra cotta dome stood at the intersection of the city's two main traffic arteries, Market and Third. James and Merritt Reid designed the building, giving extra attention to the eighteenth floor, where they would house their architectural offices. The nationally recognized bridge engineer Charles Strobe, inventor of the Z-bar structural design, ensured the building would withstand any natural disaster. The 310-foot-high steel-frame structure was, when completed in 1897, the tallest building west of Chicago, and it became the most recognizable San Francisco landmark. With its nineteen stories, it towered "majestically" over the neighboring ten-story building that housed its newspaper rival, a fact the *Call* repeatedly reported, to the chagrin of the *Chronicle*'s publisher, Michael de Young.

The *Call* extensively informed the public on every aspect of the building's progress, a reporting that was an unprecedented type of self-marketing in the city's history. Finally, on a day that readers thought would never come, the

Call asked San Franciscans to step outside their homes at dusk on December 17, 1897, to witness and celebrate a new Spreckels accomplishment, a "spectacular light show":

> As darkness fell the crowd outside grew quiet until, as if by magic, all the lights in the building were turned on simultaneously—from the basement to the lantern on the dome—and "the whole vast pile suddenly shone forth in a blaze of glory." Hundreds of people stood along Market Street or on the hills and rooftops of San Francisco to witness the spectacle. Hundreds, possibly thousands more lined the shores of the East Bay from San Pablo to what was then Hayward.[41]

Because electricity was still a novelty, the show was the most talked-about spectacle for some time and was considered to be "one of the sights of a lifetime."[42]

The most prominent men of the time pulled out of existing leases to secure office space at the Call Building and didn't mind paying a premium just to have their business cards display the prestigious address. It was an instant sensation with the public, who often ascended to the fifteenth-floor café, the Spreckels Rotisserie, known for elegant French cuisine "in the clouds." The restaurant was one of the first of its kind, and San Franciscans reveled in the panoramic view of their burgeoning city. The skyscraper became iconic the moment it was finished and was prominently featured in most postcards of the city.

The mosaic floor of the marble, domed lobby bore a circular motif bearing the monogram "C.S.," which was replicated on every doorknob throughout the building. At the top of the tower, accessed by an elevator that ascended to it in less than a minute, were the luxurious offices of J. D. Spreckels and Brothers. Claus was proud that John was becoming so well-known across the country and had the distinction of being profiled at the time of the building's construction as one of "America's successful men of affairs." The *New York Tribune*, named a long list of John's various business interests: "Such diversified interests would crush a man of ordinary talents, but Mr. Spreckels manages them all with admirable ease, coolness, skill and judgment."[43] John might have looked like he was easily handling both his and his father's interests with ease, but his health was on the wane. If the family hadn't fractured, he would've been relieved of much of the responsibilities that were now placed on his shoulders. "Damn Gus" was his familiar refrain.

Gus as a Rival

Gus, acting exactly as his father would have, used the proceeds from the sale of Hawaiian Commercial & Sugar to build a refinery in 1902 to rival Claus's operations. The Federal Sugar Refining Company of New York had advanced railroad and shipping facilities and was close to every type of industry. Like his father, he found loyal relatives to employ, including his cousins Walter, the grandson of his father's brother Peter, and Louis, the son of his father's brother Henry. The Federal became the largest and most modern refinery in the country, the only independent sugar refinery enterprise of any importance. Claus consistently declined to comment on Gus's success. While Gus was the principal owner of the company, its public face, and the main decision maker, he and his family spent half of their time either at their mansion on Avenue Foch in Paris or at their villa in on the French Riviera, as far away as he could get from his father and the squabbles in San Francisco.

Loneliness amid Luxury

Although the Spreckelses dominated the wealthy enclave of Pacific Heights, their neighbors knew the high-profile family was divided. Four generations lived in palatial mansions that were the envy of many, but geographic close-ness meant nothing relationally. The Spreckels family was fractured, impaired, and disgruntled, cracks obvious from one generation to the next. Pondering the future of the family, the *Town Talk* said it all:

> As a consequence of the alienation of affections in the Spreckels family the palatial home of the parents in Van Ness avenue is a very lonesome place. It is a large family, three of the sons and one daughter being married, several grandchildren having come into the world, but only a small section of it has the entrée to the big brownstone house in Van Ness avenue. J.D. Spreckels and his brother Adolph have retained the confidence and love of their parents and their business interests are entwined but there is no cordiality between them and their brother or the families of any of them.[44]

When there came about a report that Rudolph in his early thirties was "dangerously sick," just down the street, Anna purportedly begged Claus to let her visit him. But it was reported that Claus was a "good hater" because he "sternly forbade his wife to visit her son" despite his illness.[45] Despite Claus's mandates, it's easy to imagine Anna's secret visits to her youngest child's back door with her arms full of mother's "medicines." Her visits would have to be conducted stealthily because, as one newspaper story aptly reminded the public, "until Claus Spreckels forgives and forgets the house of Spreckels will remain divided."[46]

15   *Large and In Charge*

When Claus landed on the cover of *Harper's Weekly* in 1891, America's number-one illustrated magazine signified the impact that he was having on the country. Accompanying the twelve-by-sixteen-inch sketched portrait of him at age sixty-two was a feature-length story that traced his life from humble beginnings to "sugar king," giving color to his black-and-white image:

> Mr. Spreckels has been aptly called a very young old man. He is of medium height, but is very strongly built, and despite the burden of his years is as active and seemingly as capable of supporting fatigue as a strong man of half his age. In fact, almost the only outward indication of that age is the growing whiteness of his hair and beard. In manner and appearance, he makes little manifestation of that business ability which has carried him through so many years successfully. Perhaps the expression of his eyes is the most characteristic feature of his appearance. They are of a clear blue, and are at once shrewd and searching, but they are so quick in movement that they give the observer a distinct impression of his secretiveness and even of cunning.[1]

Even though Claus looked hale and hearty on the outside as he pushed through his seventh decade, he was dealing with the chronic illness of diabetes, a medical condition that few doctors totally understood. Excessive thirst, fatigue, frequent urination, and weight loss might have been symptoms that would lead to this diagnosis. His family physician, the eminent Dr. Levi Cooper Lane of Cooper Medical College, monitored the condition as best he could and prescribed a "rigid diet." Claus had recently gifted $25,000 ($810,000 in today's money) toward the founding of his doctor's project, Lane Hospital (forerunner to the Stanford University School of Medicine).

24. Claus Spreckels, large and in charge. The immigrant Claus was proud to be illustrated for "Living Makers of American History." Courtesy of the Society of the California Pioneers, CO28761.

Since Claus was a major benefactor, his medical needs were prioritized by Dr. Lane whenever the sugar king slowed down enough for a medical visit. Even with his diabetes, he showed no outward signs of minimizing his business ventures—in fact, just the opposite. Nobody outside selected family members were told of his condition. Claus hated pity. To be pitied would've put him in a humbled and lowly position in business negotiations, so he insisted that his condition be kept secret.[2]

The Spreckels Republican Club

During the final years of the 1890s, a rise in the Republican Party was John's chance to step out from his father's long shadow. In 1893, with the onset of a national economic depression and the resultant repeal of the Sherman Silver Purchase Act, whose unintended consequence had been a severe depletion of the nation's gold reserves, currency issues became more intensely divisive than in years past. As the 1896 presidential election approached, Republicans geared up to retake the White House. The contest largely came down to economic conditions and monetary policy. The Republican candidate was William McKinley, the former congressman who had removed all duty from raw sugar and benefited the domestic cultivation of beet sugar. Candidate McKinley, with the support of the rich eastern establishment, was in favor of a strict gold standard; he believed the "free coinage of silver" (the unlimited coinage of silver on demand) would bring financial ruin to the country. The Democratic candidate, William Jennings Bryan, had developed a reputation as a defender of the working class, especially farmers; he believed that bimetallism, allowing both gold and silver as legal tender (with silver dollars produced at a fixed-weight ratio of sixteen to one against dollar coins made of gold), was necessary for the nation's economic health.

The Spreckels family, in a state where silver mining was prolific, favored the gold standard but wanted the coinage of silver to also be considered, which was necessary in their views for a more equitable economy. John's foray into politics at age forty-two was pitched as a charitable endeavor, but economic issues were actually the catalyst for a western industrialist such as himself. The anticorruption issue—deploring the widespread corruption between San Francisco's prominent businessmen and politicians—was the other moral incentive to get involved.

The Republican Party's state central committee secured John's services as vice-chairman as both an elected delegate at large to the national convention and a member of the national committee from California.[3] John's ascension to the party leadership in California was celebrated by those who hoped that silver would remain legal tender, and as he made plans to leave for the convention, he pompously told his supporters through the *Call*: "We propose to have one final standard, gold, and on that standard, we will circulate the two metals, gold and silver, besides paper money. Could anything be plainer?"[4]

The Republican National Convention in St. Louis, Missouri, in the summer of 1896 was an embarrassment for John, and therefore his father. Behind the scenes, established Republicans had already settled among themselves that a monetary system based on gold alone would be the campaign focus and that any other ideas, especially from a California upstart, would be quickly squelched. Specifically, the wealthy Marcus "Mark" Hanna, McKinley's campaign manager, had promised to uphold the gold standard to the Wall Street crowd and was determined to protect that standard at all costs.[5] Aware of the Spreckels platform of "free silver," he was prepared to meet the "great nerve of the California's leaders" and "force them into line" because it was in direct conflict with his strategy.[6] And he did.

After being formally introduced to Hanna, John brought up his concerns over corruption and patronage in California, believing that he'd have full sympathy. Hanna, however, was not interested in California's problems. Anticipating the topic of silver next, Hanna brusquely silenced John and told him in no uncertain terms to forget about silver because McKinley would be promoting a strict gold standard and then walked away. When the word got out that John had been publicly silenced, the *San Francisco Examiner* was delighted to illustrate his humiliation by showing a contented cigar-smoking tiger (Mark Hanna) after eating a canary (John Spreckels) at the convention.[7]

Back at home, John might have retreated from supporting the party, but he increased his efforts to deliver the state for McKinley even as support for the Republican candidate had sputtered over the monetary issue. The secretary of the National Republican League took steps to remedy this situation; he established Republican clubs throughout California to "organize and educate" their districts. Because John didn't retreat after the public humiliation, they named their club the Spreckels Republican Club.

Backing Opposite Candidates

John was often mentioned for the office of governor or a seat in the U.S. Senate, but he always declined in favor of family and work. The truth was, he was known to be profoundly tongue-tied in front of an audience. He was bold, sagacious, and self-assured until he had to give a speech. John was not reticent or retiring in his political views, but he was more likely to oppose his political rivals with the written word rather than the spoken one. He needed a front man, a master orator.

The man he chose was Samuel Morgan Shortridge, a staunch Republican and Masonic brother, who had become his personal attorney and then close friend. They became too close in the opinion of Claus. And despite Claus's strong objections, John proclaimed he was backing Shortridge for senator during the 1896 campaign. This infuriated Claus who was backing incumbent George Clement Perkins for the same senate seat, and he told anyone who would listen to him, including the press, that he would "call down hard" on his son and demand that he fall in line.[8] John flagrantly disregarded his father's concerns and continued to use his money and the *Call* to promote his friend Sam, who he believed would fight graft and reform "the wild west of his father's generation."[9] Claus insisted that his son was attempting to buy himself a senator and that Shortridge "must have hypnotized him" and would harm John's reputation while feathering his own nest.[10]

Claus had thrived in an age where one man could capitalize on the triumphs of industrial progress and bend the politics of a city or state. In the 1880s he was one of the most powerful men in California and was looking to pass that baton on to his firstborn son. Unfortunately, that son was not cooperating: John was tired of the corruption that was so prevalent in the politics of his father's era. Aligning himself with Shortridge may have been the first time John did anything his father was diametrically opposed to.

In his unabashed support of Shortridge, though, many came to agree with Claus that John was indeed attempting to buy a senator to be his mouthpiece.[11] With false bravado in the *Call*, John assured readers up to the day of the nomination that Shortridge would easily defeat Perkins. This arrogance angered Claus as well as the dozens of the state's politicians firmly behind Perkins, who had served them not only as the fourteenth governor of California but also already in the U.S. Senate. Because Shortridge didn't get a single vote, many newspapers chastised John for backing a candidate who had no legislative experience and never had a chance.[12] Locally, many called John and his newspaper "ridiculous enough to be pathetic."[13] Claus was both angered and deeply embarrassed for his son.

On Board with Levi Strauss

One of Claus's biggest accomplishments in the mid-1890s was the building of the San Francisco and San Joaquin Valley Railroad, a rail line between Stockton and Fresno. Crucial in this accomplishment was the help of his good friend Levi Strauss. Like other founders of West Coast industries, both Claus and Strauss had long nursed a grudge against the monopoly of the Southern Pacific Railroad (the SP). Both born in Germany, Strauss, a faithful Jew, and Claus, a faithful Lutheran, were alike in so many ways. They both had grown up with the city they loved and were still working after a half century to make San Francisco the commercial capital of the West. But the SP, the only link with the rest of the United States, controlled freight rates on such goods as Claus's sugar and Levi Strauss's riveted denim clothing. The rate structure made it impossible for their goods to compete with eastern goods or even with goods out of Southern California.

A decade earlier, a Board of Railway Commissioners had been elected from all regions of the state to regulate freight rates. The board was acclaimed as a giant leap forward in "commerce and common decency," but the triumph was short-lived. It soon became painfully obvious the elect commissioners were easily corrupted by payouts from the SP, and there was never any real headway in reducing the prices. Many a tale was told about the violence that had erupted after San Joaquin Valley farmers learned they had been cheated out of their land by the SP only to watch the SP offer the same land at a higher price to others who would then allow the railroad to lay tracks on their property.[14]

The first successful competition came in 1887 when the Santa Fe Railroad arrived in Los Angeles. This sparked a frenzied rate competition with the Southern Pacific, each side undercutting the other, dropping the price of a $125 ticket from Chicago to Los Angeles down to a "single, solitary dollar." This rate war between the two lines enabled growth never seen before. The population of Los Angeles grew from eleven thousand in 1880 to at least fifty thousand by 1890.[15]

It was clear that San Francisco needed its own Santa Fe, a competing railroad. A group calling themselves the Traffic Association of California, led by the upright educator Isaac Upham, sought out Claus after many failed attempts to get such a railroad off the ground.[16] A meeting on January 22, 1895, was called, and because Claus Spreckels had agreed to attend, there was an air of jubilant expectancy. Not only did Claus have capital, but he also had actual railroad experience and seemed to never fail at anything.

At the meeting, Claus was appointed chairman of the fundraising committee because his participation was predicated on money in hand before beginning any construction. He himself pledged $50,000 to get the Stockton-to-Fresno railroad up and running, with an equal amount pledged on behalf of John and Adolph.[17] Strauss said, "The new railroad is by no means a money-making scheme; it is a necessity," and with that pledged $25,000.[18] In just a couple of weeks, the goal of $5 million ($168 million in today's money) was amazingly over-pledged, raised largely from small California investors, thereby giving the line yet another moniker: the People's Railroad. Claus Spreckels and Levi Strauss—their very names inspired confidence.

The name San Francisco and San Joaquin Valley Railroad was chosen, generally known as the Valley Road. As construction began, Claus released a statement:

> I believe that with new and improved methods of construction, and with the use of new motor power, transportation speed will be immensely increased. Electricity will take the place of steam and a single track will take the place of the present double rails, and whereas 60 miles an hour is now the very limit of speed, 150 miles an hour, and possibly more than that, will be attained with more safety and comfort to the travelers. It may be thought that such a prophecy is chimerical, but assuredly it is no more chimerical at this day than was the telegraph, the telephone, or the steam railway in the days of their infancy.[19]

While Claus was president of the new railroad, John, a major stockholder through his father's pledge on his behalf, would sit on the board of directors so his father could concentrate on the sugar beet industry.

Claus, the Agriculturalist

Americans love their sugar, which required that in 1896, $9 million worth of sugar had to be imported.[20] Not having a reliable large domestic source was a danger to price stability and a problem Claus wanted to solve with his running mantra:

> Wherever I find the farmers sufficiently interested in the subject, if the climate and soil is suitable, I am ready and willing to assist them in developing the industry, not alone by the establishment of factories in their immediate vicinity, but also in the way of assisting them financially in the cultivation of the raw product. In other words, I am willing to back up my faith in beet sugar by all the capital that may be required.[21]

In September 1897, following the July 25 passage of the Dingley Tariff, an article in the *Sacramento Bee* with the headline "May Mean Millions for Our Farmers" caught the attention of struggling farmers up and down the state. The purpose of the tariff was to protect American businesses and industries from foreign competition. Imported products, including sugar (tax rates for sugar doubled!), became more expensive than those made in America. This, said the *Bee*, was the time for California farmers to get in the game of making sugar with beets.

Claus, through the *Bee*, declared that "California surpasses all other states in possessing all of the conditions suitable to the industry of beet cultivation." The time, he told farmers, is now, before other states watching his success in Watsonville beat them. He described how he had already proved California was more than admirably suited to agriculture. The region's variety of soils and climate, including the fact that rainfall is concentrated in one season, made both specialty and diversified farming highly profitable. Sugar beet was also influencing the development of other row crop industries. As John Spreckels said, "Strawberries and sugar beets go together very nicely."[22]

With the protective tariff in place, Claus emphatically stated there was no other time like the present for California farmers to leave grain behind and prosper with row crops. "Land adapted to sugar-beet growing will average fourteen of fifteen tons to the acre from which the farmer will realize about $60. The cost varies with varying conditions and localities but will in general range from $30 to $40 per acre. The farmer will thus net from $20 to $30 per acre on his crop. No grain crop can be compared with the sugar-beet for results."[23]

Claus began writing other articles for agricultural magazines and sat for multiple interviews about his groundbreaking sugar-making methods. He beamed in the hard-earned role of an agriculturalist. His success was a big deal for the California State Agricultural Society, who hoped beet cultivation would spread throughout the struggling agricultural state and bring it much needed prosperity.

Suddenly, newspapers were filled with articles about farmers expanding into beet production. Soon others in California began manufacturing sugar from beet roots: Los Alamitos Sugar Company, American Beet Sugar Company, Alameda Sugar Company, Union Sugar Company, and more.[24] (Across the country others were being inspired by Claus's sugar beet culture, and in a few years, there would be ninety-one factories in eighteen states.)

Salinas Valley

After only a few years, sugar beet crops overwhelmed the capacity of the Watsonville factory, and because there was not room to expand, it was time to move locations.[25] Claus knew that by abandoning the Watsonville factory he'd incur ill will. Even though he'd continue to contract with the farmers in the Pajaro Valley, the factory was "really the heart which pumps the life blood of the city's trade through every artery and vein of the whole community. Remove the factory, and Watsonville would be struck a staggering blow."[26] But he was left with little choice. The rumors that Claus was looking around for a new sugar factory location stunned the community of Watsonville, especially those who had deeded the land to him for the Watsonville refinery. So many laborers had relocated to Watsonville for the steady income; now what would they do?

Pajaro Valley farmers had learned much from Claus, such as irrigation techniques and rotating beets with other crops (lettuce, for example) to enrich the soil, which in turn increased crop yields and profits. Their beet crop would still be needed despite Claus's plan for relocation. The city of Watsonville was booming, and Claus hoped the progress would continue; after all, because of the life blood pumped by his enterprise, Watsonville had installed electric and telephone systems, built a new city hall and a library, and constructed hospitals and schools. But the location that had been selected for him left him no room to expand—and besides, many of the farmers he contracted with lived near Salinas.

As before, after hearing of Claus's desire to build a massive plant in one central location using updated technology, a number of cities expressed interest. Likewise, Claus knew he wanted one place only: the Salinas Valley, a tried-and-true venture, since he was already milling high-quality beets from farmers there. And most importantly, with his health needs, the Salinas Valley was still reasonably close to his Aptos Ranch. He felt in his bones that the long, narrow Salinas Valley, with the Gabilan and the Santa Lucia mountain ranges on either side and a long meandering river running through, would become one of the richest agricultural regions in California and was the best place to house the large-scale enterprise that would be his final parting gift to the state.

From the inception of Salinas in the 1860s, its founders knew the key to its success would be to entice the Southern Pacific Railroad to put a major stop in the town. But the founders had their work cut out for them. The Salinas Valley was dusty and windy, and it had no obvious attributes that would benefit industry or agriculture. Yet the valley had already become a sort of crossroads, a place where stagecoach drivers raced to as an approximate midway point between San Francisco and Los Angeles.[27] According to local lore, Elias Howe, on the road in 1856, had an accident that caused his entire wagonload of lumber to fall to the ground. Rather that reload it, the enterprising pioneer built a small stagecoach stop, which he named Howe's Halfway House, giving Salinas its start.[28] The founders who followed worked hard to create a town around the stagecoach stop that would attract the attention of the SP as it was planning its route to Los Angeles. Salinas's tenacious entrepreneurs quickly built a real town and managed to get a railroad station placed there; this in turn attracted new residents and businesses to the city, solidifying Salinas as a major metropolitan center in California.

So, the founders had their train stop, and now they wanted Claus. They had seen how his beet sugar enterprise had brought greater wealth to Watsonville in a thousand different ways. Salinas business leaders caught whiffs of rumors that Claus had his eye on *their* valley to expand his enterprise. Jesse D. Carr, president of the California State Agricultural Society, knew what a beet refinery would do for Salinas, and he and others congregated privately to discuss ways to ensure the rumors would become fact—namely, to offer Claus free land for his refinery and the assurance that farmers would convert their cereal grain crops to the high value beet crop.

Working behind the Scenes

Claus didn't believe in luck. Establishing the sugar beet enterprise in Watsonville had been done not by risky and chaotic moves or with fingers crossed but by carefully laid-out plans. It was well known he lived by the Lutheran motto "What is worth doing is worth doing well." He had a lot to consider. As a businessman, he knew full well the advantages of controlling the transportation of his product. First, he needed to gather and analyze facts and figures about expanding his small-scale but impressive twenty-four-mile Pajaro Valley Railroad, with its 3 locomotives, 1 passenger car, 16 boxcars, 19 flatcars, and 126 other cars, which had been hauling beets from the factory to the wharf at Moss Landing since 1890.[29] To support a bigger facility elsewhere, either the PVR would have to be extended, or Claus would need to use the SP for transport, his last choice because he had built the PVR specifically to thumb his nose at the SP's extortionate freight rates, and local farmers had lauded him for his ingenuity because they also benefited.

By 1896 Claus's railroad was well established in the valley. The PVR had become far more important than originally planned once it had started its passenger service by caboose, which left from the Watsonville factory and arrived at the shipping port at Moss Landing on Monterey Bay. The name Claus Spreckels brought nothing but deep respect from farmers for "beating" the SP and for giving them cheaper transportation.[30]

Considering all of this, Claus sent engineers to map out a possible railroad extension to the Salinas Valley. He also sent several engineers to the valley to investigate the quality of available water and real estate in the surrounding areas. He even went so far as to hire a tug company to take depth soundings off the mouth of the Salinas River.[31] As he suspected, he was assured that "at light expense" he could bore artesian wells and install pumping plants along the river for irrigation of the dry valley.[32] He was encouraged with the results, but as a good poker player, he knew to keep his cards close to his chest for negotiation purposes with the Salinas Valley stakeholders.

The Word's Out

A reporter for the *Santa Cruz Sentinel* was sent to Aptos on Sunday afternoon, March 22, 1896, in regard to the rumors that Claus was pulling operations out of Watsonville. The reporter had undoubtedly heard the sugar king was brusque and impatient and was therefore surprised to spot him puffing on a cigar and reposing on "the veranda admiring the scenery." The reporter was "cordially" invited into the house "to have a chat" before being introduced to Anna. According to the reporter, Claus, "by his ease of manner[,] makes one forget that he is in the presence of a man whose name is known to all in the financial institutions of the world, and who counts his wealth by the millions; a man to whom nearly every county in California is coquettishly looking to with the expectation of inducing him to build sugar factories."[33]

Before the interview started, Claus stretched his arms out wide and said that after being all around the world, there was no place like Aptos for him. Here, where the climate was mild, he said, was where he would rest his weary bones when he returned from an upcoming July trip to Germany to see firsthand if "any improvements, if any, have been made" in beet sugar refining. His specific plans to collaborate with Grevenbroich's engineers on developing a monster sugar machine were not revealed. This might be his last trip overseas, he told the reporter. "I am 68 eight years old," and "I have all I can do in California," he explained.[34]

The reporter was surprised when the heretofore "calm" Claus moved forward his chair with an abrupt change in demeanor to irritably describe a situation contributing to his dissatisfaction in Watsonville: one of the members of the Hans Christian Struve household (a prominent family) complained that one of Claus's silos was partially encroaching over their property line, and they were expecting remuneration. Only "some of the silo," Claus said, had encroached, and he was being pressured to buy an entire acre at a ridiculous price: "I will fight before I give a twenty-five cent piece more for a thing than it is worth. That's my nature. The Struve land isn't worth any sum near $1,000 an acre, and I will not give it!"[35] It's unknown if the boundaries were clearly revealed when the land had been deeded to Claus, but on principle alone, he made it clear, he wasn't paying! He told the reporter how he alone had built up Watsonville's economy and echoed what was being reported about the beet sugar refinery: "The monthly wages distributed to employees find their way into the hands of business and keep alive the prosperity which does not desert Watsonville in any stress of financial or industrial depression."[36] Damn the Struves! How dare anybody try and take advantage of him!

When pointedly asked, "Have you decided to build a factory at Salinas?" he replied, "Not yet." But, without any details, he reported, "I recently purchased 7,000 acres of land in Monterey County." This he wanted known to the decision makers in Salinas: "I have purchased land to be prepared if we [Salinas and Claus] can not agree on terms. I always believe in being prepared."[37]

Claus and the ever-faithful Anna packed their well-used trunks for Germany. Before he left, he said:

> I circulated a pamphlet throughout California, sending a copy to every farmer and land owner in the state. I showed them as clear as daylight that they must start growing beets in California if they mean to keep their heads above water. They are growing wheat at a loss, and I will put them in the way of growing beets at a profit. With every pamphlet I sent a quantity of beet seed. The more they grow the richer they will be. I can take all they can raise and my scheme will be the salvation of the country, but there is much to do to insure this end.[38]

Partnering with the Enemy

Claus spent two months in Europe, ordering the machinery from Grevenbroich, "the largest order for sugar machinery in one package ever to be received by the firm."[39] He arrived home on July 16, 1896, looking, as the family-owned *Call* said, "as fresh and vigorous as a young man just out of school."[40] On his previous trips to Europe, he had gone as a young man to study beet sugar refining, once on the job as common laborer. Now he was an honored client who brought big business to the Grevenbroich Machine Factory, Germany's leading manufacturer of refinery machinery. Carl Langen, the manager, invited the Spreckelses to stay at his home and even offered his own carriage, pulled by beautiful high-stepping horses, for his personal use, making neighbors wonder who this important man was.[41]

The very next day after his return from Europe, before the sun came up, Claus was back at his desk in the Call Building, furiously attending to business. The Western Beet Sugar Company report from Watsonville awaited him on his desk and informed him that in the company's eighth year of operation, it had produced 19,750 tons (39.5 million pounds) of sparkling white sugar—more than ten times its first year's output![42] He was proud and knew he was going to do better than even that.

Also, dozens of letters responding to his pamphlets awaited Claus from farming communities all over the state, trumpeting their merits and hoping to be selected for the site of his next mammoth project. But his sights were on the Salinas Valley. He had too many investments there. Back in March 1896 he had purchased some seven thousand acres of flat land along the Salinas River at a point where the river skirted high hills in a district known as Llano de Buena Vista, its Spanish grant name.[43] Those acres would be perfect for the size of factory he envisioned.

While Claus was in Europe, construction of the Valley Road had been going full steam ahead and was projected for completion in October 1896, now just weeks away. With his return, he granted interviews in the hopes to share his grandiose plans for the institution of a massive beet culture industry for the good of the country. However, reporters frequently veered him away from the topic of beets to other topics, especially the lawsuits with his sons. "There is no reason to question that!" was a common refrain when he was taken away from the subject of sugar beets.[44] It's hard to blame the press because the Spreckels clan had become publicity shy after the family's dissension following the "sugar war" in Philadelphia. Claus was now sixty-eight and had just completed the construction of an epic mansion in Pacific Heights, purchased over a million dollars' worth of downtown real estate, purchased a newspaper, transformed the Pajaro Valley into virtually one irrigated beet farm, launched yet another railroad, acquired ranches and other acreage in Monterey County, and built the tallest skyscraper on the West Coast—but the press was over-interested in the emotional costs of legally battling with his younger sons.

Now he needed a partner, because after this extensive development, he was worried about working capital so that he could freely develop in Salinas without, as the *Watsonville Pajaronian* had said, looking for "dividends one minute after the first toot of the whistle."[45] Both John and Adolph were chief officers and directors in the Western Sugar Refining Company and his remaining Hawaiian plantation companies, but by now, Claus had stopped fooling himself they would ever share his same passion for the sugar industry. They were looking to make their own marks in separate industries, John in shipping and Adolph in horse breeding. He concluded that his former enemies, the Sugar Trust, now the American Sugar Refining Company, would be an excellent choice. They were already his 50-percent partners in the Western Sugar Refining Company and had been nothing but helpful by staying out of his way and, when asked, providing occasional technical advice. One of the officers of the American reported, "We stayed out of there, so as not to do anything to upset the old man [Claus]." They were perfect "silent" partners. They, unlike the Spreckels sons, enjoyed being in the game of making sugar. Claus asked John Searles for $7–8 million to help fund his dream in Salinas.[46] He proposed that American buy half of the stock in all his beet sugar operations: the Western Beet Sugar Company at Watsonville, the soon-to-be-extended Pajaro Valley Railroad, and the new Spreckels Sugar Company. Claus promised to make one of the American's representatives an officer on the board of directors of each company.

Havemeyer and Searles had originally looked down their noses at the beet as an orphan child of the sugar industry. But by now many states had been following Claus's success; in fact, Utah, Idaho, Colorado, and Michigan were in the game.[47] This, along with the power that farmers were gaining in Washington DC with the establishment of the American Farmers Industry, seemed to be the right time to protect themselves by investing in Claus's beet industry.

All Aboard the Pajaro Valley Consolidated Railroad!

On December 9, 1897, Claus and his new partners consolidated the Pajaro Valley Railroad and its extensions as the Pajaro Valley Consolidated Railroad Company (PVCRRC), with roughly forty-two miles of track, four locomotives, and 170 cars in service, with its northern terminus at the Watsonville factory.[48] Claus's little beet line had now become a full-fledged railroad with fine Baldwin locomotives, baggage and freight cars, and four designated stations with two points where freight could be transferred to the main line of the SP. The line now connected all the Spreckels operations (the farmers) in both the Pajaro and Salinas Valleys. Because beets begin losing their sugar content shortly after harvesting, it was imperative to get the train up and running to the fields, where anxious farmers waited to unload their harvest. Claus established beet dumps along the track where farmers could deliver their loads. Once the farmer received verification of delivery from a company representative, he was absolved of further responsibility.

Already, with the founding of the Watsonville refinery, real estate sales in Salinas had been soaring. "The beet sugar factory in Watsonville has increased the value of land from $300 to $600 per acre and the enterprise has many investments to be made."[49] Now, with the PVCRRC, people realized they

25. Miles of farmers waiting their turn to dump their beets. Because beets begin losing sugar content shortly after harvest, Claus established beet "dumps" along his train track, where farmers could deliver their loads. Courtesy of the Monterey County Historical Society.

could live and farm in Salinas and commute to Watsonville, and Salinas real estate values soared even higher.

Claus had brought not only a beet industry to the area but a modern transportation system that generated further jobs for the people of the valley. And he was already in conversation with John and Adolph to turn the management of the railroad company over to them. Claus kept piling on the tasks for John—as his eldest, so like him in business—to do more and more. He seemingly disregarded his son's preoccupation with developing San Diego—especially when San Francisco, not San Diego, was his home. Publishing newspapers, for example, was a profitable commercial venture, mainly due to the revenue from advertisements, but that isn't what drove both Claus and John to purchase them. Their philosophy, dating back to Claus's providing the funds for Walter Murray Gibson to purchase Hawai'i's *Pacific Commercial Advertiser* in 1880, was akin to "If you can't beat them, buy them." The *San Francisco Call* had served and was serving its purpose for influencing public opinion: endorsing the Spreckels business investments and representing the Republican Party's viewpoints. With his assets multiplying in Southern California, John was quick to purchase the *San Diego Union* in 1890 for similar purposes. When the rival *San Diego Evening Tribune* began to warn the public that a rich San Franciscan was turning their community into a "one-man town," John solved the problem in 1901 by buying the *Tribune* after considerable litigation and settlements. With major newspapers owned by the Spreckels family from the top to the bottom of the state, Spreckels was a household name in California.

As Claus made plans to expand into the Salinas Valley, word leaked out the American Sugar Refining Company had bought an interest in the Watsonville plant, but nobody could have guessed that its stake was as much as 50 percent, and Claus didn't feel the need to reveal that fact. He was large and in charge. Regardless how much money partner Havemeyer invested, he and everybody else at the American knew, based on their Philadelphia experience, not to step on Claus's toes. No investor was ever really considered by Claus as a "real" partner; his only real partners were farmers. He was well aware that his success depended on them alone. Salinas Valley farmers—this is where he would place all his energies in the upcoming days.

16   *Sweet Success in the Salinas Valley*

On August 1, 1896, Claus arrived in Salinas to lead an informational session for farmers, with the singular purpose of selling them on the idea of growing beets. The Salinas Valley at this time was teeming with 213,000 acres of grain. He needed only 30,000 of those acres to produce beets, but the labor intensiveness of growing beets was always a hard sell, yet he was up to it.

Claus enjoyed talking farmer to farmer on his favorite topic—the infinitesimal details required in cultivating beets. Farmers were his people, and they always responded favorably after learning that Claus had grown up on a farm and in midlife had become a self-taught agronomist. His concerns for the farmer were genuine; he knew about rising costs, falling prices, drought, plagues, high interest rates, and generally how difficult the life of a farmer was. With California in the throes of a depression, he hoped that sugar beets might be seen as a savior to the struggling farming industry.

Wooing and Wooed in Salinas

Claus beamed at the delegation of Salinas civic leaders awaiting him on the platform when he stepped down from the train, a delegation that included Mayor Thomas Harris. Claus was accompanied by William Waters, factory manager in Watsonville and his right-hand man. Waters had agreed to not only supervise construction but relocate permanently to superintend the new factory, *Spreckels style*. Claus was whisked off to a buffet in the city's elegant hotel, the Abbott House. With refreshments over, he knew a celebration awaited him when the Salinas Military Brass Band showed up at the hotel door to musically escort him down the street to the agricultural hall known as the Pavilion, where two thousand people waited expectantly to applaud him the second he walked through the door.[1] Claus was overwhelmed not only by the rousing cheers and applause but by the multitude of sugar beet tops, the harvest of which had just begun for the Watsonville refinery. The boughs were wrapped in colorful ribbon and strung across the entire hall. He was led to the stage, shaking as many hands as he could along the way. With a wave of his hand, he acknowledged his delight to see that beets had been creatively arranged on the wall in the back of the stage to spell out "Our Future Industry."[2]

Mayor Harris walked up to the podium, quieted the crowd, and solemnly reminded his "fellow citizens" that despite the gaiety around them, the event at hand was "fraught with meaning and deep significance to the future and prosperity of this whole valley." After reciting the Spreckels family's accomplishments in industries outside sugar, Claus was given a familiar introduction: "He has arisen from a poor farmer-boy to occupy by force of his own dauntless spirit, to a place in the industrial forces of the world that is unsurpassed. Yet, with all this, he is a plain American citizen whose sympathies go out for the laborer." With this, Mayor Harris warmly invited "California's greatest friend" to the podium, with the caveat that Mr. Spreckels was not a "great speech maker" but gave "great speeches." Claus was quick to the point: "There are two things essential to the manufacture of beet sugar: one is the beets, the other the factory. Now, if you farmers will guarantee to grow the beets, I'll guarantee to turn 'em into sugar."[3]

He continued, "Mark my words. . . . I propose to build here at your door the greatest sugar factory and refinery in the world!" After the applause died down, he told the crowd that his refinery would "eat up 3,000 tons of beets every day and turn out every day 450 tons of refined sugar." But more importantly, he said, "that means the distribution of $12,000 every day." He then proceeded to go into beet cultivation in practical language that only a farmer would understand. At the end of it, implying that nobody but a German like himself could transform their valley with beets, he told them a joke: "Two Englishmen talked of starting the beet-sugar industry. They inquired of an expert if sugar-beets could be grown there. 'Yes,' was the reply, 'but the first thing to be done is to get a shotgun and kill off all the English farmers and put Germans in their places.'" After the laughter subsided, he got serious: "Now, beets, my friends, are the salvation of the farmer. Cereals have been overworked and they need a rest. Its cultivation [beets] will go far toward making this the greatest State in the Union, which I am sure is its ultimate destiny."[4]

William J. Hill, a former mayor of Salinas, stood up next to give a short speech on the importance of the beet cultivation topic, which included the following famous words from Shakespeare's *Julius Caesar*: "There is a tide in the affairs of men. Which, taken at the flood, leads on to fortune." The "tide," of course, was Claus Spreckels, and the farmers shouldn't miss the once-in-a-lifetime opportunity (the "flood") for a "fortune." To lighten the tone, Hill shouted a jingle he had made up: "To banish hard times and increase our shekels, let us grow sugar-beets and sell them to Spreckels!" It seemed the applause would never die down.[5]

Soon Mr. Waters, the future refinery foreman, stepped up to tell them about their excellent remunerations, which prompted Claus to interrupt with a story about how the weather conditions at Watsonville the previous year had prevented beets from being harvested on time, which meant a loss of sugar, and contractually, they wouldn't have been "purchasable." But he realized that he could stand the loss "better than the poor farmers," so he had paid the full amount anyway. He wanted to relay the fact that, in his advanced age, he was beginning to realize that people were more important than profit. He concluded by telling the crowd, "I am an old man, but I keep learning."[6]

When the meeting adjourned, Claus remained behind to shake hands all around and to answer any questions that hadn't been fully answered. So moved by the whole evening's events and the warm reception, he pronounced the following to the crowd standing around him on the floor: "All I ask is that farmers produce the beets. I will buy them. I ask no favors of any kind. I shall buy and pay for the site and put up the factory myself. I ask no presents or bonuses from the people."[7]

The fact that Claus said he wouldn't need any donated land for the refinery was music to the ears of Salinas leaders. After hearing this, a committee was instantly formed and they spread out among the contingency of farmers in an effort to engage them before they left the event. Before Claus left the building, the committee gleefully reported to him that they received verbal pledges for an astonishing 100,000 acres to be planted for beets.

Following the meeting, everyone was in good humor, and they returned to the Abbott House to enjoy "oysters and cigars." As the clock inched toward midnight, a toast was finally proposed to "Sir" Claus Spreckels. Likely pausing for a sad second with memories of his departed friend King David Kalākaua, who had enabled this title, and full of drink, he boasted, "When I shall have built this big refinery, I will no longer be the Sugar King but the Emperor of the sugar industry."[8]

Empty Promises

Two weeks later the disappointing word came to Claus that only 5,000 acres had resulted in written contracts, the verbal pledges for 100,000 acres notwithstanding, and those contracts had been made by small-time farmers. Since the goal was for 30,000 acres a year, which equated to 90,000 acres on a three-year rotation, this news was dismal.[9] Apparently, after the enthusiasm of the mass meeting in Salinas, reality had set in. Large landowners who were growing thousands of acres of wheat, barley, and oats went home and did the math. For every one man employed by them to plant, tend, and harvest their grain, about forty-one men would now be needed for the leafy-topped root crop.[10]

Meanwhile, Woodland growers near Sacramento had written pledges in hand for 40,000 acres of what they described as "the best beet land in California."[11] Not only that, but they would also donate land for the factory in Yolo County. This, along with the pleasing samples of beets that had been grown with the seeds Claus had sent out, gave him the leverage he needed.[12]

Claus telegrammed Salinas growers that he was giving them exactly two weeks to provide 30,000 acres a year (90,000 acres on a three-year rotation), or he'd be "moving on and building in Woodland."[13] This ultimatum put city leaders into action with editorials in the town's two newspapers, which hysterically proclaimed, "A Crisis Is Upon Us" and "We Must Not Fail!"[14] The small farmers who had pledged the 5,000 acres pointed their angry fingers at the big landholders who hadn't pledged and were therefore keeping them from prospering in a new venture.

An emergency mass meeting was again called for August 22. Three highly respected men were gathered to motivate the farmers again, with big landowners as their target audience. The first speaker was the distinguished British grower Edward Berwick, famed for his experimental farming. He supplied the elegant Hotel Del Monte with his famous pears and other homegrown fruit and was a friend of Robert Louis Stevenson. His presence brought a deep credibility to the topic at hand. The second influencer was California senator William J. Hill, who had spoken at the August 1 meeting in the Pavilion welcoming Claus to Salinas and who was the popular publisher of the

Salinas Index (he was also described as "sheriff, Indian fighter, mayor, post-master"). When it was all said and done, though, it was pioneer cattle rancher and farmer Jim Bardin who, in giving the first speech of his life, cinched the deal. Bardin was currently a major sugar beet grower for the Spreckels refinery in Watsonville. He was well known among farmers up and down the valley for his toughness and honesty. He lived by the western philosophy "Live each day so you can look every damned man in the eye and tell him to go to hell."[15]

Bardin stood up at the meeting and with a quivering voice said, "You all know I'm scared [giving a speech], but the time has come when I believe it the duty of every farmer to raise his voice in support of the sugar factory." He then pulled out his ledgers and told of the "cost and the profit of his big beet crop." Aside from beets, he even told his listeners how he fattened his heretofore skinny cattle with "beet tops" and sold the fattened stock for the greatest profit he had ever realized.[16] Before he sat down, he said, "Gentlemen, Mr. Spreckels can live handsomely without us, but I am not so dang sure we can all live without him."[17] This lengthy and detailed firsthand account by one of their own, a well-respected farmer, was all those assembled needed to hear to sign up at the end of the meeting.

Good News!

Claus had never been so pleased than when he received the urgent telegram from Salinas that they had signed pledges in hand exceeding all expectations.[18] On September 3, 1896, he arrived in Salinas, with the press in attendance, to hype up and announce the location of the soon-to-be "largest sugar beet factory in the world." It was to be four miles southwest of their town on the eastern bank of the Salinas River.[19] Many questioned why Claus would select a site so far from the center of Salinas, considering the only way to get there would be by horse and buggy. But he explained that he'd be expanding his Pajaro Valley Railroad to the location.

As summer turned into fall, there wasn't an agricultural community in California that wasn't buzzing with the news that the sugar king was building not only a massive beet sugar factory on the banks of the Salinas River but a namesake town, Spreckels, to go along with it! The projected date for construction was January 1897, and the first campaign at the new refinery was projected to begin with the 1898 season. Never a woolgatherer, Claus had the entire project well coordinated and in production by the end of September.

In March 1897, in an attempt to get Adolph excited about the new venture, Claus brought him along to see the selected site.[20] It was likely that Anna had convinced Adolph to travel to Salinas with his father because Claus's health had become a complicating factor, and with her own heart issues, she worried mightily. Neither Adolph nor John was often seen with their father, so this made the news. With all four of his sons branching off in many different directions, Claus was losing control over the name of Spreckels, and it was a good reminder to the press that his sons, at least one of them, was still standing beside him in the sugar business. But in reality, Claus was relying on the loyal managers who had been beside him since the early days of building the California Sugar Refinery.

On August 6, 1897, the articles of incorporation of the new venture, the Spreckels Sugar Company, were filed in San Francisco with a capital stock of $5 million. There were five directors: John and Adolph Spreckels, Walter D. K. Gibson (extended family member), attorney Alexander Francis Morrison, and Merrit Herman Weed, manager of the California Sugar Refinery (then leased by Western Sugar Refining Company). Each subscribed $1 million ($34 million apiece in today's money).[21] The remaining 49,950 shares were divided equally between the American Sugar Refining Company and J. D. Spreckels and Brothers.

On His Deathbed

On February 15, 1898, Spain's alleged sinking of the USS *Maine* in Havana Harbor set off a series of explosive events that led the United States to declare war on Spain. During the ensuing spring, young patriotic Americans gathered at Fisherman's Wharf in San Francisco, ready to fight for their country. The U.S. Navy needed ships, and three of the Spreckels tugs as well as the steamer *Alameda* were conscripted.

During this time of great uncertainty and in the middle of his Salinas Valley venture, Claus collapsed into his bed at the Brownstone at the end of March 1898. Dr. Lane had been closely monitoring his diabetic condition in the months preceding the episode. At the end of April, the sugar king's battle with diabetes was leaked to the public. One headline proclaimed, "Claus Spreckels Dangerously Ill with Diabetes," and another, "He May Be on His Deathbed." It was reported that John and Adolph were alternating their visits to their father's bedside to assure him that business was going on fine and to keep him in bed. Not only was Claus suffering from complications of high blood sugar, he developed a painful carbuncle (infected cluster of boils under the skin). One reporter brazenly telephoned the Brownstone inquiring about his health and was told that Dr. Lane had ordered complete bed rest, with no visitors outside the family allowed to see him. The doctor was quoted: "Diabetes is incurable, its course may be extended before the fatality results, and for the time the malady may be stayed, but is recurrent in form until at last comes an attack from which the sufferer is unable to recover." Dr. Lane then went on record: "You may say that Mr. Spreckels has been very ill. His sickness was aggravated by business and family affairs, but we believe that he will recover."[22] The news story then pointed to the "bitter quarrel with the two sons" as likely one of the aggravating factors the doctor was referring to.

Hearing that Claus was sick in bed, Rudolph swallowed his pride and visited the Brownstone to attempt a reconciliation. The door was answered by a servant who declared that nobody was allowed to visit the ailing Claus. Rudolph replied, "He is my father," and with that handed the servant his calling card to be taken to his father's bedside. The servant returned with the announcement that his father didn't wish to see him. Rudolph went home and sent word to his parents that he "was willing to waive all claims to his share in the estate" to prove he was sincere in his efforts for a reconciliation. Complete silence from the Brownstone. *Town Talk*, reporting on this story, likened it to a "medieval tale, one of those tales of a stern and unrelenting sire, filled with a sense of the duty a child owes to a parent, and unwilling ever to forgive an aspersion upon his honor, even though the rash offender be of his own flesh and blood."[23]

The reporter sought out Gus to ask for a comment regarding his father being on a "deathbed," to which Gus replied: "I have heard that he is very seriously ill. But why do you ask me? I know nothing about it." The news story ended with the hopes the "city's most public-spirited citizens will be able to postpone the visit of the grim messenger."[24]

In the midst of Claus's staving off "the grim messenger," the news came that on July 7, 1898, President McKinley had signed a congressional joint resolution formally annexing Hawai'i. Years of arduous debate in the U.S. Congress over the advantages and disadvantages of annexing the Hawaiian Islands had quickly ended with the start of the Spanish-American War. Ostensibly, the resolution was justified as a move by the United States to protect its national security. It certainly dashed all of Lili'uokalani's hopes for being restored to her throne. As much as Claus tried to wield his influence with the envious sugar planters, he hadn't been able to prevent the annexation. His warnings to the planters that annexation would bring about the demise of the contract labor system throughout Hawai'i would be realized.

Three years earlier, an attempt to restore Lili'uokalani to her throne had ended horribly with her imprisonment in her palace. As part of her efforts to stave off annexation and give journalists her own views, she published *Hawai'i's Story by Hawai'i's Queen Lili'uokalani* in early 1898. She memorialized a significant show of support from the Spreckels family. Even though they were not speaking to one another, they were all apparently like-minded in their loyalty to the queen. Recalling her arrival in San Francisco, she recounted, "Many friends had hastened to call upon me; amongst these were Mr. and Mrs. Claus Spreckels, Mrs. J. D. Spreckels and her lovely daughter, Miss Emma Spreckels, Mr. and Mrs. C. A. [Gus] Spreckels."[25]

John had generally liked David Kalākaua but didn't respect him as a ruler. In contrast, Lili'uokalani had earned his deep respect. In a letter to her business manager in Honolulu, Joseph Oliver Carter, the ex-queen anxiously reported that because the Spreckels ships had been conscripted for the war and transportation service to Hawai'i had been heavily curtailed, she was stranded in "financial embarrassment" in Washington DC. Unable to reach Honolulu from San Francisco (which she reached by train), she was left with only one option, that of going home via Vancouver, Canada, at a cost she couldn't afford, since her funds had been seized. With great relief, the queen reported on July 8 that John Spreckels had sent her $2,000 (about $68,000 in today's money) to enable her to return home the alternate way and have some cash reserve.[26] After the point of no return for the monarchy, the Spreckels bank in Honolulu lent Lili'uokalani $70,000 ($2.2 million in today's money) to pay off her remaining property mortgages and, more importantly, to fight the United States Congress to win compensation for the crown lands it had taken.[27] The Spreckels family had proven their loyalty to the Hawaiian monarchy when many had abandoned it.

During the years the Provisional Government had ruled Hawai'i—while Claus was engaged in manufacturing sugar from beets—he had been saddened that he and Anna had been forced by the annexationists to abandon their tropical mansion in Honolulu. Now that the islands belonged to the United States, however, he wondered if he'd ever be well enough to see his beloved house once again, or the islands he loved.

The Refinery

Encouraged by Claus's success, beet sugar refineries began to pop up across the country, and Claus welcomed all efforts outside his territory. In December 1898 President McKinley told Congress that "the number of sugar beet factories has been doubled in the last two years, the ability of the United States to produce its own sugar from this source has been clearly demonstrated."[28] Claus was so proud.

From the summer of 1897 to the summer of 1899, construction of the Spreckels Sugar Company's refinery and new town of Spreckels continued, with nearly six hundred men working on the refinery and the many buildings surrounding it.[29] The sheer number of "ironworkers, brick masons, and other craftsmen" meant a boom to Salinas business owners, who provided housing, meals, and entertainment for hundreds of men. Almost instantly, Salinas was permanently transformed and lifted out of a depression that at the time held most of the county in its grip.

Those workers who lived in Salinas could pick up the "Spreckels Dinky," as it was called because of its small engines for narrow-gauge tracks, on its thrice-daily runs to the refinery. Since the Dinky stopped in front of the Jeffery Hotel on Main Street, the enterprising mother of the owner, James Jeffery, saw an opportunity to earn a little money by putting together pail lunches in the hotel's kitchen. She walked up and down the line in the mornings, selling her lunches to workers waiting for their turn to board the Dinky. To celebrate the "marriage" of Salinas with Claus Spreckels, the Jeffery also created a new menu: "New Enterprise Soup, Prosperity Crab Salad, Sugar Factory Stew, Chicken à la Claus Spreckels, Breast of Mutton Refinery Style, and Fricandeau of Veal au Sugar Beets."[30]

At the same time the refinery was going up, beets were being grown on thirty thousand acres in and around the Salinas Valley. Just as he had done in the Pajaro Valley, Claus installed irrigation systems where dry farming had previously prevailed. To the wonderment of all, it was Maui all over again: he turned the arid brown plains to a vibrant green. According to one observer-turned-poet, Claus transformed "the floor of the great central valley

26. The Salinas refinery was producing granulated, powdered, and liquid sugar on a massive scale and in a variety of sizes for both industrial and household use. Courtesy of the Monterey County Historical Society.

to an emerald sheen in winter, a golden sea in spring, and a tawny vastness after the time of the harvest."[31]

A headline in the *Santa Cruz Surf* summed up the new refinery for curious citizens who had watched hundreds of construction workers pass through their town: "Dimensions and Details That Stagger the Mind." Because beet sugar refineries contain a maze of pipes, machines, flumes, and tanks, with duplicate sets of equipment, the buildings had to be massive. The enormous complex spread over twenty-two acres, and the main brick building was 582 feet long and 102 feet wide. Since the process used gravity to draw the beets through production, the 2.5-million-square-foot refinery was five stories high and could be seen for miles around.[32] The *Index* called the factory one of the "wonders of modern achievement," comparing it to the Brooklyn Bridge and the Eifel Tower.[33]

Claus had optimistically announced the refinery would be ready to "eat beets," one of his favorite phrases, in the summer of 1898. However, the worst drought since the 1860s meant that the total beet harvest was half of what it had been the previous year. As the dry winter gave way to a dry spring, Claus ordered one more season for refining beets at the Watsonville refinery—with his fingers crossed the rain would come so he could finally leave Watsonville behind. The importance of irrigation for California's Salinas Valley had never seemed more important than when the rains came the following year. A dam, several pumping plants, and a fourteen-mile irrigation canal were soon working, and Claus advised other independent farmers he contracted with to follow suit or risk ruination if another disastrous drought were to come along.

On August 26, 1899, a long, loud blast from the Spreckels refinery whistle signaled the steam boilers, powered by engines of nine thousand horsepower, were at long last making sugar in the Salinas Valley. While the Watsonville plant had been putting out an average of 50 tons of sugar per day, the Salinas operation was daily slicing and crushing 3,000 tons of sugar beets and producing a staggering 450 tons of sugar.[34] With an annual yield of 120,000 tons of sugar, Claus had finally achieved his dream of refining beets on a scale that was unparalleled in this country. He was producing on a massive scale granulated, powdered, and liquid sugar in a variety of sizes for both industrial and household use. Refining beets necessitated enormous amounts of fresh water, and the refinery consumed 13 million gallons of water, as much in a single campaign day as the entire city of San Francisco.[35]

It's hard to overstate the value of Claus's enterprise to the economy of the entire region, considering that when the beet sugar operation began, the refinery employed 1,300 people at a time when Salinas had a population of 3,034.[36] And that's a lot of beer to supply: Claus insisted that in German tradition, a pint of steam beer that he originated was to be served to each of the hardworking laborers at noon.

In the beginning Claus had to rush the raw beets to his San Francisco refinery. But he perfected a process that would enable the factory to create its own pure and fine white sugar on site in Salinas.[37] Originally, Claus's machines sliced the beets, and the juice was extracted by centrifugal force. But with the new diffusion process, sliced beets were submerged in hot water so the sugar passed through the beet's cell walls, leaving behind the pulp, 80 percent of the weight of the beet. Not only was this more efficient, but the diffusion process extracted a far higher quantity of sugar.

Claus, in record time (or in "Spreckels time"), had become an industrial leader in California and the entire United States because sugar beet refining was an undeveloped industrial venture, and the nation took notice. The innovation of processing sugar beets at the location where they were grown was innovative and worth emulating for other crops across the country. Claus's success taught agriculturalists that to function most effectively, factories should be moved to the countryside, near the fields. In this way, transportation costs were cut down and the quality of the product and the rapport between factory and farmer were greatly improved.

Waste Not, Want Not

Claus had been raised with a "waste not, want not" philosophy. He was thrilled to find that he could capitalize on the by-products of beet refining. Right from the start, he took full advantage of the lavish number of by-products—the mountains of beet pulp that formerly went straight into the garbage pile. He found a separate market for the dried beet pulp to be used as cattle feed. Waste molasses, another by-product that remains after the crystallizable sugar has been separated from the concentrated beet juice (molasses), found a separate market as a valuable fertilizer. Another important use for the waste molasses was in the manufacture of alcohol, which added considerably to Claus's revenues.[38] A significant amount of lime is required by manufacturers to capture and remove impurities in the juice of sugar beets. Claus determined to no longer buy and ship limestone from Santa Cruz at appalling prices, so he bought the Silacci limestone quarry in the Gabilan foothills east of Salinas.[39] The limestone by-products were then also used for foundation purposes in his building projects.

Claus had also been raised with an ethic of land stewardship. On the island of Hawai'i, he had a major interest in the Pa'auhau Sugar Plantation on the northeast coast. He had been appalled at the way the leased land was treated by cattle ranchers, such as those who ran the huge Parker Ranch. In Claus's mind, they were contributing to the deforestation of the island in harmful ways. They balked at the expense of fencing, instead allowing their large herds to trample everything in their paths as they went deeper into the hills looking for water. This worried Claus, and he "presented a detailed proposal for forest protection" to King Kalākaua. The king wouldn't even need to replant if he'd only force ranchers to fence the forests and let nature perform a vegetative recovery. Too slowly, in Claus's mind, the government had finally responded in 1887 by naming "forest keepers."[40] So, when he now learned that his refinery, only a few days into production, polluted the water and killed some fish, he went into action. The county health officer promptly investigated the stench from twelve miles of the coffee-colored Salinas River and found that Claus's men were already in the throes of remediation, digging new and improved "settling ponds."[41]

The Little City of Spreckels

It was said the "little City of Spreckels," four miles south of Salinas and eighteen miles east of the sparkling Monterey Bay, seemingly popped up overnight.[42] From the beginning, the town was planned on a grid system that included three rows of five rectangular blocks each, with each block divided into twenty lots, leaving acreage for future expansion. Indoor plumbing, with hot and cold water, and electric wiring were rare, but the houses in Spreckels had both. Just as he did with the building of the factory, Claus was frequently onsite, overseeing the creation of his namesake town.

In Watsonville Claus had been introduced to the imaginative work of rising young architect William Henry Weeks. Tall, handsome, blond-haired, and blue-eyed, Weeks certainly reminded Claus of his sons. He was a strategic choice to design and build in Spreckels what Claus certainly believed would be his final and revolutionary venture. Not only was Weeks creative and ornamental in his design, but he paid close attention to practical details and kept costs within his original bids. He was conscientious and hardworking, traits Claus greatly respected; these two were brought together in a mutual relationship of respect and friendship.[43] Claus, hoping to include a variety of structures in Spreckels, "stole" Weeks from Watsonville for the entire project, which ultimately required Weeks to open up a branch office in Salinas. The development was done in several phases, starting with forty houses as well as a store, a school, and a hotel. Claus had his abandoned hotel in Aptos torn down and reused the materials in Spreckels to defray costs.[44]

27. Claus paternally loved the tiny town of Spreckels, California. He may have built the town in 1898 for practical reasons, but his love of the town, his namesake, always brought a smile to his face when he heard it spoken. Courtesy of the Monterey County Historical Society.

The first examples of Weeks's forty prototypical residential houses were built in 1898 for the average company worker. All had shingled roofs with redwood siding. Some had slight variations, such as "flipping the plan, or producing a gable roof instead of a hip roof."[45] The charming prototypes were either single-story or two-story, two- or three-bedroom, wood-framed houses with horizontal siding and small front porches.

The practice of building from one plan with variations (hallways, fireplaces, slightly larger rooms) were used in all of the construction phases. Every house had an adjoining empty lot for the purpose of gardening or raising chickens. (That is, until the town needed to expand and other small houses that Claus had built on nearby ranches—all designed by Weeks—were moved into the empty lots adjacent to the original forty houses. These "newer" houses in Spreckels were distinguished by the adornment of a wooden sugar beet posted on the front gable.) [46]

Outside of the cottages, everything was maintained by the Spreckels Sugar Company, including house painting (sixteen colors of approved paint from which to choose from), street maintenance, landscaping, and so forth. There were hierarchies, though; that is, there were larger houses built for those like Charles "Charlie" Pioda, who as a young surveyor had staked out the Pajaro Valley Railroad extension to the factory in Salinas. He had risen to plant manager and was given a beautiful two-story house just in time for his son, Paul Lawrence Pioda, the first baby born in Spreckels on November

28. Claus, with his ever-present cigar, touring the Salinas Valley with his fellow countryman Charles Romie, owner of Paraiso Hot Springs. Courtesy of the Monterey County Historical Society.

26, 1898.[47] For Superintendent William Waters, Claus commissioned a gorgeous and expansive Victorian dwelling, including "two rooms furnished in the finest style for use by Claus Spreckels whenever he visit[ed] the factory."[48]

But those rooms in the Waters house would go unused because once Claus discovered the nearby Paraiso Hot Springs, operated by fellow countryman Charles Theodore Romie, that would be where he would bunk down. Paraiso Hot Springs had become a recognized retreat, with cultivated gardens and lodgings considered luxurious. Just as with Germany's spas, the warm natural waters on the eastern slope of the Santa Lucia Mountains were reputed to cure a multitude of ailments, from rheumatism to nervous complaints. Claus constructed his own personal redwood cabin on the property, distinguished by a shingle reading "Spreckels" above the door.[49] Claus and Romie made heads turn when they were together. They could have easily passed as brothers, laughing and conversing in their native tongue.

The first structure in town—before the houses—was the three-story, sixty-one-room Spreckels Hotel, which opened in August 1898 to house and feed

29. The sixty-one-room Spreckels Hotel was the social center of life in the town of Spreckels when it opened in 1898 to house and feed unmarried workers. Beets are shown passing through the Spreckels depot on their way to the refinery. Courtesy of the Monterey County Historical Society.

single workers. It was eventually necessary to expand the hotel with two two-story annexes. The rate was six dollars a week, which included three daily meals.[50] The hotel faced Railroad Avenue (on the site of today's St. Joseph's Catholic Church). On the first floor were a large meeting room, barbershop, bar, kitchen, and dining room.[51] One of the features most noted in the Salinas journals was that it boasted ten bathrooms, because "Cleanliness is next to Godliness."[52] Ten might have not been enough considering that working in a sugar refinery was not only hazardous but sticky and that every laborer went back to the hotel covered in sugar dust.

The hotel was the social center of life in Spreckels: it hosted weddings, celebration dinners, and even election polls—all of which helped knit the tiny community together. Those who didn't live in Spreckels and wanted a hot lunch could get one for a dollar a week in the hotel's dining room, whose tables were covered in crisp snowy linens and where a "fifty-gallon coffee pot and a sixty-gallon stew pot" were always ready.[53]

On September 8, 1898, Charles Maguire, a young hotel worker, went to his third-floor room at the end of his shift. Once he fell asleep, he dreamed the hotel was on fire. He flung himself out the window to escape into a net that he dreamed was waiting for him to jump into. Instead, he hit the ground; when he was found, he relayed the dream before dying from internal injuries.[54] Maguire's nightmare became reality on June 17, 1899: only a year after being built, the hotel burned down. In her private room in the hotel, a "servant girl" curling her hair knocked over a "lighted lamp," which ignited the bed covers and turned the beautiful hotel to ashes. One hundred and eighty-seven boarders were then transferred to Salinas to find new accommodations.[55] The hotel was quickly rebuilt (Claus had no insurance as of yet).[56]

Unlike most factory towns that were owned and operated by the company that built them, Claus decided early on the town of Spreckels would belong to the employees. Likewise, all businesses would be owned and operated by unaffiliated entrepreneurs, and Claus's employees wouldn't need to support them as a condition for employment, as required by other company towns.[57] A small commercial district was set apart around Spreckels Boulevard to encourage outside merchants to lease space and provide their services.[58] Right from the beginning, the town of Spreckels and the refinery were virtually separate entities. The only linkage between the two was the stipulation that one be an employee to rent a house.

Claus had a two-story general store built in 1889 (still standing today). The brick building with a cast-iron storefront included a huge dance hall on the top floor.[59] Recognizing the opportunities the town offered, the popular Ford & Sanborn retailers out of Salinas became the first store lessee, in 1899. When circumstances later required that company to pull out, several Spreckels employees bought out the lease and renamed the store the Emporium. But it proved too much for all but one, Jesse M. Juhler, to handle. He left the factory, and he and his wife ran the store. The mail used to arrive in horse-drawn carriages from Salinas until the U.S. government allowed a part of the Emporium to serve as the community's post office, and Henrietta Juhler, Jesse's daughter, became the town's first postmistress.

In 1899 a charming, red, two-story schoolhouse with a central bell tower was added. A separate social life developed around the school activities of the children. Later, Trinidad Gutierrez recalled, "We couldn't wait for school to be let out. We'd run as fast as we could to the Emporium and see who could get there faster because we would get free hot dogs and ice cream cones."[60] It was remembered that "all the kids who grew up in Spreckels were good kids" because parents were strict and everybody knew each other.

Claus set aside acreage for a playground, a baseball field, and a park. Following the school in quick succession, Spreckels acquired a church, a theater, and then the town's very own newspaper, the *Spreckels Courier*, which was dedicated to promoting the town of Spreckels:

> It is a lovely spot on the Salinas River, seventeen miles from Monterey Bay [with] a very mild climate, and cool, healthful breezes from the ocean in summer. The town is thoroughly sewered and supplied with the purest water. Spreckels has a fine school and the most skilled physicians and surgeons. It has the largest sugar factory in the world and has a very large payroll year around. No better place or opportunity for building a new home or for entering into business anywhere.[61]

Propaganda or not, the *Courier*, the first of two newspapers,[62] was successful in luring a variety of businesses: a meat market, a harness and livery shop, a men's shoes and clothing store, a Chinese laundry, a lumberyard, a barbershop, a husband-and-wife doctor team, a saloon, and a bicycle shop. The State Bank in Spreckels started in the Emporium with a capital of $50,000 ($1.7 million in today's money) and lent money to beet farmers, and the loans were approved and guaranteed by the Spreckels Sugar Company.[63]

As the town evolved with independently owned businesses, Spreckels developed its own unique and charming character. Through the spring and summer, as the beets were being planted and ripened, Spreckels was like any other small rural farming community. In their free time, the permanent employees of the sugar refinery who lived in the town year-round organized a volunteer fire company, worked in the gardens, exchanged vegetables with their neighbors, and drank beer on their porches under the setting sun. The women shopped at the Emporium, shared recipes, and organized clubs of all kinds under the banner of culture. The women's pride in their town was seen in the formation of a Spreckels Improvement Club. Many wives and daughters earned a little money themselves by sewing burlap sacks (cotton on the inside) to hold fifty pounds of sugar. The Spreckels men formed the Board of Trade to look after the general interests of the community and ensure the town would remain "a nice, quiet place with no robberies or killings."[64]

At the end of every summer, however, the character of Spreckels changed when the annual sugar beet campaign opened, and throngs of laborers brought the town to life. The annual campaign began with a frenzied harvest in September and continued over the ensuing months to bring together the delicate dance of harvesting, transporting, storing, measuring, and processing the ugly vegetable to turn it into beautiful white granules.

It was well known that Claus paternally loved the town of Spreckels and took an active interest in the lifestyles of his regular employees and the seasonal laborers, who in turn became loyal and returned every year. He might have built his village for practical reasons, a means of keeping employees productive and stable, but his love of the town, his namesake, always brought a smile to his face when he heard it spoken.

The Chinese Exclusion Act of 1882 and its extension, the Geary Act of 1892, limited Chinese immigration to the United States, so Claus predominantly employed "German, Slovenian, Irish, Swedish and Danish workers."[65] Scottish, Welsh, English, and Portuguese immigrants were also represented and lived in Spreckels year-round.[66] Both the town and the refinery were important sources of income and helped inculcate American ideals in immigrants. But to those Chinese who were already in California, who were suffering greatly from anti-Chinese hostility, the farms around Salinas were functioning as one of the population's safety valves. The Chinese were being irrationally blamed for everything from the epidemics of smallpox and typhoid to the bubonic plague—with specific threats directed toward Claus and others who hired them.[67]

Colonies Spoiled by the Drought

Claus had plenty of everything to run a great beet sugar enterprise—except people. He needed farmers to grow the beets, field laborers to cultivate and harvest the beets, and refinery workers to extract the sugar. The population of Monterey County was sparse, and therefore the Salinas Valley was more or less undeveloped. The paucity of farmers able and willing to contractually fulfill the required obligations led Claus to create some innovative ways of accomplishing his goals.

He purchased thousands of acres around King City, Soledad, and Hollister, with a plan that future tenants would develop and farm the land for him. The Salvation Army, acting on Claus's encouragement and an 1898 donation of $1,000 ($34,000 in today's money), leased with the option to purchase "600 acres of rich agricultural land" to resettle homeless families.[68] The land was divided into small lots of ten or twenty acres and sold to needy families, mostly from San Francisco, on long-term payments.[69] The colony, called Fort Romie, provided a second chance to these families to establish themselves in life.[70] Some were hired by Claus to work either in the refinery or in harvesting the beets. Others took contracts for hoeing, thinning, and topping sugar beets. Unfortunately, the colonization coincided with the severe drought of 1897 and 1898. Due to the hardship brought about by the drought, many colonists left, and by 1903, there were only seventy working under contract, a shortage that forestalled any real success of the colonization effort.[71] Still, Claus's Fort Romie experiment, while not ultimately successful, was the first attempt made in California to resettle the unemployed where they could perhaps gain a foothold in life.

On the other side of the valley, St. Joseph's Colony, widely promoted by Claus, developed around the same time. Eleven thousand acres were purchased by the German Colonization Association at the foot of the Gabilan Range, about fifteen miles northeast of Salinas. Almost daily, it was said, trains loaded with middle-class families from Germany by way of Chicago arrived to settle in the Salinas Valley.[72] They began creating homes and, more important, getting their land in "shape for the cultivation of beets."[73] By 1899 many of these settlers were working in Claus's mammoth refinery. Some even moved into the town of Spreckels, or they relocated to Salinas and commuted to work. They "tended beet machinery, hauled beets, and shoveled beets into the sluice boxes alongside the plant. Many became sugar beet contractors or went to work for other famers in their fields."[74]

Unfortunately, the poor soil coupled with the drought of 1897 and 1898 also caused grief for the Germans who had come as tradesmen, merchants, and carpenters but not as farmers. Their enterprises collapsed. Some of the Germans returned home, and some moved to the city of Salinas to form the backbone of a devout German Catholic group.

The drought hit the Salinas Valley hard, not just those in the colonization programs that Claus sponsored. Hit the hardest were the people in the low hills south of King City, near one of the ranches Claus had bought to raise beets. The parched land caused cattle to die of starvation, and their owners were reportedly eating animal fodder to survive. A citizens' relief committee under the San Francisco Merchants Association was formed in San Francisco, and Claus, through Governor James Budd, donated $25,000 in cash. Farmers made their way to the makeshift headquarters in King City to receive "cash and hay." They could have taken their share of cash in either a loan or a donation, but most, if not all, refused a charitable donation. Three years later, the fiercely proud farmers attempted to repay the $25,000 in full, but Claus refused to accept it, declaring that it was a gift, to the lasting endearment of farming families in the valley. Demonstrating their collective independence, the farmers donated to the library of the University of California to finance a long list of notable acquisitions.[75] All the while, Claus was demonstrating new technologies and teaching skills that would dramatically transform agriculture in the Salinas Valley forever with his systems of irrigation.

Selling Off the Valley Road

The same time construction was going on in the Salinas Valley, construction continued on the San Francisco and San Joaquin Valley Railroad (the Valley Road). It was a celebrated day in 1896 when locomotive engine number 1, the Claus Spreckels, with Claus Spreckels himself on board, pulled its first excursion train over the new tracks from Stockton to Fresno, a one-hundred-mile trip. Waiting for the train was Governor Budd, who proposed "three cheers" for President Claus Spreckels after he disembarked. Humbled, Claus said, "I feel more strongly than ever that this is the people's enterprise," and when he projected the valley's population to grow from 1,500 people to 5,000,000 due to this venture, champagne corks popped in the air.[76]

In July 1898 the line was extended to Bakersfield, with a spur into Visalia. At every railroad stop, the train had been met with great fanfare by those relieved to be out from under the tyranny of the SP. But when the SP immediately lowered its rates far below those of the Valley Road, independent farmers and merchants chose savings over loyalty. Rumors had begun to swirl even during the construction of the Valley Road that the Santa Fe Railroad would be interested in purchasing the line to extend its service into San Francisco. So, in December 1898, just four years after it had been conceived, Claus and his partners voted to sell it because it was not a moneymaker. The deal was quickly done, with stockholders receiving the par value of their stock and the Santa Fe acquiring rail lines that merged easily with their own. The legal transfer of the Valley Road was completed on December 4, 1900, and many farmers up and down the valley cussed the name of Spreckels because the sale of "the People's Railroad" (as the Valley Road was known) meant the railroad won out in the end. Some pointed their fingers angrily at Claus for selling out, but like Levi Strauss, he believed, "If the deal is an honest one and a competing line is to be brought into the state, then the Valley Road was not built in vain. Its purpose will be accomplished no matter who may be the owners so long as it is not the Southern Pacific."[77]

In the end, Claus was tired. He didn't mind pulling out one more of his "irons in the fire," as he used to refer to his many ventures. He was now in his eighth decade, and priorities were becoming all too important. Right around the corner another threat—so small, it could only be seen under a microscope, but large enough to destroy all of his plans and dreams—would need his full attention.

17   *Too Many Irons in the Fire*

In June 1899 superintendent Percy Morse was on his routine inspections of fields for the Spreckels Sugar Company at the King City ranch, forty miles south of the town of Spreckels. Strolling through rows of growing sugar beets under the warm sunshine, ledger in hand, he looked for anything amiss, particularly irrigation problems. He hadn't gotten far when he was stopped in his tracks by the sight of severely curled leaves on several plants. Alarmed, he moved in closer to notate "yellow spots on the leaves." When he began to dig below the soil to determine the health of the beet, he was alarmed at the vegetable's withered state. Morse noted in one of his reports that he saw a large number of small insects on the beets and speculated they might be the culprit. Not knowing anything else to do, he ordered the fields to be sprayed with a variety of insecticides and germicides. After several days he observed the application had had no effect and the disease continued to spread throughout the crop. He abandoned the idea that insects were the root of the problem.[1]

Fighting a Mysterious Enemy

This situation demanded Claus's full attention, and he was forced to put another iron in the fire. Unchecked, this disease threatened to bring his great dream to ruin. Any disease at all could reduce the sugar yield by more than 20 percent.[2] But if the entire crop died, he had bigger problems. Claus ordered that "samples of the blighted beets be sent to universities, to federal and state agencies and even to laboratories in Germany and Hungary."[3] The answer from abroad was that the disease was totally unknown to both European plant pathologists and American beet growers.

Utilizing the advice he passed on to his grandchildren, Claus knew that "hard cash, expert advisers and common sense" had to be employed when he didn't thoroughly understand a business problem.[4] Soon, the entire farming industry knew that Claus's burgeoning sugar beet industry had a serious problem when the *Botanical Gazette* reported, "Dr. Albert Schneider has resigned the professorship of botany, pharmacognosy, and materia medica in the California College of Pharmacy, to accept the position of pathologist and physiologist of the Spreckels Sugar Company and he is devoting his entire time at present to the investigation of the so-called California sugar-beet blight."[5]

In Spreckels time, a new breed of employees was hired to fight the war on the mysterious and unknown enemy. In the "experimental station" led by Dr. Schneider were pathologists, biochemists, and entomologists all contracted to keep the great Salinas Valley enterprise alive.[6] As the days of experimentation went on, the blight went unchecked, and Claus ordered that a "quarter of the acreage" around King City to be plowed in the hopes that it wouldn't spread to nearby healthy crops. In time, the decision was made to abandon beet growing operations altogether there and instead invest in a herd of Holstein cows. They could be fed at no cost with beet pulp, their milk would feed people, and their manure could fertilize beet fields. Claus hoped the King City beets would be the first and last to be plowed under. Meanwhile, he put all his trust in his expensive experts as he returned to another iron in the fire.

The Smokestack Revenge

In the spring of 1898 soot from a 175-foot-high smokestack at one of the San Francisco Gas and Electric Company's plants on Stevenson Street had begun to blacken the stunning white marble of the outside walls of Claus's namesake skyscraper on Market Street.[7] Of course, Claus issued a formal complaint to the offending company. If what was happening to his building's exterior wasn't enough to raise the hair on the back of Claus's neck, complaints began to pour in from his building's tenants, whose expensive rental offices were being impacted by both smoke and ash-smudged windows. Apparently, Claus's repeated formal complaints were not getting the attention he hoped for.

As Claus was contemplating what further action he'd take, he was lunching at the exclusive Pacific-Union Club and happened to spot at a nearby table Joseph B. Crockett, the president of the offending utility company. According to an account by another club member, Charles Coleman, Claus left his table to present his complaint personally to Crockett: "When are you going to do something about the smoke from your power houses? The soot is blackening the wall of my building and filling my tenants' offices." Claus was instantly and publicly rebuffed by Crockett, who turned his back on him and coldly stated, "I make it a practice not to discuss business at the club." The widely circulated story of Claus's revenge went like this: Embarrassed and angry, he left his lunch unfinished and stormed back to his office. Within two hours, he had a meeting with a lawyer and his engineer. With the pledge of $15 million ($505 million in today's money), he finalized plans to start his own gas-and-light venture with the declaration of a rate war and the sole intent to put Crockett out of business for good.[8]

While Claus was seeking vengeance for the public rebuff and a permanent solution to the problem at hand, he knew that profits could be made in this field and the public would benefit from an upgraded system. Seeing that Claus meant business, the board of SF Gas and Electric elected one of their wealthy stockholders, Claus's son Rudolph, to the board of directors. They clearly understood the only way to stop the trajectory to ruin was to hire a Spreckels to beat a Spreckels.

Claus's new Independent Light and Power Company, organized on March 29, 1899, was, of course, upgraded in every way and performed exactly as its founder had envisioned.[9] Claus liked beauty. He believed that overhead electric wires were ugly and would have none of that with his new company. In the course of buying terra-cotta conduits to be placed underground, he was appalled at the quoted prices. Forthwith, he established a pottery company and manufactured his own conduits.[10]

Attracted by lower prices for their utilities, San Franciscans saw the benefit of breaking the back of the ten-year-old monopoly of the overpriced and outmoded San Francisco Gas and Electric Company, and switched their services over to Independent. Crockett's stockholders were dismayed as they watched their stock plummet in value. Crockett's poor management came to light, and the rate wars put the decade-old company near bankruptcy. Stockholder Rudolph Spreckels watched his $100-per-share investment sink to $30, thanks to his father's rate wars. Officers of SF Gas and Electric were rebuffed when they tried to reach a settlement. They even sent politicians and respected city leader Levi Strauss, Claus's friend, to "take him out of the game." But Claus wouldn't budge.[11]

Rudolph was determined to regain value of his stocks even if that meant going up against his father publicly again. A chip off the old block, he won control of the board of directors. He eliminated the corrupt practices that had previously infected its management, forced the resignation of Crockett, and efficiently reorganized the company to enable it to profit in spite of its continued rate war with his father's Independent Light and Power Company. The *San Francisco Chronicle* gleefully reported that Joe Crockett was now "without work and flat broke" and gave the "formidable old sugar king" one more hard-earned victory.[12]

Within two years Claus was enjoying immense profits, and he extended his utilities operations by organizing them on January 3, 1901, adjacent to his refinery at Potrero Point. His two plants were more than well equipped, efficient, and modern by industry standards. Everyone close to him beseeched him to pull back an iron from the fire. He was not looking well. So, with his point made, and receiving many hearty slaps upon the back, Claus sold his utility company to SF Gas and Electric on September 1, 1903. He received a profit of $2.5 million in cash and $5 million in bonds ($78 million and $156 million, respectively, in today's money). The record also shows that "he made a clear profit of $1,214,000 [about $38 million in today's money] as recompense for the coal smoke that had smudged the walls and windows of his office building at Third and Market Streets."[13] His bank account and the public both benefited mightily when costs were brought down to more realistic levels with his upgraded facilities. After this buyout, all competing companies were consolidated under the efficient management of a single company, which within two years merged with Pacific Gas and Electric Company. (Today PG&E serves most of northern and central California.)

Rudolph had been a worthy adversary, and Claus was impressed with his youngest son's tactical strategies, the business moves that could have been learned by his side. Not long after this episode, Rudolph disposed of much of his utilities interests at a huge profit, and both father and son were gratefully out of the utility business.[14] This experience proved beneficial because Claus was slowly growing in respect for his youngest son and Rudolph was beginning to find his passion: speaking out against the corrupt alliance between politics and the big business that had taken hold in San Francisco.

The Temple of Music

When Golden Gate Park opened in 1870, nature-starved San Franciscans were elated. They had never found much delight in the few small public squares in the city: Union Square, Portsmouth Square, and Washington Square. The idea of an urban park, a public pleasure ground for use by all classes of people, was a new and democratic concept. New York had Central Park (1858), Philadelphia had Fairmont Park (1865), and Brooklyn had Prospect Park (1866). It was time for San Francisco to have a park on the "great sand waste" in the city's "Outside Lands."[15] It was constructed on 1,017 acres of a half-mile-wide, mostly windblown rectangle stretching for three miles to the Pacific Ocean. The pastoral landscape, with more than thirty thousand trees, fulfilled its purpose to be a sylvan retreat for San Franciscans, both rich and poor, to escape the pressures of the noisy city.

Adolph had become ardent about his role in the park after being appointed a park commissioner by Governor James Budd in 1898. Alongside Adolph in 1899 was fellow park commissioner Reuben Hedley Lloyd, the attorney who had unsuccessfully prosecuted him fourteen years earlier for the attempted murder of Michael de Young.[16] Clearly Lloyd had reversed his attitude toward him, because he was the one who nominated Adolph to be the president of the Golden Gate Park Commission in 1900.

Band shells were popular across the country and provided entertainment for their respective communities. On Sundays, people flocked to their indoor or outdoor music concourses to hear musical conductors present everything from waltzes and polkas to overtures from famous operas or movements from symphonies. Adolph successfully nudged Claus into donating the entire amount for constructing a band shell in the park. Designed by the Reid Brothers architectural firm, the Spreckels Temple of Music is a 75-foot-high, 160-foot-wide neoclassical masonry structure, composed of "California sandstone of bluish gray tint." Of course, since the name Spreckels was attached ("go big or go home"), the Temple of Music was said to be "unexcelled by any structure used for a similar purpose in the world." The half-dome band shell, with its two flanking colonnades of eight pairs of ionic columns, was built in the Music Concourse, designed to be the cultural center of Golden Gate Park. The Spreckels Temple of Music was engineered so that up to seventy-five thousand people would be able to hear "the range of the most delicate shades and tones of music."[17]

30. The Spreckels Temple of Music was a gift to the city of San Francisco. It was designed to be the cultural center of Golden Gate Park and was touted to be "unexcelled by any structure used for a similar purpose in the world" ("Electric Illumination," *San Jose [CA] Mercury-News*, September 10, 1900). Courtesy of Terrence and Virginia Wilson private collection.

In 1900 almost a half century had passed since Claus had made San Francisco his home, and September 9, California's Admission Day, was sentimentally chosen for the dedication of the Spreckels Temple of Music. Claus's dedication speech reveals that he was reminiscing over the day when as a young, twenty-eight-year-old immigrant grocer, he had arrived just six years after California had in 1850 become the thirty-first state to join the Union. Even though the structure was built with terraces around the perimeter capable of seating twenty thousand, it was standing room only for ten thousand others for the official "music stand presentation."[18]

At the appointed time of 1 p.m., Claus, who was never late to anything, stepped up to the stage and stood between the columns. Following in his steps were Anna, Adolph, John, and Lillian, along with their children: twenty-two-year-old Grace, nineteen-year-old Lillie, eighteen-year-old John Jr. "Jack," and twelve-year-old Claus Jr. Most in attendance had never seen Mr. Spreckels in person, but his image was well known, and the crowd recognized him at once and went crazy with applause.[19] Certainly there were whispers in the crowd that two branches of the family were conspicuously absent on this momentous day: Gus and Oroville along with fifteen-year-old Lurline, and Rudolph and Nellie along with their two-year-old son, Howard.

As Claus was ushered to center stage, the multitude of thirty thousand slowly grew silent, shushing each other so they could hear what San Francisco's famous septuagenarian had to say.[20] Nervous, he cleared his throat and began to read his carefully prepared speech, which demonstrated the full depth of his passion for the city he had been instrumental in building:

> California has been for 50 years a state of the American Union, and I have been for nearly fifty years a citizen of California. I was among those who came in early manhood to take part in the development of the rich resources of this golden land and to lay the foundations upon which the fabric of her prosperity rests. Whatever may have been the experience of others, my labors in California have been abundantly rewarded. . . . I have found its people as generous as the soil and society here as rich in human virtues as are the mountains with gold. My experience has been that whoever works in California with the honesty of a true industry and meets the opportunities she offers with a fair degree of sagacity will not fail to find ample reward for all work of hand and head and heart.[21]

A small portion of his speech was memorialized on a stunning silver plaque alongside his etched image and ceremoniously presented to him at his home two weeks after the dedication by the Merchants Association. Claus's eyes filled with tears after they told him, while they were grateful for the band shell, the city was indebted to him more for the thousands of San Franciscans he employed, to which he responded: "I have never wished for any other home nor longed for anything on earth that California could not give."[22]

Adolph recounted that his father had agreed to only $60,000 ($2 million in today's money) for the construction, and when the Reid Brothers' invoice crossed his desk, he was dismayed to see the cost exceeded the architect's estimate by $15,000. Adolph, "confident his father would pay no more than the price originally agreed upon," quickly and quietly paid the balance.[23]

Continuing the Fight against Curly Top Virus

The Golden Gate Park event was one of the highlights of Claus's life, but there was still an iron in the fire that needed his attention. The blight of his beet crops remained a puzzle. It was serious and active one year, mild in another. Curiously, there was no blight found in any field in the Pajaro Valley, near his former Watsonville refinery.

One Watsonville farmer switched out Claus's German beet seeds for American-grown seeds and produced approximately 36.33 tons per acre, double what most farmers considered excellent. In time, the Spreckels Sugar Company determined the successful production of curly-top-resistant beet seed showed the need for producing varieties adapted to local and diverse regions, and not from European seeds. This reversal in policy resulted in the development of a new breeding program and domestic seed industry for the country.[24]

Rather than celebrating and rewarding the Pajaro Valley's farmers, who were providing a bumper crop of beets for the refinery, the Spreckels Sugar Company, with decisions being made by John Spreckels and William H. Hannam of the American Sugar Refining Company, made a foolish mistake. Anxious to make up profits out of their blight-stricken operation in the Salinas Valley, they announced to the Watsonville farmers that their free ride was over. The Spreckels Sugar board decided the Pajaro Valley farmers would now pay fifty cents a ton for hauling to the refinery, just like everybody else.[25]

As Claus's first beet growers, they had been enjoying free transport according to their original contracts, and now they were deeply offended. Passing daily by the abandoned refinery sitting on the land they had contributed to only increased their resentment. The region's farmers met in Watsonville to hold an "indignation meeting," which resulted in the founding of the Pajaro Valley Beet-Growers Association in 1902.[26] Empowered with their healthy, unblighted crops, they came up with demands. Primarily, they wanted the price they were paid for their beets raised by fifty cents a ton, to cover the freight cost. Second, they demanded that one of their own act as "representative," to ensure that farmers were being credited for an accurate weight after their loads were washed and weighed. Unbeknown to Claus, these demands were ignored.[27] The farmers' actions were louder than words when instead of the 5,352 acres of beets planted in 1902, only 288 acres were planted in 1903.

The blight spread in the Salinas Valley unevenly, but now a large number of small wedge-shaped insects were easily observed on the plants, and the investigation switched from soil and seed to insect. It would be several more years until it was learned the insect, dubbed the beet leafhopper, was indeed the culprit of the virus. The "thickening of the veins of the leaf" was referred to as "curly leaf" or "blight" or "curly top." Ultimately, Dr. Elmer Ball, a nationally renowned entomologist, demonstrated that curly top virus occurred when insects fed on other diseased vegetables or plants in the wild, then transmitted the disease to a young crop of insect-enticing sugar beets.[28]

While Claus relished being first in everything, this was a first he disliked being attached to. The first virus disease of plants in America, coined "curly top," would be forever linked to Claus's sugar beets in 1899.[29] A great deal of attention and subsequent study by several scientists would be needed as curly top rapidly emerged as a threat to American sugar beet production in the West.

Battling C&H Sugar

On April 29, 1898, another iron was put in the fire. A new threat, a serious one, had appeared when the California Beet Sugar and Refining Company started refining sugar in a little settlement north of San Francisco called Crockett. Led by Canadian Robert Paterson Rithet, the company produced its first refined white sugar, not from beets but from raw Hawaiian cane. (The company never actually refined beets, as they had hoped—because of bad timing [the drought], fears of the curly top disease, and location [the Crockett refinery was too far from the beet fields].) Rithet was assured a good supply of Hawaiian cane due the connections he made with the missionary-descended planters in Hawai'i as consul for British Columbia. The sugarcane-refining company bowed to reality in 1899 and switched its name to California and Hawaiian Sugar Refining Company (C&H).[30] Rithet knew what he was doing, and by 1902 C&H was manufacturing one-sixth as much sugar as the Spreckelses' refinery in Potrero.

Sharing the western market was not an option for the Spreckels family. With C&H entering the picture, it was obvious the supply of sugar would exceed demand, and this threat would have to be dealt with. With John now president of Western Sugar Refining—and with Claus up and down with diabetes and consumed with his Salinas Valley venture, and with Adolph ailing sporadically with syphilis—it would be up to him and William Hannam (representing the 50-percent partnership) to fight for survival. But as Claus's firstborn son, John held his father's legacy on his shoulders.

The price war began earnestly in 1902, with both refineries cutting prices and cutting prices again. As a sugar refiner in Canada, Rithet had faced rivalry before, when a smear campaign against him had been carried out in the newspapers, claiming "smallpox germs were being carried by bugs" that were found in his sugar from China.[31] But the Spreckels family would never resort to this type of rivalry; dirty tricks had never been their style. They had enough capital to just keep slashing prices until C&H could realize no profits. Not only did the Spreckels family have more capital to sustain a price war, but more importantly, Claus had established relationships with his San Francisco jobbers (wholesalers), who knew better than to deal with the opposition lest they incur his ill will.

The sugar war ended in record time, the same year it started. To repay their loyalty, at Christmastime Claus withdrew half a million dollars ($16.2 million in today's money) to give each one of his jobbers a very Merry Christmas: a check equal to "a quarter of a cent of every pound of sugar they handled during the struggle with C&H." Their response was appropriate: on January 7, 1903, the Wholesale Grocers' Association, with one hundred distinguished representatives from three West Coast states, gave a sumptuous banquet at the Palace Hotel to honor Claus. When the toastmaster of the evening referred to him as "the grand old man of California," the seventy-four-year-old Claus loudly interrupted, "Hey! I consider myself as young as anyone present," to great laughter across the room.[32] At each table setting, a miniature sugar barrel and a satin ribbon was imprinted with a portrait of Claus and an image of the Golden Gate Park band shell. Following a very short speech on the greatness of California, Claus held on tightly to his walking cane and strolled around the tables, clinking glasses with each guest. It was a happy evening.

In early 1903 C&H waved the white flag. They presented Claus, through John, with an interesting proposition. They offered a three-year lease of their C&H refinery for $150,000 a year. After having lost $600,000 in the price war, C&H could recoup some of that money in the yearly lease, which would buy them time to reorganize more efficiently. The Spreckels interests agreed they had to do this deal because it included presigned contracts for fifty thousand tons a year of raw Hawaiian sugar. When they then discovered the contract for the purchase price of Hawaiian sugar was a quarter cent a pound under the going price, they estimated that this alone would be a savings of $250,000 a year ($7.8 million a year in today's money). When the deal was done, Claus was content because "his people" had eliminated the competition for a three-year period and had made a profit out of the whole deal. With his Western Sugar Refining again in control of the market, Claus hoped that John, Adolph, and Hannam were keeping a sharp eye out for any other rivals, including the resurrection of the humbled c&h.

Stress and Stroke

In July 1903 Claus's daughter, Emma, initiated a lawsuit against him for the possession of a business block in Honolulu valued at $400,000, and for $100,000 in damages. In the days following her elopement, to prove that Tom Watson had married her only for love, she had quitclaimed the real estate. She had settled in the village of Lower Kingsford, Surrey, England, in a mansion where no children came along. But by all accounts, Emma was happy living in the "magnificent old manor house situated in a vast and beautifully terraced park" surrounded by animals.[33] Every Christmas, she invited the entire village to a lawn party and gave each guest a present, winning the hearts of both the young and old.

Claus undoubtedly read the news article in 1901, stating, "Mr. Watson is fast taking on himself all the airs and the honors of a lord of the manor. Both he and Mrs. Watson have been giving dollars and time to the charities and the poor funds of Lower Kingsford."[34] Having the real estate back would be helpful, so she sued her father to recover the prime parcels in Hawai'i. With this legal action, which would ultimately be unsuccessful on the part of Emma, the heartbroken Claus felt betrayed all over again.

This lawsuit brought on more untold stress, and in September 1903 Claus suffered "a slight stroke of paralysis . . . in such a manner that he could scarcely speak."[35] On October 19, 1903, to avoid any publicity, John and Lillian whisked his parents, along with two of their servants, down to the Hotel del Coronado for complete rest, relaxation, and medical care.[36] John kept the hotel's staff on their toes attending to his father. The hotel ledger indicates that meals were sent to the rooms, indicating that Claus was following doctor's orders to rest.[37] Ten days later, when they railed back to San Francisco, it was hoped by all that the worst was behind Claus.

Unfortunately, Claus then suffered a second stroke the following month, which left him unable to speak, thus forcing him to turn business negotiations over to others. This was a staggering blow to Claus, who liked to be in control; the temporary loss of speech meant he was no longer able to ensure that his demands were being met. The finest doctors that money could buy were brought to the mansion, creating a spectacle in Pacific Heights. The sugar king's strokes sent reporters to John's nearby doorstep at midnight in the hopes of landing a headline story. John, obviously cranky, told the press, "Reports of his serious illness are exaggerated. I have nothing more to say." He then slammed the door.[38]

C & H behind the Scenes

As Claus struggled to regain his health and his sons were distracted, Robert Rithet at C & H was making great plans. He quietly talked to the prominent sugar factors in Hawai'i and invited them to invest in the Crockett refinery to specifically "participate in the refiners' margin."[39] They jumped at the chance to establish a cooperative refinery.

Sugar Factors Company Ltd. was organized under the laws of the territory of Hawai'i on June 16, 1904, with $3 million in capital, which rapidly increased to $5 million. Thirty-seven different plantations held stock, which represented a whopping 80 percent of the total sugar production in Hawai'i.[40] The Sugar Factors Company bought stock in C & H. They hired expert engineers and mechanics and invested in modern machinery with plans to overhaul the Crockett refinery. With the reorganization and reopening of the refinery when the lease with the Spreckels family was up, C & H began planning to take over the sugarcane business from the Spreckels family, and there was nobody to stop them.

The Reconciliation of 1905

Retaliation instead of forgiveness was a theme in the life of Claus Spreckels, even when it involved his children. But after the strokes, the actions by C & H, his dissatisfaction with John's and Adolph's mishandling of his affairs, and intense reflection at the start of a New Year, Claus sought to repair the fractured relationships with his younger children in January of 1905. Rudolph, age thirty-three, living just down the street, was first on Claus's list to make amends with. Rudolph was eager to restore relationships with his elderly parents and assured his father that he'd urge Gus, forty-six, and his saddened sister, Emma, a recent widow at thirty-seven, to also be amenable to a reconciliation.

Both Claus and Anna had been pining for their only daughter, especially after learning that she had no children and her husband had died. Once Emma heard about their failing health, she was easily encouraged to reconcile with her parents. Headlines such as "Spreckels Feud Happily Ended" were broadcast in February 1905: "Rudolph Spreckels and his father, millionaire Claus Spreckels, have made up after having been bitter enemies since 1899. Claus's health is failing, he is in his eighties and is becoming at peace with his children. It is said his only daughter, Mrs. Emma Watson, is on her way from London to effect a reconciliation with the richest man in California."[41] After Emma's arrival, the *Oakland Tribune*, on March 11, 1905, reported that Claus Spreckels looked "ten years younger" since the reunion with his only daughter.[42] Neither one was sorry for their previous actions, but it was nonetheless the sweetest reunion for both.

A reconciliation with Gus was harder to obtain. He was living a very separate life far away from the San Francisco hostilities. As Gus remembered it, "He [Claus] sent for me and told me that he had discovered his mistake and was sorry. He said it was the biggest mistake of his life, and to rectify it as far as possible he intended to make me the executor of his will."[43] Soon, the following news came via the *Sacramento Daily Union*: "Gus Spreckels has been forgiven by his father. All the old differences have been forgotten and all the bitterness that was engendered has been assuaged. I hear that even Mrs. Gus Spreckels has been forgiven by her mother-in-law for that little faux pas that was reported to have taken place in New York some years ago."[44] That "faux pas" was Anna's very public exit from the Palace Hotel after she overheard Oroville harshly refer to her as "that old woman" some years back. It was well known that Anna disliked even the mention of Oroville's name after that episode.

But all was forgiven when Gus, Oroville, and their beautiful twenty-one-year-old Lurline arrived in San Francisco and checked into the brand-new luxurious St. Francis Hotel at Union Square for the planned reconciliation. This would be the last chance to see her grandparents as a "Spreckels," since she was engaged to marry the prominent Spencer Eddy, serving as an attaché at the American embassy in Saint Petersburg. Lurline, who hadn't seen her grandparents since she was seven years old, remembered the moment when the phone in their suite rang: "That was my grandmother—she wants to see all of us!"[45]

And just like that, the end of the fourteen-year estrangement was over between Claus and his three younger children. The reconciliation confused the San Francisco elite, who for more than a decade had ensured that Claus's younger sons were never on the same invitation list with him or with the elder sons. "Society hosts and hostesses had to be very particular about dinner invitations to the members of the Spreckels family."[46] It's unknown whether Claus took one bold last move to unite all five of their warring children in their final years, but such a move would've been futile in the case of John. He wouldn't consider making amends with siblings he considered disloyal troublemakers. He was astonished and angry that his parents could easily forget and forgive, considering all that they had endured because of their vengeance.

Aloha of 1905

A little later, Claus, with speech returned but only slightly stable enough to travel, decided it was time to return to Hawai'i to continue his rehabilitation in the mild climate and to enjoy the relative privacy. The plan was for Anna to follow as soon he could arrange the reopening of the mansion and hire the requisite help.[47] Traveling from San Francisco with Claus was the ever-faithful William Irwin, who at sixty-one, was much younger and much help.

As the *Australia* pulled into Honolulu Harbor on Friday, April 21, 1905, Claus's "snow white hair" was spotted; he was sitting in his easy chair on the deck. Once the ship docked, it was reported that Claus rose up and walked slowly up and down clutching the handrail, eager to notice any changes that had occurred in his long absence. Looking down at the wharf, he was astounded at the great crowd assembled to greet him, including members of the legislature. It was big news the former "power behind the Hawaiian throne," the "uncrowned king of Hawai'i," had returned to the islands, and the *Evening Bulletin* proclaimed, "Hawaii Welcomes the Sugar King Claus Spreckels!" It was reported that "his feeble step," which required the aid of a cane, showed "only too well that he need[ed] rest."[48]

One journalist for the *Hawaiian Gazette* interviewed Captain Thomas Dowdell about Claus's condition during the journey. He recalled, "Why, during the worst of the storm into which we ran, Mr. Spreckels sat in my cabin smoking a cigar as complacently as if he were in his office in San Francisco. You can't get him seasick!"[49]

It had been nearly twelve years since his previous visit, and curious journalists followed his moves. One reporter described, "[He is of] medium height, compactly built, and dresses neatly. His round head is covered with a thick growth of hair, now white." The journalists were surprised that soon after arriving at Irwin's home in Waikiki, Claus left almost immediately for Chambers Drug Store on the downtown corner of Fort and King Streets, the hub of the city and the point of departure for the new electric cars. While waiting and seated at the counter, he shook hands all around, and when asked what his initial thoughts were, he replied, "Honolulu is greatly improved since I left and there have been buildings erected which would do credit to a large city on the mainland." When asked what he thought about the electric car system he was about to board, he answered, "[It's] a great improvement over the mule car system we used to have." The reporter noted that he said "we" like the "old Kamaaina he is." Standing by was the aged hackman Manuel Reis, who used to drive Claus "scores of times" in the old days, when he pulled the tram by mule, who said, "I wish Mr. Spreckels would have let me drive. I would do it for nothing just for old-time's sake." Everywhere he went, Claus was the "cynosure of all eyes," and repeatedly stated, smiling, that despite all rumors, he had no "financial deals" on his mind but that he had come to Honolulu for strictly the benefit of his health, believing the "island climate would improve his health in a place he well knew." The reporter was skeptical, saying, "His heart is in his business, and he will die working." The entire page was devoted to his life but showed that missionaries still ruled the island; the article curiously ended, "Spreckels is not a church-goer."[50]

Claus was honored in every news story in Hawai'i. He was no longer the "ruthless interloper" or an "invader" but a loyal supporter of the monarchy and the greatest entrepreneur to ever have landed on their shores. Claus, the mellowed royalist, would've been warmly welcomed by Lili'uokalani at her private home, Washington Place. Even as the life of old Hawai'i was slipping away, the former queen remained as loyal to her culture and as "royal" as she had ever been. She was the most high-profile personality in Honolulu, beloved by both residents and visitors. This was not only out of sympathy;

indeed, she was revered and given more respect and ceremonial courtesy after her dethronement than she had ever received as the sitting monarch. She became a cherished link with Hawai'i's past, and many notable figures paid homage to her throughout her life.

In the midst of directing repairs and whatnot for his mansion, Claus "received a letter saying that Mrs. Spreckels was too ill to join him."[51] With that, he hastily returned to San Francisco on May 23, 1905, to attend to his beloved Anna, who had been besieged by heart problems for some time, and he was mightily worried. Anna was well enough to return to Hawai'i with Claus a month later. They arrived together, along with four servants, on June 23. The *Alameda* docked at the Oceanic Wharf at 7:45 a.m. after a newsworthy time of five days and eighteen hours due to perfect weather and smooth seas.[52] Anna found the mansion untouched, just as they had left it twelve years earlier, "as if the host and hostess and guests had been away for merely a night."[53]

Kamaaina (longtime Hawaiian residents) who had remembered Claus and Anna from years gone by awaited an invitation to visit with their old friends, but none came. Anna was still ailing and soon wanted to return to San Francisco to be near her doctors. It had been Claus's plan that he and Anna might spend their last days in their opulent tropical home and let the warm and balmy weather soothe their weary souls and body. But it was noted, "[The] climate here does not agree with Mrs. Spreckels, hence the plan of remaining here permanently has been abandoned."[54]

Unbeknown to many, their son Rudolph had been with them in Honolulu for the entire month of July, discussing a business proposition, while his wife, Nellie, and the children vacationed at the Hotel Del Monte in Monterey. Interestingly, however, Rudolph didn't accompany his ailing parents' home at the end of August; John, the dutiful eldest son, was put upon to be the escort. John was met at the dock by the usual reporters and briskly said, "I came down just for the trip and to accompany my people back on the *Alameda* on her return trip."[55] He then looked around for the family's business partner, William Irwin, who had come to escort him to his parents' home. Once hands were shaken, it was noted they engaged in a lengthy hush-hush conversation before taking off. Most likely, John was hearing firsthand reports pertaining to his enemy brother Rudolph and his parents' health condition. At the mansion, John helped his parents get ready to go home on August 30, 1905. The windows were shuttered, the doors locked, outside gates bolted, and both Claus and Anna looked painfully back at their beautiful mansion sitting sadly in a lush tropical setting. They both knew they would never be back.

Elder Brothers Ailing

Adolph was consumed with horses, and Claus was undoubtedly aware of the fact that he was spending a lot of time with his mistress, Alma de Bretteville, a San Francisco icon. In her teenage years, Alma had delivered the laundry her mother washed for the gentry, but she had also posed nude for paintings that hung in private homes and in some of the city's better restaurants. Legend holds that the six-foot-tall Alma had modeled for the figure of scantily clad Nike (the ancient Greek goddess of victory), which stands atop the eighty-five-foot monument in San Francisco's Union Square that was dedicated in 1902 to Admiral George Dewey, hero of the Spanish-American War.[56] Aside from this, in a high-profile court case, Alma at twenty-one had sued the millionaire Charles Anderson for breach of a marriage contract—or, as she later told her friends, "personal defloration."[57]

Alma was resolved to marry a rich man. "I'd rather be an old man's darling than a young man's slave," she once said.[58] In private rooms upstairs at the Poodle Dog Restaurant, Alma got to know Adolph Spreckels, more than two decades her senior. It was said, "Their knees touched, and they dined no more."[59] He became her "sugar daddy," as she called him, in 1903. He insisted the relationship remain secret, though, knowing his parents and his elder brother would never approve of Alma. Adolph's business partnership with John had yielded a formidable bank account, and in John's eyes, a serious relationship with a known "gold digger" could threaten their business relationship.

Just as his relationship with Alma started to blossom, Adolph suffered a stroke and went to Berlin in July 1904 for an undisclosed operation to treat his "apoplexy."[60] Syphilis-induced strokes were common. With the social stigma attached to having syphilis, a sexually transmitted disease, Adolph ensured the "stroke" became a bout with "appendicitis," and the *San Jose Mercury News* reported that Adolph had gone to Berlin for treatment.[61] Where he was likely going was Berlin's Charité Clinic, where doctors Fritz Schaudinn, a zoologist, and Erich Hoffman, a dermatologist, were working

31. Alma de Bretteville was determined to marry a rich man, and Adolph, twenty years her senior, became her "sugar daddy" in 1908. Library of Congress Prints and Photographs Division, George Grantham Bain Collection, LC-DIG-ggbain-36207 DLC.

hard to identify the cause of syphilis (in 1905 they zeroed in on the bacterium *Treponema pallidum*). It's unknown what treatment Adolph was given. As the bacterial disease moved from the secondary stage to the latent (hidden) phase, Adolph might have exhibited no symptoms, and this stage could last for years, but what Adolph feared was that his disease could progress to its third, often fatal, stage.

When John entered his fifties, he had a great deal of money, power, and fame, but his health was also waning. Even so, he was in better shape than his father, who hadn't improved much from his two strokes and was suffering more complications from diabetes. In 1905 Claus importuned John to assume the role of president of the Spreckels Sugar Company. Meanwhile, the best physicians couldn't pinpoint the source of John's persistent illness and ultimately diagnosed an "obscure and obdurate digestive disorder."[62] His family and friends were more than alarmed with his drastic weight loss: "From nearly 200 pounds he can now scarcely budge the scales at the 140 mark."[63]

The press, during this time of sickness, couldn't refrain from commenting on John's former status as an amateur boxer and speculated the "former athlete" was "paying the price."[64] The chronic pain in his spine along with the intestinal issues had all become too much. News of John's illness had already become public in June 1904, when he was unable to attend the Republican National Convention in Chicago.[65] Those who ran C&H were well aware of the medical problems of the Spreckels family and quietly awaited the day of April 1, 1906, when the Spreckels lease was due to expire, so they could jump into action and implement their operations in Crockett, California, with the single-minded purpose to beat Claus Spreckels once and for all.

Not only was unwanted news of John's private illness being published, but his public losses were also receiving attention. In 1904 the stockholders of the Oceanic Steamship Company were told by John that a drought in Australia had "seriously affected the business of all steamship lines." He told them things were looking bad and they had suffered a net loss of $234,672.01 along with a net loss for the preceding year of $439,303.72.[66] But he optimistically encouraged his stakeholders that Australia was recovering from the "misfortune" and the situation was improving for resumed service. Unfortunately, between late 1905 and early 1906, the press circulated stories that the Oceanic Steamship Company had suffered yet another money-losing year. John defensively provided a statement indicating the loss was due to strong competition and the effects of Australia's and New Zealand's unfavorable tariffs. A year later, the Oceanic Steamship Company lost the mail contracts to Australia, and the *Pacific Commercial Advertiser*, no longer under the Spreckels influence, reported the Oceanic was in a "hapless condition," with no comment from its owners, neither John nor Adolph.[67]

Likely, the stress of his beloved steamship company losing millions and his forced reentry into leading his father's sugar business didn't help John's state of mind. In January 1906 he was unable to digest food and stopped eating. He was intravenously nourished for three months, but it was said that he kept his sense of humor throughout. At a very low point, he asked to see his lawyers, despite the fact that his legal affairs had already been put in order. When Lillian questioned the request, he retorted, "Why shouldn't I have a lawyer too? There is a doctor in the next room all the time; the undertaker has been sitting impatiently at the front door for weeks and you know the cast of this show isn't complete without a lawyer."[68]

In early March the entire family was deeply alarmed by John's "precarious condition," which had left him unable to get out of his bed.[69] The *Oakland Tribune* reported that his son Jack was moving up and "familiarizing himself with the business" due to his father's "dying condition."[70] At the end of March Grace was summoned home from her trip abroad to see her father one last time.[71] By all accounts, John was dying of some unknown malady.

Claus and Rudolph's Only Collaboration

As alarmed as he was over John's failing health, Claus found a new irritation to distract him in early 1906: overhead electric trolley lines in San Francisco. In 1902 most of the city's street railways were controlled by a syndicate of eastern investors and consolidated as the United Railroads of San Francisco. Patrick Calhoun, the grandson of the notorious John C. Calhoun, was its president. Prior to United's purchase, the former streetcar magnates, led by Henry E. Huntington, had dealt firmly with labor problems by sacking any man rumored of trying to organize a union. When ownership changed, workers unionized and won substantial wage increases. It was universal gossip that the eastern capitalists had overpaid, and now Calhoun and his eastern colleagues were disinclined to put any more money into advancements or wages.[72]

When United Railroads took over the system, it was only halfway converted to overhead-cable wires. Calhoun was determined to complete the conversion, thus standardizing the system, but he was met with strong public opposition. Most large cities had abandoned the cable car in favor of electricity when Frank Sprague invented an electric motor that turned cable cars into cheaper, faster, and larger streetcars. So why not San Francisco? And the sentiment in favor of electricity involved placing the electric wires in underground conduits, where, it was argued, they would be less dangerous and less unsightly than overhead wires.[73]

Soon after purchasing the railroad, United had begun to pay attorney Abraham Ruef a "regularly secret monthly fee" to "be on call" for the company. Ruef was the driving force behind the founding of the Union Labor Party. In a unique position of power, he was instrumental in getting an unknown musician, Eugene Schmitz, to run for mayor on the Union Labor Party ticket. Ruef's campaign was successful, and the charismatic and handsome Schmitz became mayor of San Francisco and Abraham Ruef's puppet.

In 1904 United Railroads began a public promotion to endorse expansion of the system with overhead-cable wires. To demonstrate the advantages, Calhoun proposed the electrification of Sutter Street. Not only did Rudolph own real estate at the corner of Sutter and Powell, but his home was also on the Pacific Avenue part of the Sutter Street Line. No way was this going to happen without a fight. This was the fight he took to his father in Hawai'i, knowing that Claus felt as he did: that the tall poles and ugly wires would not only mar the loveliness of their beautiful city by the bay but decrease the property values everywhere they were added. In the 1899 fight against his father with the utility company, Rudolph had secretly admired Claus's stance for placing conduits underground in the name of beauty, no matter the price.

In the spring of 1905 Rudolph organized the Sutter Street Improvement Club and went on public record in favor of underground conduits. This club teamed up with ex-mayor James D. Phelan, whose Association for the Improvement and Adornment of San Francisco was also against a citywide system of overhead-cable trolleys. Calhoun was incensed. He told attorney Ruef that the opposition to his plans came from "a group of petty, selfish, local financiers" who hated interlopers messing around with their "feudal province." Calhoun offered Rudolph "highly valuable inducements" to cease opposition to the overhead-cable trolley projects, inducements that Rudolph declined. Calhoun argued not only that conduit pipes were expensive but that they could be problematic in the rainy season. Rudolph insisted this could be easily solved by ordinary drainage pipes and even offered to pay the cost of constructing drainage pipes, an offer that Calhoun rejected.[74]

In February 1906 Ruef was paid $200,000 ($6.2 million in today's money) by Calhoun to get his puppet, Mayor Eugene Schmitz, to push forward his proposal for overhead wires. Schmitz's ordinance of 1906 permitted the street railway system to convert most of its remaining cable car lines to overhead-cable trolleys.[75] This move made it clear the Schmitz-Ruef administration was corrupt.

As a last resort, Claus and Rudolph, in their first father-son collaborative scheme, decided to organize a competing street railway company. Because Claus had been reported to be in a critical condition following his strokes, the community was shocked at his recovery, when on March 24, 1906, he made a public announcement informing United Railroads of San Francisco that if they persisted in their "overhead wire policy," he'd build a competing street railway and give the city a modern underground-wire system of street transportation. "Poles are cheap. We have a beautiful city, and I do not want to see it disfigured by more trolley lines!"[76]

The *Sacramento Daily Union* published an open letter to United Railroads reminding them of Claus Spreckels's track record with specific references: "He has an unequaled record for doing what he sets out to do, therefore, we advise the United Railways of San Francisco to do a little back-tracking in the matter of their overhead wire plans. . . . [Claus Spreckels] is not as young as he used to be but has the same old game spirit."[77] Calhoun didn't listen to the *Daily Union*'s advice, and Claus and Rudolph's Municipal Street Railways of San Francisco filed articles of incorporation in California on April 17, 1906. On the very next day, a catastrophic event would place the trolley pole controversy on the back burner, so Calhoun's company would count as the only monopoly Claus Spreckels didn't have a chance to break to his and the community's advantage.

18   *Claus's World Crumbles*

At 5:12 a.m. on Wednesday, April 18, 1906, a deep, foreboding rumble jolted Claus and Anna from their slumber, along with most every other San Franciscan. Twenty seconds later a massive earthquake followed. This tremendous shaking caused the crystal chandelier in their bedroom to fall and shatter, barely missing both himself and Anna.[1] The violent trembling, which seemed to go on forever but lasted less than a minute, drove the couple to the window as fast as their age allowed them. It's likely Anna arrived first, as Claus recounted having gashed his foot on a shard of chandelier glass. From their elevated vantage point, they witnessed the skyline swaying from the aftershocks. As they rushed to their front door, they could see the streets down below them buckle, chimneys snap off, and countless buildings collapse and crumble into rubble.

James Burgess Stetson, one of the wealthy founders of the notable mercantile firm Holbrook, Merrill & Stetson, was not only Claus and Anna's next-door neighbor but also their close friend. Stetson, age seventy-five, lived in a spectacular mansion at 1801 Van Ness and "jotted down" what he saw and experienced in the neighborhood during those initial terrifying moments and the ensuing weeks. Many of those accounts were about the Spreckels family. The shaking sent Stetson to his bedroom window, where through the "white dust," he was shocked to see "the chimneys of the Spreckels mansion were gone, the stone balustrade and carved work wrecked."[2]

Near to Claus and Anna, at the northwest corner of Washington and Gough Streets, lived their niece Emma Mangels Tillmann and her prosperous husband, Frederick Tillmann Jr.[3] (Claus had stepped into a surrogate role of both father to the Mangels brood and grandfather for their children after brother-in-law Claus Mangels had died suddenly at the age of fifty-five in 1891.) Seventeen-year-old Agnes Lily Tillmann recorded the event in her well-loved diary:

> At 5:12 we were all awakened by a terrific earthquake. It lasted 48 seconds and we all thought the world had come to an end. Every ornament fell and broke. Things went crashing down on all sides. We all rushed downstairs bare-footed. People ran out of their houses half crazed with fright. After the first shock, we ran up stairs and grabbed some clothing and then ran down and dressed in the parlor. There were shocks all during the day. . . . Both water and gas, were broken and every chimney was down. . . . Went out on the steps and porch. Soon rising above the hill we saw clouds of smoke and heard that there was an immense fire. The clouds of smoke grew larger and larger and soon we heard the fire could not be controlled. There was no water. The militia was sent out to fight the fire. They blasted. . . . We sat outside waiting for another earthquake every moment. . . . The fire came nearer and nearer and in the night instead of growing darker it grew lighter. The city was a roaring furnace, and it was a wonderful indescribable sight to see our own dearly beloved city burning. The fire caught one building after another—Call, Flood, Crocker, City Hall, etc. . . . Hundreds of people were camping opposite our house. China town burnt before sun down and the Chinese passed our house. No one cried or screamed—all suffered the same fate. I walked up the hill several times and had oh such a sight! Never shall I forget that night—Farewell to our beautiful S.F. in whose prosperity we were glorifying.[4]

The Great San Francisco Earthquake, with a moment magnitude scale of 7.9 (seismologists designate an earthquake as "great" if the magnitude is higher than 7.8), was felt as far north as southern Oregon, as far south as beyond Los Angeles, and as far inland as central Nevada. In the San Francisco area, it killed up to four thousand people instantly, displacing many more. The earthquake occurred when the San Andreas Fault, which bisected the San Francisco Peninsula, shifted just to the west of the city. The land along the eastern side of the fault, where the Spreckels family lived, moved southward, while land on the western side pushed northward. In the short period of time, the ground shifted twenty feet.[5]

A City Ablaze

One of those killed instantly was an essential first responder: San Francisco's fire chief, who never left his bed after his entire chimney fell on him.[6] In the aftermath of the earthquake, countless fires erupted simultaneously. Without a leader to guide them, San Francisco's firefighters still turned out in force but found most of the hydrants dry because the underground water mains had ruptured. Efforts to pump water from the bay were hampered by a myriad of complications.

Without water, they resorted to using dynamite and even gunpowder to create firebreaks in areas that were deemed important. On Thursday, the day after the quake, a decision was made to blow up residences along Van Ness Avenue where Claus and Anna lived. Because the street was wide, it was seen as a potential firebreak that could prevent the flames from engulfing the western part of the city.[7] This action did halt the fire's westward trek. Due to inexperience, incompetence, and lack of leadership, however, their firefighting tactics resulted in more deaths, and the use of dynamite caused even more fires to spread.[8]

In the interest of public safety, a mandate was issued by stressed-out mayor Eugene Schmitz for people to stay outdoors. Stetson, however, snuck back inside his mansion. He speculated that if Claus had done the same, rather than following the mandate, he might have saved his home:

> I saw smoke coming out of the chimney of the Spreckels mansion. I went out and spoke to a fireman, and he said that he had been into the house and that it was full of smoke and on fire. At 1 o'clock the house was on fire in the upper rooms, at 1:30 it was blazing out of the upper windows, and in a short time afterwards was wholly on fire. . . . I feel quite sure that if anyone had been on guard inside with a bucket of water the fire could have been put out.[9]

Though Claus may not have been inside, he was nearby when the fire brigade stormed by his property. The handwritten caption on an archival photo of his burned-out mansion tells a compelling story: "One time when money did not count. The offer of a million dollars by Spreckels to the firemen had no effect."[10] Claus and Anna's priceless collection of art and opulent furnishings were "reduced to heaps of ashes and charred stones in

32. The Brownstone after the earthquake. The Spreckelses' "fireproof" mansion had been built to withstand fire when the windows were closed, but explosions had blown the windows out, reducing the family's priceless collection of art and furnishings to "heaps of ashes and charred stones in less than an hour" ("Spreckels Mansion to Be Restored," *Los Angeles Herald*, August 12, 1906). Courtesy of Terrence and Virginia Wilson private collection.

less than an hour."[11] The Spreckels "fireproof" mansion had been built to withstand fire if the windows were closed, but, unfortunately, the explosions had blown them out.

San Francisco was in peril. The disaster's combined forces destroyed almost the entire city infrastructure. In addition to broken water mains, all streetcar lines were out of operation, and the telephone and telegraph offices were destroyed, as were banks, hotels, apartment buildings, thousands of houses, and all but a scattering of outlying small stores and bakeries.[12]

Food and provisions were in short supply, and San Franciscans grew desperate. Rich and poor alike were reduced to scavenging for food and supplies. Douglas Wilson, a photographer for the *Los Angeles Herald*, arrived the day after the earthquake to memorialize the disastrous scene for Southern

California readers. Wilson wrote that he encountered the "famous Claus Spreckels whilst he was digging under a bakery with several laborers for bread." Wilson noted that, unlike the others, Claus was "protected by armed men."[13] However, it's unlikely that Claus did any digging himself—he would only be supervising—and he described being in immense pain for days due to stepping on the crystals from his fallen bedroom chandelier.[14]

Shoot to Kill!

Within hours of the initial tremors, the acting commander at San Francisco's Presidio, Brigadier General Frederick "Fighting Fred" Funston, not waiting for martial law to be declared, dispatched troops into the city. Some proclaimed him a hero and others accused him of inciting "legal lawlessness" after his soldiers shot harmless citizens who were confused about the lines of authority. Mayor Schmitz added to the disorder and lawlessness when he ordered deputized citizens to shoot looters on the spot. To ensure public safety, the mayor issued a proclamation on leaflets posted throughout the city stating: "The Federal Troops, the members of the Regular Police Force and all Special Police Officers have been authorized by me to KILL any and all persons found engaged in Looting or in the Commission of Any Other Crime."[15] The consequences "were the hasty abandonment of democracy and the legal system, and instant death for some."[16]

A *Los Angeles Herald* reporter happened to be on the scene and shocked his readers by recounting law enforcement's swift and deadly reaction to an incident of price gouging in front of a bakery: "I had gone but a few blocks up Market Street when one of the troopers shot a negro for attempting to collect 65 cents for a loaf of bread" (more than $20 in today's money). Wilson's shock soon turned to horror:

> When I reached the vicinity of the mint on Fifth street. I saw eleven men shot down in rapid succession. Several of these were negroes who were believed to be the colleagues of three men who had gained entrance to the mint with the intention of robbing it. Guards inside the mint had discovered the three and had killed them instantly. Hearing the shots, soldiers rushed up to the building and when the eleven men outside the building were suspected of being accomplices they were shot to death without further questioning. The picture of those eleven

men as they dropped, one after the other, to the ground, will never be forgotten by me.[17]

Agnes Lily Tillmann, granddaughter of Claus and Anna Mangels, recorded that when the hat was passed around by some unknown official, "several prominent men refused to throw bucks when they were ordered and were shot immediately. All men found stealing or doing violence were shot."[18]

These instances of enforcement of the mayor's proclamation exemplify the mass hysteria that followed the earthquake. In a four-day period, the city was largely consumed by fires that couldn't be contained. It's estimated that over 250,000 people, many still in their nightwear, became refugees. They were forced to live without food in makeshift tents and shacks in parks, beachfronts, and vacant lots outside the burned area. On their way to those refugee camps, many heard heart-wrenching cries for help amid the rubble— until there was deathly silence. The unimaginable sights and loss of life sent many survivors into shock, which in turn caused more deaths.

Ruins and Hope

Within three days approximately twenty-five thousand buildings on 490 city blocks were destroyed. Unfortunately, for the citizens of San Francisco, in 1906 most of the city's wooden buildings had been haphazardly constructed. Additionally, when shoddily built chimneys toppled, they crashed down onto the homes they were attached to or onto neighboring houses, and the results were disastrous to both the structure and the inhabitants inside.[19]

By noon on April 18 the city's most recognized structure, the Claus Spreckels Building—only nine years old—spewed large plumes of black and gray smoke from its iconic dome. Structurally, the building had withstood the earthquake's jolts, and at first the damage was minimal. But fire soon ravaged the interior, by blazing through the elevator shaft and blowing out windows floor by floor, as horrified spectators looked on.[20] Only twenty-four hours after disaster struck, the city's most celebrated structure was one of the few buildings still standing, albeit a smoldering and hollow shell against a darkened sky. In the days that followed, however, the skyscraper stood proud in the ruins. For San Franciscans, its silhouette became a symbol of hope and the indestructible nature of their city as well as a reflection of their determination to survive.

33. The Claus Spreckels Building after the quake. By noon on April 18, 1906, fire had ravaged the interior of the iconic building, blazing through the elevator shaft and blowing out windows floor by floor, as horrified spectators looked on. By permission of Adolph Rosekrans.

The Impact of the Family

The tragedy also had a profound effect on the greater Spreckels family, many of whom lived within walking distance of Claus and Anna. Only John and Rudolph were in San Francisco on that fateful morning.

John

On James Stetson's walk around the neighborhood, he stopped in front of John and Lillian's mansion. He noted the exterior "had cracked and crumbled and fallen like spun sugar out of a wedding cake and . . . blocks of cement had fallen from the entrance ceiling." Glancing up, Stetson saw "at one of the upper windows a wan, white face, peered from the rich lace curtains within."[21] The "wan" face looking out on the horror below undoubtedly belonged to the ailing owner, who hadn't been seen in public for three months. Two weeks before the catastrophe, the press had reported that John was "critically ill" and had been advised by his physicians "to get his affairs in order, as they could not say how much longer he had to live."[22]

On that dark Wednesday John felt that his entire world had crashed down around him as he watched the smoking ruins of his home and discovered the burned-out shell of the Spreckels skyscraper, which housed every one of his numerous business interests. John didn't need to wonder where to find a comfortable bed. He owned an entire island and a luxurious place in which to take refuge: the Hotel del Coronado.

John was so weak that Lillian and their eldest daughter, Grace, practically carried him to the harbor, where they boarded an Oceanic ship, thankfully stationed there. He was assisted on his journey to San Diego by his wife; his married daughters, Grace Hamilton and Lillie Holbrook; and eighteen-year-old son Claus Jr. The other men in John's family, including his son Jack and sons-in-law, Alec Hamilton and Harry Holbrook, stayed behind to protect their business interests.

Perhaps it was due to his relocating to San Diego's island of Coronado, a place with happy holiday memories and a warmer climate, that John's health, to the astonishment of his family, revived. As his health began to return, no question remained: they would stay permanently in the mild climate of San Diego, away from the stresses of San Francisco. By all accounts, John's miraculous recovery gave him a sense that he was starting life anew, away from his feuding brothers and domineering father. He had been to hell and back, and now it was time to retake his life.

John found a five-acre bluff in Coronado overlooking the picturesque Glorietta Bay. To design his and Lillian's personal residence, John enlisted Harrison Albright, a self-trained architect who had earned a reputation for his use of reinforced concrete. This method of encasing steel in concrete so that a structure could withstand both an earthquake and fire was more than appealing to John and Lillian after what they had lived through in San Francisco.

Rudolph

In the aftermath of the earthquake, San Francisco was under martial law, and soldiers were stretched thin as they struggled to guard public property and assist with the distribution of relief supplies that poured into the city. The catastrophe pushed domestic life outside, giving the public unforeseen access to the private lives of the rich, such as Rudolph and Nellie Spreckels, who lived at the corner of Pacific and Gough, within minutes of Claus and Anna's home. Rudolph, well-armed, stayed put to guard his family and property. James Stetson wrote of the scene he encountered when he passed their home the day after the earthquake. Nellie, eight months pregnant—with the baby soon to be named Anna Claudine Spreckels, after her formerly estranged mother-in-law—was camped in the yard on items dragged from their mansion. Amid the blocks of crushed cement, Rudolph, his son and daughter, mother-in-law, sisters-in-law, and servants "had set up their household on the sidewalk, the women wrapped in rugs and coverlets and huddled in easy chairs hastily rolled out. They were having their morning tea on the sidewalk and the silver service was spread on the stone coping."[23] Rudolph found refuge in Oakland, where little Anna was soon born.

Spreckels Family Helping

When Mayor Schmitz named several prominent citizens to a Committee of Safety to manage the crisis, among them was Rudolph. To facilitate relief efforts, Rudolph donated $10,000 ($312,000 in today's money) to the mayor's newly formed finance committee, and Claus gave $25,000 ($780,000 in today's money).[24]

An archival photograph bears the caption "Claus Spreckels breaking into his vault," in which Claus is seen, along with Rudolph, surrounded by rubble, directing the efforts to breach a vault when they were able. When Adolph returned to San Francisco, he was drafted as chairman of the committee to restore lighting for the city by the end of April; all plans for the restoration of light and power needed to be reviewed and approved by him. Under his oversight, powerhouses in certain areas of the city were able to get the trolleys back on track.

Refuge in Aptos

Upon hearing Aptos had been spared from San Francisco's mass devastation, Claus used his innumerable resources to cut through the chaos and board a train going south to Aptos. During the preceding decade, he and Anna had considered their ranch, more than anywhere else, as a respite from life, and now it would prove its worth as a refuge. Their usual method

CRACKING FOR SPRECKLES' SAFES.

34. Cracking the safe after the earthquake. Claus's back is to the camera and Rudolph is wearing a light hat. The pair are supervising the cracking open of the Spreckels safe (1906). Online Archive of California, UC Berkeley, Bancroft Library, BANC PIC 19xx.112:064b.

of going the eighty miles to Aptos was by boarding a luxury yacht for the Santa Cruz harbor. Then Claus would send word to the Cardiff livery stable, owned by brothers Robert and George Cardiff, that he needed a team and surrey to transport them to Aptos where George would always stay over at the ranch until it was time to leave. George was always overpaid with a $20 gold piece and thought the great big "whiskered German" a "wonderful man, an awful nice fellow." While Anna was a "lovely woman," George found it hard to communicate with her because she "spoke English very brokenly."[25]

But neither the yacht nor George was available, and Claus and Anna entered the mass fray of people exiting the disaster. Not without incident, they made it on a train, where Claus struck up a conversation with a fellow passenger, a *Santa Cruz Sentinel* reporter who recognized the "famous Mr. Spreckels." With some emotion, Claus told him the worrisome story of how he had been separated and then reunited from Anna during the melee at the train station. He then relayed, for the record, his commitment to the

35. A family meal in Aptos. Claus was his happiest when surrounded by his family on the porch of his home in Aptos. Courtesy Tillmann Family Archives, privately held by Mark H. Reed.

city, claiming that he'd "rebuild all his structures in San Francisco and there would be a new San Francisco inside of three years." Incredibly, the reporter published what was likely "off the record," telling readers, before leaving the Brownstone on Van Ness, the "richest man in California" had "buried" salvaged valuables in an underground "tunnel, which runs under the garden of the Spreckels home."[26]

Sadly, in the days before the earthquake, Claus and Anna were planning a grand celebration to host their reunited daughter's second marriage to John Wakefield Ferris, a civil engineer, twenty years her senior.[27] It seems she had a preference to father figures who were British, because Ferris and Watson were curiously similar in that regard. The earthquake rearranged her plans, so she stayed over in New York and wed Ferris there, depriving Claus a second chance to give his daughter away in marriage. Though Emma herself was lucky to be away from San Francisco, the building her father had named after her, the beautiful Emma Spreckels Building at 927 Market, was not so lucky. It was reduced to rubble.

Forging Ahead

With great relief Claus learned the sugar refinery in the Potrero district was running at "full blast with all the working men that [could] be found."[28] It's a mystery why Potrero would be safe when many other smaller towns within a radius of over one hundred miles were shaken to their core, including Claus's special treasure in the Salinas Valley: the Spreckels sugar factory and his namesake town of Spreckels. Claus must have been devastated when he read in the paper that the Salinas refinery was a total loss. However, Claus Jr., Claus's eighteen-year-old grandson, on behalf of his ailing father in San Diego, refuted the report. He telegraphed his grandfather in Aptos that the refinery would be up and running soon, and this was soon verified by the *Santa Barbara Morning Press*: "The machinery of the Spreckels sugar refinery was apparently not damaged in the least, and the refinery building was not injured to any very large extent. The refinery is all right, and we will be able to resume operations in a short time without much difficulty and with very little to be expended for repairs."[29]

With every family member safe and assurances that both refineries could be fixed and put in working order, Claus was well positioned to rise again, as he had so many times before. When a reporter from the *Sacramento Daily Union* caught up with the seventy-seven-year-old and asked him about his enormous material losses, Claus's response was steadfast: "In spite of my losses I can still afford to return to my native land of Germany and to live as liberally as the Emperor William, but I propose to stay right here in San Francisco, and to devote my fortune and what is left of my energy to the upbuilding of this city, where my fortunes were made." Humbled by his response, the reporter wrote of Claus's character and fortitude: "Men do not do such things, at such an age, from love of money. It is the spirit that loves to wrest victory from defeat, to redeem disaster."[30]

When it was safe for Claus and Anna to return to San Francisco, the decision of where to reside was an easy one. Claus had never settled easily into the beautiful, art-filled Van Ness mansion, the Brownstone, which was more of a museum than a home, and had always regretted having left the old neighborhood. He had pined for the days when he walked through the commotion of the South of Market neighborhood, smoking his cigar and bantering with fellow immigrants in his native tongue. Fortunately, Claus had never sold their comfortable old house on Howard Street, full of his most precious memories, as it was one of the few houses on the street to escape major damage. When an old friend asked Claus how he liked being back on Howard Street, he said, "I wished I had never left it and I never intend to leave it again."[31] He never did.

19

Auf Wiedersehen

Weary San Franciscans labored hard to rebuild their city in the days, weeks, and months following the earthquake. The city received emergency aid appropriated by Congress, and donations were solicited from around the country for the massive disaster relief effort. Railroads were still taking refugees wherever they wanted to go free of charge, and close to one hundred thousand people fled the city. For an estimated three hundred thousand men, women, and children, and their pets camping out, mainly in Golden Gate Park, food, water, tents, blankets, medical supplies, hay for horses, and warm clothing were sent in from all over the world to meet basic needs. Emergency relief switched to long-term care in the camps of "earthquake cottages" by July, when the number of "campers" dropped to twenty-five thousand.[1]

As the city was rising from its ashes with miraculous speed, so was Patrick Calhoun's above-ground trolley system, complete with its poles and overhead wires. With the aid of Mayor Schmitz, Boss Abraham Ruef used the emergency status the earthquake gave them to enable Calhoun to quickly reestablish transport after the earthquake. Seeing this opportunity to get ahead of the Spreckels men, Calhoun wasted no time and moved aggressively before Claus and Rudolph could start building their rival Municipal Street Railways.

It was a bold move by Mayor Schmitz, who had learned in the days before the earthquake that he was being investigated for corruption. His own appointee, district attorney William Langdon, had begun assembling compelling evidence of graft and bribery against him and his partner in crime, Boss Ruef. Theodore Roosevelt, the nation's reformist president, was persuaded by Fremont Older, managing editor of the *San Francisco Bulletin*, to launch a federal probe, but he needed funds to supply two federal investigative employees. Rudolph, in the name of "clean government," bankrolled the crusade to bring down Schmitz and Ruef.

Two weeks after the earthquake, the public learned of the extent of the Spreckelses' grandiose project to have their entire railroad system—not just the cables—moving underground. Claus and Rudolph worked out a plan that their subway would be "turned over to the city at the end of ten years."[2] Both Claus and Rudolph, defeated in their only joint project, to move not only the cable conduits but the entire railroad below and out of the line of sight, were both saddened and infuriated when the earthquake rearranged their plans. In the days after the earthquake, Mayor Schmitz had organized a Committee of Fifty, which included Rudolph Spreckels, to supervise subcommittees for San Francisco's reconstruction. When Rudolph found out the "crooked" mayor Schmitz had appointed the "crooked" boss Ruef to be on the same committee, he resigned.[3]

c & h Out Ahead in the Aftermath of the Quake

While Claus was distracted with incorporating the fight for an underground railroad system with Rudolph, George Morrison Rolph, president of the newly reorganized California and Hawaiian Sugar Refining Company (c & h) was ensuring that Claus Spreckels's West Coast domination of sugar refining had finally and irrevocably come to an end. With the demise of their three-year lease with Spreckels of their Crockett refinery, they were back in control of all operations. Crockett had suffered only trivial damage from the earthquake, and in days Honolulu's Sugar Factors Company was now fully operating in California. The missionary-descended sugar planters had banded together and successfully curtailed Claus's source of raw sugar from Hawai'i forever. For Claus, it was beets or nothing, but he was getting weary and was shocked that John and Adolph had not seen this coming. He was nothing but grieved at being beaten by his longtime enemies in Hawai'i.

Contemporary businessmen outside of Hawai'i wondered at their hatred for Claus. It seemed out of place considering the millions of dollars he poured into their islands. The sugarcane planters in Hawai'i had benefited more from Claus's activities there than they had suffered. By demonstration, he showed them that climate, soil, and transportation advances combined made the sugar trade in the islands an empire unto itself. He improved cane cultivation; elevated milling; created railroads, irrigation reservoirs, and canals; expanded shipping; and more. Claus had almost single-handedly advanced the kingdom's economy with sugar as the chief item of commerce, to the planters' direct benefit. But even though the planters had been paid—some say overpaid—by Claus for their raw sugar, it had been his high-handed nature of "all or nothing" they never could get over. Furthermore, Claus was a crusty outsider, not aligned with the Congregationalist Church. This along with his stalwart alliance to the Hawaiian monarchy and his attempts to stop annexation—they would never forgive.

The tables were now irrevocably turned, and the turning happened under his two eldest sons' watch. The Western Sugar Refining Company, which Claus had turned over to his boys, now had access to "less than 51,000 tons of sugar out of the island's [Maui's] annual output of 425,000 tons."[4] This meant that 375,000 tons of sugar were off limits, because his boys weren't paying attention. Claus's vertical integration in Hawai'i was now over. He had thought that by this point in time, the family would no longer be relying on sugarcane from Hawai'i, since the domestic beet was supposed to have supplanted their need for cane. The problem was the beet yield in California didn't meet expectations. Claus had hoped that during the time he was leasing the factory in Crockett, he'd have solved the agricultural issues that limited beets during imperfect seasons. Now Western Sugar Refining would need to find cane elsewhere and pay to transport it. Meanwhile, during the confusion following the earthquake, C & H successfully launched itself toward ultimate preeminence in the sugar business. The planters in Hawai'i had won. It must have been excruciatingly painful for Claus to watch his legacy fade after turning over a thriving enterprise to his boys.

Claus's refineries in San Francisco and Salinas had both suffered damage, but not significant enough to shut down production for long. But finding product to refine in the days following would be a challenge because all stored product in the warehouses had been lost in the fires caused by the quake. He'd have to prevail upon top managers to ensure that a multitude of Spreckels employees would remain employed in these times of great uncertainties.

It took three long and expensive years of managing the curly top virus by "conquering the soil" on ten thousand Salinas Valley acres. The Spreckels Sugar Company employed four highly trained agriculturalists to run the experimental station at the Salinas refinery. John reported that after a "series of experiments and analysis of the soil, good crops were produced, and beets [were] made to grow on additional soil that [had been] thought to be unfitted for their cultivation."[5] It seemed that now, with C & H having the advantage of sourcing all of its sugar from Hawai'i and turning Crockett into "Sugar Town," beets had to be the future focus of all Spreckels refining operations.

Postquake Reevaluation

The completely gutted but structurally intact Claus Spreckels Building— the Call Building—the city's iconic domed skyscraper standing forlorn on Market Street, became a metaphor in both commentaries and sermons across the country. Like the eviscerated tower, Claus, too, was nothing but a shell of his former self, with his fortune reduced to $10 million ($312 million in today's money). That reduction was due not only to the heavy losses he had incurred from the earthquake but the distribution of money to John and Adolph in the preceding years.[6] In these dire circumstances, he knew he had little chance of recouping his fortune. He told Rudolph, "I'm aging. I've given your two eldest brothers $25,000,000 in the past few years and they haven't used it wisely."[7] What Claus meant was that in his mind, neither John nor Adolph, who had been passed the mantle of stewardship of his sugar enterprises, cared enough to reinvest their profits back into those enterprises to ensure his legacy.

The business partnership of John as president and Adolph as vice-president of J. D. and A. B. Spreckels Securities Company was a successful one, however. With their combined assets, the two owned and operated their own companies at the same time their father required them to manage his business interests in the wakes of his strokes. But after Adolph's own stroke in 1904, he was also ailing—a fact that required more leadership from John, who had also been ill.

After the earthquake, John, now permanently relocated in Coronado, was pulled in many different directions. He was president of more than fifteen separate companies, most of which involved his San Diego ventures. John was known by his employees as a kind man but "a gruff fellow." When entering his office with a question or concern, "it was 'Yes' and 'No' and 'Goodbye' and that was it."[8] Claus, while often viewed as "gruff," was different. He was noted for engaging in small talk with all employees and rolling up his sleeves to work alongside any of them on a whim.

At the height of building his multiple sugar entities, Claus had understood that running multiple companies came with financial rewards but also with a lot of risks. To ameliorate the risks, he had surrounded himself with loyal managers, many of whom were part of his extended family, and responsible employees. Because they were respected, well paid, and fairly treated, his employees worked hard and stayed for years.

Claus was impatient with stupidity in all forms and chose his employees for their intellect. His philosophy for hiring, as described by John, was simply matching talent to task: "I believe that every man should work according to his ability and opportunity."[9] Claus's tenacity was legend, his working style systematic and structured. He despised waste and worshipped efficiency. Once employees had proved themselves, they knew they had a hands-on boss who led by example, and that example was typified by hard work, day in and day out. Long hours were the norm for him and his employees alike. Drinking beer at the end of the day, a common cultural practice in Germany with a name of its own, *Feierabendbier* (end-of-work beer), was financially supported by Claus for refinery workers both in San Francisco and Salinas. The daily beer breaks, oftentimes enjoyed by Claus alongside his men, brought much-needed levity as workers bumped their glasses of steam beer together in whatever toast came to mind.

Once Claus retired, *Feierabendbier* became a thing of the past. John viewed the various sugar ventures his father established as an indifferent investor and left the superintendence of them to others, mainly those longtime and faithful managers who had worked side by side with Claus for decades. In Salinas one of Claus's oldest and most reliable managers, Superintendent William Waters, suddenly quit in 1905 when he no longer felt valued once the blight-fighting scientists began interfering in his daily operations of beet sugar refining, operations he felt they knew nothing about.[10]

In Hawaiʻi William G. Irwin was equally frustrated. Even though John and Adolph controlled two-thirds of a few Hawaiian sugar plantation interests, they left the lion's share of the work to Irwin, their financial equal partner. The following correspondence that Irwin sent to his friend Walter M. Giffard in 1908 reveals John's complete lack of interest in plantation problems in Hawaiʻi:

John D. [Spreckels] has simply lost all interest in business matters, so far as the Islands are concerned and he seems to have taken up his residence in San Diego, where I trust he may make a better success of it than he has the Island business. I have held business for the firm single-handed for many years past, but there is a limit to what I can do, especially when the firm with which we have been so intimate, fails to do their share of the work.[11]

In San Francisco the ever-faithful William H. Hannam, managing director of the Spreckels Sugar Company, also grew impatient because "J. D. Spreckels was spending most of his time, and the company's money, on his interests in San Diego."[12] Irwin and Hannam were right. In the aftermath of the earthquake and the decision to permanently leave San Francisco, John had "lost all interest in business matters" outside of San Diego—but especially in the sugar business, a career path he had been forced into. John now focused all his energy—his whole heart and wallet—to build his legacy in San Diego. In every sugar venture, those loyal men Claus had hired and partnered with grew weary of shouldering all the responsibilities without the Claus Spreckels pat on the back, while John and Adolph Spreckels grew richer from the men's labors.

Just as bribery and extortion on a grand scale were being linked to Abraham Ruef and Mayor Schmitz, it became known that Ruef, Claus's archenemy, was allied in a business venture with Adolph—on the "black gold" oil industry. In and around California the development of that industry was helping to put the nation on wheels and was frenetically enticing investors. Adolph saw the enormous promise of oil and asked John to join in the venture. John, however, declined to speculate. Adolph, the horse man, was a betting man and had taken a flier in April 1903 that led him to buy $25,000 ($780,000 in today's money) worth of stock in the Sunset Monarch Oil Company.[13] The company had originally been incorporated by four men, including Abraham Ruef, and it had remained in their control until 1904, when Adolph and his friend Grove P. Ayers assumed charge. The company acquired a refinery in Berkeley, began operations under the name of Monarch Oil Refining Company, and rapidly announced its intention to expand with a board of directors that included Ruef, a major stockholder.[14] By February 1907 Adolph owned more than 40 percent of Sunset Monarch when it went under reorganization. Nevertheless, with his passions elsewhere (horses), he remained in the background of the oil operations, putting in place officers who were connected with J. D. & A. B. Spreckels Securities Company. At a meeting of the Monarch stockholders Adolph, by now the single Monarch owner in control of a substantial block of shares in the company—giving him absolute control—elected Abe Ruef, his father's enemy and a known criminal, to the board of directors.[15] Claus was livid.

After five years as Adolph's mistress, Alma de Bretteville, more than two decades younger than himself, became Mrs. Spreckels in Philadelphia on May 11, 1908. It had taken that long to convince the confirmed fifty-one-year-old bachelor, living with syphilis, that they should marry. Only after the fact did he inform John, who was appalled. It was well known that John hated Alma; he thought her crass and worried that she'd drain the company's bank account. Adolph hoped to keep the news private, but the "bride's family" had other ideas, and the news of the marriage hit all the newspapers in San Francisco and sent tongues wagging.[16] It leaked out in San Francisco that Claus and Anna were also agitated about this entanglement with Alma and her known reputation as a "gold digger." In Claus's mind, Adolph was doing the same thing that Emma had done: he eloped with a gold digger with a twenty-year age difference.

Claus's New Will

The trauma of living through the earthquake and the discontent with the choices his eldest sons were making shifted Claus's perspective about his priorities in relationship to his five children. He decided, along with Anna's full support, to split their remaining $10 million ($312 million in today's money) in equal shares to their youngest children. According to Rudolph's account, Claus explained that "age" had caused a reassessment of his feelings toward John and Adolph, and he sought to make it right.[17]

Rumors flew high in Hawai'i after Rudolph's San Francisco accountants arrived in Honolulu in October 1907 to scrutinize the financial ledgers of Claus Spreckels & Company Bank and those of W. G. Irwin & Company. The examination was undertaken silently to avoid any publicity. No questions from any nosy journalist in Hawai'i received a single answer as to the purpose of the visit. The *Gazette*, with its story headline "Is Spreckels Making a Will?" speculated that Claus needed the financial information to change his existing will. Their readers were informed, "Rudolph Spreckels is now the power behind the throne," and "John D, who for years was his father's favorite son and business confidant, has been displaced."[18]

Little did they know, Claus had already had his will redrawn in New York on May 11, 1907. The location was likely strategic, so that his eldest sons, with their many San Francisco connections, wouldn't catch wind of what was happening and stir up trouble. Not only did he name Rudolph and Gus as executors, but he stipulated that upon Anna's death, his estate was to be split among the three younger children; he was leaving the older brothers completely out: "I have made no provision in this will for my sons John D. Spreckels and Adolph B. Spreckels for the reason that I have already given to them a large part of my estate."[19]

Claus's Passing

Early in December 1908 Claus caught a nasty cold traveling from New York, where he had been visiting with Gus and discussing end-of-life-matters. Because of Claus's weakened immune system from diabetes, that cold turned into acute pneumonia. By the time he got back to San Francisco, he was feverish, coughing, and having trouble catching his breath. Two doctors were summoned to the house. "Acute Pneumonia" was the diagnosis. An assembled medical team hovered over the bedridden patient around the clock before shaking their heads at the inevitable.[20]

There was forced holiday cheer throughout the house, but it was clear to all in attendance that this would be Claus Spreckels's last Christmas. During the final week, Anna put everyone on alert, but John was the only child who could spend a week at his father's side before Claus died from his condition on Saturday, December 26, at 4:30 a.m. Rudolph, who had been in Honolulu, barely made it to his father's bedside; he arrived just a few hours before the passing. He had been in the islands, doing "quick work" under "extreme secrecy" negotiating the sale of Claus's extensive real estate holdings, including the Spreckels Bank, in "one of the largest single real estate transactions ever negotiated in Honolulu."[21] Because Adolph was traveling with his new bride, Alma, and Gus and Emma were abroad at that time, they all missed the final farewell.

Since John, always the dutiful son who ran whenever he was called for, had stayed by his father's deathbed, it's hard not to wonder what that long goodbye held for both of them. Notwithstanding their conflicts and differences, their relationship had endured over mutual respect for each other's self-directed nature and independence. There was no question that throughout the years, John had been Claus's preferred child, but that all changed when that child chose a different career path and moved to San Diego.

The Reverend Julius Fuendeling of St. Markus Kirche officiated at Claus's brief and simple service in the living room of the Spreckels home at 2027 Howard Street. St. Markus played a vital role for Claus and Anna, who could hear Sunday sermons in their native tongue. Its outreach to San Francisco's German community had flourished because it preserved the tenets of Evangelical Lutheranism and the German culture. Because the earthquake had damaged the church, the funeral service was conducted at home, not under the beautiful German sparkling chandelier Claus had donated nor surrounded by the music of the Schoenstein organ he had shipped from Germany as a gift for the congregation.

Claus employed thousands of people, so almost every household in San Francisco had been touched by his life in some way. For two consecutive days, from early morning until late night, there was a continuous line of mourners waiting their turn to enter the Howard Street home to view Claus Spreckels's body, his coffin placed on top of "white satin in a sea of flowers" in the bay window. The ornate, lead-lined, bronze coffin had a full-length French plateglass top that rivaled that of the assassinated president McKinley. Many grievers were surprised the "body laid out in a Prince Albert suit" looked so "lifelike."[22] It was noted that "the octogenarian's face" hadn't been ravaged by sickness and instead looked as if Claus were merely peacefully slumbering.

Since Claus's dire condition was published in the days before his death, newspapers across the country were ready to front-page lengthy obituaries on the very same day he died. The eulogies played up the story of a poor immigrant boy who chased the American dream as far as he could take it to become the "Sugar King of California." Many San Francisco office buildings, banks, stores, and factories flew the American flag at half-mast for the passing of their "sugar king." Even "numerous deep sea vessels" berthed along San Francisco's water front "drooped" their national colors at half-mast.[23]

The funeral procession left the home on Howard Street and walked solemnly to the corner of Valencia and Twenty-Eighth Streets, where a private funeral car awaited to carry the casket to the Cypress Lawn Cemetery, where only "a few close friends" were invited to the interment. Although John and Rudolph, bitter enemies, acted as pallbearers at their mother's request, they neither looked into each other's eyes nor exchanged a single word.[24]

Fighting the Will

When John discovered the remarkable turn of affairs following his father's December 1908 funeral—that he had been disinherited—his hurt and fury were unmatched by any other point in time. Not only had he been replaced as the executor, but in a sense, he had been disowned by the father whom he alone, almost in servile obedience, had stood by throughout his life, particularly when the youngest children, who were now replacing him, had disrespected and sued their father. John and Adolph jumped into action; through their lawyers, they declared Claus's will invalid due to coercion. They claimed their father had been "mentally and physically incompetent" and that Gus and Rudolph had forced their father to sign over bequests to them.[25]

In the midst of the contentious legal battles, Anna, unable to battle with her sons, especially with John's feelings of betrayal, or with the lingering effects of the grippe (flu) she had contracted after Claus died, took to her bed. She had for years suffered from myocarditis, but the stress of the situation exasperated the "irregular action of [her] heart."[26] Some believed she never favored recuperation because she felt adrift without her husband.[27] Emma, now married to John Ferris, and living in England, made a three-week visit home in January 1909 to see her ailing mother for the first time in many years. This reunion, according to Anna's niece and bedside companion, Anna Brommer, gave Anna a fresh impetus to live.[28]

Anna had been given title to the Pacific Heights mansion before Claus's death, and she mentioned that she might restore the Brownstone to live her life out. Sorting out the insurance after the mansion had been damaged by "fire and dynamite" during the earthquake had been a legal fiasco. Rudolph had been given power of attorney over his father's business affairs on April 16, 1906, three days before the earthquake, which amounted to a total loss of $410,000 ($12.8 million in today's money). Rudolph was handed a renewal policy by the insurance brokers on April 17, informing him the policy on the Brownstone would expire on April 19. Rudolph handed it back to the brokers with the recorded response, "We don't want those policies. I intend making some changes in my father's insurance." He allowed the policy to lapse; therefore, the insurance company refused to pay on an expired policy. On his first order of business for Claus, Rudolph blundered. Claus had been outraged and took the legal stance that since the home had been put in Anna's name, "Rudolph had no legal right to control his mother's insurance."[29] A negotiated settlement was far into the future.

Almost immediately after Emma's departure, it was reported that Anna was "dangerously ill" and that two doctors were in constant attendance at her bedside, reporting the grippe had "developed into heart trouble complications" and that she'd have to be closely watched.[30] In the same month, Gus and Oroville arrived and moved into the Howard Street home to reside with Anna. Their primary purpose was to supervise her health; the secondary purpose was likely to safeguard her from John and Adolph's influence.[31]

On May 19, 1909, John told a journalist that he'd never compromise with his brothers and would contest the validity of the will to "the bitter end": "This proceeding has been started with no idea of a compromise. It is a matter of principle and there can be no settlement. I haven't spoken to Rudolph or Claus A. [Gus] for 14 years; nor do I think Adolph has, neither are we likely to."[32]

After Emma returned to England, Anna was desolate. She was now being forced to take a side once again between her children, this time on the opposite side. In the protracted span of fifty-six years, she had delivered twelve children and had buried seven of them. She had stood by and watched her surviving children and husband fight for decades and thus had been deprived of establishing a relationship with some of her grandchildren. She had lived through the horror of the earthquake and had watched her home and city tumble around her, only to bury her husband when she needed him the most. It was a miserable Christmas in 1909, with no hopes for a happy new year.

Anna's doctor, Dr. Clemons Max Richter, a well-known heart doctor, had been treating her myocarditis throughout 1909. He reported that "she had very irregular action of the heart and short breath, and weak feeling, troubles of circulation in all parts of the body."[33] He visited her almost daily and found her stable until December of 1909. On January 10, 1910, he visited Anna and solemnly reported the end was near and ordered complete bedrest and a strict diet. John and Adolph, hearing the news directly from the doctor, concerned for her emotional well-being, abandoned their proposed contest of the will. A public statement by Rudolph and Gus downplayed their elder brothers' "altruistic" move:

> There were absolutely no grounds upon which a successful contest of the will could be maintained. If there were it is most improbable that any consideration for their mother could have prevented it in view of the fact that since our father's death neither John nor Adolph ever called upon or communicated with her. During his lifetime Claus Spreckels advanced to his sons, John D. Spreckels and Adolph B. Spreckels, property of great value by millions of dollars than the combined value of all the property he gave to his widow and all other children in his lifetime and by his will. Any sense of wrong that they may feel is inconsistent with the honor they claim to have extended to their father as the neglect of their mother in her old age is inconsistent with their declaration of consideration for her.[34]

Anna's Passing

Purportedly "impatient" and unhappy with Dr. Richter's diagnosis and course of prescribed treatment, which included staying bedbound on a restrictive diet, Anna discharged herself from his care, and Dr. Rudolph Baum, from the San Francisco Board of Health, replaced Dr. Richter. Rudolph said that his mother was "restive" under Richter's treatment and was anxious to get up and get around, believing it would help her constitution. Her motivation was that she wanted to be with Emma in England when her first child was to be born in June.

But then she went downhill fast. On February 16, 1910, in the midst of the contention between her sons, Anna Christina Spreckels, aged seventy-nine, closed her weary eyes for good. Unlike her husband's public funeral and memorial service, Anna's (according to her well-known wishes), though also officiated by Reverend Julius Fuendeling, was private, open only to select family members. Anna's remains were placed beside Claus at the impressive Spreckels mausoleum at Cypress Lawn Cemetery with only a few people in attendance. Conspicuously absent were her two eldest sons.

Contradicting Rudolph and Gus's published statement that implied his neglectful absence, John stated that neither he nor Adolph were notified that their mother had been "in any imminent danger [of passing] until after [she]

36. Anna Christina Mangels Spreckels (1830–1910) delivered twelve children and buried seven of them. She was caught in the middle of the decades-long fights between her husband and her surviving children. Courtesy of Terrence and Virginia Wilson private collection.

was dead." If that weren't bad enough, John was not even informed she had died until after her funeral. This withheld information left him with "intense bitterness."[35] Since there weren't any public causes that she championed, there were few comments in Anna's memorial outside of her being the sugar king's wife. Justifying the lack of accolades, one death announcement noted, "Mrs. Spreckels never cared for the gayety of society. She preferred the home."[36]

Anna's Will, Following Claus's Wishes

Following Anna's burial, John learned why he might have been intentionally left out of the funeral. He might have learned that his mother, despite his and Adolph's hopes, had fulfilled his father's last wishes and left her entire estate to Gus, Emma, and Rudolph. Her will made it very clear that her two eldest sons were intentionally omitted from sharing a single dime of her $6 million estate ($181 million in today's money):

> I intentionally omit making any provision in this will for my sons John D. Spreckels and Adolph B. Spreckels . . . because I do not desire my said two sons or any of their issue to take any part of my estate. This I do for the reason that my deceased husband, Claus Spreckels, prior to his death, had already given and advanced to my said sons a large part of his estate, and for other reasons satisfactory to me.[37]

It was reported in the *Call* that Anna was in "frail physical health" when the document was signed, as evidenced by a "barely decipherable" signature.[38] The press urged the public to prepare for "the hottest legal fight ever staged in San Francisco." Readers were guaranteed the ongoing litigation would "develop into one of the biggest will contests the West has ever witnessed" and were reminded of the irony, noting the peculiarity and the reverse of allegiance between parents and the children.[39]

John and Adolph had reopened the contest over their father's will, and on the same day that Anna died, their legal efforts paid off (but only temporarily): the will was declared invalid.[40] But in March 1910 the three youngest children appealed the decision, and *their* legal efforts paid off permanently on April 10, 1911, when the state supreme court reversed the lower court's February 16, 1910, decision, which had favored John and Adolph, and stated the $10 million estate was to be distributed per Claus Spreckels's wishes.[41] (This decision, too, must have been contested, unsuccessfully, because on

April 11, 1912, John's *Call* impartially declared that Claus's will was judged valid. However, the article held out the possibility, almost in a warning, that the attorneys for John and Adolph might petition the state supreme court for a "rehearing and reconsideration of the case."[42] And they did. Still, the four long years of litigation ended with a final decree for distribution in June 1912. That is, Claus's will was once again declared valid.)

Feeling victorious and perhaps a little vindictive, Gus, Emma, and Rudolph, together as executors of the wills of Anna and Claus, turned the tables and sued John and Adolph in December 1911, asserting that each of them should return $12 million ($361 million in today's money), which was one-half of the money on record previously gifted to each by their father. The suit alleged that Claus had provided lifetime gifts to the two older sons of community property valued at roughly $26 million total ($782 million in today's money), while the property remaining at the time of their father's death was valued at less than $10 million.[43] In their lawsuit, the three youngest alleged that because their mother hadn't provided written consent to the monetary gifts made by their father, those gifts were void, had to be accounted for as part of the community estate, and had to be returned to the estate, as it rightfully belonged to them under their mother's will. The irony that their legal objection was based on the written-consent statute made the public scratch their heads in disbelief because the younger siblings were using the same legal weapon their father had unsuccessfully used against Gus in 1897.

John and Adolph legally objected and provided sufficient evidence their mother had known about the money—specifically, that Anna had been well aware of the total money that Claus had given to John and Adolph—because in their father's will, admitted to probate in 1909, the gifts Claus had made to John and Adolph were specifically mentioned, indicating that she had known exactly her husband's desire. The court ruled in favor of John and Adolph: on May 30, 1912, Superior Court Judge James V. Coffee ordered the Spreckels estate distributed according to the terms of the will of Claus, thereby invalidating the younger siblings' demand that John and Adolph each return $12 million. This decision did make it possible, however, for Gus, Emma, and Rudolph to appeal the decision to the state supreme court.[44] Finally, at the end of a long legal struggle, that court upheld the will in *Spreckels v. Spreckels*, 172, Cal. 775 (1916).

It's unknown if, in those last bedbound days, Claus took any responsibility for shattering the relations between his children. Did he wonder if his gesture of reconciliation in leaving his estate to his younger children would continue the shattering down the generational lines? Did he regret renaming the executor and changing his will, particularly knowing how it would affect John who had always stood by his side through the storms of life, even as he took his last breath? But once Claus made up his mind, he persevered until he got what he went after, with his familiar refrain: "I never yet have gone into anything unless I could have it all my own way." If John and Adolph would've been successful in their lawsuit to undo his will, Claus wouldn't have had the last word. So, right or wrong, his last wishes were respected and he got his way.

Epilogue

After Claus's death in 1908, millions of dollars changed hands over the years—years that included a number of shattered relationships. Anna, who inherited most of Claus's empire, placed her assets into the San Christina Corporation, with Rudolph president of the trust. Moving the assets into a single trust corporation would facilitate giving away slices of her net worth while she was alive without having to itemize each business or property, because a gift of shares was not taxable. According to an initial ruling of the state, however, Anna had been coerced by her children to form the corporation for their financial benefit—as a ploy to avoid paying inheritance taxes, considering that Anna lived only a month after forming the San Christina Corporation. The state imposed its inheritance tax (enacted five years earlier) and placed tax liens on the children's inherited property. One clause in the tax law aimed to capture more money: If someone transferred assets in "anticipation of their death," that gift was to be included in the inheritance tax. The three heirs of Anna (Rudolph, Gus, and Emma), the "prodigals," refused to pay and instead sued the state of California for tax relief. The prodigals won; the state appealed and lost.[1] The state's lawyers couldn't prove that Anna expressly formed the corporation to avoid taxes.

The Sugar Beet Industry: Claus's California Legacy

The disinherited eldest sons, John and Adolph, retained control of the sugar beet operation and profited handsomely. John, preoccupied as he was in building San Diego, owned 25 percent, which he chose not to reinvest in the Spreckels Sugar Company. Adolph, who also owned 25 percent (the American Sugar Refining Company of New York owned the remaining 50 percent), guided the affairs of Spreckels Sugar. Dividends, which were 90 percent of the earnings, were all paid out rather than reinvested in the company, contrary to Claus's practice. The company did, however, expand from Salinas, building a second factory in Manteca, California, which started operations in 1917.

The J. D. & A. B. Spreckels Securities Company was the prime source of income for the two branches of the family after the deaths of the brothers. Adolph's widow, Alma, however, had the controlling interest over John's heirs. Even though she liquidated many of the investments, she held onto the crown jewel, Spreckels Sugar. Adolph's will stipulated that the income from operations be distributed half to her and half to their three surviving children, while the entirety of the principal would be held in trust for the children, so she had nothing to gain by selling the company.

Spreckels Sugar flourished until the curly top virus again reared its ugly head. In 1922 the Manteca factory temporarily closed due to the blight. The 1926 crop was the worst on record, and the company nearly declared bankruptcy.[2] Crop problems, wild fluctuations in sugar prices, tariff reforms in the Progressive Era—all diminished the Spreckels competitive edge both domestically and in the world market, and the future looked dim for Spreckels Sugar.

Then in 1930 Katherine Esau, a botanist at the College of Agriculture at UC Davis and former Spreckels employee, developed a curly-top-resistant strain of beet.[3] With this "cure" and with careful crop rotation—sugar beets in the spring, lettuce and peas in the fall—the Spreckels company successfully eliminated the blight and expanded operations just at the beginning of the Great Depression. The Spreckels beet sugar business was flourishing in 1932 with three factories, and the new "Honeydew Sugar" label was marketed only in California in consumer-size packaging. In and around Spreckels, California, and the Salinas factory, there were "1,250 factory workers working 8-hour shifts."[4] Even in the midst of the Great Depression, the Manteca factory was reopened, and a third refinery, the Spreckels Woodland factory, was built in 1936.

At the very time the company needed capital to run three factories, some in the Spreckels family continued to drain company resources. In 1947 Adolph Jr. sued his mother, Alma, for $1.5 million of distributions ($20.2 million in today's money) that she had taken, which he argued was return of principal rather than dividends.[5] Her lawyers had achieved this by increasing debt through a holding company over the years. In 1948, while the Central Valley celebrated the fiftieth anniversary of the Spreckels Sugar Company, there was a battle for the company behind the scenes. Alma didn't want to return the cash and threatened liquidation. John's granddaughter Harriet Holbrook recorded that she and his other heirs attempted to stabilize proposed liquidation proceedings. The "hectic family situation" on the "other side" (meaning Adolph Bernard's side of the family) would prevail.[6] Adolph Jr., with five marriages and ex-wives who were perpetually in the news, didn't have the experience to control the company.

There was a stock offering and an attempt to recapitalize the company, using the proceeds to pay off over $6 million in debt ($81 million in today's money) owed by a holding company, the Spreckels Realization Company. Claus's grandchildren and great-grandchildren in both the J. D. and A. B. branches bought the offering to keep Spreckels Sugar in the family. But Alma retaliated by selling her stock to an investment company, Blair Holdings, owned by Virgil Dardi. They installed Charles Edouard de Bretteville, thirty-six years old, a nephew of Alma, who eventually took over as head of the company in 1949 and led a group that purchased control. In a small, green-carpeted room of San Francisco's Bank of America, one of the biggest sugar deals in West Coast history was quietly sealed: "Last week, for $5,250,000 [$66,250,000 in today's money], husky, handsome Charles Edouard de Bretteville, 36, and associates announced that they had picked up the choicest pieces of the disintegrating J.D. & A.B. Spreckels companies, a sprawling empire founded by bearded Claus Spreckels in 1863, which once held some 50 companies worth $60 million."[7]

In 1963 Charles sold the company to the American Sugar Refining Company of New York, which already held 50 percent of the stock, giving them control and himself a fat bank account. American Sugar was one of the original twelve stocks in the Dow Jones Industrial Average. Its most popular brand was Domino Sugar, and it was the legacy of the Sugar Trust created by Henry O. Havemeyer, Claus's onetime archenemy. In the same year, American absorbed the Spreckels Sugar Company (including the Western Sugar Refining Company of San Francisco) as a fully owned subsidiary. As the company focused on developing the high-fructose corn syrup industry, they rebranded as Amstar Corporation in the early 1970s. The name "Spreckels" remained a division of Amstar until 1987, when it went private and separated itself during a period of leveraged buyouts. The Salinas Valley operations were shuttered because of "transportation and fuel cost, high dept payment due to ubiquitous corporate buyouts started by such investment companies as Kholberg, Kravis, and Roberts."[8] In 1996 Spreckels Sugar merged with Holly Sugar Corporation. In 2005 Southern Minnesota Beet Sugar Cooperative purchased Holly Sugar from Imperial Sugar Company, and the name Spreckels Sugar Company Inc. was chosen for the purchased entity.

Even though Ebenezer Dyer had been the first to make a go of a beet sugar operation in America, he didn't succeed. Claus is the undisputed father of beet sugar growing and refining in the United States. His legacy is well documented in the fact that there are "20 highly efficient operating sugarbeet factories in 9 states processing over 30 million tons of sugarbeets grown on approximately 1.1 million acres. Approximately 5 million tons of sugar are produced each year in the U.S. from sugarbeets and beet sugar represents 54 percent of domestic sugar production in the U.S."[9]

But only one of those factories is left in California. It's located in Brawley, the geographic center of the Imperial Valley, and it does bear the name "Spreckels." Recognizing the historical significance, Native Sons of the Golden West, a fraternal service organization dedicated to preserving the state's past, just as they had for Claus Spreckels more than a century earlier, saw fit in 2020 to honor and celebrate California's last surviving beet sugar plant in a special plaque ceremony.

The ceremony consisted of a special mix of materials: sand and gravel from every county in California, cement from all the mills of California, and water from every mission in the state. After the materials were mixed, the grand officer smeared part of the mixture onto the top right corner of the plaque as a final dedication.[10] It seems fitting the Spreckels name is still associated with at least one sugar operation, and it's in Claus's beloved state of California.

Hawai'i's Sugarcane Industry: Sweet to Sour

The sugar industry played a major role in Hawai'i's economy for over a century. The advent of jet travel coincided with statehood in 1959, and tourism in Hawai'i exploded. Land values soared, as did the cost of labor. Sugar production peaked in 1965, and Hawai'i growers lost market share to lower-cost providers in Brazil, India, and Cuba, and domestically to those in Florida.

The very last sugar harvest took place in the islands in 2016 by Hawaiian Commercial & Sugar, the company named by Claus and then taken over by Alexander & Baldwin in 1898. The news of the cessation was welcomed by critics who had been relentless with their concerns about the environmental impact, including air pollution caused by cane burning, the use of pesticides, and the diversion of streams in East Maui from sugar farming.

The end of Hawaiian Commercial & Sugar marked the end of an industry that had strongly influenced Hawai'i's politics, economy, and culture for more than a century. The legacy of the Spreckels family, who had dominated the sugar industry during its formative years, is reflected in Hawai'i's diversity today. The state is proud to hold the nation's top ranking for racial and ethnic diversity.[11] The descendants of Hawaiian sugar laborers play a large role in modern-day Hawai'i. Even though hardship and backbreaking work are two principal features of the accounts told and retold by sugar laborers and their descendants, the stories about plantations such as Spreckelsville tend to sentimentalize the laborers' close-knit community. Tales of children running barefoot on unpaved roads and thus developing calluses, the clever attempts to collect rainwater, the evening glow from kerosene lamps, the distinctive smell of burning sugar, the odors from the stables, and nostalgia over sharing food with one another seem to reveal a sense of pride in their unique place in the history of Hawai'i.[12] This pride is illustrated by an elderly "sugar boy" who proudly explained to an oral historian, "With my bare hands and callused heart and patience, I helped build Hawai'i."[13]

Spreckels, California

There's not any other place that captures the final dreams of Claus Spreckels more than the historical town of Spreckels.[14] Approaching the town through a long tunnel of towering, century-old black walnut trees hints at something special to follow. When history seekers emerge from the tunnel of trees, they are not disappointed by the 1899 redbrick building with the faded word "Spreckels" on its side. It's clear the tiny town (0.122 square mile) is a time capsule, virtually unchanged from the days Claus himself walked around, cigar in hand, shaking hands and barking out orders during its creation in 1898. He built Spreckels in the Salinas Valley for his refinery workers and their families to embody his ideas of independence, efficiency, and beauty.

Just like then, Spreckels embraces a slower pace of life, and neighbors know and take care of one another in times of need. A few townspeople ensure that Claus's legacy lives on. For example, James Ross Riley III is fiercely proud of the Victorian cottage that was passed down to him through the generations, beginning with his Scottish grandparents, James and Mary Riley, whom Claus personally recruited from his plantation in Hawaiʻi to live and work in Spreckels. Others recall for the younger generation the "sickening, delicious, overpowering, subtle smell of sugar" after the blow of the whistle.[15]

Small-town mercantilism generated most of the basic goods and services required by its community in the early days, but with the exception of the Emporium, all the shops are gone. So today Spreckels is more a pastoral neighborhood than a town. The bucolic street scenes reflect a Norman Rockwellian wholesomeness rarely seen these days. The heart of Spreckels is at its center—the beautiful tree-filled park, designed by Claus to provide pleasure and a safe haven for the town's children.

Spreckels is an "island," and Claus's legacy is seen from all sides of the town's borders in the surrounding verdant agricultural land. He built a vast underground irrigation network to water the beet fields and transformed the valley into fertile farmland for row crop farming, making the introduction to lettuce possible during the 1920s, when it replaced the sugar beet as the Salinas Valley mainstay. The imagination of Nobel and Pulitzer Prize–winning novelist John Steinbeck was captured in the author's seasonal farm work for the Spreckels Sugar Company, and immigrants found their travails and struggles famously chronicled in his fiction. The town of Spreckels and the then working beet sugar factory was the location for Steinbeck's 1955 film *East of Eden*, set in the Salinas Valley.

Generally speaking, company towns such as Spreckels that relied for their economic sustainability on single industries (sugar beets, for instance) didn't fare well with cyclical changes in the local, regional, national, and world economies. This town is the exception. It has not stopped thriving. The last beet was refined in 1982, allowing Tanimura & Antle to establish the headquarters of its produce empire in the long shadows of the towering Spreckels Sugar Company silos, which still stand today. A seventy-three-home subdivision, originally subdivided by Claus but never developed, was completed in 2006 by the Tanimuras on the western edge of town, and the number of households jumped by nearly 30 percent. These new architectural designs echo that of the craftsman style for houses of the 1910s, and at first glance they are not easily distinguishable from the earlier versions.

When demolition of the world's largest sugar factory began on the wind-swept banks of the Salinas River in 1992, it was a harder feat than any contractor imagined, causing the first company to quit the project after the failed attempts to bring the overly well-built factory down. The factory, so well-constructed, refused to be easily demolished; it took an extraordinary amount of time and effort to bring it down, its demolition almost a metaphor for the man who built it.

America's Anti-German Delirium

Shortly after Claus Spreckels died, World War I stirred an anti-German sentiment that reached into all parts of the United States, distressing those German immigrants who loved America and had brought to their newly adopted homeland an expertise in farming, education, science, the arts, and more. When Americans went to war in 1917, Germans were the largest non-English-speaking minority group in the country. The 1901 census had counted more than 8 million first- and second-generation German Americans in the 92 million population. But now a steady stream of actions, official and private, were taken against citizens of German descent and German resident aliens. For example, Claus's grandnephew Walter Spreckels was classified as an "enemy alien" and was barred from the refinery he was managing in New York for Gus.[16] Theodore Roosevelt had been happy to take the Spreckels money prior to the war, but the American Defense Society, which the former president presided over, assailed Germans as the most treacherous, brutal, and loathsome people on earth and characterized the very "sound of the German language" as repulsive.[17]

With sentiments like that from on high, German-language newspapers were forced out of business, and colleges dropped the German language from the curriculum (this at a time when 25 percent of high school students studied German). Churches, mainly Lutheran, were denounced for their supposed allegiance to the German state. Words and phrases that sounded German were changed; as an example, the hamburger became a "liberty steak," and dachshunds became "liberty hounds." German culture had seeped into American life, but now such German composers as Bach, Beethoven, and Brahms were banned from orchestra programs. From this wholesale persecution, many German Americans concealed their ethnic identity and "over-proved" their loyalty to America.

Claus would have been crushed to his core during America's anti-German delirium, especially after he had displayed such a public show of patriotism for America and love for his adopted state whenever given the opportunity:

> Whatever may have been the experience of others, my labors in California have been abundantly rewarded. . . . I have found its people as generous as the soil and society here as rich in human virtues as are the mountains with gold. My experience has been that whoever works in California with the honesty of a true industry and meets the opportunities she offers with a fair degree of sagacity will not fail to find ample reward for all work of hand and head and heart.[18]

Claus was an unapologetic cutthroat businessman who dearly loved his adopted state and believed "Spreckels success is California's success."[19] He spotted opportunities, pioneered new technologies, bested and busted rivals—all for California. There are probably few men who were as pragmatic about making money as he was. He publicly stated many times that he didn't go into the sugar business as a philanthropist, though he was delighted with the far-reaching impact of this agricultural industry on the life of rural California. He didn't create his sugar industries out of ego either; he developed them, as he did with all of his ventures, only if he believed he could elevate or advance them with the latest technology of the time. He reached the pinnacle of success in his ventures because of his self-assurance, his inexhaustible ambition, and, more importantly, his nerve. Sadly, the two world wars lowered sentiments toward German Americans, and rather than Claus being remembered as an innovator of California agriculture or as a titan of industry, the tabloids gossiped with distain and hostility about the exploits of his wealthy grandchildren and their marriages and divorces, gossip that drove the subsequent generations further apart.

In the Footsteps of Their Father

At the time of his death, Claus had made amends and was on speaking terms with all five of his children, but they were not all speaking to one another. Sadly, his gesture of reconciliation in leaving his estate to his younger children continued the family wars down the generational lines. There was no forgiving and forgetting, and the rift in family relations was never repaired. All four sons went to extraordinary and irrational lengths to pursue their passions separately from one another.

John Diedrich Spreckels (1853–1926)

Claus's first son, John, was the employer of thousands and at one time paid 10 percent of San Diego's property taxes. He was president of companies in five industries: steamships, drinking water, transit, railroads, and sugar refining. He was passionate about modernizing San Diego and spearheaded the development of dams and pipelines to provide consistent water to the dry city. He donated to the arts, music, and literature, and built theaters and a library. He led the transformation of Balboa Park for the 1915 Panama-California Exposition, donating the Spreckels Organ Pavilion and its pipe organ, one of the few things retaining the Spreckels name. In many ways, that fact is a sad commentary on a once-great legacy and vital chapter in San Diego's history.

Considering his prominence, it was shocking the empire of John Diedrich Spreckels was broken up so quickly. Many speculated that if his eldest son, John D. "Jack" Spreckels Jr., had not died in a car crash at the age of thirty-nine in 1921, his empire might have survived. Five years after John's death, Adolph's widow, Alma Spreckels, controlled the majority of the brothers' joint companies. To get quick cash, she seemed to delight in undervaluing and selling short the prized holdings of the brother-in-law who had never fully accepted her; the liquidation of John's biggest assets appeared to be retaliatory because they were sold "at ridiculously low prices."[20]

Oceanic Steamship Company was the venture that had given John the impetus to chart his own course in life. The company had thrived with a fleet of passenger cargo steamships that operated from California to New Zealand and Australia via Hawai'i, but it was economically dependent on government transpacific mail contracts, which, during John's era, were awarded by acts of Congress. Thus, the company prospered when it had the contracts but fell into deep economic problems when it did not, such as in the year that John died. On May 17, 1926, John's beloved steamships *Sierra*, *Sonoma*, and *Ventura* became subsidiaries of the Matson Navigation Company.

John's final estate was appraised for the inheritance tax levy at $16,740,264 (more than $285 million in today's money). After all legacies, beneficiaries, and creditors were paid, the estate was divided evenly among his children and grandchildren, without the favoritism that John's parents had shown. Grace, Lillie, and Claus each received a quarter of the amount, with the fourth quarter going to the children of his deceased son, Jack: Marie, Adolph, John, and Geraldine.

When John's coffin was driven through downtown San Diego, white flags had been hung at half-mast throughout the city. Every ferry, streetcar, and even the train was stopped in silent tribute.[21] The mayor of San Diego went as far as to issue a proclamation that public buildings were to be shut down during John's memorial service. After his death, what remained in San Diegans' memory of John D. Spreckels was the one short, unscripted sentence he had spoken at the conclusion of his only formal speech to the city leaders on May 19, 1923. With trembling hands and tear-filled eyes, he had looked straight into the eyes of his audience, many of them his strongest critics, justifying his great expenditures by saying, "Gentlemen, I love San Diego."[22] John's remarkable life is covered in my monograph *Empire Builder: John D. Spreckels and the Making of San Diego* (2020).

Adolph Bernard Spreckels (1857–1924)

Claus's second son, Adolph, was able to hide from his wife, Alma, his dark secret of having contracted syphilis. It wasn't until their first child, Alma Emma, was born in 1909 that she learned. Elated at being a father in his fifties, Adolph purchased a Victorian home in a prime area of Pacific Heights (2080 Washington Street) as a present for Alma. But it wasn't large enough, so he tore it down and bought the neighboring lots for their new mansion, a French château that locals referred to as the "Sugar Palace," which took up an entire block. Alma enjoyed all the material benefits of her new role as Mrs. Spreckels, but she was, for the most part, snubbed by San Francisco society, who couldn't forgive her dubious past. Never a wallflower, Alma embraced the arts and philanthropy; she wouldn't allow San Francisco to ignore her.

By 1911 Adolph had had two syphilis-induced strokes that kept him home, often confined to a wheelchair, with the children, whom he smothered with love and adoration. He instilled in his daughter Alma Emma (1909–83) a love of horses, and she was a prizewinning show rider. Dorothy Constance (1913–2000) had a love for the arts and was a fixture in the world of fine couture. Adolph Bernard Jr. (1911–61) was a prize-winning polo player. The children were chronicled breathlessly in tabloids as they came of age.

Today, Adolph's most visible legacy is the Adolph B. and Alma de Bretteville Spreckels Gallery inside the California Palace of the Legion of Honor, where Auguste Rodin's sculptures dominate. A replica of the original Palais de la Légion d'Honneur in Paris, the building, in San Francisco's Lincoln Park, is a memorial to the California soldiers who fell in World War I. Adolph died on June 28, 1924, a few months before the Armistice Day opening of the structure.

On January 9, 1925, John, quite ailing, made his last visit to San Francisco to dedicate a magnificent municipal organ for the museum as his last tribute to his brother. Immediately following his death the following year, his sister-in-law Alma, only forty-five, looked for money to indulge her passions and became a tabloid celebrity. Considering the liquidation possibilities with her inherited interests in the J. D. and A. B. Spreckels Securities Company, the choice was easy: she began selling off John's San Diego empire without appraisals. Her personal haul from the estate was $8 million ($136 million in today's money), with another $8 million to her children.

Big Alma: San Francisco's Alma Spreckels chronicles her colorful life of unrestrained excess (she was the richest woman in the West, but she wanted more) until her death in 1968 at age eighty-seven.[23] Her excesses reduced her inherited $8 million fortune to a paltry $1 million. An unpublished fanciful biography, "The Story of A.B.," written by Clay M. Greene and commissioned by Alma soon after Adolph's death, has been "freshened up" and privately published with wonderful pictures in 2022 by Adolph and Alma's grandson Adolph Spreckels Rosekrans.

Claus Augustus "Gus" Spreckels (1858–1946)

Claus's third son, Gus, was constantly referred to as a "chip off the old block" after he created the largest independent sugar refinery in the United States in 1905. Like his father, he found loyal relatives to employ, including his cousins Walter, the grandson of his father's brother Peter, and Louis, the son of his father's brother Henry. Until World War I, the operations of Gus's Federal Sugar Refining Company in Yonkers, New York, were very profitable, employing more than 1,500.

The war changed everything, however. Gus was enraged when his cousin and manager of the business, Walter Spreckels, due to his being a German, was classified as an "enemy alien and barred from the refinery."[24] Following the war, global agricultural overproduction hit the sugar business hard. Prices tumbled to a record low in 1920, and Cuba's rise to become the world's largest sugar producer kept prices depressed. U.S. tariff politics favored American investments in Cuba because it was often cheaper to import refined sugar from that U.S. protectorate than to refine raw sugar in New York. In 1922 the Yonkers refinery was forced to temporarily close, and 1,000 men were laid off.

Gus, frustrated with the sugar business, turned the company over to Pierre J. Smith on January 1, 1923, changing his own role from president to chairman of the board. By 1927 refiners faced serious difficulties, including the worldwide government subsidization of beet production. Federal Sugar Refining was struggling along with a drastic reduction of workforce when Smith died, leaving Federal without a president.

In 1927, when he was sixty-eight, Gus persuaded Rudolph, fifty-five, who was already a heavy stockholder in Federal, to move to New York and take over the company as president so he could move to France. While it was an easy sell for Rudolph, it wasn't for Nellie who insisted on remaining in California with their children and grandchildren. Federal was reorganized as the Spreckels Sugar Corporation in 1929. Rudolph then invested millions of dollars into the new company. But all came to a crashing halt on Black Thursday, October 24, 1929, followed by Black Tuesday on October 29, when the stock market crashed. Rudolph lost millions, as did Gus, when his assorted holdings dwindled to nothing. The Spreckels Sugar Corporation was liquidated in 1930.

Gus and his wife, Oroville "Orey" (1863–1933), and their only child, Lurline Elizabeth Eddy Kuznik (1886–1969), expatriated to France during the booming economy and explosion in consumerism after World War I. Gus and Orey spent millions, living a carefree, high-profile life among Europe's rich and famous—Orey especially as a Paris and Riviera socialite. She loved to gamble and made the news in 1926 by exposing dishonesty among the dealers at the Monte Carlo Casino. Gus's passion was collecting art.

The *San Francisco Examiner* on November 30, 1930, hinted the "French" Spreckels family was having money problems: "Word comes that as a result of the decision of Mr. and Mrs. Claus A. [Gus] Spreckels to sell the Villa Baratier, their home on the Riviera, many notable pieces of fine Eighteenth Century French furniture, sculpture and bronzes will be dispersed at auction."[25] Once their magnificent mansion at Saint-Jean-Cap-Ferrat (in the Alpes-Maritimes) was sold, along with their mansion in Paris, they moved into an apartment in Paris nearby Lurline and her second husband, Colonel Joseph Kuznik. Orey, at seventy, died from an infection of the pancreas. After his wife's death, Gus lived an obscure and quiet life in Paris, being looked after by the Kuzniks.

In March 1940, when Gus was eighty-one years old, his obscurity was compromised: he was hauled into court by R. E. Titus, who sought to collect a judgment for $3,808,208 ($81,677,569 in today's money) on delinquent promissory notes. Gus testified in court that his money was gone and that his living expenses were paid by his daughter and son-in-law. Questioned about a private bank in Paris he used, he responded, "I have no bankers." In response to "When did they cease to be your bankers?" he said with some of his old swagger and humor: "When I had no more money."[26]

Gus returned to Paris after the trial. He died there from a stroke in the fall of 1946 at the age of eighty-seven. One death announcement from a San Francisco reporter imagined for the readers that Gus might meet his father, Claus Spreckels, in heaven. After learning that Gus died broke, Claus would "demand to know what the devil Gus did with the fortune [he had] left for him?!" Then the *Examiner* opined that it was a good thing that Gus didn't have any sons, because "had there been a young Spreckels to inherit nothing from him, then the cynical world could have pointed out this as another case of the old aphorism of 'From shirt-sleeves to shirt sleeves in three generations'"—meaning the older generation started with nothing, worked hard, amassed wealth, but by the time their grandchildren are in charge, the family would be back where they started, with nothing.[27]

Emma Claudine Watson Ferris Hutton (née Spreckels) (1870–1924)
In Emma's era it was said that a lady would have her name in a newspaper only when she was born, married, and buried—unless she was seeking publicity for a charitable event. Since there is simply little on record about how Emma lived or any public causes that she championed, there were few substantial remarks made after her death outside of her being the only daughter of Claus

Spreckels and of her three marriages. So, if it's true that well-behaved women rarely make history, in Emma's case there are no truer words.

Claus's only daughter, Emma, was married three times and was twice made a widow in England. After her first husband Tom Watson died in 1904, she married John Ferris (in 1906). Emma's only child, daughter Jean Ferris, was born in 1910, and the family lived in Kingswood Manor in Reigate, Surrey, England (today's exclusive wedding venue). Ferris died in 1920 at seventy-one, making Emma a young widow again at fifty, but now with a nine-year-old daughter to raise alone. Prior to Ferris's death, they had purchased a new estate, Nutfield Priory in Surrey (today's luxury hotel destination). Emma married for the third and last time in 1922 to Arthur Hutton.

Emma died in 1924 at age fifty-four, from complications after a surgery to treat "peritonitis," leaving the fourteen-year-old Jean Ferris with her step-father, Arthur Hutton, as her legal guardian, and in the care of her lifelong nanny, Sarah Pullen.[28] In 1926 Jean, fifteen, was living an unremarkable life at an English boarding school in Bournemouth, a coastal resort town in southwestern England, until she was notified that she had come into the inheritance left by Claus Spreckels, the grandfather she'd never met.[29] The news of a "schoolgirl" inheriting this $2,500 fortune ($42,575 in today's money) made headlines across the globe, reminding readers of how a pen-niless immigrant had become the world's sugar king. The media attention directed to the "Spreckels Heiress" was not well received by the reserved girl. Jean was described as a "tall, slender, blue-eyed" girl who was "English in all her ways" and was "not excited about the money." It was speculated that Jean could never be persuaded to return to the United States and abandon her passion, horses.[30]

But when Jean came of age, she wanted to reunite with her Spreckels fam-ily. While visiting her uncles Gus and Rudolph in New York, she was swept off her feet, at age nineteen, by a thirty-two-year-old divorced architect from Texas, Irving Drought Harris. They married in 1929, but it was a "stormy," short-lived marriage. In 1938 Jean married a French "phony nobleman," Prince de Broons, going by the name of Charles Marquis d'Espinay de Durtal, cousin of the French royal pretender, the Duke de Guise. Jean thereby gained for herself the lofty title of Marquise d'Espinay de Durtal, Princesse de Brons.

Jean died at the age of thirty-one in 1941 in Nazi-occupied France after an unknown operation. The antique correspondence of Nancie Thomson, the nanny of Jean's daughter Mimi Harris, describes Jean as obstinate as her grandfather Claus: "a lady who liked her own way, whether it be in the choice of a yacht or a husband" and "woe betide anyone who crossed her!" Mimi noted that "all that money did not bring her a lot of happiness."[31] The historical novel *Forsaken Kings: Emma Spreckels, the Surfer of Asbury Park* (2022), by Vincent J. Dicks, chronicles the life of Emma and hews closely to the actual events.

Rudolph Spreckels (1871–1958)

Claus's youngest child, Rudolph, lost millions in the disaster of the 1906 San Francisco earthquake and fire. He left the San Francisco Gas and Electric Company that year to become president of the First National Bank of San Francisco. He organized and financed with a quarter of a million dollars ($8.4 million in today's money) the San Francisco graft prosecutions of 1906–9, which ultimately "freed the city from the ring that had robbed it for many years."[32]

He became famed throughout the country as the young millionaire who fought grafters and won. Rudolph's war on graft and civic corruption in San Francisco made him a national figure. But after the "house cleaning" of San Francisco, Rudolph was ostracized, and many businessmen tried to brand Rudolph as a traitor to his class. His wife, Nellie, was also shunned in society circles, which was a deep blow to one who loved to socialize. Because of the ostracism he endured, Rudolph in 1914 told a reporter how "his eyes were opened." "Before that, my whole life was bounded by dollars. My only ambition was to amass more millions. Human beings were unimportant except in so far as they were party to a bargain I happened to be driving. I was just the ordinary rich man."[33] During World War I Rudolph, like many liberals, was a pacifist and was furious at the First National Bank's board of directors for voting funds for military preparedness. After seventeen years as bank president, he was voted out in 1923.

The news of John's serious health diagnosis in 1926 prompted Rudolph to seek amends with his long-estranged eldest brother. Four years earlier, he and Adolph had mended their estrangement publicly in San Francisco society; evidently, "their mutual admiration for horses" had inspired them to "discard their differences."[34] Rudolph apparently hoped for a similar outcome with John, but it was not to be. When he arrived in Coronado from San Francisco, hat in hand, he was refused entrance to the Glorietta Bay mansion. John couldn't bury the resentments he had long harbored against his brother.

Rudolph floundered about trying to reinvent himself. His business activities were numerous and varied: whaling, radio, promotion of inventions, and more. He then became president of a group of banks in the Sacramento and San Joaquin Valleys until he was persuaded in 1927 by his brother Gus to accept the presidency of the Federal Sugar Refining Company in Yonkers, New York. He lost his entire fortune in the crash of 1929 and with the liquidation of Federal. Over the next decade, it was discovered that a large part of his fortune had been built on borrowed money. He was left owing about $4 million (about $88 million in today's money) to banks and another $1 million ($22 million today) to the federal government.

Rudolph moved back to California, and during World War II, he entertained his numerous grandchildren with his escapades at raising chickens and rabbits with Nellie, who died in 1949. Before he died in 1958 at the age of eighty-six, Rudolph was impoverished, having spent his widower years living alone in a three-room apartment in San Mateo. Grandchildren recalled their grandfather always had a bowl of sugar cubes nearby, reminding them that it had been Claus Spreckels who gave America their first sugar cube. A journalist who wanted to interview the "last Spreckels" took great delight describing Rudolph as he puttered around his small kitchen, making a sardine-on-toast sandwich for lunch. He looked straight at the reporter and said, "I have never been happier than I am now. . . . Some financiers jumped out of windows when they found themselves bankrupt. I never lost a night's sleep over it."[35] Rudolph's life as a business reformer is highlighted extensively in *Upbuilders* (1968), by Lincoln Steffens, which has undergone numerous reprints.

Lessons Learned

The longing for wealth and success, the myth of streets paved with gold, the notion that New York's harbor was open to all comers have always been at the heart of what propelled thousands of immigrants like Claus Spreckels to America. It was the dream of riches that precipitated Columbus's voyage to the shores of the new continent. At the time of Claus's death, his fortune was estimated by the *New York Times* to be $50 million ($852 million in today's money).

In 1996 Claus made "The Wealthy 100" list of the richest Americans in history, a fact that illustrates there are a hundred different ways to build an American fortune.[36] In this elite list, relative wealth is expressed as a ratio of the person's total wealth to the U.S. gross national product (GNP) at the time of his or her death (or to the current GNP if the person is living). Claus ranks fortieth on the list, with a 554 ranking. To illustrate his wealth today, Warren Buffett is just one step above our Claus, at number thirty-nine, and Bill Gates is only nine places above at thirty-one. Claus outranks others we recall as the richest of the rich, such as J. Paul Getty, Joseph Pulitzer, Frank Woolworth, and Howard Hughes.

Claus Spreckels made his fortune in an unsettled country, in an era when there were far fewer rules. There were no signs pointing to the path of fortune either, so he couldn't follow the herd. He charted a new direction with his innovations, and he pushed his inventions into commercial success, paving the way for his sons to follow. Judged by current standards of business, the moves that Claus made to amass his fortune appear ruthless. It wasn't that he was the smartest or most creative entrepreneur, but it's clear from his words and actions that he pursued a vision that was more important than the money itself. Sam Walton, Walmart's founder, had this to say about people like Claus: they "just got after it and stayed after it."

Claus's sons learned the hard way that the sugar business, like most businesses dealing in commodities, had an insatiable appetite for scale that eventually surpassed any individual's ability to provide capital. Only his oldest, John, would be able to carve his own path and establish a lasting legacy beyond sugar. For many of Claus's descendants, the great wealth was not a blessing but a curse, as seen in comments by Rudolph, who had "never been happier" than when it was all gone. Some in the family couldn't get rid of the Spreckels fortune fast enough, while others carefully managed it, leaving the "haves" and the "have nots" to this day with strained relations.

The lessons are many. Hard work alone did not protect Gus and Rudolph from financial ruin. Claus had a tremendous work ethic, but it was combined with his ability to learn from his past, to adjust from failure, to anticipate trends correctly, and to build a loyal army of employees. He was perfectly suited for his period. There can never be another Claus Spreckels, but every age presents unique opportunities for those with the right mix of skills and grit.

NOTES

Introduction

1. "Living on Twenty Dollars a Week: Our Millionaires Tell the People How They Could Do It," *San Francisco Morning Call*, November 12, 1892, 3.
2. "The New Refinery," *Hawaiian Gazette* (Honolulu), June 22, 1881.
3. *Watsonville (CA) Pajaronian*, November 10, 1887, quoted in Conway, "Spreckels Sugar Company," 12n13.
4. San Francisco Journal of Commerce, *Builders of a Great City*, 317, quoted in Goldberg, "Cauldron of Anger," 241–79.
5. "The Spreckels Trial," *Los Angeles Times*, June 6, 1885, 4; "The Spreckels Case," *Daily Evening Bulletin* (Honolulu), June 8, 1885.
6. Steffens, "Rudolf Spreckels: A Business Man," 391.
7. "Welcome and a Token for Claus Spreckels," *San Francisco Call*, September 26, 1900.
8. "The Touchstone of Calamity," *Sacramento Daily Union*, April 25, 1906.
9. "Welcome and a Token."
10. "Living on Twenty Dollars a Week," 3.

1. Chasing the American Dream

1. O'Brien, "Claus Spreckels, the Sugar King," 517.
2. Claus's five brothers were Barthold (also called Bernhard, 1830–61), Johann (1833–35), Died(e)rich (1837–1920), Peter (1839–1922), and Hinrich "Henry" (1842–77). His sister was Anna Margarethe (Henning) (1845–1913).
3. Wagner, *History of Migration*, 57.
4. Wagner, *History of Migration*, 55; O'Brien, "Claus Spreckels, the Sugar King," 516.
5. Cohn and Wegge, "Overseas Passenger Fares," 401.
6. Mehrländer, *Germans of Charleston*, 16.
7. You can appreciate Claus's experience in steerage by reading Downey, *Levi Strauss*, 20.
8. Cohn and Wegge, "Overseas Passenger Fares," 402.
9. Downey, *Levi Strauss*, 20.

10. "Traveling through Time: Archived Articles of Shelby County People, Places and Events," Shelby County Historical Society, Sidney OH, retrieved March 18, 2022, https://www .shelbycountyhistory.org/schs/immigration/thejourney.htm.

11. Downey, *Levi Strauss*, 21.

12. Downey, *Levi Strauss*, 22–23.

13. H. Adams, *The Man, John D. Spreckels*, 131.

14. Terry, "*Die Deutschen in Kalifornien*," 15.

15. Strickland, "How the Germans Became White Southerners," 54.

16. Mehrländer, *Germans of Charleston*, 39.

17. Strickland, "How the Germans Became White Southerners," 58.

18. Mehrländer, *Germans of Charleston*, 39.

19. Newhall, "Spreckels" (unpublished manuscript, privately circulated, about the history of the Spreckels Sugar Company and its founder, Claus Spreckels), 3.

20. H. Adams, *The Man, John D. Spreckels*, 31–32.

21. "Living on Twenty Dollars a Week," 3.

22. "Living on Twenty Dollars a Week."

23. Located on the southeast corner of Anson and Society Streets, 60 Anson Street is the historic Robert M. Venning House, which was owned by Robert Murrell Venning (1789 –1856). Historic Charleston Foundation, *60 Anson Street*, 1960, Lowcountry Digital Library, https://lcdl.library.cofc.edu/lcdl/catalog/lcdl:64323.

24. "The City: Bringing Back the Heritage," *Time*, September 1, 1967, http://content.time .com/time/subscriber/article/0,33009,837255,00.html.

25. Historic Charleston Foundation, *60 Anson Street*; Green, "Martin Dowd's Brick Tenements," Lowcountry Digital Library.

26. "Council Chamber," *Charleston Courier*, October 1, 1852, 1.

27. Carrie Berger (daughter of John G. Belcher, descendant of Claus and Anna Spreckels), personal communication with author, April 23, 2018.

28. "The Weather," *Sumter (SC) Banner*, August 16, 1853, 2.

29. Barbara Tieken, "Many German Immigrants Opposed Slavery in Texas," letter to *Victoria (TX) Advocate*, October 12, 2017, updated February 22, 2018, https://www.victoria advocate.com/opinion/many-german-immigrants-opposed-slavery-in-texas/article_0cfd 665c-a9d3-5d00-8617-a9e291ed1fb7.html.

30. "Customer Services and Site Information: About Us," *New Braunfels (TX) Herald-Zeitung*, March 20, 2022, https://herald-zeitung.com/site/about.html.

31. Strickland, "Ethnicity and Race in the Urban South," 21, 28.

32. Strickland, "How the Germans Became White Southerners," 60.

33. Adolph Rosecrans (great-grandson of Claus and Anna Spreckels), personal communication with author, March 1, 2018.

34. Newhall, "Spreckels," 4.

35. Wilson, *Trow's New York City Directory*.

36. "Tribeca: Commercial and Industrial Development," Wikipedia, retrieved March 20, 2022, https://en.wikipedia.org/wiki/Tribeca#Commercial_and_industrial_development.

37. Twarog, "Heights and Living Standards in Germany," 288.

38. Meyer, *Die Verwandten des Zuckerkönigs*, 130–37.

39. Cordray, "Claus Spreckels of California," 6.

40. "Living on Twenty Dollars a Week," 3.

41. Cordray, "Claus Spreckels of California," 26.

42. *San Francisco*, 26–27.

43. Terry, *"Die Deutschen in Kalifornien,"* 19, 47.

44. Newhall, "Spreckels," 5.

45. Terry, *"Die Deutschen in Kalifornien,"* 66.

46. St. Clair, "Gold Rush," 196.

47. Downey, *Levi Strauss*, 58.

48. "Living on Twenty Dollars a Week," 3.

49. *San Francisco Directory*, 256.

50. Newhall, "Spreckels," 6a.

51. H. Adams, *The Man, John D. Spreckels*, 44, 45, 46.

52. Allen and Avery, *California Gold Book*, 360.

53. "Beer and Bullets: The History of Beer in the Civil War," American Battlefield Trust, November 5, 2018, updated March 25, 2021, https://www.battlefields.org/learn/articles/beer-and-bullets-history-beer-civil-war.

54. St. Clair, "Gold Rush," 194.

55. Peter and Anna Spreckels had four children who survived childhood: Agnes (1861), Minna (1868), Martha (1870), and Alfred (1872).

56. U.S. Census Bureau, *Eighth Census of the United States, 1860*, population schedules, Roll 0067, 10th District San Francisco, page 108, NARA M653.

57. Yenne, *San Francisco Beer*, 28.

58. "Spreckels Was Started by Corner in Sugar," *San Francisco Examiner*, December 27, 1908.

59. "Living on Twenty Dollars a Week," 3.

60. Yenne, *San Francisco Beer*, 28.

61. "District Fair," *Daily National Democrat* (Marysville CA), September 21, 1859.

62. "Albany Ale," *San Joaquin Republican*, February 24, 1859.

63. Libby Ingalls, "George Gordon: Historical Essay," *Shipping San Francisco's Digital Archive Found*, retrieved March 20, 2022, https://www.foundsf.org/index.php?title=George_Gordon.

64. Strickland, "Ethnicity and Race in the Urban South," 8. The first stage of processing raw sugar is to soften and then remove the layer of mother liquor surrounding the crystals with a process called "affination."

2. White Gold

1. Gritz, "Unsavory History of Sugar."

2. Edwards, "Sugar Racket."

3. Rehder, "Sugar Plantation Settlements of Southern Louisiana," 111–12; "Quarter Miles Travel—Louisiana Purchase," *Travel with Annita and Friends* (radio show), retrieved April

16, 2022, https://www.travelwithannita.com/episode-6-quarter-miles-travel-louisiana
-sugar-cane-plantations-louisiana-purchase/.

4. Khalil Gibran Muhammad, "The Sugar That Saturates the American Diet Has a Barbaric History as the 'White Gold' That Fueled Slavery," *New York Times Magazine*, August 14, 2019, https://www.nytimes.com/interactive/2019/08/14/magazine/sugar-slave-trade-slavery.html.

5. Riquelmy, Currie, and Robinson, *Sugar at LSU*.

6. University of Pennsylvania, Wharton School, and Philadelphia Social Science Association, *Publications of the University of Pennsylvania*, 9.

7. H. Adams, *The Man, John D. Spreckels*, 37.

8. Phelps, *Contemporary Biography*, 410.

9. "Claus Spreckels" in *Planter and Sugar Manufacturer*, 37:82.

10. "Living on Twenty Dollars a Week," 3.

11. H. Adams, *The Man, John D. Spreckels*, 48.

12. Newhall, "Spreckels," 12–13.

13. H. Adams, *The Man, John D. Spreckels*, 48.

14. "New York Draft Riots," History.com, October 27, 2009, updated April 16, 2021, https://www.history.com/topics/american-civil-war/draft-riots.

15. H. Adams, *The Man, John D. Spreckels*, 57.

16. "Living on Twenty Dollars a Week," 3.

17. Though Claus eventually sold his shares, the brewery remained in the family until 1879, when Claus Mangels's good friend Frederick Hagemann Jr. from Hanover bought the enterprise.

18. Claus Mangels resided at a mansion at 2518 Howard Street. He was connected with the firm Tillman & Bendel, cigar dealers on Battery Street. He died in April 1891 at the age of only fifty-eight.

19. Allen and Avery, *California Gold Book*, 361.

20. Greene, "Story of A. B.," unpublished biography, 13.

21. Ira G. Hoitt, "Education in California," *Sunset*, May 3, 1899, 1.

22. *History of the College of California*, 104.

23. It's unknown if Gus went, or when Adolph followed, but it was before 1867, when the school closed.

24. Greene, "Story of A. B.," chap. 2, p. 4

25. "Insurance Statement of the Pacific Insurance Company of California," *Vicksburg (MS) Daily Times*, July 9, 1871.

26. Newhall, "Spreckels," 14.

27. Merleaux, "Spectacles of Sweetness," 55–80.

28. Amy McDonald, "A Bitter Look at the Sweet History of Brown Sugar," *The Devil's Tale: Dispatches from the David M. Rubinstein Rare Book & Manuscript Library*, February 25, 2016, citing Eichner, *Emergence of Oligopoly*, 68–69, https://blogs.library.duke.edu/rubenstein/2016/02/25/amari-stokes/.

29. Merleaux, "Spectacles of Sweetness," 58.

30. J. P. Green, *Fact Stranger Than Fiction*, 114; Merleaux, "Spectacles of Sweetness," 72.
31. Pigman, *Carbohydrates*, 503.
32. Newhall, "Spreckels," 15.
33. Newhall, "Spreckels," 15.
34. Newhall, "Spreckels," 15.
35. Roth, "Cholera, Community," 528.
36. Alexandra, "Mindblowing Tales."
37. "There's Money in It," *San Jose Weekly Mercury*, April 6, 1865.
38. "Beet Sugar," *Sacramento Daily Union*, September 27, 1861.
39. "There's Money in It."
40. "Beets and Beet Sugar," *Weekly Colusa (CA) Sun*, February 23, 1867.
41. Terrie Todd, "Lazy Farmers Don't Grow Sugar Beets," *Hanna (AB) Herald*, September 2, 2021, https://www.hannaherald.com/opinion/columnists/lazy-farmers-dont-grow-sugar-beets/wcm/e7156777-c726-47cc-8a6f-71914b2b10a1/amp/.
42. Spreckels Sugar Company, *Sugar from Western Farms*, 11.
43. Schmitt, "Prussia's Last Fling," 316.
44. Spiekermann, "Claus Spreckels," 4; Magnuson, "History of the Beet Sugar Industry," 68–69.
45. "Births," *Sacramento Daily Union*, May 28, 1866.
46. "Beets and Beet Sugar."
47. Newhall, "Spreckels," 25.
48. Spiekermann, "Claus Spreckels," 4.
49. Cordray, "Claus Spreckels of California," 26.
50. Downey, *Levi Strauss*, 118.
51. U.S. Department of the Interior Patent Office, *Report of the Commissioner of Patents for the Year 1868*, 716, patent number 75,656: "Claus Spreckels, San Francisco, Cal.—*Manufacture of Crushed Sugar.*—March 17, 1868.—The sugar is removed from the centrifugal machine to the molds and immediately pressed; after this it is subjected to a moderate heat and then to a greater heat in an oven. It is then ready for crushing and pulverizing. *Claim.*—The manufacture of the crushed sugar of commerce directly from the centrifugal machine, in the manner substantially as herein described."
52. Cordray, "Claus Spreckels of California," 14.
53. Adler, *Claus Spreckels*, 23.
54. "The California Sugar Refinery, Its Founder, and His Work," *San Francisco Merchant*, May 27, 1881.
55. Ingalls, "George Gordon."
56. Cordray, "Claus Spreckels of California," 23.
57. H. Adams, *The Man, John D. Spreckels*, 49.
58. Cordray, "Claus Spreckels of California," 16.
59. "California Sugar Refinery."
60. "Sugar-Refining," *Weekly Commercial Herald Annual Review* (Vicksburg MS), January 15, 1880.

3. Too Much Too Fast

1. Phelps, *Contemporary Biography*, 410–11.
2. Barke, Fribush, and Stearns, "Nervous Breakdown," 567.
3. Phelps, *Contemporary Biography*, 410–11.
4. The term *nervous breakdown* wouldn't be introduced until 1901.
5. "Living on Twenty Dollars a Week," 3.
6. "Living on Twenty Dollars a Week," 3.
7. Phelps, *Contemporary Biography*, 410–11.
8. "Ocean Holidays," 775.
9. Bonura, *Light in the Queen's Garden*, 174.
10. "The West," *New North-West* (Deer Lodge, Montana Territory), July 9, 1869.
11. "News," *San Francisco Chronicle*, June 18, 1869, 3.
12. "Taking the Cure," *Bismarck Tribune*, November 2, 1911.
13. J. M. Adams, "Development and Marketing," 92.
14. Greene, "Story of A. B.," chap. 3, p. 5.
15. H. Adams, *The Man, John D. Spreckels*, 50.
16. H. Adams, *The Man, John D. Spreckels*.
17. David Lewis (great-great-grandson of Claus and Anna Spreckels), personal communication with author, 2018.
18. Newhall, "Spreckels," 21.
19. H. Adams, *The Man, John D. Spreckels*, 52–53.
20. Phelps, *Contemporary Biography*, 411.
21. "Received Amid Palms," *San Francisco Call*, February 13, 1896.
22. Hefner, "Sugar Beet Roots," Coronado Museum of History & Art.
23. Jones, *Economic History*, 25.
24. Walker, "Industry Builds Out the City," 100.
25. Wiggin, *My Garden of Memory*, 108.
26. "Mission Dolores," *Sacramento Daily Union*, May 12, 1877.
27. Uwe Spiekermann, personal communication with author, February 11, 2019.
28. Greene, "Story of A. B.," chap. 4, p. 1.
29. Gregory, *History of Solano and Napa Counties*.
30. H. Adams, *The Man, John D. Spreckels*, 58, 60, 71, 60.
31. Steffens, "Rudolph Spreckels: A Business Reformer."
32. Greene, "Story of A. B.," chap. 3, p. 3.
33. Lyles and Thibodeaux-Lyles, *Historical Development of Capitalism*, 115.
34. "Millionaires of San Francisco," 3.
35. Ben Ratliff, "The Octopus and the Big Four: Historical Essay," *Shipping San Francisco's Digital Archive Found*, retrieved March 29, 2022, https://www.foundsf.org/index.php?title=The_Octopus_and_the_Big_Four.
36. Pollock, *San Francisco's Golden Gate Park*, 19.
37. "Spreckels et al. v. State," 22:775.

38. Steffens, "Rudolph Spreckels: A Business Reformer."

39. Swenson, *Alvarado Sugar Beet Factory*, 26.

4. Between Heaven and Hell

1. Kevin Newhouse and Michael Oppenheimer, "The Meaning of 'Aptos,'" *Aptos (CA) Times*, January 20, 2014, https://tpgonlinedaily.com/meaning-aptos/.

2. John Hibble, "The First Family of Aptos," Aptos History Museum: Local People Preserving Local History, August 3, 2020, https://aptoshistory.org/?p=486

3. John Hibble, "The First Family of Aptos: History Corner," Aptos Life, February 4, 2020, https://aptoslife.com/the-first-family-of-aptos-history-corner/.

4. Bethel, "Golden Skein," 255–76.

5. Collins, "Spreckels Era."

6. Stevens and Schwantes, "Frederick Augustus Hihn."

7. "Capitalist Clashes with Church People," *San Francisco Call*, August 1, 1905.

8. Lydon and Swift, *Soquel Landing*, 8; Payne, "Howling Wilderness."

9. "Charley Parkhurst," Wikipedia, retrieved April 2, 2022, https://en.wikipedia.org/wiki/Charley_Parkhurst.

10. Snodgrass, *Settlers of the American West*, 127.

11. Vivian Underhill, Stanley D. Stevens, Jennifer Fosgate, and Alix Norton, "Guide to the Frederick A. Hihn Records MS.201," Online Archive of California, 2020, https://oac.cdlib.org/findaid/ark:/13030/c8n58tfx/entire_text/.

12. Angel, *History of San Luis Obispo County*, 154.

13. Hamman, *California Central Coast Railways*, 7–8.

14. C. O. Cummings, editorial, *Watsonville (CA) Pajaronian*, April 11, 1872, https://americanhistory.si.edu/america-on-the-move/community-dreams.

15. Hamman, *California Central Coast Railways*, 10, 13–14.

16. Powell, *Reign of the Lumber Barons*, 13–15, 41.

17. Gendron and Domhoff, *Leftmost City*.

18. "Articles of Incorporation of the Santa Cruz R. R. Company," Hihn Records, certified copy from county clerk's office, Museum of Art and History, McPherson Center, Santa Cruz.

19. John Hall, "Santa Cruz Railroad," Pacific Coast Narrow Gauge, updated February 28, 2015, http://www.pacificng.com/print.php?page=roads/ca/scrr/index.htm.

20. Magnuson, "History of the Beet Sugar Industry," 75.

21. Swenson, *Alvarado Sugar Beet Factory*, 40–41.

22. Wiley, *Sugar-Beet Industry*, 35–36.

23. San Francisco Journal of Commerce, *Builders of a Great City*, 167.

24. Swenson, *Alvarado Sugar Beet Factory*, 27.

25. Hachten and Allen, *Flavor of Wisconsin*, 112.

26. Soquel Pioneer and Historical Association, *Soquel (Images of America)*, 34.

27. S. B. Smith, *Adobe Days*, 70.

28. "Sheriff's Sale," *Santa Cruz (CA) Sentinel*, September 13, 1879.

29. "Soquel Sugar Works," *Santa Cruz (CA) Sentinel*, December 4, 1880.

30. "Carpenter Gothic Architectural Style," Encyclopedia Britannica, February 11, 2016, https://www.britannica.com/art/Carpenter-Gothic.

31. Stevens and Schwantes, "Frederick Augustus Hihn," 20.

32. Hansen, *California*, 337.

33. Mark Reed, personal communication with author, July 15, 2022.

34. John Hibble, "Mural of Aptos Polo Matches," *Aptos (CA) Times*, August 7, 2017, https://tpgonlinedaily.com/mural-aptos-polo-matches/.

35. "Aptos Stock Farm."

36. Steffens, "Rudolph Spreckels: A Business Man," 393.

37. "Newport of the Pacific," *Santa Cruz (CA) Sentinel*, June 12, 1875.

38. Collins, "Spreckels Era," 3.

39. "A Case of Assault," *Santa Cruz (CA) Sentinel*, May 22, 1875.

40. John Hibble, "The Grand Hotel of Aptos," Aptos History Museum: Local People Preserving Local History, July 13, 2020, https://aptoshistory.org/?p=481.

41. Hamman, *California Central Coast Railways*, 16.

42. Preston Sawyer, "Santa Cruz Yesterdays," *Santa Cruz (CA) Sentinel*, August 15, 1954.

43. John Hibble, "The Santa Cruz Rail Road, Built by Giants," Aptos History Museum, August 13, 2021, https://aptoshistory.org/?p=589.

44. Sawyer, "Santa Cruz Yesterdays."

45. Hibble, "Grand Hotel of Aptos."

46. "Guest Ledger (1876–78, 1880, 1884), Aptos Hotel," Aptos History Museum.

47. Cordray, "Claus Spreckels of California," 39.

48. "Living on Twenty Dollars a Week," 3.

49. Hall, "Santa Cruz Railroad."

50. Hamman, *California Central Coast Railways*, 25.

51. Stanley D. Stevens, compiler, *F. A. Hihn's Rail Road Researcher's Digest*.

52. Hihn v. Spreckels, 59 Cal. 315 (1881), Caselaw Access Project: Harvard Law School, https://cite.case.law/cal/59/315/.

53. Hall, "Santa Cruz Railroad."

54. "Hotel Del Monte: History," Wikipedia, retrieved April 20, 2022, https://en.wikipedia.org/wiki/Hotel_Del_Monte#History.

55. Hibble, "Grand Hotel of Aptos."

56. "Schoolhouse for Aptos," *Los Angeles Times*, October 25, 1899.

5. Threats, Opportunities

1. "Living on Twenty Dollars a Week," 3.

2. Kuykendall, *Hawaiian Kingdom*, 2:147.

3. Adler, *Claus Spreckels*, 14.

4. Adler, *Claus Spreckels*, 10.

5. Twain, "Twenty-Third Letter," 398.

6. Rigby, "American Expansion in Hawaii," 363.

7. Adler, *Claus Spreckels*, 13.

8. Hefner, "Sugar Beet Roots," Coronado Museum of History & Art.

9. Speed, "King Kalakaua of Hawaii," 96.

10. Emmet, *California and Hawaiian Sugar Refining Corporation*, 1.

11. Cordray, "Claus Spreckels of California," 15.

12. Adler, *Claus Spreckels*, 14.

13. Hawaiian Mission Children's Society, *Portraits of American Protestant Missionaries*, 86.

14. Schulz, "Empire of the Young."

15. "Reciprocity," *Pacific Commercial Advertiser* (Honolulu), March 13, 1875.

16. Patterson, "United States and Hawaiian Reciprocity," 14, quoting *Reports of the Senate Committee on Foreign Relations, 1789–1901*, document 231, 56 Cong., 2 sess., 6:465.

17. Adler, *Claus Spreckels*, 15.

18. Adler, *Claus Spreckels*, 13.

19. Simonds, *Kama'aina*, 84.

20. Adler, *Claus Spreckels*, 15.

21. Adler, *Claus Spreckels*, 13.

22. Simonds, *Kama'aina*, 17.

23. Simonds, *Kama'aina*, 42.

24. Scott, *Saga of the Sandwich Islands*, 97.

25. Spreckels, "Hawaii for Tourists," 662.

26. W. D. Alexander, "Advent of Spreckels," 181.

27. Korn, *News from Molokai*, 308.

28. Bonura, "Queen Lili'uokalani's," 39.

29. Joseph Emerson (1843–1930) accepted a position with the Hawaiian Government Survey; Nathaniel Emerson (1839–1915) became president of the Hawaiian Board of Health; William Richards Castle (1849–1935) and William Neville Armstrong (1835–1905) each served as attorney general; Samuel Mills Damon (1845–1924) served as minister of finance; Albert Francis Judd (1838–1900) and Sanford Ballard Dole (1844–1926) received appointments to the Hawaiian Supreme Court.

30. Bonura, *Light in the Queen's Garden*, 34.

31. Creighton, *Lands of Hawaii*, 32.

32. Takaki, *Pau Hana*, 4.

33. Takaki, *Pau Hana*, 6–7.

34. William Hooper diary and correspondence, William Hooper Papers, quoted in Takaki, *Pau Hana*, 5.

35. Takaki, *Pau Hana*, 7.

36. Max Roffman, "History of Labor in Hawai'i," Center for Labor Education and Research, University of Hawai'i–West O'ahu, 1974, https://www.hawaii.edu/uhwo/clear/home/HawaiiLaborHistory.html.

37. Fleischmann and Tyson, "Interface of Race and Accounting," 12.

38. Roffman, "History of Labor in Hawai'i."

39. "At Last!," *Pacific Commercial Advertiser* (Honolulu), August 26, 1876.

40. "At Last!"

41. Adler, *Claus Spreckels*, 285.

42. Siler, *Lost Kingdom*, 72.

43. Adler, *Claus Spreckels*, 33.

44. Wilcox, *Sugar Water*, 16.

45. Wilcox, *Sugar Water*, 16.

46. "The Career of Claus Spreckels," *Indianapolis Journal*, November 21, 1884.

47. Adler, *Claus Spreckels*, 49–50.

48. Kuykendall, *Hawaiian Kingdom*, 1:59.

49. Haleakalā Crater, retrieved April 8, 2022, https://haleakalacrater.com/; Twain, *Roughing It*, 409; London, *The Call of the Wild*.

6. Storming into Hawai'i

1. Siler, *Lost Kingdom*, 72.

2. Wakeman, *History and Reminiscences*, 81, 104.

3. H. Adams, *The Man, John D. Spreckels*, 72.

4. "Spreckels in Queer Tangle," *Hawaiian Star*, June 16, 1909.

5. Carrie Prudence Winter to Charles A. Kofoid, August 21, 1890, Kofoid Papers.

6. Angell, *Theatres of Hawai'i*, 9.

7. Elson, *Musical Herald*, 205.

8. H. Adams, *The Man, John D. Spreckels*, 74.

9. When the Music Hall burned to the ground in 1895, John and Adolph Spreckels subsidized the rebuilding of it, giving it a new name: the Hawaiian Opera House.

10. O'Shaughnessy, "Reminisces of Hawaii," typescript, 24–25.

11. H. Adams, *The Man, John D. Spreckels*, 75.

12. Hackler, "Princeville Plantation Papers," 67.

13. W. F. Allen to E. H. Allen, September 29, 1879, in Hackler, "Princeville Plantation Papers," 79.

14. Hackler, "Princeville Plantation Papers," 81.

15. Sullivan, *History of C. Brewer*, 144.

16. Sullivan, *History of C. Brewer*, 144.

17. *Address by the Hawaiian Branches*, 5.

18. In 1882 sugar agencies formed the Hawaiian Labor and Supply Company, which would soon reorganize into the Hawaiian Sugar Planters' Association.

19. "Mr. Spreckels' Projected Enterprise on Maui," *Pacific Commercial Advertiser* (Honolulu), October 12, 1878.

20. Scott, *Saga of the Sandwich Islands*, 125.

21. "A California Notable," *Pacific Commercial Advertiser* (Honolulu), May 25, 1878.

22. The Ahupuʻa of Waikapu and of Pūlehunui together are known as the Waikapu Commons.

23. Adler, "*Spreckelsville Plantation*," 34.

24. "Mr. Spreckels' Projected Enterprise."

25. Wianecki, "Great Diversion."

26. "Sandwich Island Sugar Raising," *Daily Evening Bulletin* (Maysville KY), December 1, 1881.

27. Spiekermann, "Claus Spreckels," 5.

28. Wianecki, "Great Diversion."

29. "Mr. Spreckels' Projected Enterprise."

30. Hittell, *Commerce and Industries*, 548.

31. Van Dyke, *Who Owns the Crown Lands?*, 107.

32. Kuykendall, *Hawaiian Kingdom*, 1:197.

33. W. D. Alexander, "Advent of Spreckels," 181.

34. Wilcox, *Sugar Water*, 16.

35. Kuykendall, *Hawaiian Kingdom*, 3:201.

36. Scott, *Saga of the Sandwich Islands*, 126.

37. Scott, *Saga of the Sandwich Islands*, 126.

38. Van Dyke, *Who Owns the Crown Lands?*, 108.

39. W. D. Alexander, "Advent of Spreckels," 181.

40. W. D. Alexander, "Advent of Spreckels."

41. Wilcox, *Sugar Water*, 16.

42. Kiyosaki, *Talk Pidgin*, 11, 10.

43. Scott, *Saga of the Sandwich Islands*, 173.

44. Adler, "*Spreckelsville Plantation*," 35–36.

45. "Commercial," *Pacific Commercial Advertiser* (Honolulu), October 26, 1878.

46. Adler, "*Spreckelsville Plantation*," 34, 35–36.

47. "Unfounded," *Pacific Commercial Advertiser* (Honolulu), October 19, 1878.

48. Newhall, "Spreckels."

49. Hittell, *Commerce and Industries*, 548.

50. Hoʻokuleana, *Hawaiʻi's Big Five (Plus 2)*, 20.

51. Brainerd, "Man of Millions," 715.

52. H. Adams, *The Man, John D. Spreckels*, 65.

7. Branching Out

1. Greene, "Story of A. B.," 41; chap. 4, p. 2.

2. Greene, "Story of A. B.," 35.

3. Pryor, *Little Known Tales*, 156.

4. Pryor, *Little Known Tales*, 156.

5. H. Adams, *The Man, John D. Spreckels*, 65.

6. Newhall, "Spreckels," 49.

7. H. Adams, *The Man, John D. Spreckels*, 66.

8. Greene, "Story of A. B.," 43.

9. Adler, "Oceanic Steamship Company," 258.

10. The *Claus Spreckels* was wrecked on California's Duxbury Reef on January 21, 1888, with a sugar cargo valued at $40,000. "Wrecked on Duxbury Reef," *New York Times*, January 22, 1888, 5.

11. *Daily Alta California* (San Francisco), June 11, 1879, quoted in Delgado and Haller, *Submerged Cultural Resources Assessment*.

12. Adler, "Oceanic Steamship Company," 258.

13. Greene, "Story of A. B.," 61

14. Adler, "Oceanic Steamship Company," 258.

15. H. Adams, *The Man, John D. Spreckels*, 66.

16. Greene, "Story of A. B.," 44.

17. H. Adams, *The Man, John D. Spreckels*, 68.

18. U.S. passport application for Claus August Spreckels, November 14, 1898.

19. Kyselka and Lanterman, *Maui*, 88.

20. "The Big Ditch of Maui," *Pacific Commercial Advertiser* (Honolulu), May 10, 1879.

21. "Mr. H. Schüssler," *Pacific Commercial Advertiser* (Honolulu), October 4, 1879.

22. Adler, "*Spreckelsville Plantation*," 35.

23. Teisch, *Engineering Nature*, 140.

24. "Act Rendering the Crown Lands Inalienable, January 3, 1865," in Van Dyke, *Who Owns the Crown Lands?*, appendix 5, https://www.degruyter.com/document/doi/10.1515 /9780824865603-036/pdf; Peter T. Young, "Claims to the Crown Lands," Images of Old Hawai'i, March 7, 2016, https://imagesofoldhawaii.com/claims-to-the-crown-lands/.

25. Hobbs, *Hawaii*, 74.

26. Dicks, "Princess Ruth," unpublished paper.

27. Van Dyke, *Who Owns the Crown Lands?*, 101.

28. Adler, "*Spreckelsville Plantation*," 156.

29. Kanahele, *Emma*, 325.

30. Van Dyke, *Who Owns the Crown Lands?*, 102.

31. Lili'uokalani, *Hawai'i's Story*, 360.

32. Van Dyke, *Who Owns the Crown Lands?*, 104.

33. Van Dyke, *Who Owns the Crown Lands?*, 103.

34. Dicks, "Princess Ruth."

35. Van Dyke, *Who Owns the Crown Lands?*, 103.

36. Forbes, *In Haste with Aloha*, 208.

37. King and Roth, *Broken Trust*, 26.

38. Van Dyke, *Who Owns the Crown Lands?*, 110.

39. "Spreckels' New Refinery," *Pacific Commercial Advertiser* (Honolulu), December 25, 1880.

40. American Society of Mechanical Engineers, *Journal*, 37:731.

41. "Spreckels' New Refinery."

42. Christopher VerPlanck, "The Story of Dogpatch: Historical Essay," *Shaping San Francisco's Digital Archive @FoundSF*, 2001, https://www.foundsf.org/index.php?title=The _Story_of_Dogpatch.

43. "The New Refinery," *Hawaiian Gazette* (Honolulu), June 22, 1881. Today this capstone sits poolside at the residence of Adolph Rosekrans Runnymede.

44. "The New Refinery."

45. "A Great Sugar Refinery," *Daily Evening Bulletin* (San Francisco), March 9, 1881.

46. "Spreckels' New Refinery."

47. "Great Sugar Refinery."

48. Cordray, "Claus Spreckels of California," 20.

49. Teisch, *Engineering Nature*, 149.

50. VerPlanck, "The Story of Dogpatch."

51. The Punahou mansion was later purchased by Jonah Kumalae, who dismantled the three-story structure by sections to move it from Punahou Street to Mōʻiliʻili and reassembled on Isenberg Street. The St. Louis Alumni Association purchased it in June 1937. It was named Dreier Manor, in honor of philanthropist August Dreier. It then served as the St. Louis Alumni Clubhouse until it burned in 1954. Peter T. Young, "The Mansion," Images of Old Hawaiʻi, October 9, 2018, https://imagesofoldhawaii.com/the-mansion/.

52. "Claus Spreckels," *Hawaiian Star*, December 26, 1908.

53. Adler, "Spreckelsville Plantation," 41.

54. "Signs of the Zodiac Were Consulted by Spreckels," *Star Bulletin* (Honolulu), May 6, 1938.

55. Adler, "Oceanic Steamship Company," 259.

56. Armstrong and Williams, *Impact of Technological Change*, 198.

57. Armstrong and Williams, *Impact of Technological Change*, 198.

58. Adler, "Oceanic Steamship Company," 259.

59. Greene, "The Story of A. B.," chap. 6, pp. 1–2.

60. "The Most Important Maritime Event of This Kingdom," *Pacific Commercial Advertiser* (Honolulu), August 4, 1883.

61. Adler, "Oceanic Steamship Company," 262.

62. Spreckels, "Hawaii for Tourists," 661–62.

63. Carrie Prudence Winter to Charles A. Kofoid, August 27, 1890, Kofoid Papers.

64. Winter to Kofoid, August 27, 1890, Kofoid Papers.

65. O'Connell, *Inner Man*, 19.

66. H. Adams, *The Man, John D. Spreckels*, 146.

67. Tate, *Transpacific Steam*, 52.

68. Spreckels, "Hawaii for Tourists."

69. Spreckels, "Hawaii for Tourists."

8. Vilified for Overnight Monopoly

1. Stamberg, "How Andrew Carnegie Turned His Fortune."

2. LeRoux and Feeney, *Nonprofit Organizations*, 176.

3. Brainerd, "Man of Millions," 716.

3. Brainerd, "Man of Millions," 716.

4. "Notice of Partnership," *Pacific Commercial Advertiser* (Honolulu), August 14, 1880.

5. Daws, *Shoal of Time*, 229.

6. "The Fraudulent Treaty," *Pacific Commercial Advertiser* (Honolulu), October 18, 1879.

7. "Fraudulent Treaty."

8. Henry A. Brown, "Hawaiian Treaty Chicanery Clearly Presented to the Honorable Senators and Representatives Assembled in Congress to Legislate for the People. (Signed) Henry a. Brown, Ex-Special Treasury Agent. Washington, D.C. May 20, 1886," 4, https://www.loc.gov/resource/rbpe.2070360a/?sp=4.

9. "Interesting Ceremonies," *Hawaiian Gazette* (Honolulu), April 23, 1879.

10. "Yesterday's Argument," *Daily Alta California* (San Francisco), June 25, 1885.

11. Jessie Kratz, "Unratified Amendments: Titles of Nobility," *National Archives Pieces of History*, January 30, 2020, https://prologue.blogs.archives.gov/2020/01/30/unratified-amendments-titles-of-nobility/.

12. *Internal Revenue Record*, 169.

13. *Congressional Record*, 4479.

14. Cordray, "Claus Spreckels of California," 212.

15. "The Sand Lot," *Sacramento Daily Record-Union*, March 23, 1880.

16. "Dennis Kearney Jailed for Cussing Claus Spreckels Name in Public," *Pacific Commercial Advertiser* (Honolulu), April 3, 1880.

17. "Sand Lot."

18. "Claus Spreckels Refuses Quarantine, 1881," *Pacific Commercial Advertiser* (Honolulu), June 18, 1881.

19. "Pehea Keiahana?" [Rich treated differently?], *Ko Hawaiʻi Pae ʻAina*, June 18, 1881.

20. Quoted in Newhall, "Spreckels," 47.

9. Raising Cane in Spreckelsville

1. Takaki, *Pau Hana*, 31.

2. "Maui Notes," *Pacific Commercial Advertiser* (Honolulu), December 10, 1881.

3. Adler, "Spreckelsville Plantation," 35.

4. "Spreckels Case," *San Francisco Examiner*, June 25, 1885.

5. "Maui Notes."

6. Nordhoff, *Northern California*, 27.

7. "The Sugar King: How Claus Spreckels Became a Millionaire," *Burlington (VT) Free Press*, January 6, 1885.

8. Fleischmann and Tyson, "Interface of Race and Accounting," 12.

9. Hawaiian Sugar Planters' Association, *Story of Sugar*, 59.

10. Takaki, *Pau Hana*, 58.

11. Kessler, "Planter's Paradise," 71.

12. Takaki, *Pau Hana*, 60.

13. Kessler, "Plantation upon a Hill."

14. Jones and Osgood, *From King Cane*, 49.

15. Adler, "Spreckelsville Plantation," 40.

16. Jones and Osgood, *From King Cane*, 47.

17. Fleischmann and Tyson, "Interface of Race and Accounting," 12.

18. Adler, "Spreckelsville Plantation," 36.

19. Newhall, "Spreckels," 45.

20. Jones and Osgood, *From King Cane*, 53.

21. Adler, "Spreckelsville Plantation," 37.

22. Hawaiian Sugar Planters' Association, *Story of Sugar*, 65.

23. Adler, "Spreckelsville Plantation," 9.

24. "Our Story: From Plantations to Power," Hawaiian Electric Company, retrieved September 5, 2022, https://www.hawaiianelectric.com/about-us/our-history/1881-from -plantations-to-power.

25. Adler, "Spreckelsville Plantation," 37.

26. Takaki, *Pau Hana*, 24, 92–93.

27. J. G. Smith, *Plantation Sketches*, 51.

28. "A Visit to Maui," *Pacific Commercial Advertiser* (Honolulu), August 25, 1883.

29. Takaki, *Pau Hana*, 103.

30. Smith, *Plantation Sketches*, 50–51.

31. Takaki, *Pau Hana*, 133.

32. Takaki, *Pau Hana*, 114–15.

33. Adler, *Claus Spreckels*, 74.

34. Adler, *Claus Spreckels*, 74.

35. Queen Emma to Mrs. Pierre Jones, November 17, 1881, Queen Emma Collection.

36. Jones and Osgood, *From King Cane*, 39.

37. Kanahele, *Emma*, 345–46.

38. Kanahele, *Emma*, 346.

39. Newhall, "Spreckels," 45.

40. Quoted in Adler, "Spreckelsville Plantation," 35.

41. Adler, "Spreckelsville Plantation," 35–36, 41.

42. Quoted in Adler, "Spreckelsville Plantation," 36.

10. The Kingdom in Crisis

1. Kuykendall, *Hawaiian Kingdom*, 3:228.

2. Quoted in "Visit to Sacramento," *Pacific Commercial Advertiser* (Honolulu), February 26, 1881.

3. "The King in the United States," *Hawaiian Gazette* (Honolulu), November 2, 1881.

4. Kuykendall, *Hawaiian Kingdom*, 3:235.

5. Quoted in Kuykendall, *Hawaiian Kingdom*, 3:241.

6. Kuykendall, *Hawaiian Kingdom*, 3:241, 242.

7. Hussey, *Hawaii History*, 164.

8. Scott, *Saga of the Sandwich Islands*, 197.

9. "Wao Lani > Gown of Princess Liliʻuokalani> Invitation to the Coronation of King Kalākaua and Queen Kapiʻolani," Bishop Museum, 2020, https://hawaiialive.org /invitation-to-the-coronation-of-king-kalakaua-and-queen-kapi%CA%BBolani/.

10. Hussey, *Hawaii History*, 66, 67.

11. Newhall, "Spreckels," 48.

12. Hussey, *Hawaii History*, 67.

13. Scott, *Saga of the Sandwich Islands*, 199.

14. Gonschor and Bousquet, "Showdown at Honolulu Harbor," 146–47.

15. Vecoli, Durante, and Venditto, "Destiny of Hawaii," 160.

16. Newhall, "Spreckels," 50.

17. Gonschor and Bousquet, "Showdown at Honolulu Harbor," 145.

18. Chapin, "Newspapers of Hawaiʻi," 68.

19. Andrade, "Hawaiian Coinage Controversy," 98.

20. Andrade, "Hawaiian Coinage Controversy," 97–98.

21. Twigg-Smith, *Hawaiian Sovereignty*, 41.

22. Adler and Kamins, *Fantastic Life of Walter Murray Gibson*, 144.

23. Adler and Kamins, *Fantastic Life of Walter Murray Gibson*, 144.

24. Adler and Kamins, *Fantastic Life of Walter Murray Gibson*.

25 Adler, *Claus Spreckels*, 131.

26. W. D. Alexander, "Advent of Spreckels."

27. Adler, *Claus Spreckels*, 174.

28. Kuykendall, *Hawaiian Kingdom*, 3:85. William G. Irwin's nephew Edward "Irwin" Spalding would hold the position for thirty-five years. In 1908 Claus sold out to Irwin, who then incorporated under the name of Bank of Honolulu, Ltd., which on March 31, 1920, merged with the Bank of Bishop & Co.

29. Newhall, "Spreckels," 57.

30. Adler and Kamins, *Fantastic Life of Walter Murray Gibson*, 172.

11. Adolph Shoots to Kill

1. *New York Times*, November 20, 1884.

2. "Island Slavery," *San Francisco Chronicle*, October 16, 1881.

3. "Editorial," *Hawaiian Gazette* (Honolulu), November 2, 1881.

4. "Spreckels Case: Hall McAllister Concludes His Eloquent Speech," *San Francisco Chronicle*, November 17, 1884.

5. Secrest, *California Feuds*, 92.

6. Secrest, *California Feuds*, 95.

7. Brechin, *Imperial San Francisco*, 190.

8. Bob Calhoun, "Yesterday's Crimes: Murdered by the Son of the Sugar King," *SF Weekly*, April 21, 2016, https://www.sfweekly.com/news/yesterdays-crimes-murdered-by-the-son -of-the-sugar-king/.

9. Brechin, *Imperial San Francisco*, 179.

10. Marzorati, "Need for Alarm," 62.

11. Richard Rodriguez, "Final Edition: Twilight of the American Newspaper," *Harpers*, November 2009, 33, https://malavika.pbworks.com/f/Richard+Rodriguez-+The +Twilight+of+the+American+Newspaper.pdf.

12. "More Blood," *San Francisco Examiner*, April 24, 1880.

13. Cutler, *Mysterious Death*, 135.

14. Brechin, *Imperial San Francisco*, 177.

15. McAllister was from a long line of prominent attorneys. His father, the legendary Matthew Hall McAllister (1826–88), had been the U.S. circuit judge for California for many years and had mentored his son well.

16. "Old Days at the Bar Described by Lawyer," *Humboldt (CA) Times*, August 28, 1912.

17. Shuck, *History of the Bench and Bar*, 514.

18. "The Spreckels Case: A Synoptical Report of the Arguments. Campbell's Able Address. The Novel and Contradictory Plea of Self-Defense and Insanity," *Placer (CA) Herald*, July 25, 1885.

19. "The Spreckels Trial," *Los Angeles Times*, June 6, 1885; "The Spreckels Case," *Daily Bulletin* (Honolulu), June 8, 1885.

20. "De Young–Spreckels," *Daily Alta California* (San Francisco), April 2, 1885.

21. "Hall McAllister," *San Jose Mercury-News*, December 2, 1888.

22. "The Spreckels Trial," *Daily Alta California* (San Francisco), May 30, 1885.

23. "The Spreckels Case," *Daily Bulletin* (Honolulu), June 8, 1885.

24. "Sugar King of the Sandwich Islands," *Sonoma (CA) Democrat*, March 21, 1885.

25. Spiekermann, "Labor as a Bottleneck."

26. "To-Day's Supplement—The Spreckels Case," *Pacific Commercial Advertiser* (Honolulu), July 10, 1885.

27. "Spreckels Trial," supplement, *Pacific Commercial Advertiser* (Honolulu), July 19, 1885.

28. "The Spreckels Trial," *Daily Alta California* (San Francisco), June 4, 1885.

29. "The Spreckels Trial," *Daily Alta California* (San Francisco), June 17, 1885.

30. "The Spreckels Case," *San Francisco Examiner*, June 26, 1885.

31. Newhall, "Spreckels," 60.

32. "The Spreckels Trial," *Daily Alta California* (San Francisco), June 17, 1885.

33. Adler, *Claus Spreckels*, 81.

34. "The Spreckels Trial," *Daily Alta California* (San Francisco), June 25, 1885.

35. "The Spreckels Trial," *Daily Alta California* (San Francisco), June 24, 1885.

36. "Spreckels Case," *San Francisco Examiner*, July 1, 1885.

37. "The Spreckels Case: A Fraud upon the Law," *Folsom (CA) Telegraph*, July 18, 1885.

38. "The Spreckels Case: A Synoptical Report of the Arguments."

39. "A.B. Spreckels Acquitted," *Daily Bulletin* (Honolulu), July 8, 1885.

40. "A.B. Spreckels Acquitted."

41. "A.B. Spreckels Acquitted."

42. "Comments on the Spreckels Verdict," *Sacramento Record-Union*, July 3, 1885 (quotations special to the *New York Times*, July 2, 1885).

12. Beets Now or Never

1. Siler, *Lost Kingdom*, 114.
2. Quoted in Kent, *Charles Reed Bishop*, 117.
3. Siler, *Lost Kingdom*, 114.
4. Adler and Kamins, *Fantastic Life of Walter Murray Gibson*, 177.
5. Siler, *Lost Kingdom*, 116.
6. Adler and Kamins, *Fantastic Life of Walter Murray Gibson*, 177.
7. Newhall, "Spreckels," 63.
8. Correspondence with Hawaiian Officials Abroad, Washington D C, October–December 1866, Foreign Office and Executive Records, 1790–1900, series 404, box 50, folder 807, Hawai'i State Archives, Honolulu.
9. Adler and Kamins, *Fantastic Life of Walter Murray Gibson*, 182.
10. Adler and Kamins, *Fantastic Life of Walter Murray Gibson*, 183.
11. "Hawaiian Finance: How it is Discussed Abroad," *Evening Bulletin* (Honolulu), November 18, 1886.
12. "Lying in State," *Pacific Commercial Advertiser* (Honolulu), February 4, 1887.
13. Swenson, *Alvarado Sugar Beet Factory*, 40–41. Dyer reorganized as the Alameda Sugar Company in 1889.
14. *Watsonville (CA) Pajaronian*, November 10, 1887, quoted in Conway, "Spreckels Sugar Company," 12n13.
15. Cordray, "Claus Spreckels of California," 104.
16. Spiekermann, "Claus Spreckels," 19.
17. H. Adams, *The Man, John D. Spreckels*, 290.
18. McPhail, *Story of New San Diego*, 101.
19. Spiekermann, "Expanding the Frontier(s)," 179.
20. McPhail, *Story of New San Diego*, 101.
21. "Coronado: History of the Charming Seaside Resort," *Coronado (CA) Mercury* 7, no. 27 (November 23, 1893): 2.
22. H. Adams, *The Man, John D. Spreckels*, 292.
23. Newhall, "Spreckels," 75.
24. Newhall, "Spreckels," 76.
25. Cordray, "Claus Spreckels of California," 104.
26. "Beet Sugar," *Los Angeles Daily Herald*, September 24, 1887.
27. "Telegraphic Brevities," *Sacramento Daily Record-Union*, September 17, 1887.
28. Ware, *Sugar Beet*, 1:31.
29. Kent, *Charles Reed Bishop*, 118.
30. Circa, *Historic Context Statement*, 15.
31. Newhall, "Spreckels," 77.
32. Lewis, "Watsonville Remembered," typescript, 6, Watsonville Public Library.
33. Circa, *Historic Context Statement*, 10.
34. "The Santa Cruz Tragedy," *Sacramento Daily Union*, November 6, 1856.

35. Circa, *Historic Context Statement*, 10, 53.
36. "Local Brevities," *Santa Cruz (CA) Weekly Sentinel*, March 18, 1876.
37. Fabing and Hamman, *Steinbeck Country Narrow Gauge*, 7.
38. Wyckoff, *Memoirs*.
39. Wyckoff, *Memoirs*.
40. Circa, *Historic Context Statement*, 15.
41. Fabing and Hamman, *Steinbeck Country Narrow Gauge*, 26.
42. Verardo, *Salinas Valley*, 56.
43. Nader, "Recovered Interview," 80.
44. Glass, *From Mission to Microchip*, 104, 105.
45. "Agricultural Notes, "*Pacific Rural Press and California Farmer* 34 (October 29, 1887), 341.
46. "The State's Beet-Sugar Future," *Sacramento Daily Record-Union*, November 17, 1887.
47. *Pacific Rural Press and California Farmer*, 341.
48. Newhall, "Spreckels," 78.
49. "King of the Sugar Trade: Claus Spreckels and the Power He Wields, How from Selling Cheese and Crackers in New York Spreckels Became the Master of Millions," *Knowersville (NY) Enterprise*, February 14, 1885.
50. Harrison, *History of Santa Cruz County*, 373.
51. Newhall, "Spreckels," 80.
52. Pfingst, *Memories of Pajaro Valley*, 5.
53. Pfingst, "Scattered Leaves," 4, handwritten chronology of the Western Beet Sugar Company.
54. Pfingst, *Memories of Pajaro Valley*, 5.
55. Newhall, "Spreckels," 81, 82.
56. Newhall, "Spreckels," 81.
57. Newhall, "Spreckels," 82.
58. "Watsonville Wins!," *Los Angeles Daily Herald*, December 15, 1887.
59. "Claus Spreckels Meets President," *Los Angeles Times*, March 25, 1888.
60. "Carl Spreckels Appears Before a Committee," *Buffalo (NY) Times*, March 24, 1888.
61. "Claus Spreckels Meets President."
62. "Beet Sugar," *San Jose (CA) Mercury-News*, March 25, 1888.
63. Pfingst, "Scattered Leaves," 10, 9, 11, 10.
64. Allen and Avery, *California Gold Book*, 397.
65. Allen and Avery, *California Gold Book*, 397.
66. Fabing and Hamman, *Steinbeck Country Narrow Gauge*, 23.
67. "The Lincoln-Roosevelt League's Avowed," *Santa Cruz (CA) Weekly Sentinel*, August 19, 1907.
68. "Sugar Beet Cultivation," *San Francisco Daily Morning Call*, December 1, 1895; Sacramento Bank, *Beet Sugar Industry*.
69. Osborne, "Claus Spreckels and the Oxnard Brothers," 118.
70. "Claus Spreckels Life Work," *Philadelphia Times*, May 14, 1888.

71. *Watsonville (CA) Pajaronian*, November 10, 1887, quoted in Conway, "Spreckels Sugar Company," 12n13.

72. Osborne, "Claus Spreckels and the Oxnard Brothers," 117.

73. Osborne, "Claus Spreckels and the Oxnard Brothers," 120.

74. Osborne, "Claus Spreckels and the Oxnard Brothers," 119–20.

13. Sugar and Strife

1. San Francisco Journal of Commerce, *Builders of a Great City*, 317, quoted in Goldberg, "Cauldron of Anger," 241–79.

2. "The Sugar Trust's Foe," *New York Times*, May 18, 1888.

3. Cordray, "Claus Spreckels of California," 84.

4. Newhall, "Spreckels," 89.

5. "The Sugar King Wept," *Daily Alta California* (San Francisco), May 6, 1888.

6. Cordray, "Claus Spreckels of California," 85.

7. Newhall, "Spreckels," 89, 90, 92.

8. Quoted in Cordray, "Claus Spreckels of California," 92.

9. Newhall, "Spreckels," 91.

10. Cordray, "Claus Spreckels of California," 85.

11. "The Spreckels Slander Suit," *Hawaiian Gazette* (Honolulu), April 26, 1895.

12. Bean, *Boss Ruef's San Francisco*, 73.

13. "Mr. Spreckels Wants War," *New York Times*, February 12, 1890.

14. "The Sugar Combine," *Wall Street Journal*, April 11, 1891.

15. "The King Abroad," *Daily Bulletin* (Honolulu), December 26, 1890, 5.

16. Quoted in "The King Slept Here," *Honolulu Star Bulletin*, January 11, 2009.

17. Baur, "When Royalty Came to California," 252.

18. McDermott, Choy, and Guerrero, "Last Illness and Death," 62–63.

19. Coffman, *Nation Within*, 107.

20. McDermott, Choy, and Guerrero, "Last Illness and Death," 62–63.

21. Newhall, "Spreckels," 93.

22. "John E. Searles Will Leave the Sugar Trust," *Los Angeles Herald*, December 23, 1898.

23. "Down an Embankment," *Saint Paul (MN) Globe*, August 30, 1888.

24. Newhall, "Spreckels," 96.

25. "C. A. Spreckels Denial," *Daily Alta California* (San Francisco), April 1, 1891.

26. Scott, *Saga of the Sandwich Islands*, 564.

27. "Our Clever Men," *San Francisco News Letter*, February 1, 1896, 17.

28. "The Spreckels Row," *San Francisco Chronicle*, November 26, 1893.

29. "The Spreckels Row."

30. "Taught by His Son," *Inter Ocean* (Chicago), January 6, 1894.

31. Twigg-Smith, *Hawaiian Sovereignty*, 134.

32. Adler, "Claus Spreckels' Rise and Fall," 19.

33. The Claus Spreckels & Company Bank was later incorporated as the Bank of Honolulu Ltd., which still later merged with the Bank of Bishop & Co.

34. Twigg-Smith, *Hawaiian Sovereignty*, 178.

35. Scott, *Saga of the Sandwich Islands*, 564.

36. Gonschor, review of *Sun Yatsen*, 90–91.

37. "Spreckel's [*sic*] Send-Off: The Ex-King Leaves for 'Frisco," *Hawaiian Star*, July 19, 1893, 5.

38. Scott, *Saga of the Sandwich Islands*, 707.

39. "The Man Who Bought Arms," *Los Angeles Herald*, February 8, 1895.

40. "Lili'uokalani Is on Trial," *San Francisco Call*, February 16, 1895, 1.

41. Quoted in Bonura, *Light in the Queen's Garden*, 121–22.

42. Cordray, "Claus Spreckels of California," 66.

43. "All Trouble Ended," *San Francisco Chronicle*, January 6, 1894.

44. Adler, "Spreckelsville Planation," 44.

45. "Estrangement of Father and Sons," *Town Talk* (San Francisco), October 3, 1903, 9.

46. "Taught by His Son," *Inter Ocean* (Chicago), January 6, 1894.

47. Adler, "Spreckelsville Planation," 44.

48. "Estrangement of Father and Sons."

49. Goldberg, "Cauldron of Anger," 255.

50. Steffens, "Rudolf Spreckels: A Business Man," 393.

51. Goldberg, "Cauldron of Anger," 256.

52. "Claus Spreckels' Hot Wrath," *San Francisco Examiner*, March 24, 1895, quoted in Goldberg, "Cauldron of Anger," 257. The $2 million refers to the Hawaiian Commercial deal.

53. "Claus Spreckels' Hot Wrath."

54. "Pretty Family Row," *Indianapolis Journal*, April 4, 1895.

55. Steffens, "Rudolf Spreckels: A Business Man," 392–93.

56. Goldberg, "Cauldron of Anger," 258.

57. "Claus Spreckels to His Son Rudolph Spreckels," *Oakland Tribune*, October 24, 1907.

58. "Claus Spreckels to His Son Rudolph Spreckels."

59. "Claus Spreckels to His son Rudolph Spreckels."

60. Goldberg, "Cauldron of Anger," 254.

61. Cordray, "Claus Spreckels of California," 234.

62. Goldberg, *Community Property*, 189.

63. Cordray, "Claus Spreckels of California," 235.

64. "Some New Law for California Married Women," *San Francisco Call*, March 24, 1897, quoted in Goldberg, "Cauldron of Anger," 268.

65. Goldberg, "Cauldron of Anger." The *Chronicle* suggested that the decision "might not have the support of Susan B. Anthony and Rev. Anna Shaw."

14. The Divided House of Spreckels

1. William Issel and Robert Cherny, "Nob Hill and Pacific Heights at the Turn of the 20th Century," *Shaping San Francisco's Digital Archive @FoundSF*, retrieved August 1, 2022,

https://www.foundsf.org/index.php?title=Nob_Hill_and_Pacific_Heights_at_Turn_of
_20th_Century.

2. "Van Ness & Washington," private essay courtesy of Lynn Wilsons, 3.

3. "Chat with C. Spreckels," *Santa Cruz (CA) Sentinel*, March 24, 1896.

4. "Residence of Sir Claus Spreckels," *San Francisco News Letter*, January 1, 1898.

5. "Spreckels Mansion to Be Restored," *Los Angeles Herald*, August 12, 1906.

6. "A 10,000 Dollar Bathroom," *Topeka (KS) State Journal*, January 25, 1897.

7. "The New Mansion Home of Claus Spreckels," *San Francisco Call*, December 19, 1897.

8. *Town Talk* (San Francisco), January 7, 1905.

9. Retan, *Iretta Hight Retan Collection*, 47.

10. Bonura, *Light in the Queen's Garden*, 19–20.

11. Tinker Swiss Cottage Museum, "Understanding Spinsters," *A Truly Victorian Experience*, February 12, 2017, https://tinkercottagemuseum.wordpress.com/2017/02/12/understanding-spinsters/.

12. "They Quietly Married," *Hawaiian Star*, January 14, 1897.

13. "Miss Spreckels Elopes," *New York Journal*, January 3, 1897, 1.

14. "They Quietly Married," *Hawaiian Star*, January 14, 1897.

15. "Papa Claus Cruel," *Los Angeles Times*, February 8, 1898, e.

16.   "They Quietly Married," *Hawaiian Star*, January 14, 1897.

17. "Alone in her Sorrow," *Town Talk* (San Francisco), January 20, 1904, 17.

18. *The Wasp* (San Francisco), September 23, 1905, 39.

19. *The Wasp* (San Francisco), July 5, 1902, 28.

20. *Pacific Commercial Advertiser* (Honolulu), July 7, 1902, 6.

21. Marie Spreckels came into this world on September 12, 1903, followed by Adolph Bernard Spreckels II in 1906 and John Diedrich Spreckels III in 1910.

22. "A Rumor Restored," *Town Talk* (San Francisco), March 8, 1902, 17.

23. "The Week's Sensation," *Town Talk* (San Francisco), January 7, 1905, 22.

24. *The Wasp* (San Francisco), November 4, 1905, 56.

25. *The Wasp* (San Francisco), September 23, 1905, 39.

26. *The Wasp* (San Francisco), September 23, 1905, 39.

27. "To Be a Quiet Affair," *San Francisco News Letter*, October 14, 1905, 16.

28. The wedding was on November 27, 1905. It was a happy marriage, which was completed when they had two daughters, Grace Alexandria, born in 1907, and Mary Leila, who always went by "Happy," born in 1909.

29. "Further Startling Disclosures of the Plot to Capture the Islands," *Los Angeles Times*, August 6, 1895.

30. "Were Wedded in Haste," *San Francisco Examiner*, August 6, 1895.

31. "Sad Loss," *Town Talk* (San Francisco), February 16, 1901, 11.

32. Graham, "Will Miss Spreckels?," 15.

33. Gretchen de Limur, personal correspondence with author, July 12, 2022.

34. Greene, "Story of A. B.," chap. 2, p. 1.

35. Harned, *Palace Hotel*, 25.

36. Kirk, *Flier in Oil*, 20.
37. Jim Smith, "Tales of San Francisco—The Poodle Dog Restaurant, Part II." *HistorySmith: Tales of California and San Francisco*, retrieved August 3, 2022, http://www.historysmith .com/tales_lost_poodledog_01_part2.html.
38. Details from hand-typed essay, likely by Harriet Hamilton (Claus and Anna's great -granddaughter).
39. Bernhard, *Porcupine, Picayune, and Post*, 78.
40. "Comments on Day's News," *San Pedro (CA) Daily News*, June 11, 1926.
41. Ellen Klages, "The Call Building: San Francisco's Forgotten Skyscraper: Historical Essay," *Shaping San Francisco's Digital Archive @FoundSF*, retrieved August 5, 2022, https:// www.foundsf.org/index.php?title=THE_CALL_BUILDING:_SAN_FRANCISCO %27S_FORGOTTEN_SKYSCRAPER.
42. Klages, "Call Building."
43. Hall, *America's Successful Men of Affairs*, 750.
44. "The Saunterer," *Town Talk* (San Francisco), October 3, 1903, 9–10.
45. "Family Differences," *The Wasp* (San Francisco), January 2, 1909, 9.
46. "Sad Loss," *Town Talk* (San Francisco), February 16, 1901, 11.

15. Large and In Charge

1. "Claus Spreckels," *Harper's Weekly*, 87.
2. "He May Be on His Deathbed," *Sacramento Bee*, April 30, 1898.
3. "John D. Spreckels Is Doubly Honored," *San Francisco Call*, October 19, 1896.
4. "Bimetallism, Not Bi-standard-ism," *San Francisco Call*, May 7, 1896.
5. Hanna had also promised the benefits of patronage to their Southern delegates for their support.
6. "They Met at St. Louis," *Los Angeles Herald*, June 26, 1896.
7. "Unhappy End of John D. Spreckels as Meat for the Cat," *San Francisco Examiner*, September 23, 1896.
8. Perkins was already in that seat, having been appointed senator on the death of Senator Leland Stanford in 1893. That he was the established incumbent goes far to explain Claus's support of him.
9. Dicks, "J. D. Spreckels," unpublished paper.
10. "Shortridge vs. Perkins and Claus," *Santa Cruz (CA) Evening Sentinel*, October 6, 1896.
11. Dicks, "J. D. Spreckels."
12. "Perkins on the First Ballot," *San Francisco Examiner*, January 13, 1897. Before the 1913 ratification of the Seventeenth Amendment, which established the direct election of U.S. senators, most were selected by state legislatures.
13. "Voice of the Press," *Sacramento Record-Union*, January 18, 1897.
14. Downey, *Levi Strauss*, 212, 213.
15. Sedgwick, "How the Santa Fe Railroad Changed America."
16. Downey, *Levi Strauss*, 215.
17. Newhall, "Spreckels," 114.

18. Downey, *Levi Strauss*, 216.

19. Newhall, "Spreckels," 113–14.

20. "May Mean Millions for Our Farmers," *Sacramento Bee*, September 17, 1897.

21. "Beet Farming," *Sausalito (CA) News*, March 7, 1896.

22. "May Mean Millions for Our Farmers."

23. "May Mean Millions for Our Farmers."

24. Magnuson, "History of the Beet Sugar Industry," 76–77.

25. Fabing and Hamman, *Steinbeck Country Narrow Gauge*, 49.

26. Francis, *Santa Cruz County*, 108.

27. McKibben, *Salinas*, 6.

28. Verardo, *Salinas Valley*, 48.

29. Cordray, "Claus Spreckels of California," 166; Fabing and Hamman, *Steinbeck Country Narrow Gauge*, 32.

30. Fabing and Hamman, *Steinbeck Country Narrow Gauge*, 36.

31. Fabing and Hamman, *Steinbeck Country Narrow Gauge*, 50.

32. "Pumping Plants in Salinas Valley," 408.

33. "Chat with C. Spreckels," *Santa Cruz (CA) Sentinel*, March 24, 1896.

34. "Chat with C. Spreckels."

35. "Chat with C. Spreckels."

36. Francis, *Santa Cruz County*, 108.

37. "Chat with C. Spreckels."

38. "Markets of the World," *Los Angeles Herald*, July 31, 1896.

39. Cordray, "Claus Spreckels of California," 114.

40. "Claus Spreckels Is Home Again," *San Francisco Call*, July 17, 1896.

41. Cordray, "Claus Spreckels of California," 114.

42. Newhall, "Spreckels," 119.

43. Newhall, "Spreckels," 118, 125.

44. "Claus Spreckels Is Home Again."

45. Newhall, "Spreckels," 120.

46. Newhall, "Spreckels," 121.

47. Newhall, "Spreckels," 122.

48. Fabing and Hamman, *Steinbeck Country Narrow Gauge*, 50. The Southern Pacific bought the Pajaro Valley Consolidated in 1929.

49. "Salinas Has a Boom," *Sacramento Daily Record-Union*, January 23, 1889.

16. Sweet Success

1. Cordray, "Claus Spreckels of California," 114.

2. "Greet the Sugar King," *San Francisco Call*, August 2, 1896.

3. "Greet the Sugar King."

4. "Greet the Sugar King."

5. "Greet the Sugar King."

6. "Greet the Sugar King."

7. "Greet the Sugar King."
8. Newhall, "Spreckels," 123.
9. Newhall, "Spreckels," 124.
10. Nader, "Recovered Interview," 79–82.
11. Newhall, "Spreckels," 124.
12. Spreckels Sugar Company, "Spreckels Sugar History," retrieved August 9, 2022, https://www.spreckelssugar.com/history.aspx.
13. Spreckels Sugar Company, "Spreckels Sugar History."
14. Newhall, "Spreckels," 124.
15. Verardo, *Salinas Valley*, 170.
16. "Sugar Beet Crops: Convincing Figures Presented by James Bardin, of Blanco," *Chico (CA) Weekly Enterprise*, September 11, 1896.
17. Newhall, "Spreckels," 125.
18. Newhall, "Spreckels."
19. Fabing and Hamman, *Steinbeck Country Narrow Gauge*, 50.
20. "Spreckels Plant Is Marking 50th Year," untitled clipping from the *Salinas Index* files of 1897, Monterey County Historical Society.
21. "Spreckels Sugar Company Incorporated," *Philadelphia Times*, August 7, 1897.
22. "He May Be on His Deathbed," *Sacramento Bee*, April 30, 1898.
23. "Father and Son," *Town Talk* (San Francisco), July 13, 1901, 12.
24. "He May Be on His Deathbed."
25. Liliʻuokalani, *Hawaiʻi's Story*, 308.
26. "To Honorable J. O. Carter from Liliʻuokalani, Ebbit House," July 8, 1898, Hawaiʻi State Archives, Honolulu.
27. "Ex-Queen Secures Loan," *San Francisco Call*, November 23, 1908.
28. Newhall, "Spreckels," 163.
29. "Spreckels Started by Greatest Sugar Daddy of All," *Salinas (CA) Californian*, August 5, 1978.
30. Breschini, Gudgel, and Haversat, *Spreckels*, 17.
31. Glass, *From Mission to Microchip*, 102–13.
32. Perry, "Lime's Sweet History," 4.
33. "Spreckels Sugar Factory," *Salinas (CA) Index*, April 17, 1899.
34. Perry, "Lime's Sweet History," 4.
35. Breschini, Gudgel, and Haversat, *Spreckels*, 8.
36. McKibben, *Salinas*, 2.
37. "The Good Old Days in Nearby Spreckels," *Salinas (CA) Californian*, March 4, 1967.
38. Townsend, "By-Products of the Sugar Beet," 447.
39. Fabing and Hamman, *Steinbeck Country Narrow Gauge*, 50.
40. Tucker, *Changing Pacific Forests*, 118.
41. Newhall, "Spreckels," 162.
42. "Good Old Days." Claus Spreckels got Monterey County's official approval for the map of the company town that bears his name in 1907, just one year before his death.

43. Lewis, "W. H. Weeks," 226–29.

44. Breschini, Gudgel, and Haversat, *Spreckels*, 35.

45. Mathews, *Spreckels, California*, 18.

46. James Ross Riley III, personal communication with author.

47. Charlie Pioda served until 1912 in engineering, construction, irrigation, and railroad and agricultural work. From 1912 to 1919 he was general agriculturist; then he became resident manager at Spreckels until 1945.

48. Breschini, Gudgel, and Haversat, *Spreckels*, 31.

49. Cartier, *Revised Evaluation*.

50. *Duty on Sugar: Hearings on H. R. 21213, Before the Committee on Finance, United States Senate*, 62nd Cong. 533 (1912), Google Books.

51. "Spreckels Started by Greatest Sugar Daddy of All."

52. Newhall, "Spreckels," 130.

53. "Good Old Days"; "The Birth of a Town," *Salinas (CA) Californian*, September 17, 1977.

54. "Fatal Plunge of Young Somnambulist," *San Francisco Call*, September 8, 1898.

55. "Spreckels Hotel Razed by Flames," *San Francisco Call*, June 18, 1899.

56. The second hotel was razed in 1939.

57. Fabing and Hamman, *Steinbeck Country Narrow Gauge*, 57.

58. Breschini, Gudgel, and Haversat, *Spreckels*, 35.

59. McWilliams, *Factories in the Field*, 89–90.

60. Laureen Diephof, "Trine and Agnes Discuss Growing Up in Spreckels," *Salinas (CA) Californian*, October 21, 2015, https://www.thecalifornian.com/story/life/2015/10/22/trine-agnes-discuss-growing-spreckels/74372872/.

61. "Birth of a Town."

62. The *Spreckels Enterprise* saw publication from 1908 to 1918.

63. "Birth of a Town."

64. Diephof, "Trine and Agnes."

65. Teisch, *Engineering Nature*, 149.

66. Riley, personal communication with author.

67. Chris Carlsson, "The Workingmen's Party and the Denis Kearney Agitation: Historical Essay," *Shaping San Francisco's Digital Archive @FoundSF*, retrieved September 6, 2022, https://www.foundsf.org/index.php?title=The_Workingmen%E2%80%99s_Party_%26_The_Denis_Kearney_Agitation.

68. "Salvation Colonies," *Los Angeles Herald*, December 14, 1898.

69. McKibben, *Salinas*, 35.

70. Most of them sold off their land by the 1910s, when land values fell and when the new irrigation practices gave rise to lettuce and row crops—practices that attracted investment of farmers.

71. "Colony Settlements," Monterey County Historical Society, 2010, http://mchsmuseum.com/colonysettlements.html.

72. Verardo, *Salinas Valley*, 75.

73. *Weekly Statistical Sugar Trade Journal* 21 (January 7, 1897): 3.

74. Street, *Beasts of the Field*, 393.

75. Newhall, "Spreckels," 142.

76. Newhall, "Spreckels," 114.

77. Downey, *Levi Strauss*.

17. Too Many Irons in the Fire

1. Newhall, "Spreckels," 164.

2. Spikes and Stout, "Photochemical Activity," 375.

3. Newhall, "Spreckels," 164.

4. Hamilton and Hamilton, *Villa Calafia*, 2:133.

5. "News Items," 78.

6. Boncquet, "*Bacillus morulans*, n. sp.," 269–89.

7. Cordray, "Claus Spreckels of California," 189.

8. O'Donnell, *Guilty Environmentalist*, 20.

9. Cordray, "Claus Spreckels of California," 194.

10. Newhall, "Spreckels," 111.

11. O'Donnell, *Guilty Environmentalist*, 20, 21.

12. "Claus Spreckels Triumph," *The Wasp* (San Francisco), July 4, 1903.

13. Cordray, "Claus Spreckels of California," 199.

14. Bean, *Boss Ruef's San Francisco*, 75; Goldberg, "Cauldron of Anger."

15. California Office of Historic Preservation, "Golden Gate Park," section 8, page 46.

16. "Park Commissioners Meet and Organize," *San Francisco Call*, January 9, 1900.

17. "Electric Illumination," *San Jose (CA) Mercury-News*, September 10, 1900.

18. "Electric Illumination."

19. "Electric Illumination."

20. Kamiya, *Spirits of San Francisco*, 91.

21. Newhall, "Spreckels," 151.

22. "Welcome and a Token for Claus Spreckels," *San Francisco Call*, September 26, 1900.

23. Greene, "Story of A. B.," chap. 8, p. 9.

24. Harveson, *Beet Curly Top*.

25. Newhall, "Spreckels," 165–66.

26. Cordray, "Claus Spreckels of California," 126.

27. Newhall, "Spreckels," 166.

28. Cook, "Insect Transmission," 174, 176.

29. Cook, "Insect Transmission," 175.

30. Newhall, "Spreckels," 170–71.

31. V. Green, *Above Stairs*, 101.

32. Newhall, "Spreckels," 171, 172.

33. "Alone in Her Sorrow," *Town Talk* (San Francisco), January 30, 1904, 16.

34. "Emma Spreckels-Watson and Her English Prospects," *Pacific Commercial Advertiser* (Honolulu), June 6, 1901.

35. "Family Not Alarmed at Magnate's Illness: No Apprehension over Condition of Claus Spreckels," *San Jose (CA) Mercury-News*, November 22, 1903.
36. "Personal," *San Francisco Call*, October 18, 1903.
37. Hotel del Coronado, *Boarders' Ledger no. 3 (1901–1905)*.
38. "Claus Spreckels Has a Second Paralytic Stroke," *Pacific Commercial Advertiser* (Honolulu), December 2, 1903, 1.
39. Newhall, "Spreckels," 173.
40. Buffum, "Sugar Industry of Hawaii," 372.
41. "Spreckels Feud Happily Ended," *Los Angeles Herald*, February 12, 1905.
42. "Claus Spreckels Buys a Fine Picture," *Oakland Tribune*, March 11, 1905.
43. "Family Differences," *The Wasp* (San Francisco), January 2, 1909, 9.
44. "San Francisco Gossip," *Sacramento Daily Union*, April 8, 1906.
45. Newhall, "Spreckels," 177.
46. "Family Differences."
47. "Claus Spreckels," *Evening Bulletin* (Honolulu), May 27, 1905.
48. "Hawaii Welcomes the Sugar King Claus Spreckels," *Evening Bulletin* (Honolulu), April 21, 1905.
49. "Claus Spreckels Here to Recuperate for His Health," *Hawaiian Gazette* (Honolulu), April 25, 1905.
50. "Claus Spreckels Here to Recuperate."
51. "Claus Spreckels," *Evening Bulletin* (Honolulu), May 27, 1905.
52. "*Alameda* Makes Quick Voyage," *Evening Bulletin* (Honolulu), June 23, 1905.
53. "Burglars Missed Chance," *Hawaiian Star*, June 25, 1906.
54. "The Capitalist and Wife Will Leave on the *Alameda* Next Week," *Hawaiian Star*, August 26, 1905.
55. "John D. Spreckels," *Hawaiian Star*, August 25, 1905.
56. But see "Graceful Figure Modeled in Clay," *San Francisco Chronicle*, January 24, 1902, which asserts that the model was Clara Petzold, later a noted photographer.
57. Christopher Craig, "Anna Spreckels Historical Essay: Spreckels (née de Bretteville), Alma Emma—Philanthropist, Socialite, and Patron of the Arts," *Shaping San Francisco's Digital Archive @FoundSF*, retrieved November 9, 2019, from https://www.foundsf.org/index.php?title=Alma_Spreckels.
58. G. Alexander, *America Goes Hawaiian*, 231.
59. Starr, *Dream Endures*, 154.
60. "Adolph Spreckels III," *Los Angeles Herald*, July 14, 1904.
61. "A. B. Spreckels in Carlsbad Is Dying," *San Jose (CA) Mercury-News*, July 14, 1904.
62. H. Adams, *The Man, John D. Spreckels*, 219.
63. "San Francisco Runs Wide Open," *Marysville (CA) Daily Appeal*, June 22, 1904.
64. "San Francisco Runs Wide Open."
65. "John D. Spreckels Reason for Absence," *San Francisco Call*, June 14, 1904.
66. "Australia Is Rapidly Recovering from Drought," *San Francisco Call*, January 22, 1904.

67. "Oceanic Is in Hapless State," *Pacific Commercial Advertiser* (Honolulu), March 20, 1907, 1.

68. H. Adams, *The Man, John D. Spreckels*, 215–16.

69. "Men and Women," *The Wasp* (San Francisco), March 24, 1906.

70. "Young Spreckels Managing the Call," *Oakland Tribune*, March 24, 1906.

71. "Men and Women."

72. Bean, *Boss Ruef's San Francisco*, 108, 109.

73. Bean, *Boss Ruef's San Francisco*, 112–13.

74. Bean, *Boss Ruef's San Francisco*, 115, 116.

75. Bean, *Boss Ruef's San Francisco*, 117, 108.

76. "Spreckels," *Sacramento Daily Union*, March 25, 1906.

77. "Spreckels."

18. Claus's World Crumbles

1. "Claus Spreckels Says 'Three Years': Tells a 'Sentinel' Representative That San Francisco Will Rebuild in That Time," *Santa Cruz (CA) Evening Sentinel*, April 24, 1906.

2. Stetson, *San Francisco during the Eventful Days*, 4.

3. Tillmann was president of German Savings and Loan and senior partner of the wholesale grocery firm of Tillmann & Bendel.

4. Tillmann diary, Tillmann Family Archives.

5. National Park Service, "1906 Earthquake Centennial."

6. Bolton and Unger, "Housing Reconstruction," 217–40.

7. Miller, *Music and Politics*, 21.

8. Hopkins, *Into the Firestorm*, 198.

9. Stetson, *San Francisco during the Eventful Days*, 21–22.

10. Author's collection.

11. "Spreckels Mansion to Be Restored," *Los Angeles Herald*, August 12, 1906.

12. Bolton and Unger, "Housing Reconstruction."

13. "Language Fails to Tell Tragedy: Correspondent Appalled by Devastation," *Los Angeles Herald*, April 25, 1906.

14. "Claus Spreckels Says 'Three Years.'"

15. "A Perspective on the San Francisco Earthquake, 1906: A Spotlight on a Primary Source by Silas Mack," History Resources, Gilder Lehrman Institute of American History, retrieved August 27, 2022, https://www.gilderlehrman.org/history-resources/spotlight-primary-source/perspective-san-francisco-earthquake-1906.

16. Fradkin, *Great Earthquake*, 6.

17. "Language Fails to Tell Tragedy."

18. Tillmann diary.

19. Slavicek, *San Francisco Earthquake*, 35.

20. Linthicum and White, *San Francisco Earthquake Horror*, 35.

21. "Story of San Francisco Horrors," *Green Forest (AR) Tribune*, April 28, 1906.

22. "John D. Spreckles [*sic*] Ill," *Minneapolis Journal*, March 19, 1906.

23. Banks and Read, *History of the San Francisco Disaster*, 118.
24. "How a Great Nation Rose to Emergency," *Honolulu Advertiser*, May 4, 1906.
25. Cardiff and Calciano, *Santa Cruz*, 28.
26. "Claus Spreckels Says 'Three Years.'"
27. "Spreckels Daughter to Wed John Ferris," *Sacramento Daily Union*, April 10, 1906.
28. "Business Resumed in the Potero [*sic*] District," *Santa Barbara (CA) Morning Press*, May 11, 1906.
29. "Spreckles [*sic*] Factory Not Destroyed," *Santa Barbara (CA) Morning Press*, April 27, 1906.
30. "The Touchstone of Calamity," *Sacramento Daily Union*, April 25, 1906.
31. "Social Jottings," *The Wasp* (San Francisco), July 14, 1906, 10.

19. Auf Wiedersehen

1. *Army Pack Train Bringing.*
2. "May Delay New Railway," *Los Angeles Herald*, May 4, 1906.
3. Older, "Story of a Reformer's Wife," 281. The Committee of Fifty remained active until early May 1906, when it was replaced by the Committee of Forty for the Rebuilding of San Francisco.
4. "The Crockett Refinery," *Hawaiian Star*, March 28, 1906.
5. "Sugar Combine Admitted by Spreckels," *San Francisco Examiner*, June 27, 1911.
6. Goldberg, "Cauldron of Anger," 275.
7. Newhall, "Spreckels," 184.
8. Anderson Borthwick, interview by Robert Wright, San Diego Historical Society Oral History Program, February 28, 1979, https://library.uscd.edu/dc/object/bb2902188s/_1.html (site discontinued).
9. Brainerd, "Man of Millions," 716.
10. Newhall, "Spreckels," 204.
11. William G. Irwin to Walter M. Giffard, November 4, 1908, quoted in MacLennan, "Kilauea Sugar Plantation," 6.
12. Conway, "Spreckels Sugar Company," 112–13.
13. Kirk, *Flier in Oil*, 27.
14. Segur, "From Crude to Refining," 243.
15. Kirk, *Flier in Oil*, 53.
16. "Nansen to Entertain Spreckels and Bride," *Stockton (CA) Independent*, June 9, 1909.
17. Goldberg, "Cauldron of Anger," 278.
18. "Is Spreckels Making a Will?," *Hawaiian Gazette* (Honolulu), October 18, 1907.
19. "Spreckels Will Sole Evidence of Two Heirs," *San Francisco Call*, June 4, 1910, 18.
20. "Grief for Demise of Sugar King," *San Francisco Call*, December 27, 1908.
21. "Sale of Claus Spreckels' Block," *Hawaiian Gazette* (Honolulu), December 18, 1908.
22. "Pay Last Tribute to Departed Financier," clipping, unnamed, undated, private collection, courtesy of the estate of Eleanor Walsh de Limur.
23. "Plain Funeral for Spreckels." *Los Angeles Herald*, December 28, 1908.

24. "Warm Fight over Sugar King's Wealth," *Tacoma (WA) Times*, May 19, 1909.

25. Birmingham, *California Rich*, 64.

26. "Spreckels et al. v. State."

27. "Death of Mrs. Claus Spreckels," *The Wasp* (San Francisco), February 19, 1910, 4.

28. "Spreckels et al. v. State."

29. "Policies Expired as Fire Swept Spreckels Manion: Loss Unpaid," *San Francisco Examiner*, April 11, 1907.

30. "Mrs. Spreckels Dangerously Ill," *Napa (CA) Weekly Journal*, April 23, 1909.

31. "Of Social Interest," *The Wasp* (San Francisco), April 10, 1909.

32. "Warm Fight over Sugar King's Wealth."

33. "Spreckels et al. v. State."

34. "Answer to Announcement Made by Brothers," *Wenatchee (WA) Daily World*, January 17, 1910.

35. "Shocked by Spreckels' Quarrel," *The Wasp* (San Francisco), February 26, 1910, 4.

36. "Follows Beloved Husband to Grave," *San Francisco Call*, February 16, 1910.

37. Goldberg, "Cauldron of Anger," 274.

38. "Will of Mrs. Anna C. Spreckels Filed," *San Francisco Call*, February 20, 1910.

39. "Death of Mrs. Claus Spreckels."

40. "Death of Mrs. Claus Spreckels."

41. "Executors Win against John D. and Adolph," *Sacramento Union*, April 11, 1912.

42. "Will of Claus Spreckels Is Judged Valid," *San Francisco Call*, April 11, 1912.

43. Goldberg, "Cauldron of Anger," 275.

44. "Test of Claus Spreckels's Will in Supreme Court," *Santa Fe New Mexican*, June 1, 1912.

20. Epilogue

1. "Spreckels et al. v. State."

2. Spreckels Sugar Company, "Spreckels Sugar History."

3. "New Variety of Beet Developed," *Sacramento Bee*, May 31, 1930.

4. Spreckels Sugar Company, "Spreckels Sugar History."

5. "Spreckels to Sue Mother over Fortune," *San Francisco Examiner*, December 24, 1947.

6. Hamilton and Hamilton, *Villa Calafia*, 2:150–51.

7. "Corporations: Sugar Plum," *Time*, June 27, 1949, https://content.time.com/time/subscriber/article/0,33009,800482,00.html.

8. Conway, "Spreckels Sugar Company," vi.

9. "Sugarbeet History," American Sugarbeet Growers Association, retrieved February 21, 2023, https://americansugarbeet.org/who-we-are/sugarbeet-history/.

10. Katherine Ramos, "Imperial Valley Sugar Beet Industry Honored," *Desert Review* (Brawley CA), February 10, 2020, updated April 16, 2021, https://www.thedesertreview.com/news/imperial-valley-sugar-beet-industry-honored/article_10de3da6-4c09-11ea-bb2d-1f3fc2af9b8f.html.

11. "Just How Diverse Is Hawaii? There's a List for That," *Hawaii News Now*, September 14, 2022, https://www.hawaiinewsnow.com/2022/09/15/list-known-melting-pot-hawaii -is-ranked-one-most-diverse-states/.

12. Kinoshita, "Storied Identities," 175.

13. Takaki, *Pau Hana*, 2.

14. Spreckels, California, achieved a historical designation from the Monterey County Board of Supervisors in 1991.

15. "Spreckels Sugar Factor Gone, but Not Forgotten," *Salinas Californian*, December 28, 1992.

16. "W. P. Spreckels Barred from Big Sugar Plant," *New York Times*, May 1, 1918.

17. Quoted in Commission on Wartime Relocation and Internment of Civilians, *Personal Justice Denied*, 291.

18. Newhall, "Spreckels," 151.

19. "The New Refinery," *Hawaiian Gazette* (Honolulu), June 22, 1881.

20. Borthwick, interview by Robert Wright.

21. "Tribute Paid Spreckels," *Los Angeles Times*, June 10, 1926.

22. Quoted in "Spreckels, John," MSS 81, box 27, folder 8, General Correspondence, Ed Fletcher Papers.

23. Chapman, Karlstrom, and Scharlach, *Big Alma*.

24. "W. P. Spreckels Barred from Big Sugar Plant."

25. "Spreckels Sale," *San Francisco Examiner*, November 30, 1930.

26. "Spreckels Sued," *Oakland Tribune*, March 30, 1940. During the trial, Gus mentioned that he planned to leave the U.S. to "visit" his daughter, but Titus's lawyers pounced on him, and the court prevented his return to France.

27. "Gus Spreckels' Spectacular Dissolving Act with the Family Sugar," *San Francisco Examiner*, November 13, 1946.

28. "Spreckels Kin Dies in Britain," *San Francisco Examiner*, May 3, 1924.

29. "Fortune Left to Girl of 14," *Maitland (Australia) Weekly Mercury*, January 7, 1926. Contradicting the headline, Jean's age in 1926 was fifteen, not fourteen.

30. "Young Heiress Not to Leave England," *Gazette* (Montreal), January 6, 1926.

31. Lyn Huntingford McCulloch, "Jean Harris Marries Charles d'Espinay in 1938," *Fairford*, May 22, 2018, http://lynhuntingford.blogspot.com/2018/05/jean-harris-marries-charles -despinay-in.html.

32. Hunt, *California and Californians*, 4:148.

33. "Rich Man Has His Eyes Opened," *Day Book* (Chicago), January 6, 1914.

34. "Spreckels Are Reunited," *Coronado (CA) Eagle and Journal*, January 21, 1922.

35. "Spreckels: From Riches to Recluse," *(London) Times*, February 19, 1983.

36. Klepper and Gunther, *Wealthy 100*.

BIBLIOGRAPHY

Archives/Manuscript Materials

Dicks, Vincent J. "J. D. Spreckels and the Reform Movement in California." Unpublished paper, 2019.

———. "Princess Ruth." Unpublished paper, 2022.

Fletcher, Ed. Papers, 1870–1955. University of California, San Diego, Libraries.

Green, Louis, III. "Martin Dowd's Brick Tenements, c. 1845, 48–50 Anson Street." Paper submitted at the Historic Charleston Foundation, April 17, 1969, Lowcountry Digital Library, https://lcdl.library.cofc.edu/lcdl/catalog/lcdl:93584.

Greene, Clay M. "The Story of A. B." Unpublished biography, [early 1920s?]. Courtesy of Adolph Rosekrans.

[Hamilton, Harriet?]. Hand-typed essay. Courtesy of Adolph Rosekrans.

Hawai'i State Archives, Honolulu.

Lili'uokalani. Correspondence: Lili'uokalani to J. O. Carter, from Washington DC, March 24–December 19, 1899. Lili'uokalani Trust Folder M-397-8-11.

Foreign Office and Executive Records, 1790–1900.

Hefner, Don. "Sugar Beet Roots." Unpublished papers of the Coronado Historical Association. Coronado Museum of History & Art, Coronado CA.

Hihn, Frederick A. Records. University of California, Santa Cruz.

Hooper, William. Diary and correspondence. William Hooper Papers. Hawaiian Collection, University of Hawai'i, Honolulu.

Kofoid, Charles A. Papers. University of California, San Diego, Libraries.

Lewis, Betty. "Watsonville Remembered: A Selection of KOMY-Radio Broadcasts." Typescript. Watsonville Public Library, Watsonville CA, retrieved July 28, 2022, https://archives.santacruzmah.org/wp-content/uploads/2013/11/Watsonville-Remembered7A29.pdf.

Newhall, Ruth W. "Spreckels: The Man and the Company." Unpublished manuscript, privately circulated. Courtesy of Adolph Rosekrans.

O'Shaughnessy, M. M. "Reminisces of Hawaii." Typescript, February 1920. National University of Ireland, Galway, Digital Collections. https://digital.library.nuigalway.ie/islandora/object/nuigalway%3A21673#page/1/mode/2up.

Pfingst, Edward Porter. "Scattered Leaves in Pajaro Valley History." Handwritten chronology of the Western Beet Sugar Company, 1957. Pajaro Valley Historical Association, Watsonville CA.

Queen Emma to Mrs. Pierre Jones, November 17, 1881. Queen Emma Collection, Archives of Hawaii, Honolulu.

Tillmann, Agnes Lily. Diary. Tillmann Family Archives, privately held by Mark H. Reed.

"Van Ness & Washington: A Family Record." Private essay courtesy of Lynn Wilsons.

Published Works

Adams, H. Austin. *The Man, John D. Spreckels.* San Diego: Frye & Smith, 1924.

Adams, Jane M. "The Development and Marketing of Specialist Water Cure Resorts." In *Healing with Water: English Spas and the Water Cure, 1840–1960,* edited by Jane M. Adams, 92. Manchester, UK: Manchester University Press, 2015. http://www.jstor.org/stable/j .cttlmkbd1x.9.

An Address by the Hawaiian Branches of the Sons of the American Revolution, Sons of Veterans, and Grand Army of the Republic to Their Compatriots in America Concerning the Annexation of Hawaii. Washington DC: Gibson Brothers, 1897.

Adler, Jacob. *Claus Spreckels: The Sugar King in Hawaii.* Honolulu: University of Hawai'i Press, 1966.

———. "Claus Spreckels' Rise and Fall in Hawai'i with Emphasis on London Loan of 1886." In *Sixty-Seventh Annual Report of the Hawaiian Historical Society for the Year 1958.* Honolulu: Advertising Publishing, 1959.

———. "The Oceanic Steamship Company: A Link in Claus Spreckels' Hawaiian Sugar Empire." *Pacific Historical Review* 29, no. 3 (August 1960): 257–69.

———. "The *Spreckelsville Plantation*: A Chapter in Claus Spreckels' Hawaiian Career." *California Historical Society Quarterly* 40, no. 1 (March 1961): 33–48.

Adler, Jacob, and Robert M. Kamins. *The Fantastic Life of Walter Murray Gibson, Hawaii's Minister of Everything.* Honolulu: University of Hawai'i Press, 1986.

Alexander, Geoff. *America Goes Hawaiian: The Influence of Pacific Island Culture on the Mainland.* Jefferson NC: McFarland, 2018.

Alexander, W. D. "The Advent of Spreckels." In *Foreign Relations of the United States, 1894,* appendix 2, "Affairs in Hawaii," 181. Washington DC: United States Government Printing Office, 1895.

Alexandra, Rae. "Mindblowing Tales from San Francisco's (Long) History with Epidemics." *KQED Arts & Culture,* April 13, 2020. https://www.kqed.org/arts/13878268/mindblowing -tales-from-san-franciscos-long-history-with-epidemics.

Allen, William Wallace, and Richard Benjamin Avery. *California Gold Book: First Nugget, Its Discovery and Discoverers, and Some of the Results Proceeding Therefrom.* San Francisco: Donohue & Henneberry, 1893.

American Society of Mechanical Engineers. *Journal of the American Society of Mechanical Engineers,* vol. 37. New York: American Society of Mechanical Engineers, 1915. Google Books.

Andrade, Ernest. "Hawaiian Coinage Controversy—Or, What Price a Handsome Profile." *Hawaiian Journal of History* 11 (1977): 97–109. https://evols.library.manoa.hawaii.edu /bitstream/10524/415/2/JL11103.pdf.

Angel, Myron. *History of San Luis Obispo County, California: With Illustrations and Biographical Sketches of Its Prominent Men and Pioneers.* Oakland CA: Thompson & West, 1883. Reprint, San Luis Obispo CA: EZ Nature Books, 1986, 2000.

Angell, Lowell. *Theatres of Hawai'i.* Charleston SC: Arcadia, 2011.

"Aptos Stock Farm." *Breeder and Sportsman,* September 9, 1899.

Armstrong, John, and David M. Williams. *The Impact of Technological Change: The Early Steamship in Britain.* Research in Maritime History 47. St. Johns, Newfoundland: International Maritime Economic History Association, 2011.

Army Pack Train Bringing Supplies. Film by Thomas A. Edison, 1906. Library of Congress American Memory: Remaining Collections. http://www.sfmuseum.org/loc/movie4.html.

Banks, Charles Eugene, and Opie Percival Read. *The History of the San Francisco Disaster and Mount Vesuvius Horror.* San Francisco: C. E. Thomas, 1906.

Barke, Megan, Rebecca Fribush, and Peter N. Stearns. "Nervous Breakdown in 20th-Century American Culture." *Journal of Social History* 33, no. 3 (Spring 2000): 565–84. https://www .jstor.org/stable/3789211.

Baur, John E. "When Royalty Came to California." *California History* 67, no. 4 (1988): 244–65.

Bean, Walton. *Boss Ruef's San Francisco: The Story of the Union Labor Party, Big Business, and the Graft Prosecution.* Berkeley: University of California Press, 1952.

Bernhard, Jim. *Porcupine, Picayune, and Post: How Newspapers Get Their Names.* Columbia: University of Missouri Press, 2007.

Bethel, A. C. W. "The Golden Skein: California's Gold-Rush Transportation Network." In *Golden State Mining and Economic Development in Gold Rush California,* edited by James J. Rawls and Richard J. Orsi, 255–76. Berkeley: University of California Press, 1999.

Birmingham, Stephen. *California Rich: The Lives, the Times, the Scandals and the Fortunes of the Men and Women Who Made and Kept California's Wealth.* New York: Open Road Integrated Media, 2016.

Bolton, Marie, and Nancy C. Unger. "Housing Reconstruction after the Catastrophe: The Failed Promise of San Francisco's 1906 'Earthquake Cottages.'" *Annales de démographie historique* no. 120 (2010–12): 217–40. https://www.cairn.info/revue-annales-de-demographie -historique-2010-2-page-217.htm.

Boncquet, Pierre Auguste. "*Bacillus morulans,* n. sp." *Phytopathology* 7, no. 4 (August 1917): 269–89.

Bonura, Sandra E. *Empire Builder: John D. Spreckels and the Making of San Diego.* Lincoln: University of Nebraska Press, 2020.

———. *Light in the Queen's Garden: Ida May Pope, Pioneer for Hawai'i's Daughters.* Honolulu: University of Hawai'i Press, 2017.

———. "Queen Lili'uokalani's Beloved Kawaiaha'o Seminary." *Hawaiian Journal of History* 51 (2017): 31–68.

Brainerd, Erastus. "A Man of Millions." *Hearst's Magazine* 26 (July–December 1914): 715–17

Brechin, Gray. *Imperial San Francisco: Urban Power, Earthly Ruin.* Oakland: University of California Press, 2006.

Breschini, Gary S., Mona Gudgel, and Trudy Haversat. *Spreckels (Images of America).* Charleston SC: Arcadia, 2006.

Buffum, Jesse H. "The Sugar Industry of Hawaii." *Louisiana Planter and Sugar Manufacturer* 44, no. 17 (April 23, 1910): 372.

California Office of Historic Preservation. "Golden Gate Park." National Register of Historic Places Registration Form, section 8, page 46, retrieved August 19, 2022. https://docslib .org/doc/4455064/received-omb-no.

Cardiff, George, and Elizabeth Spedding Calciano. *Santa Cruz and the Cowell Ranch, 1890–1964.* Santa Cruz: University of California Library, 1965. https://escholarship.org/uc/item /2zw5t11r.

Cartier, Robert R. *Revised Evaluation of Historical Resources at the Paraiso Springs at 34358 Paraiso Springs Road in the County of Monterey.* San Jose CA: Archeological Resource Management, 2005. https://docplayer.net/82361808-Archaeological-resource-management.html.

Chapin, Helen G. "Newspapers of Hawai'i 1834 to 1903: From He Liona to the Pacific Cable." *Hawaiian Journal of History* 18 (1984): 68.

Chapman, Martin, Ann Heath Karlstrom, and Bernice Scharlach. *Big Alma: San Francisco's Alma Spreckels.* Berkeley CA: Heyday Books, 2015.

Circa. *Historic Context Statement for the City of Watsonville: Final Report.* San Francisco: Circa; Historic Property Development, 2007. https://www.cityofwatsonville.org /DocumentCenter/View/3955/City-of-Watsonville-Historic-Context-Statement-2007.

"Claus Spreckels." *Harper's Weekly* 35, no. 1780 (January 31, 1891): 87.

"Claus Spreckels." In *Planter and Sugar Manufacturer,* vol. 37, 82. New York: Spon & Chamberlain, 1906.

Coffman, Tom. *Nation Within: The History of the American Occupation of Hawai'i.* Durham NC: Duke University Press, 2016.

Cohn, Raymond L., and Simone A. Wegge. "Overseas Passenger Fares and Emigration from Germany in the Mid-Nineteenth Century." *Social Science History* 41, no. 3 (Fall 2017): 393–413.

Collins, Allen. "The Spreckels Era in Rio del Mar, 1872–1922." Santa Cruz Public Libraries Local History Collection, retrieved April 1, 2022. https://history.santacruzpl.org/omeka /files/original/aa1465611aedbbabe44a9f362d9fbbba.pdf.

Commission on Wartime Relocation and Internment of Civilians. *Personal Justice Denied: Report on the Commission on Wartime Relocation and Internment of Civilians.* Seattle: University of Washington Press, 1997. https://www.archives.gov/files/research/japanese -americans/justice-denied/chapter-12.pdf.

Congressional Record: Proceedings and Debates of the House of Representatives, May 24, 1884. Washington DC: U.S. Government Printing Office, 1884, 4479. Google Books.

Conway, Jimmy Don. "Spreckels Sugar Company: The First Fifty Years." Master's diss., San Jose State University, 1999.

Cook, Melville T. "Insect Transmission of Virus Diseases of Plants." *Scientific Monthly* 44, no. 2 (1937): 174–77.

Cordray, William W. "Claus Spreckels of California." PhD diss., University of Southern California, 1955.

Creighton, Thomas H. *The Lands of Hawaii: Their Use and Misuse.* Honolulu: University of Hawaiʻi Press, 1978.

Cutler, Robert W. P. *The Mysterious Death of Jane Stanford.* Stanford CA: Stanford University Press, 2003.

Daws, Gavan. *Shoal of Time.* Honolulu: University of Hawaiʻi Press, 1974.

Delgado, James P., and Stephen A. Haller. *Submerged Cultural Resources Assessment: Golden Gate National Recreation Area, Gulf of the Farallones National Marine Sanctuary, and Point Reyes National Seashore.* Santa Fe NM: Southwest Cultural Resources Center Professional Papers, no. 18, 1989. https://www.nps.gov/orgs/1635/upload/GOGA_641_D84_-31512 .pdf.

Dicks, Vincent J. *Forsaken Kings: Emma Spreckels, the Surfer of Asbury Park.* Sea Girt NJ: Career Gaudium Press, 2022.

Downey, Lynn. *Levi Strauss: The Man Who Gave Blue Jeans to the World.* Amherst: University of Massachusetts Press, 2016.

Edwards, Chris. "The Sugar Racket." *Tax & Budget Bulletin* 46 (June 2007). https://www .cato.org/sites/cato.org/files/pubs/pdf/tbb_0607_46.pdf.

Eichner, Alfred S. *The Emergence of Oligopoly: Sugar Refining as a Case Study.* Baltimore MD: Johns Hopkins, 1969.

Elson, Louis C., ed. *The Musical Herald.* Boston: Musical Herald, 1884.

Emmet, Boris. *The California and Hawaiian Sugar Refining Corporation of San Francisco: A Study of the Origin, Business Policies, and Management of a Co-operative Refining and Distributing Organization.* Palo Alto CA: Stanford University Press, 1928.

Fabing, Horace W., and Rick Hamman. *Steinbeck Country Narrow Gauge.* Nelson BC: Otter B Books, 2004.

Fleischmann, Richard K., and Thomas N. Tyson. "The Interface of Race and Accounting: The Case of Hawaiian Sugar Plantations, 1835–1920." *Accounting History* 5, no. 1 (May 1, 2000): 7–32.

Forbes, David W. *In Haste with Aloha: Letters and Diaries of Queen Emma, 1881–1885.* Honolulu: University of Hawaiʻi Press, 2017.

Fradkin, Philip L. *The Great Earthquake and Firestorms of 1906: How San Francisco Nearly Destroyed Itself.* Berkeley: University of California Press, 2005.

Francis, Phil. *Santa Cruz County: A Faithful Reproduction in Print and Photography of Its Climate, Capabilities, and Beauties.* San Francisco: H. S. Crocker, 1896.

Frear, Walter Francis, ed. *Mark Twain and Hawaii.* Chicago: Lakeside Press, 1947.

Gendron, Richard, and G. William Domhoff. *The Leftmost City: Power and Progressive Politics in Santa Cruz.* New York: Taylor & Francis, Routledge, 2009.

Glass, Fred B. *From Mission to Microchip: A History of the California Labor Movement.* Oakland: University of California Press, 2016.

Goldberg, Charlotte K. "A Cauldron of Anger: The Spreckels Family and Reform of California Community Property Law." *Western Legal History: The Journal of the Ninth Judicial Circuit Historical Society* 12, no. 2 (Summer/Fall 1999): 241–79.

———. *Community Property*. Aspen Casebook Series. New York: Wolters Kluwer Law & Business, 2008.

Gonschor, Lorenz. Review of *Sun Yatsen, Robert Wilcox and Their Failed Revolutions, Honolulu and Canton 1895: Dynamite on the Tropic of Cancer*, by Patrick Anderson. *Journal of Pacific History* 58, no. 1 (2023): 90–91. https://www.tandfonline.com/doi/abs/10.1080/00223344.2022.2059580.

Gonschor, Lorenz, and Louis Bousquet. "A Showdown at Honolulu Harbor: Exploring Late 19th Century Hawaiian Politics through a Narrative Biography of Celso Cesare Moreno." *Journal of Narrative Politics* 3, no. 2 (Spring 2017): 131–51.

Graham, Alice J. "Will Miss Spreckels Become Mrs. Santos-Dumont?" *Broadway Weekly* 3, no. 60 (April 7, 1904): 15.

Green, John P. *Fact Stranger Than Fiction: Seventy-Five Years of a Busy Life with Reminiscences of Many Great and Good Men and Women*. Cleveland OH: Riehl Printing Company, 1920.

Green, Valerie. *Above Stairs: Social Life in Upper-Class Victoria, 1843–1918*. Victoria BC: TouchWood Editions, 2011.

Gregory, Thomas Jefferson. *History of Solano and Napa Counties, California, with Biographical Sketches of the Leading Men and Women of the Counties Who Have Been Identified with Its Growth and Development from the Early Days to the Present Time*. Los Angeles: Historic Record Company, 1912.

Gritz, Jennie Rothenberg. "The Unsavory History of Sugar, the Insatiable American Craving: How the Nation Got Hooked on Sweets," *Smithsonian Magazine*, May 2017. https://www.smithsonianmag.com/history/unsavory-history-sugar-american-craving-180962766/.

Hachten, Harva, and Terese Allen. *The Flavor of Wisconsin: An Informal History of Food and Eating in the Badger State*, 2d ed. Madison: Wisconsin Historical Society Press, 2009, 2013.

Hackler, Rhoda E. A. "Princeville Plantation Papers." *Hawaiian Journal of History* 16 (1982): 65–85.

Hall, Henry, ed. *America's Successful Men of Affairs: An Encyclopedia of Contemporaneous Biography*, vol. 2. New York: Tribune Association, 1896.

Hamilton, Edward Morse, and Harriet Holbrook Hamilton. *Villa Calafia*. 2 vols. Privately printed, 1961.

Hamman, Rick. *California Central Coast Railways*. 2nd ed. Santa Cruz CA: Otter B Books, 2002.

Hansen, Harry. *California: A Guide to the Golden State*. New York: Hastings House, 1967. Originally Compiled by the Federal Writers Project of the Works Progress Administration for the State of California, 1939.

Harned, Richard. *The Palace Hotel (Postcards of America)*. San Francisco: Arcadia, 2009.

Harrison, Edward Sanford. *History of Santa Cruz County*. San Francisco: Pacific Press, 1892.

Harveson, Robert M. *Beet Curly Top: America's First Serious Disease of Sugar Beets.* St. Paul MN: American Phytopathological Society, 2022. https://www.apsnet.org/edcenter/apsnetfeatures/Pages/CurlyTop.aspx.

Hawaiian Mission Children's Society. *Portraits of American Protestant Missionaries to Hawaii.* Honolulu: Hawaiian Gazette, 1901.

Hawaiian Sugar Planters' Association. *Story of Sugar in Hawaii.* Honolulu: Hawaiian Sugar Planters' Association, 1926.

History of the College of California 1, nos. 1–2 (1887). In Papers of the California Historical Society, San Francisco, California.

Hittell, John S. [John Shertzer]. *The Commerce and Industries of the Pacific Coast of North America; Comprising the Rise, Progress, Products, Present Condition, and Prospects of the Useful Arts on the Western Side of Our Continent, and Some Account of Its Resources, with Elaborate Treatment of Manufactures; Briefer Consideration of Commerce, Transportation, Agriculture, and Mining; and Mention of Leading Establishments and Prominent Men in Various Departments of Business.* San Francisco: A. L. Bancroft, 1882.

Hobbs, Jean. *Hawaii: A Pageant of the Soil.* Palo Alto CA: Stanford University Press, 1935.

Hoʻokuleana. *Hawaiʻi's Big Five (Plus 2).* Kailua HI: Hoʻokuleana, 2017. https://imagesofoldhawaii.com/wp-content/uploads/Big-5-Plus-2.pdf.

Hopkins, Deborah. *Into the Firestorm: A Novel of San Francisco, 1906.* New York: Alfred A. Knopf, 2006.

Hunt, Rockwell D., ed. *California and Californians,* vol. 4. Chicago: Lewis, 1926. Google Books.

Hussey, John A. *Hawaii History 1778–1910: National Survey of Historic Sites and Buildings, Special Study.* Washington DC: U.S. Department of the Interior, 1962.

Internal Revenue Record and Customs Journal 30, no. 19 (May 12, 1884): 169. Google Books.

Jones, C. Allan, and Robert V. Osgood. *From King Cane to the Last Sugar Mill: Agricultural Technology and the Making of Hawaiʻi's Premier Crop.* Honolulu: University of Hawaiʻi Press, 2015.

Jones, Peter d'Alroy. *An Economic History of the United States since 1783.* London: Routledge & K. Paul, 2006.

Kamiya, Gary. *Spirits of San Francisco: Voyages Though the Unknown City.* New York: Bloomsbury, 2020.

Kanahele, George S. *Emma: Hawaiʻi's Remarkable Queen: A Biography.* Honolulu: Queen Emma Foundation, 1999.

Kent, Harold W. *Charles Reed Bishop, Man of Hawaiʻi.* Palo Alto CA: Pacific Books, 1965.

Kessler, Lawrence Helfgott. "A Plantation upon a Hill; Or, Sugar without Rum: Hawaiʻi's Missionaries and the Founding of the Sugarcane Plantation System." *Pacific Historical Review* 84, no. 2 (May 2015). https://doi.org/10.1525/phr.2015.84.2.129.

———. "Planter's Paradise: Nature, Culture, and Hawaiʻi's Sugarcane Plantations." PhD diss., Temple University, Philadelphia, 2016. https://digital.library.temple.edu/digital/api/collection/p245801coll10/id/374197/download.

King, Samuel P., and Randall W. Roth. *Broken Trust: Greed, Mismanagement & Political Manipulation at America's Largest Charitable Trust*. Honolulu: University of Hawai'i Press, 2006.

Kinoshita, Gaku. "Storied Identities: Japanese American Elderly from a Sugar Plantation Community in Hawai'i." PhD diss., University of Hawai'i–Mānoa, 2003.

Kirk, Anthony. *A Flier in Oil: Adolph B. Spreckels and the Rise of the California Petroleum Industry*. San Francisco: California Historical Society, 2000.

Kiyosaki, Wayne. *Talk Pidgin; Speak English; Go Local; Go American: The Japanese Immigrant Experience in Spreckelsville, Maui*. Bloomington IN: AuthorHouse, 2014.

Klepper, Michael, and Robert Gunther. *The Wealthy 100: From Benjamin Franklin to Bill Gates—a Ranking of the Richest Americans, Past and Present*. New York: Citadel Press, 1996.

Korn, Alfons L., ed. *News from Molokai: Letters between Peter Kaeo and Queen Emma, 1873–1876*. Honolulu: University of Hawai'i Press, 1976.

Kuykendall, Ralph Simpson. *The Hawaiian Kingdom*. Vol. 1, *Foundation and Transformation, 1778–1854*. Honolulu: University of Hawai'i Press, 1965.

———. *The Hawaiian Kingdom*. Vol. 2, *Twenty Critical Years, 1854–1874*. Honolulu: University of Hawai'i Press, 1953.

———. *The Hawaiian Kingdom*. Vol. 3, *The Kalakaua Dynasty, 1874–1893*. Honolulu: University of Hawai'i Press, 1979.

Kyselka, Will, and Ray E. Lanterman. *Maui, How It Came to Be*. Honolulu: University of Hawai'i Press, 1980.

LeRoux, Kelly, and Mary K. Feeney. *Nonprofit Organizations and Civil Society in the United States*. New York: Routledge, Taylor & Francis, 2015.

Lewis, Betty. "W. H. Weeks, California School Architect." *California History* 64, no. 3 (1985): 226–29.

Lili'uokalani. *Hawai'i's Story by Hawai'i's Queen Lili'uokalani*. Boston: Lee and Shepard, 1898.

Linthicum, Richard, and Trumbull White. *San Francisco Earthquake Horror: Comprising Also a Vivid Portrayal of the Recent Death-Dealing Eruption of Mt. Vesuvius*. Chicago: Hubert D. Russell, 1906.

London, Charmian Kittredge. *Our Hawaii*. New York: Macmillan, 1917. Republished, Orinda CA: SeaWolf Press, 2018.

Lydon, Sandy, and Carolyn Swift. *Soquel Landing to Capitola-by-the-Sea*. Cupertino CA: History Center, DeAnza College, 1978.

Lyles, Lionel D., and Essie Thibodeaux-Lyles. *Historical Development of Capitalism in the United States and Its Affects on the American Family: From Colonial Times to 1920*, vol. 1. Bloomington IN: iUniverse, 2003.

MacLennan, Carol. "Kilauea Sugar Plantation in 1912: A Snapshot." *Hawaiian Journal of History* 41, no. 1 (2007): 1–34.

Magnuson, Torsten A. "History of the Beet Sugar Industry in California." *Annual Publication of the Historical Society of Southern California* 11, no. 1 (1918): 68–79.

Marzorati, Guy. "Need for Alarm: The *San Francisco Call* and the *Chronicle* Cover the 1900–1904 Bubonic Plague." *Historical Perspectives: Santa Clara University Undergraduate Journal of History*, series 2, vol. 18 (2013), art. 4, 62, https://scholarcommons.scu.edu/historical -perspectives/vol18/iss1/4/.

Mathews, Glenn David. *Spreckels, California: Design Guidelines.* Monterey CA: Monterey County Planning and Building Inspection Department, 1999. https://www.co.monterey .ca.us/home/showpublisheddocument/37957/636371078696470000.

McDermott, John F., Zita Cup Choy, and Anthony P. S. Guerrero. "The Last Illness and Death of Hawai'i's King Kalakaua: A New Historical/Clinical Perspective." *Hawaiian Journal of History* 49 (2015): 59–72

McKibben, Carol Lynn. *Salinas: A History of Race and Resilience in an Agricultural City.* Redwood City CA: Stanford University Press, 2022.

McPhail, Elizabeth C. *The Story of New San Diego and of Its Founder, Alonzo E. Horton*, 2nd. ed. San Diego: San Diego Historical Society, 1979.

McWilliams, Carey. *Factories in the Field: The Story of Migratory Farm Labor in California.* Oakland: University of California Press, 1999.

Mehrländer, Andrea. *The Germans of Charleston, Richmond and New Orleans during the Civil War Period, 1850–1870: A Study and Research Compendium.* Boston: De Gruyter, 2011.

Merleaux, April. "Spectacles of Sweetness: Race, Civics, and the Material Culture of Eating Sugar after the Turn of the Century." In *Sugar and Civilization: American Empire and the Cultural Politics of Sweetness*, edited by April Merleaux, 55–80. Chapel Hill: University of North Carolina Press, 2015. https://www.universitypressscholarship.com /view/10.5149/northcarolina/9781469622514.001.0001/upso-9781469622514-chapter -003.

Meyer, Karl-Heinz. "Die Verwandten des Zuckerkönigs Claus Spreckels in der Börde Lamstedt und in den USA" [The relatives of the sugar king Claus Spreckels in the Börde Lamstedt and in the USA]. *Jahrbuch der Männer vom Morgenstern* 43 (1962): 130–37.

Miller, Leta E. *Music and Politics in San Francisco: From the 1906 Quake to the Second World War.* Oakland: University of California Press, 2012.

"The Millionaires of San Francisco." *Pilot* 37, no. 43 (October 24, 1874), 3.

Nader, Jennifer M. "A Recovered Interview with Frank Norris." *American Literary Realism* 42, no.1 (Fall 2009): 79–82.

National Park Service, U.S. Department of the Interior, "1906 Earthquake Centennial." *Point Reyes National Seashore Resource Newsletter*, 2006. https://www.nps.gov/pore/learn/upload /resourcenewsletter_1906earthquakecentennial.pdf.

"News Items." *Torreya* 6, no. 4 (April 1906): 77–80. http://www.jstor.org/stable/40594483.

Nordhoff, Charles. *Northern California, Oregon, and the Sandwich Islands.* New York: Harper & Brothers, 1875.

O'Brien, Victor H. "Claus Spreckels, the Sugar King." *Ainslee's Magazine* (February 1901): 516–23.

"Ocean Holidays." *British Medical Journal* 1, no. 1632 (April 9, 1892): 775–76. https://www .jstor.org/stable/20245784.

O'Connell, Daniel. *The Inner Man: Good Things to Eat and Drink and Where to Get Them.* San Francisco: Bancroft, 1891.

O'Donnell, Arthur J. *The Guilty Environmentalist: Essays, Musings, and Political Fantasies, from the Age of Electricity to the Collapse of Enron.* Victoria BC: Trafford, 2003.

Older, Cora Miranda Baggerly ("Mrs. Fremont Older"). "The Story of a Reformer's Wife." *McClure's Magazine* 33, no. 3 (July 1909): 281.

Osborne, Thomas J. "Claus Spreckels and the Oxnard Brothers: Pioneer Developers of California's Beet Sugar Industry, 1890–1900." *Southern California Quarterly* 54, no. 2 (Summer 1972): 118.

Patterson, John. "The United States and Hawaiian Reciprocity, 1867–1870." *Pacific Historical Review* 7, no. 1 (March 1938): 14–26.

Payne, Stephen Michael. "A Howling Wilderness: Stagecoach Days in the Mountains." Santa Cruz Public Libraries Local History Collection, retrieved April 2, 2022. https://history.santacruzpl.org/omeka/files/original/de80b293391129d77d1e511db1db9234.pdf.

Perry, Frank. "Lime's Sweet History." *Lime Kiln Chronicles.* Friends of the Cowell Lime Works Historic District newsletter, Spring/Summer 2010. https://limeworks.ucsc.edu/newsletter/issues/lkc-2010-spring.pdf.

Pfingst, Edward Porter. *Memories of Pajaro Valley: An Interview with Edward Porter Pfingst.* Watsonville CA: Pajaro Valley Historical Association, 1974.

Phelps, Alonzo. *Contemporary Biography of California's Representative Men: With Contributions from Distinguished Scholars and Scientists.* San Francisco: A. L. Bancroft, 1881.

Pigman, Ward. *The Carbohydrates: Chemistry and Biochemistry Physiology.* Cambridge MA: Academic Press, 1957.

Pollock, Christopher. *San Francisco's Golden Gate Park: A Thousand and Seventeen Acres of Stories.* Berkeley CA: West Margin Press, 2001.

Powell, Ronald G. *The Reign of the Lumber Barons: Part Two of the History of Rancho Soquel Augmentation,* edited by Derek R. Whaley. The Secret History of Santa Cruz County. Santa Cruz CA: Zayante, 2021.

Pryor, Alton. *Little Known Tales in Hawaii History.* Roseville CA: Stagecoach, 2004.

"Pumping Plants in Salinas Valley." *Pacific Rural Press and California Farmer* 51 (June 27, 1896): 407.

Rehder, John B. "Sugar Plantation Settlements of Southern Louisiana: A Cultural Geography." PhD diss., Louisiana State University, Baton Rouge, 1971. https://talltimbers.org/wp-content/uploads/2014/03/Rehder1979_op.pdf.

Retan, Iretta Hight. *The Iretta Hight Retan Collection.* Honolulu: Kamehameha Schools, 1988.

Rigby, Barry. "American Expansion in Hawaii: The Contribution of Henry A. Peirce." *Diplomatic History* 4, no. 4 (October 1980): 353–70.

Riquelmy, Christina, Debbie Currie, and Emily Robinson. *Sugar at LSU: A Chronology.* Online exhibition *Sugar at LSU: Cultivating a Sweeter Future* based on the 1995 physical exhibition. Baton Rouge: Louisiana State University Libraries, 2002. https://www.lib.lsu.edu/sites/all/files/sc/exhibits/e-exhibits/sugar/contents.html.

Roth, Mitchel. "Cholera, Community, and Public Health in Gold Rush Sacramento and San Francisco." *Pacific Historical Review* 66, no. 4 (1997): 527–51. https://doi.org/10.2307/3642236.

Sacramento Bank. *The Beet Sugar Industry in the State of California: Interviews with and Letters from Mr. Claus Spreckels, Mr. C. C. Howell, Prof. E. W. Hilgard, Mr. W. H. Holabird, Alameda Beet Sugar Co.* Sacramento CA: Sacramento State Agricultural Society, 1896. Google Books.

San Francisco. Chicago: Santa Fe Railroad, 1901. https://tile.loc.gov/storage-services/service/gdc/gdclccn/02/02/46/61/02024661/02024661.pdf.

San Francisco Directory. San Francisco: Henry G. Langley, 1858. https://archive.org/details/sanfranciscodire1858lang/page/256/mode/2up.

San Francisco Journal of Commerce. *The Builders of a Great City: San Francisco's Representative Men, the City, Its History and Commerce.* San Francisco: San Francisco Journal of Commerce Publishing, 1891.

Schmitt, Hans A. "Prussia's Last Fling: The Annexation of Hanover, Hesse, Frankfurt, and Nassau, June 15–October 8, 1866." *Central European History* 8, no. 4 (December 1975): 316–47, http://www.jstor.org/stable/4545753.

Schulz, Joy. "Empire of the Young: Missionary Children in Hawai'i and the Birth of U.S. Colonialism in the Pacific, 1820–1898." PhD diss., University of Nebraska–Lincoln, 2011, https://digitalcommons.unl.edu/cgi/viewcontent.cgi?article=1035&context=historydiss.

Scott, Edward B. *The Saga of the Sandwich Islands.* Lake Tahoe NV: Sierra-Tahoe, 1968.

Secrest, William B. *California Feuds: Vengeance, Vendettas and Violence on the Old West Coast.* Sanger CA: Ward Dancer, 2004.

Sedgwick, John. "How the Santa Fe Railroad Changed America Forever: The Golden Spike Made the Newspapers. But Another Railroad Made an Even Bigger Difference to the Nation." *Smithsonian Magazine,* July 2021. https://www.smithsonianmag.com/history/santa-fe-railroad-changed-america-forever-180977952/.

Segur, I. E. "From Crude to Refining: The Scope of the Sunset Monarch Oil Company." *Sunset Magazine* 25, no. 2 (August 1910): 243.

Shuck, Oscar T., ed. *History of the Bench and Bar of California: Being Biographies of Many Remarkable Men, a Store of Humorous and Pathetic Recollections, Accounts of Important Legislation and Extraordinary Cases, Comprehending the Judicial History of the State.* Los Angeles: Commercial Printing House, 1901.

Siler, Julia Flynn. *Lost Kingdom: Hawaii's Last Queen, the Sugar Kings, and America's First Imperial Adventure.* New York: Atlantic Monthly Press, 2012.

Simonds, William A. *Kamaʻaina: A Century in Hawaii.* Honolulu: American Factors, 1949.

Slavicek, Louise Chipley. *The San Francisco Earthquake and Fire of 1906.* New York: Chelsea House, 2009.

Smith, Jared Gage. *Plantation Sketches: A Record of Hawaiian Industries as They Appeared to an Itinerant Journalist in 1923; Published in the Columns of the "Advertiser."* Honolulu: Advertiser Press, 1924.

Smith, Sarah Bixby. *Adobe Days: Being the Truthful Narrative of the Events in the Life of a California Girl on a Sheep Ranch.* Whitefish MT: Kessinger, 2010.

Snodgrass, Mary Ellen. *Settlers of the American West: The Lives of 231 Notable Pioneers.* Jefferson NC: McFarland, 2015.

Soquel Pioneer and Historical Association. *Soquel (Images of America)*. Charleston SC: Arcadia, 2011.

Speed, John Gilmore. "King Kalakaua of Hawaii." *Harper's Weekly* 35, no. 1780 (January 31, 1891): 96.

Spiekermann, Uwe. "Claus Spreckels: A Biographical Case Study of Nineteenth-Century American Immigrant Entrepreneurship." *Business and Economic History On-Line* 8 (2010), https://thebhc.org/sites/default/files/spiekermann.pdf.

——. "Expanding the Frontier(s): The Spreckels Family and the German-American Penetration of the Pacific, 1870–1920." In *Explorations and Entanglements: Germans in Pacific Worlds from the Early Modern Period to World War I*, edited by Hartmut Berghoff, Frank Biess, and Ulrike Strasser, 171–94. New York: Berghahn Books, 2019.

——. "Labor as a Bottleneck: Entangled Commodity Chains of Sugar in Hawaii and California in the Late Nineteenth Century." In *Global Commodity Chains and Labor Relations*, edited by Andrea Komlosy and Goran Musić, 177–201. Leiden, Netherlands: Brill, 2021.

Spikes, John D., and Myron Stout. "Photochemical Activity of Chloroplasts Isolated from Sugar Beet Infected with Virus Yellows." *Science* 122, no. 3165 (August 26, 1955): 375–76.

Spreckels, John D. "Hawaii for Tourists." *Paradise of the Pacific Monthly* 8, no. 9 (September 1895): 661–62.

"Spreckels et al. v. State." In *California Appellate Divisions*. Vol. 22, California District Courts of Appeal, January–June 1916, 775. San Francisco: Recorder Printing and Publishing Company.

Spreckels Sugar Company. *Sugar from Western Farms*. San Francisco: Spreckels Sugar Company, n.d. Brochure.

Stamberg, Susan. "How Andrew Carnegie Turned His Fortune into a Library Legacy." *Morning Edition*, National Public Radio, August 1, 2013.https://www.npr.org/2013/08/01/207272849/how-andrew-carnegie-turned-his-fortune-into-a-library-legacy.

Starr, Kevin. *The Dream Endures: California Enters the 1940s*. New York: Oxford University Press, 2002.

St. Clair, David J. "The Gold Rush and the Beginnings of California Industry." *California History* 77, no. 4 (1998): 185–208. https://doi.org/10.2307/25462514.

Steffens, Lincoln. "Rudolf Spreckels: A Business Man Fighting for His City," *American Magazine* 65 (November 1907–April 1908): 390–402.

——. "Rudolph Spreckels: A Business Reformer," *American Magazine*, February 1908. Archive of American Journalism, Lincoln Steffens Collection, http://nebula.wsimg.com/a2868e7643451c06e8e7f596f36a4513?AccessKeyId=94861742399A59C7B18A&disposition=0&alloworigin=1.

——. *Upbuilders*. Seattle: University of Washington Press, 1968.

Stetson, James B. *San Francisco during the Eventful Days of April, 1906: Personal Recollections*. San Francisco: Murdock Press, 1906. Online Archive of California, Bancroft Library, University of California, Berkeley, https://oac.cdlib.org/view?docId=hb4p3007dw;NAAN=13030&doc.view=frames&chunk.id=div00002&toc.depth=1&toc.id=&brand=oac4.

Stevens, Stanley D., and Benjamin Schwantes. "Frederick Augustus Hihn." In *Immigrant Entrepreneurship: German-American Business Biographies, 1720 to the Present*, edited by

William J. Hausman. Vol. 2. Washington DC: German Historical Institute, 2014. Repro-
duced as "Frederick Augustus Hihn (1829–1913)." Immigrant Entrepreneurship: German-
American Business Biographies, 1720 to the Present, June 8, 2011, last updated August
22, 2018. https://www.immigrantentrepreneurship.org/entries/frederick-augustus-hihn/.

Street, Richard Steven. Beasts of the Field: A Narrative History of California Farmworkers,
1769–1913. Redwood City CA: Stanford University Press, 2004.

Strickland, Jeffery G. "Ethnicity and Race in the Urban South: German Immigrants and
African-Americans in Charleston, South Carolina, during Reconstruction." PhD diss.,
Florida State University, 2003.

——. "How the Germans Became White Southerners: German Immigrants and African
Americans in Charleston, South Carolina, 1860–1880." Journal of American Ethnic History
28, no. 1 (Fall 2008), 52–69. http://www.jstor.org/stable/27501881.

Sullivan, Josephine. A History of C. Brewer & Company Limited: One Hundred Years in the
Hawaiian Islands, 1826–1926, edited by Karl Clayton Leebrick. Boston: Walton Advertising & Printing, 1926.

Swenson, Timothy. Alvarado Sugar Beet Factory and the Dyer Family That Founded It. Fremont
CA: Museum of Local History, 2015. https://museumoflocalhistory.org/wordpress2/wp
-content/uploads/2015/02/AlvSugarBeetFactory.pdf.

Takaki, Ronald T. Pau Hana: Plantation Life and Labor in Hawaii, 1835–1920. Honolulu:
University of Hawai'i Press, 1984.

Tate, E. Mowbray. Transpacific Steam: The Story of Steam Navigation from the Pacific Coast of
North America to the Far East and the Antipodes, 1867–1941. New York: Cornwall Books,
1986.

Teisch, Jessica B. Engineering Nature: Water, Development & the Global Spread of American
Environmental Expertise. Chapel Hill: University of North Carolina Press, 2011.

Terry, Carole Cosgrove. "Die Deutschen in Kalifornien: Germans in Urban California, 1850–
1860." PhD diss., University of Nevada, Las Vegas, 2012.

Townsend, C. O. "By-Products of the Sugar Beet and Their Uses." Yearbook of the Department
of Agriculture, 1908. Washington DC: Government Printing Office, 1909. https://naldc
.nal.usda.gov/download/IND50000109/PDF.

Tucker, Richard P. Changing Pacific Forests: Historical Perspectives on the Pacific Basin Forest
Economy. Durham NC: Duke University Press, 1992.

Twain, Mark. Roughing It. Hartford CT: American Publishing, 1872. Republished, New York:
Penguin, 1962. http://www.online-literature.com/twain/roughing-it/77/.

——. "Twenty-Third Letter to the Sacramento Daily Union" (September 10, 1866). In Mark
Twain and Hawaii, edited by Walter Francis Frear, 398. Chicago: Lakeside Press, 1947.

Twarog, Sophia. "Heights and Living Standards in Germany, 1850–1939: The Case of Wurt-
temberg." In Health and Welfare During Industrialization, edited by Richard H. Steckel
and Roderick Floud, 285–330. Chicago: University of Chicago Press, 1997. http://www
.nber.org/chapters/c7434.

Twigg-Smith, Thurston. Hawaiian Sovereignty: Do the Facts Matter? Cohasset MA: Goodale,
1998.

University of Pennsylvania, Wharton School, and Philadelphia Social Science Association. *Publications of the University of Pennsylvania: Series in Political Economy and Public Law*, no. 21. Philadelphia: University of Pennsylvania Press, 1908.

"Unratified Amendments: Titles of Nobility." *National Archives Pieces of History* (blog), retrieved May 19, 2022, https://prologue.blogs.archives.gov/2020/01/30/unratified-amendments-titles-of-nobility/.

U.S. Census Bureau. *Eighth Census of the United States, 1860*. National Archives and Records Administration M653.

U.S. Department of the Interior Patent Office. *Report of the Commissioner of Patents for the Year 1868*, 716, patent 75,656. Washington DC: Government Printing Office, 1869.

Van Dyke, Jon M. *Who Owns the Crown Lands of Hawai'i?* Honolulu: University of Hawai'i Press, 2007.

Vecoli, Rudolph J., Francesco Durante, and Elizabeth O. Venditto. "The Destiny of Hawaii." In *Oh Capitano! Celso Cesare Moreno—Adventurer, Cheater, and Scoundrel on Four Continents*, edited by Donna R. Gabaccia, 1st ed., 155–71. New York: Fordham University Press, 2018.

Verardo, Jennie Dennis. *The Salinas Valley: An Illustrated History*. Chatsworth CA: Windsor, 1989.

Wagner, Jonathan. *A History of Migration from Germany to Canada, 1850–1939*. Vancouver: University of British Columbia Press, 2006.

Wakeman, Abram. *History and Reminiscences of Lower Wall Street and Vicinity*. New York: Spice Mill, 1914.

Walker, Richard. "Industry Builds Out the City: The Suburbanization of Manufacturing in the San Francisco Bay Area, 1850–1940." In *Manufacturing Suburbs: Building Work and Home*, edited by Robert Lewis, 92–123. Philadelphia: Temple University Press, 2004. http://www.jstor.org/stable/j.ctt14bs74p.9.

Ware, Lewis Sharpe. *The Sugar Beet: Devoted to the Cultivation and Utilization of the Sugar Beet*, 1 (February 1884).

Wianecki, Shannon. "The Great Diversion: The East Maui Irrigation System Was One of the Nineteenth Century's Major Feats of Hydrologic Engineering." *Hana Hou!* 18, no. 5 (October–November 2015), https://hanahou.com/18.5/the-great-diversion.

Wiggin, Kate Douglas. *My Garden of Memory: An Autobiography*. Boston: Houghton Mifflin, 1923.

Wilcox, Carol. *Sugar Water: Hawaii's Plantation Ditches*. Honolulu: University of Hawai'i Press, 1997.

Wiley, Harvey Washington. *The Sugar-Beet Industry: Culture of the Sugar-Beet and Manufacture of Beet Sugar*. Washington DC: Government Printing Office, 1890.

Wilson, H., compiler. *Trow's New York City Directory (1855–1856)*. Vol. 69. New York: John H. Trow, 1856.

Wyckoff, Hubert C., Jr. *The Memoirs of Hubert C. Wyckoff, Jr. Vol. 1, Watsonville Recollections*, edited by Randall Jarrell and Doris Johnson. Santa Cruz: University of California, Dean E. McHenry Library, 1978.

Yenne, Bill. *San Francisco Beer: A History of Brewing by the Bay*. Charleston SC: American Palate, 2016.

INDEX

Page numbers in italics indicate illustrations

granulated sugar, 25–26, 32

Green, John P., 26

Greene, Clay M., 307

Grevenbroich Machine Factory, 157, 217, 218

grocery-grade sugar, 65

Grosse, Agnes, 14–15, *55*; death of, 55

Grosse, Anna, 14–15

Gutierrez, Trinidad, 239

Hackfeld, Heinrich "Henry," 69, 70. *See also* H. Hackfeld & Company

Hagemann, Frederick, Jr., 30, 318n17

Haight, Henry H., 50

Haiku Ditch. *See* Spreckels Ditch

Haiku Plantation and Mill, 77

Haleakalā, 76, 78, 86, 87, 129

Hāmākua Ditch, 77, 87, 89, 97

Hamilton, Alexander "Alec," 198, 274

Hamilton, Grace Alexandria, 336n28

Hamilton, Mary "Happy" Leila, 336n28

Hanna, Marcus "Mark," 209, 337n5

Hannam, William H., 252, 253, 285

Hanover, kingdom of, 1, 29, 98

haoles, 67, 88, 89, 99. *See also* missionary families

Harper's Weekly, 67, *116*, 206

Harris, Irving Drought, 310

Harris, Mimi, 311

Harris, Thomas, 223, 224

Harrison, Benjamin, 179

Harrison, Ralph, 145

Hartwell, Alfred S., 87, 88–89

Havemeyer, Frederick D., 25

Havemeyer, Henry Osborne, 169, 171, 175, 220, 299. *See also* American Sugar Refining Company; New York Sugar Trust

Havemeyer, Theodore, 175

Havemeyer, William, 25

Hawai'i: Claus Spreckels's arrival in, xvii, 75–76; indebtedness of, 89; mail delivery to, 104–5; Provisional Government of, 180–81, 230; racial and ethnic diver-sity of, 301; republic of, 183; sugarcane exports from, 66, 69, 100, 300; U.S. annexation of, 69, 72, 132, 179, 180, 229–31. *See also* Big Island (Hawai'i); Kauai; Lāna'i; Maui; Moloka'i; O'ahu

Hawaiian Commercial & Sugar Company, 90–91, 127, 147; Alexander & Baldwin's takeover of, 188, 301; Gus Spreckels and, 178, 183–84; last harvest of, 301; press accusations against, 141; reorganizing, 129; stock assessment levy of, 178, 184; stock value of, 141. *See also* Spreckelsville Plantation

Hawaiian Gazette (Honolulu), 86, 96, 104, 129, 258, 286–87

Hawaiian Hotel, 76, 85–86, 88

Hawaiian Labor and Supply Company, 324n18

Hawaiian League, 153, 179

Hawaiian natives. *See* Native Hawaiians

Hawaiian royalty. *See specific persons*

Hawaiian Star, 181

Hawaiian sugar agents: Claus Spreckels as, 111; hatred toward Spreckels, xvii, 84, 281–82. *See also specific companies*

Hawaiian Sugar Planters' Association, 324n18

Hawaiian words for water and wealth, 86–87

Hawai'i's Story by Hawai'i's Queen Lili'uo-kalani, 230

Hawai'i Supreme Court, 98, 100

Heald's Business College, 43

Hennige, Jacob, 29

H. Hackfeld & Company, 69, 70–71, 93. *See also* Hackfeld, Heinrich "Henry"

Hight, Iretta, 192

Highton, Henry E., 144

Hihn, Frederick Augustus, 48, 49, 53, 57; contention with Claus Spreckels, 58, 62–64; railroad ventures of, 50–52

Hill, William J., 225, 226

Spreckels, Claus Johann (*cont.*)
197; "Hail to the Chief" played for, 107; in Hawai'i after coup d'état, 180–81; Hawaiian coinage and, 137–38; high blood pressure of, 155; hiring practices of, 25, 284; horse racing and, 56; hot temper of, 26, 57–58, 77, 155, 186, 217; immigration to America, xvii, 2–5; intolerance of employee disrespect, 57–58; inventions of, 30, 31, 39, 165, 233–34, 313, 319n51; keeping illness secret, 208, 228, 255, 256; King Kalākaua and, xviii, 88–89, 113–14, 131, 141, 151–52, 153–54, 173, 174, 235; leaving Hawai'i under threat, 181, *182*; loan to Hawaiian government, 137–38, 151, 152; Lorrin Thurston and, 151; losing children, 27, 29, 30, 37, 40, 45; love for California, xx, 118, 251, 254, 300, 304; love for Spreckels village, *236*, 241; managerial style of, 16, 33, 36, 57–58, 284; micromanaging by, 16, 36; monarchy restoration attempt and, 182, 282; monopolies and, xviii, 32, 68, 87, 93, 110–11, 111, 112, 117, 118; nervous breakdown of, 35, 36–39, 155; as New York grocer, 9–10; New York Sugar Trust and, 169–72, 172–73; nobility title and, xviii, 113–14; "no nonsense" parenting by, 12, 21, 33, 34, 39, 43; opportunities seized by, xvii, 14, 22, 26, 34, 44, 70, 304; *Pacific Commercial Advertiser* and, 86, 90, 112, 120, 136, 181, 221; politicians suspicious of, 68, 70, 87, 99, 139; pottery company of, 247; Princess Ruth and, 98–100; public scandals of, 112, 113–14, 116, 120, 141, 185, 204; Queen Lili'uokalani and, 180–81, 181–83, 230, 259; in railroad accident, 175; railroad ventures of, xix, 51–52, 57, 58–61, 62–63, 166, 211–12, 216, 221; Reciprocity Treaty and, xvii, 65–70, 76, 78, 112; reconciliation with younger children, 256–58; recruiting employees, 42, 101, 119–20; recruiting farmers, 29–30, 48, 160–64, 223; restless ambition of, 12, 18, 26, 34–35, 36, 78, 154–55, 157–58; retaining employees, 282, 313; *San Francisco Chronicle* and, 113, 141, 144, 145, 147, 248; San Francisco earthquake and, xx, 267, 276–77, 278; as San Francisco grocer, 12; secret deal with Sugar Trust, 175; soil improvement efforts of, 86, 97, 214, 234, 281; SP and, 166–67, 211, 216; speeches by, 163, 166, 224, 225, 251, 254; Spreckels Temple of Music and, 249–51; stock manipulations by, 129, 141; strife with Emma, 194, 195, 255; strife with Gus, xix, 183–87; strife with John, xix, 210–11, 256; strife with Rudolph, xix, 186, 187, 229, 247–48, 290; strokes of, 255–56; sugar agents' hatred toward, 84, 87, 281–82; testimony before Congress, 164–65, 168; training in sugar business, 19–21, 29, 154, 155, 156–57; transferring assets to John and Adolph, 187–88, 283, 291, 293, 294; transferring assets to Rudolph and Emma, 183, 287; travels back to Germany, 9–10, 28–29, 38–40, 155, 156–57, 176, 187, 217, 218; trekking to California, 10–11; Valley Road and, 212, 221; Walter Gibson and, 136–38, 152, 221; water rights and, xviii, 85, 87–89, 112; wealth of, xviii, 44, 88, 111, 116, 139, 283, 312–13; William Irwin and, 111–12, 138, 258, 259; work ethic of, 6, 12, 16, 36, 37, 61, 304, 313. *See also* Mangels, Anna Christina
Spreckels, "Claus Jr." (grandson), 192, 250, 274, 278
Spreckels, Died(e)rich (brother), 15, 315n2
Spreckels, Dorothy Constance (granddaughter), 306–7
Spreckels, Edward (son), death of, 45
Spreckels, Edward Henry (son), 29, 38; death of, 40
Spreckels, Eleanor (granddaughter), 199